OBSCENITY AND THE LAW

A Da Capo Press Reprint Series

CIVIL LIBERTIES IN AMERICAN HISTORY

GENERAL EDITOR: LEONARD W. LEVY

Claremont Graduate School

OBSCENITY AND THE LAW

by

Norman St. John-Stevas

DA CAPO PRESS · NEW YORK · 1974

Library of Congress Cataloging in Publication Data

St. John-Stevas, Norman.
Obscenity and the law.

(Civil liberties in American history)
Reprint of the 1956 ed. published by Secker & Warburg London.
Bibliography: p.
1. Obscenity (Law)—Great Britain. 2. Obscenity (Law) I. Title. II. Series.
KD8075.S2 1974 345'.027'4 74-8538
ISBN 0-306-70602-4

This Da Capo Press edition of *Obscenity and the Law* is an unabridged republication of the first edition published in London in 1956. It is reprinted with the permission of Martin Secker & Warburg Ltd.

Published by Da Capo Press, Inc.
A Subsidiary of Plenum Publishing Corporation
227 West 17th Street, New York, N.Y. 10011

Manufactured in the United States of America

Not available for sale from Da Capo Press in the British Commonwealth (excluding Canada), the Irish Republic, Republic of South Africa, Burma, Egypt, Iraq, Israel, Jordan, and the British Trusteeships

OBSCENITY AND THE LAW

Lydia: Here, my dear Lucy, hide these books. Quick, quick. —Fling *Peregrine Pickle* under the toilet—throw *Roderick Random* into the closet—thrust Lord Amworth under the sofa—cram Ovid behind the bolster—there —put *The Man of Feeling* into your pocket—so, so,— now lay Mrs. Chapone in sight, and leave *Fordyce's Sermons* open on the table.

Lucy: O burn it ma'am! the hairdresser has torn away as far as Proper Pride.

Lydia: Never mind—open at Sobriety.—Fling me *Lord Chesterfield's Letters.*—Now for 'em.

(Exit *Lucy*)
(Enter *Mrs. Malaprop* and *Sir Anthony Absolute*)

RICHARD BRINSLEY SHERIDAN, *The Rivals*, Act I, Sc. ii.
First performed at Covent Garden Theatre
on January 17th, 1775.

OBSCENITY AND THE LAW

by

NORMAN ST. JOHN-STEVAS

With an Introduction by
Sir Alan P. Herbert

London: SECKER & WARBURG: *1956*

Printed in Great Britain by
Spottiswoode, Ballantyne & Co. Ltd.
London and Colchester
and
first published 1956
by
Martin Secker & Warburg Ltd.

Dedicated to Professor Ronald Graveson,
Dean of the Faculty of Laws,
King's College, London,
with gratitude and affection.

CONTENTS

APPENDICES

INTRODUCTION

BY A. P. HERBERT

I AM truly glad to introduce a brilliant young barrister and his book; and I can promise from experience that he will be found not only learned and wise but entertaining.

In 1954 and 1955 there was one of those periodical swirls of trouble about 'obscene libel', or, in plainer language, 'dirty books'. Within a few months five publishers of good reputation and serious purpose found themselves in the dock with their authors, and whichever way the cases went, suffered much indignity, anxiety, and loss. The energetic secretary of the Society of Authors, Mr. Denys Kilham Roberts, got together a committee of sixteen to consider the law, and its administration, and to recommend to the Home Secretary any change on which we could agree. We were not all authors or publishers. There was Sir Gerald Barry, and Sir Herbert Read: there was Mr. Roy Jenkins, M.P. (but he is an author, too): philosophy and printing and education were represented: there was Mr. C. R. Hewitt, of the *New Statesman*, with much experience of the courts: there was, of course, the ever-watchful parent-bird, Mr. Kilham Roberts: and last, but far from least, there was Mr. Norman St. John-Stevas, a barrister-at-law.

I found myself, with no small reluctance and alarm, 'in the chair'. 'How it all comes back', I heard myself muttering as we sat down. Far back in 1929 I remember a sudden surge of trouble about Books and Bow Street, and the Old Bailey. Public tastes and standards change. The 'dirt' of today may be the art of tomorrow. One day some comic-strip artist of our time may be respectfully regarded as another Hogarth or Edgar Allan Poe. On the other hand, no one today would be allowed to put on the kind of play that rolled 'em in the aisles in the seventeenth and eighteenth centuries. But, whether the artist changes or not, every now and then Society decides that it is time for Art—or Literature—to receive a hearty slap. I do not think the writers of 1929 were more wanton or wicked than their fathers: but it was time for a slap. A powerful journalist (long dead, so I will call him Mr. D.) set himself up as the Savonarola of Fleet Street, and lashed out terribly in all directions. No novelist could be sure that one day he would not be denounced in black letters as a corrupter of the young, a 'purveyor of slime', etc. We all trembled duly.

The climax was the case of a book that I will call X. It was a sincere, well-written book on a sad, unseemly subject, though it was rather a bore (the books we battle about are nearly always rather a bore), and it was so delicately done that it could not have 'corrupted' anyone. (Indeed, when I had read the whole book through, I remember asking someone where the naughty bits were supposed to be.)

But this book was denounced by Mr. D. and prosecuted at Bow Street under the Act of 1857, which empowers a magistrate to order a book to be destroyed as 'obscene' without giving author or publisher a chance to say a word in his defence.

The tribe of authors were roused and resentful. It was hotly felt by many that the time had come to fight back, and someone organised an indignation, a mutiny, meeting at a Chelsea studio. There were about a hundred of us. The great Mr. Bernard Shaw, we were told, was to address and inspire us: and we waited eagerly for the Torch of Intellect and the Voice of Freedom. Half an hour—three-quarters—passed, but the Torch, the Voice, did not arrive. Disappointed, but not daunted, we held our meeting without the Torch, and solemnly declared, promised and (secretly) vowed that each of us would go to Bow Street, force our way into the witness-box and testify that in our opinion the book X was a sincere, worthy and artistic work, and did not deserve to be destroyed.

It is very easy to laugh at all this now; but it was very serious then, especially for a young writer beginning to grope his way into the world. We saw ourselves martyred in large black letters in Mr. D.'s column—THESE ARE THE NAMES OF THE MERCHANTS OF IMMORALITY WHO TESTIFIED IN FAVOUR OF A BEASTLY BOOK, etc.

Soon after we had dedicated ourselves to this heroic shame, the Torch of Intellect and Liberty arrived and made a long speech. Alas, he did not pat us on the backs and send us to the sacrifice inspired and happy. He told us we should do no good, and were making fools of ourselves. We all went out into the night, dedicated still but damped.

The Torch turned out to be an accurate prophet—though not, I still think, a very good Leader. We all turned up at Bow Street and sat, a valiant but uneasy mob, in some waiting-room outside the court. The late Sir Desmond MacCarthy was the first, and only, literary witness to enter the witness-box. The magistrate said politely that he was delighted to see him; he was charmed to hear that numerous other literary ladies and gentlemen were waiting outside:

but he thought that he was quite capable of deciding, without their aid, whether the book X was obscene or not. We went home, still muttering mutinously, but secretly relieved.

Meanwhile, the magistrate decided that the book X was obscene and ordered it to be destroyed. It has recently, they tell me, been published again without a word of protest, even from the Public Prosecutor. You may laugh at us—as I have laughed myself—but perhaps, after all, we were right, and the magistrate—or rather the law—was wrong.

And now—here we are again! These things come in cycles, as I have said, and there has been in the last year or two another crop of prosecutions for 'obscene publication'. Any private person can start one of these—any old lady who unluckily picks out of a twopenny library a book which shocks her. But for the last batch of five the Director of Public Prosecutions—horse, foot, and Attorney-General—accepted responsibility. In two cases he scored a conviction: in two more there was an acquittal. In the fifth, at the first trial, the jury, after long deliberation, disagreed. One would have thought that, in such an affair, the authorities would have said to themselves: 'Well, if twelve average men can't agree that this book is "depraving or corrupting" it can't be so bad. And anyhow, the more we prosecute the more we advertise it. Let it go.' But no—the Crown returned to the charge, and there was a second trial at the Old Bailey. *Again the jury disagreed.* A third trial was formally called, but this time, according to custom, the Crown offered no evidence, and the accused, author and publisher, were discharged.

So the Public Prosecutor's total score was two wins—three losses. Not very hot. You may say, 'That will teach him! Why are you worrying?'

Because, for one thing, in a few years all this will happen again. Now, let us be clear what kind of books we are talking about. I am not worrying—no member of the Society of Authors would worry—about those who deliberately write and publish what is usefully described as 'dirt for dirt's sake'. They know what they are doing and may deserve what they get. I am thinking of 'respectable' publishers and 'serious' authors—writers, who without claiming to be Maughams or Dickenses, are trying to write good books, or, if you like, 'literature', and, through inexperience or ignorance, are guilty of errors of taste—of publishers who are guilty of no more than an error of judgement. When you read of such cases, you can imagine some gross unscrupulous monster conspiring with some lewd and conscienceless writer to send forth poison and grow rich on it: and such persons may exist. But the true picture is generally different: an obscure, shy, and earnest young author whom all his friends consider 'highbrow'—a publisher who thinks the lad has quality and 'something to say' and deserves encouragement, though he is unlikely to win the publisher a profit, much less a fortune. The book, when published, attracts little attention, is not 'condemned' by any critic, sells a few thousand copies only (at 12*s*. 6*d*.), and is forgotten, even by the author. But, three or four years later, perhaps, the old lady in the library takes it home: there are outcries and 'informations', the great wheel of Justice begins to go round, and two nervous and astonished little men find themselves in the dock at the Old Bailey.

I have read two of the books concerned in the recent cases. But without the activities of the Public Prosecutor I should never have heard of either of them. One of them was worth reading: it had even a 'moral message'. It thought that young husbands who love their wives should be careful of dallying with other women. It contained passages which were perhaps unnecessarily 'frank', but nothing 'obscene' and nothing likely to corrupt the grown persons to whom (at 12*s*. 6*d*. a copy) it was addressed. That book was very sensibly acquitted, but only, I think, because it came before a particular judge. The other book was about the biggest bore in a lifetime of reading. Nobody but the Public Prosecutor could have induced me to read it to the end. No ordinary young person who picked it up would get very far with it. It was 'obscene', I thought, in the sense of shocking, but it was certainly not corrupting. Indeed, it was enough to put Casanova off sex for life. It was perhaps a mistake to publish it: but it was an honest mistake. The book was unimportant but sincere, I thought—not 'dirt for dirt's sake', but an attempt at art. The author had 'something to say', though I was not quite clear what it was.

In most countries it would have been left alone: or if it had come before the courts, it would have been judged by more just and sensible laws.

It is no joke, I imagine, to find yourself in the dock at the Old Bailey charged with any criminal offence. But the suspected murderer or robber has certain defences and advantages which are old traditions of British justice. For one thing, some damage must have been done: someone must have been slain or robbed. For another, the accused person can give some explanation of his conduct: for it is a principle of the law that there can be no criminal guilt without a guilty mind. But the publisher and author, accused of 'obscene publication', though they stand in the dock like common criminals (rightly, no doubt, if they are 'dirt for dirt's sakers'), may be confined in the cells for hours while the jury deliberate, and may, if convicted, be heavily fined or imprisoned, have not the advantages of the common criminal. No one cares, and no one will allow them to testify, about their state of mind. They may not tell the court that their intention was good (as the burglar, for example, may explain that he thought the house was on fire and popped inside to save the situation). The Rugby forward who has his shorts torn off does not get into trouble: for that was not his intention. The man who deliberately 'exposes himself' in public is another matter. But here there is no such distinction. The accused may be convicted without evidence or proof of a wrongful intention—or damage done. No father comes forward and says: 'Look at my little Evie. She was a good girl till she read *Love and Destiny*'.

The only question before the court is 'Does the book *tend to* deprave or corrupt . . .?' Observe 'tend to'. A man can be convicted of murder—or attempted murder—or manslaughter; but not of a 'tendency to homicide'. Whether there is a 'tendency to corrupt', whether a book is a work of art or an instrument of evil can only be a matter of opinion; but those whose opinion might be most helpful, experts and practitioners in the world of art and books and education, are not allowed to say a word. Nor can any expert go into the witness-box and say to the judge: 'Whatever you may think of Mr. A. and Mr. B., this, I believe, is a genuine work of art, which may one day be famous and considered precious, and ought not now to be destroyed'.

The danger of this is clear. Many a book which was howled at in Queen Victoria's reign is now regarded as a classic—Hardy's *Jude the Obscure*, for example.

In 1888, at the Old Bailey, one Vizetelly, who translated most of Zola's novels, was prosecuted and fined for publishing Zola's *La Terre* and other foreign works. Three weeks earlier Zola had been admitted to the Legion of Honour in France; eight years later he was lionized in London. In 1889 Vizetelly was imprisoned for three months, and some more dangerous books, by Flaubert, for example, were withdrawn or destroyed. Recently, *La Terre* has been republished in England. It is pretty strong meat, I should agree, but not dirt for dirt's sake. Tastes may have changed, but the law is the same as it was 100 years ago. There is nothing to prevent some old lady from running to a magistrate with the new edition of *La Terre* and demanding a prosecution. There is nothing to prevent a magistrate, who may know nothing of the fame of Zola or the worth of his work —and cannot or will not take the advice of those who do—from ordering the book to be destroyed again. No one's morals would be a penny the better, and England would have made herself ridiculous once more.

Against this kind of nonsense, the grievance of a century, we massed for mutiny anew on 26 November 1954. I do not think that when we first sat down any of us expected very much to emerge. It is one thing to fulminate generally, as I have just been doing, and quite another to frame precise proposals which can be translated into law. By a complicating chance we met at the peak of a powerful (and, for all I know, justifiable) campaign against the 'horror-comics'. Authority, and the Churches, were far more concerned with suppressing the 'horror comic' than with liberating 'literature'. Mud sticks: and a series of prosecutions, however silly and unsuccessful, must leave the author slightly muddy in the minds of those who do not study the facts and know little of the law. On the other hand, there are many—there were two or three, I think, on the Committee—who think that there should be no law at all, that Art and Truth should be utterly free. But we were meeting as practical men, whose business was not to carry a debate at the Oxford Union but to offer advice which might be acceptable to a Minister of the Crown. Authors are not supposed to be 'practical' men, and they can even disagree about the income-tax. Yet, after a couple of meetings, we had made up our minds on the fundamental matters; and very much of the credit for that is due to the research, the learning, and the lucidity of the author of this book. We decided early not to concern ourselves with the troubles of 'reputable' publishers only, but to cover the whole field of 'obscene publications' including the 'horror comic' and plain pornography. I felt strongly that we should not confine ourselves to a historical report and a series of resolutions, but put what we wanted, if we could, in the form of a Parliamentary Bill, for reports and resolutions die by the thousand in the pigeon-holes of Whitehall, but a Bill can be brought to life by any private Member. A resolution is a whine: a Bill is a weapon. I took a very rough sketch of a Bill to the first meeting: but its only merit, I fear, was to show how difficult a job it was—and the wider the field the worse it would be. But Mr. St. John-Stevas leaped upon this ambitious task like a tiger: and, with the help of Mr. Hewitt and others, he produced a comprehensive and lengthy Bill of which, I think, the Parliamentary draftsmen would not have been ashamed. Four weeks after our first meeting it was presented, with our report, to the Home Secretary—not bad going, I thought, for 'unpractical' but busy men. My old friend, Mr. Gwilym Lloyd-George, the new Home Secretary, had lunched with us and shown great interest and goodwill. But he was keen to go ahead at once with the 'Horror Comics' Bill: his advisers thought that our main proposals needed 'careful consideration'; so—not for the first time in Home Office history—the job could not be tackled as a whole. When this was known, Mr. Roy Jenkins, M.P., very ably and eloquently, asked leave to introduce our Bill under the 'Ten-Minute Rule'. Leave was granted, to my surprise, without a single dissentient voice. So the Bill was formally 'read a first time' and 'ordered to be printed'. No mention was made of this matter in the Gracious Speech with which Her Majesty opened the new Parliament; but perhaps the 'careful consideration' of the Home Office is continuing. Meanwhile, there is our Bill, not perfect, no doubt, but easily amendable, ready for some bold private Member. We may not seem to have got very far: but little did we think, when we first sat down to this unpromising, unpopular problem, that four months later our proposals would be printed at the public expense by order of the House of Commons. Mr. St. John-Stevas is entitled to regard the Bill as his first publication. I hope that his second will bring him greater rewards. He was afraid at one time, I know, that the labours of our Committee might put this book out of date: but I see no immediate danger of that. Here is a ready weapon for the law-reformer. On behalf of all those who love good art and literature, good sense, and good law, I salute and wish him well.

AUTHOR'S PREFACE

IT is now two years since I first became interested in the subject of obscenity. For some time I had been searching for a topic which would link my two interests of the law and literature, and would give scope for some original research. I found it in obscenity, the only point—apart from copyright—where the two come into contact. Obscenity raises not only intricate legal problems but also those of literary taste and freedom of expression in literature, and it is these underlying issues which make it such an important and fascinating topic. My book is, therefore, a study of changing law and taste, and I have tried to indicate the connection between the two. Perhaps the most significant point that has emerged from my study is that the law only intervened to suppress serious literature at the close of the nineteenth century, when the Victorian synthesis was breaking down and when Forster's Education Act had created a vast new reading public. I have dealt with the nineteenth century at some length, partly because of the richness of the material available, and partly because the problems then being faced were so similar to our own. The contempt for the Victorians, which reached its highwater mark with the publication of Lytton Strachey's *Eminent Victorians* is now unfashionable and on the wane. For some years the Victorians have been favourably reassessed and in my chapter on the 'Victorian Conscience' I have tried to show that much of Victorian prudery and literary reticence was a necessary means of self-defence against the newly expanded urban underworld. I am conscious that I have only touched upon this question and I hope in a later work to examine the whole Victorian notion of respectability and the part it played in preserving a stable society in what was essentially an age of revolutionary change.

I had originally intended to confine myself to an article on this subject, but I soon realised that there was enough material for a full-length study. I also discovered that there was no book which dealt with the subject from the legal point of view. There have, of course, been many books on obscenity, perhaps the best known being those by Alec Craig, but none of these have any claims to be considered works of legal scholarship. I was unable to find even an article in any of the English law journals to assist me in my research, although some American lawyers have ventured into this field. I was, therefore, thankful for one result of the recent campaign against reputable publishers—it gave me the opportunity of writing this book. Shortly after I had begun work on my article obscenity became headline news. As prosecution after prosecution was launched the literary world became seriously alarmed about the threat to the freedom of authors which was taking shape. For the first time authors took a positive step to defend their rights and the Society of Authors appointed a committee to recommend reforms of the law. The committee's conclusions are embodied in the draft Bill, reproduced at the end of the book, and which received unanimous support in the House of Commons when it was introduced by Roy Jenkins, M.P., in March 1955. Just before the Society set up its committee, Secker and Warburg, who had been triumphantly acquitted on an obscene libel charge at the Old Bailey, commissioned me to write a book on the whole subject, examining the history and present state of the law and recommending any necessary reforms. In the planning and writing of this book my publishers have given me the completest freedom and to them I tender my grateful thanks. My aim has been to produce a book that is both readable and scholarly. Wherever possible, references to sources have been given and a fully referenced table of cases and statutes has been included. The law in the United States and Southern Ireland has been set out in full in separate chapters and appendices on Commonwealth and foreign law have been added.

In the book itself I have tried as far as possible to let the facts speak for themselves, and have attempted not to intrude my own opinions until the final chapter. The chief conclusion drawn is that the law should be invoked to suppress pornography, but should leave literary expression to be determined by prevailing standards of taste. It should draw a fundamental distinction between works written with a serious purpose and those which have no other aim save the making of money by exploiting and degrading the sexual passions. It is my hope that despite its limitations this book will be of some small help in liberalising the law in this sense, and will be a contribution towards the achievement of reforms which are now long overdue.

Harley Street,
January 1956.

NORMAN ST. JOHN-STEVAS.

ACKNOWLEDGMENTS

I SHOULD like to acknowledge with gratitude the help afforded me by the following: K. Tillotson for her book *Novels of the 1840's*, one of the outstanding works of literary criticism of this century and M. J. Quinlan for his book *Victorian Prelude*, from both of which I have derived great profit; G. M. Young for suggesting the frontispiece to the book; John Hayward for his advice about Rochester; John Crow for his advice and help on licensing problems during the sixteenth and seventeenth centuries; David Low for advice on Swinburne; Robert Burchfield, of Christ Church, for his help with Anglo-Saxon literature; I. Raknem and Vincent Brome for their help in relation to H. G. Wells; Walter Allen for continual encouragement and advice about the literary side of the book.

For help with the legal problems raised by the book I am deeply grateful to Professor Gerald Nokes, LL.D., of London University, who has helped me continuously over the past year, and to Anthony Bland, Visiting Professor at Tulane University, Louisiana, who advised me throughout and read the final manuscript. Both made many valuable suggestions which I have incorporated. Professor Ronald Graveson of King's College, London, Professor Raphael Powell of University College, London, Professor E. C. S. Wade of Downing College, Cambridge, and F. J. Odgers, Fellow of Emmanuel College, Cambridge, have also afforded me valuable assistance.

In the field of foreign law I would like to thank the following: Dudley Collard of the Anglo-Soviet friendship society for help with Soviet law; the Assistant Commissioner of the Danish Police for help with Danish law; Sten Rudholm, Associate Judge of the Court of Appeal in Stockholm, for help with Swedish law; the late Professor Dr. Werner Lüthi, Procurator-General of the Swiss Confederation, for help with Swiss law; the French Minister of the Interior, and M. Michel Richaume-Lambert of the Institut de Droit Comparé of the University of Paris, for their help with French law; Dr. Kanter of the Federal Ministry of Justice, German Republic, and Herr William Knaf for their help with German law; the Director-General of the Ministry of Justice, Brussels, for his help with Belgian law; Mr. Kazuo Yamanouchi, Counsellor of the Japanese Cabinet Legislation Bureau, Mr. Shozo Kadota and Mr. M. Takashima, both of the

Japanese Embassy in London, for their help with Japanese law, and Dr. A. D. Kalovidouris, of Athens, for his help with Greek law.

In compiling the appendices on Commonwealth law I have been assisted by Professor B. Beinart of Capetown University; Sir John Lienhop, Agent-General for Victoria; the Agent-General for Tasmania; Professor Norval Morris of the University of Melbourne, and Professor R. S. Mackay of Toronto University. For my chapter on United States law I am greatly indebted to Robert B. McClure and Professor William B. Lockhart of the University of Minnesota.

For the chapter on Ireland I owe a debt to Mr. Sean O'Faolain, who placed all his knowledge at my disposal; to Senator Sheehy Skeffington, who gave me every assistance during my visit to Ireland; to the Librarian of Trinity College, Dublin; to Professor Otway Ruthven of Trinity College, and Dr. Smyth, formerly of the Irish Censorship Board, who helped me in an endless number of ways. I am also grateful to the Secretary of the Irish Censorship Board, who gave me much information and arranged a meeting with a member of the Board.

Among others I would like to thank are Sir Alan Herbert for his kindness in writing an Introduction to this book; Fredric Warburg, David Farrer and John Pattisson of Secker and Warburg, who have been both kind and patient; Roy Jenkins, M.P., for obtaining statistical information for me about prosecutions and destruction orders; Rupert Hart-Davis for lending me a copy of a rare book by Vizetelly; Professor David Knowles, O.S.B., of Peterhouse, and Fr. Brasell, S.J., of Heythrop College, for help with the Roman Index; V. S. Pritchett for lending me his copy of *Cw.* v. *Gordon*; C. H. Rolph for his help in drafting the Obscene Publications Bill; Denys Kilham Roberts, Secretary-General of the Authors' Society for continual help and advice; Sir Theobald Mathew, Director of Public Prosecutions, for telling me of the work of his department; Cadness Page, President of the Booksellers' Association, for advising me as to the position and views of booksellers; Gerald Gardiner, Q.C., for his advice about drafting Bills, and George Tomlinson, Secretary of the Public Morality Council, for placing the Council records at my disposal.

At the British Museum Angus Wilson, then Superintendent of the Reading Room, and his staff, gave me every assistance, as did Mr. Witney and his staff at the Institute of Advanced Legal Studies. I must also thank Mr. Horne of the King's College law library, who took a keen personal interest in the book.

Last of all, I should like to thank the Honourable Rose Talbot of Malahide Castle, Dublin, and the Reverend Michael Canavan of Grace Dieu Manor, Whitwick, in whose hospitable houses much of this book was written.

CHAPTER I

OBSCENITY: ITS EARLY HISTORY

WHAT is meant by 'obscenity'? The dictionaries attempt to define the word 'obscene', but provide little more than an unhelpful list of synonyms. 'Offensive to modesty or decency', says the Oxford English Dictionary, 'expressing or suggesting unchaste or lustful ideas; impure, indecent, lewd'. Webster's International Dictionary suggests: 'offensive to chastity or modesty; expressing or presenting to the mind or view something which delicacy, purity and decency forbid to be exposed: impure, as obscene language, obscene pictures'. Dr. Johnson offers: 'immodest; not agreeable to chastity of mind; causing lewd ideas; offensive; disgusting; inauspicious; ill omened'.

Obscenity's etymology is disputed and is not enlightening. It is a Latin word derived possibly from 'ob' (on account of) and 'cænum' (filth). Havelock Ellis suggested that the word is a modification of 'scena', and means literally what is 'off the scene', and not normally presented on the stage of life.[1] Pornography on the other hand is Greek in origin, coming from *πορνογράφος* (the writing of harlots).

In truth 'obscenity' is impossible to define. The 'how do you define?' question, expecting a one-sentence answer differentiating between genus and species, is only appropriate for a word such as 'table' which corresponds to some tangible and verifiable reality. 'Obscenity', on the other hand, has no such correspondence to a tangible object, being a relative and subjective term, describing the reaction of the human mind to a certain type of experience. In an unpublished letter to Schroeder, Havelock Ellis wrote:

> There can be no doubt whatever regarding the soundness of your view of 'obscenity' as residing exclusively not in the thing contemplated, but in the mind of the contemplating person. The case has lately been reported of a young schoolmaster who has always felt tempted to commit criminal assault by the sight of a boy in knickerbockers—must we therefore conclude that all boys in knickerbockers shall be forcibly suppressed as 'obscene'?

[1] *Revaluation of Obscenity. More Essays in Love and Virtue* (1931).

D. H. Lawrence was expressing the same thought when he wrote: 'What is pornography to one man is the laughter of genius to another'.

Apart from its subjective aspect, it must be remembered that a statement that a certain book is obscene is more than a plain statement of fact. It conceals a deduction based on certain unstated premises, the code of manners prevalent in a community at any particular time. To understand the meaning fully one must be familiar with the customs of the social system in question.

The attempt to understand 'obscenity' in the terms of a simple definition is fruitless and best abandoned, but when this has been said certain constant elements in its meaning can be isolated. Obscenity has always been confined to matters related to sex or the excremental functions. Although there is an ideological element in the word and it is sometimes used to describe unconventional moral attitudes, the word is normally related to the manner of presenting a theme or idea rather than to the theme itself. A book is usually said to be obscene, not for the opinions which it expresses, but for the way in which they are expressed. Further, 'obscene' is an emotive word, conveying a feeling of outrage. Mere offensiveness is not enough to constitute words or books obscene. If 'immodest' is taken as the positive, 'indecent' may be described as the comparative, and 'obscene' as the superlative.

A pornographic book can be easily distinguished from an obscene book. A pornographic book, although obscene, is one deliberately designed to stimulate sex feelings and to act as an aphrodisiac. An obscene book has no such immediate and dominant purpose, although incidentally this may be its effect. A work like *Ulysses* certainly contains obscene passages, but their insertion in the book is not to stimulate sex impulses in the reader but to form part of a work of art.

GREECE AND ROME

At every stage of its development European civilisation has known both pornography and obscenity. Erotic songs and poems were popular in ancient Greece and were an accepted part of the nation's culture. Thus in Sparta, on the feast of Dionysius, it was customary for poets and others to take part in the public processions and to rally the populace with obscene and licentious songs and jokes. Greek drama, which it must be remembered was closely connected with religion, was frequently obscene, the best-known surviving examples being the plays of Aristophanes,* especially *Lysistrata*,

* St. John Chrysostom (d. A.D. 407) is alleged to have slept with twenty-eight plays of Aristophanes under his pillow.

The Thesmophoriazusæ and *The Assembly of Wo.*   Greek dramatists were not inhibited by fears of shocking feminine delicacy since women did not attend the plays. Pornography was also popular in Greece and we know the names of two pornographic writers of the ancient world although we possess none of their work, Dindyme and Sotate. The censorship debate raged in Greece, and in 378 B.C. Plato was advocating the expurgation of the Odyssey to make it more suitable for young readers.[2] Thus Socrates (in a passage applicable to 'horror comics'):

> Then we must also get rid of all the fearful and terrifying titles belonging to those subjects, 'wailing Cocytus', and 'loathed Styx', and 'infernals', and 'sapless dead' and all the words of that type, the very sound of which is enough to make men shiver. These will probably be useful enough for other purposes, but for our guardians we are afraid that this shivering fear will make them more emotional and softer than they ought to be.

He advised the omission of passages such as those describing the lust of Zeus for Hera since they were 'not conducive to self-restraint'.[3]

In Rome both Plautus and Terence wrote obscene plays with characters such as libertines and prostitutes, while adultery and seduction were among the subjects bawdily treated. These plays were also religious in origin, descending from the 'attellanes' or farces performed as part of the cult of the goddess of fertility. Petronius wrote the subsequently banned *Satyricon*, and Ovid was banished from Rome for writing *Ars Amatoria* and for the commission of some obscure offence. Musaeus and Sabellus were Roman pornographic writers, but we know of their works only by hearsay, since they were destroyed when the Empire became Christian. A popular Roman diversion was writing obscene inscriptions on the bases of statues in the public places. Despite, or perhaps because of, the general licentiousness the Romans of the middle class were curiously reticent and prudish in their conversation. Thus phrases such as 'cum nobis' were avoided because they might be confused with words like 'cunnibus', a verbal prudery which is not encountered again until Victorian times.

ANGLO-SAXON LITERATURE

In English literature obscenity makes an early appearance. The Exeter Book, the manuscript of which with that of Beowulf, the

[2] See *The Republic*, Everyman edition (1935), p. 71.
[3] *Op. cit.*, p. 67.

Vercelli Book and the Junian manuscript, form the earliest sources of Anglo-Saxon literature, contains a fine collection of obscene riddles of which the following is a typical example:

Wrætlic hongao bi weres þeo
frean under sceate foran is þyrel
bið stiþ ond heard stede hafað godne.
þonne se esne his agen hrægl
ofer cneo hefeð wile þæt cuþe hol
mid his hangellan heafde gretan
þæt he efelang ær oft gefylde.

Translated this reads:

A strange thing hangs by a man's thigh
under its master's clothes. It is pierced in front,
is stiff and hard, has a good fixed place.
when the man lifts his own garment
up above the knee, he wishes to visit
with the head of this hanging instrument the familiar hole
which it, when of equal length, has often filled before.

The answer to the riddle is, of course, 'key'.

Another robust riddle is the following:

I am a wonderful creature, bringing joy to women,
and useful to those who dwell near me. I harm
no citizen except only my destroyer.
My site is lofty; I stand in a bed;
beneath, somewhere, I am shaggy. Sometimes
the very beautiful daughter of a peasant,
a courageous woman ventures to lay hold on me,
assaults my red skin, despoils my head,
clamps me in a fastness. She who thus confines me,
this curly haired woman, soon feels
my meeting with her—her eye becomes wet.[3a]

The answer to the riddle is 'onion'.

It is worth noting that these and other incredibly gross riddles were lovingly collected by a monk, and included in a book intended to be a work of piety. For the most part the Exeter book is made up of devotional, penitential and didactic works. Anglo-Saxon readers, even the pious, were apparently not prudes.

MEDIEVAL TIMES

Robustness and lack of inhibition characterised not only Anglo-Saxon but medieval literature. Even those writers who had an

[3a] Anglo-Saxon Riddles, Nos. 44 & 25.

explicitly didactic purpose did not hesitate to describe the vices they were denouncing in vigorous and vivid language. Ballads, the most popular form of literature, were frank and unashamed, as were the lyrics of the thirteenth and fourteenth centuries, many of which have come down to us.[4] Chaucer, a court poet, was in no way inhibited, as a reading of 'The Miller's Tale' will remind, but there is no record of shocked contemporaries. The pilgrims were not scandalised by the revelations of 'The Wife of Bath', and bawdiness was not considered incompatible with religious devotion. Such broadmindedness was not confined to England: the fourteenth century was that of the subsequently much banned Boccaccio, who anticipated his critics in the Epilogue to his tales.

> Most noble damsels, [he wrote] corrupt mind did never yet understand any word in a wholesome sense . . . everything is in itself good for somewhat and being put to a bad purpose may work manifold mischief. And so I say it is with my stories. If any man shall be minded to draw from them matters of evil tendency or consequence they will not gainsay him.

The Medieval Church concerned itself with heresy and not obscenity, and although the faithful were warned against the writin of heretics, an ecclesiastical censorship was not instituted until aft the Reformation at the Council of Trent. Ovid's works were studie in English monasteries and although certain works of John Eruye and later William of Ockhàm were condemned, this was for reasons of faith, not morals. Savonarola threw *The Decameron* into his Florence bonfire in 1497, but he was a fanatic, untypical of his age. When *The Decameron* did fall under the papal ban in 1559 this was not because of its obscenity, but because it satirised the clergy. The Church authorised an expurgated edition, but the references expunged were those relating to the saints and the clergy; the obscenities remained. Accordingly monks became magicians, nuns were turned into noblewomen and the Archangel Gabriel transformed into the king of the fairies.*

PRINTING

During the fifteenth century book production in England steadily increased. Reading spread and professional scribes supplemented

[4] See the manuscript collection Harley 2253, and the volumes of lyrics published by the Early English Text Society, e.g. Chambers and Sidgwick's *Early English Lyrics*.

* The change in attitude subsequent to the Reformation is well illustrated by the views of St. Alphonsus Liguori who maintained that *The Decameron* had done more harm than all the works of Luther!

the work of the monks. In 1403 the Stationers' Guild was granted a charter of incorporation. The guild's origin is considerably earlier, but its incorporation is a significant pointer to the increased importance of books. Books were steadily if not rapidly increasing in numbers and circulation, when the invention of printing revolutionised the position. One of the first books to issue from Caxton's printing press at Westminster (1476) was a translation of Ovid's *Metamorphoses*. Printing presses were set up at Oxford in 1478: at St. Albans the following year; and in London itself in 1480. The reaction of the government was favourable, and Richard III passed a statute in 1483 encouraging not only the printing of books, but also their importation.[5] At first the Crown did not realise the importance of the new invention, but when printing became more general in the sixteenth century its power was better appreciated. Henry VIII repealed the liberal statute of 1483 and passed a measure to protect the English printers, but it was also the first step towards their control. The statute [6] referred to

> the marvellous number of printed books imported to the prejudice of the king's natural subjects [who] have given themselves so diligently to learn and exercise the said craft of printing that at this day there be within this realm a great number cunning and expert in the said science or craft of printing as to be able to exercise the said craft in all points as any stranger in any other realm or country.

As for the bookbinders they were declared to be 'destitute of work and like to be undone, except some reformation herein be had'. After this the Crown assumed the power of granting printing privileges as part of the prerogative and exercised it through Henry VII's court of Star Chamber.

LICENSING

The first licensing decree was issued by the King through Star Chamber in 1538.

> Item that no persone or persons in this realme, shall from hensforth print any boke in the englyshe tonge, onles vpon examination made by some of his gracis priuie counsayle, or other suche as his highnes shall appoynte, they shall haue lycense so to do, and yet so hauyinge, not to put these wordes Cum privilegio regali, without addying ad imprimendum solum and that the hole copie, or els at the least th effect of his license and priuilege

[5] 1 Ric. 3, c. 9.

[6] (1533) 25 Hen. 8, c. 15.

> be therewith printed, and playnely declared and expressed in the Englyshe tonge vnderneth them.*

The decree, however, does not appear to have been enforced.

In 1556 a decisive step was taken, destined to influence the whole Tudor and Stuart censorship, when Philip and Mary incorporated the Stationers' Company. In return for the charter which confined printing, apart from special licence, to members of the Company, the members undertook to search out and suppress all undesirable and illegal books. This was a royal master-stroke, since the company was the one instrument by which the government's policy could be successfully carried out. The Master and Wardens of the Company were given power

> to make search whenever it shall please them in any place, shop, house, chamber, or building of any printer, binder or bookseller whatever within our kingdom of England or the dominions of the same of or for any books or things printed or to be printed and to seize, take hold, burn or turn to the proper uses of the foresaid community, all and several those books and things which are or shall be printed contrary to the form of any statute, act or proclamation made or to be made.[7]

Besides ordering the destruction of the books the Wardens were empowered to commit to three months' imprisonment anyone who attempted to hinder them in the exercise of their duties. In addition a fine of one hundred shillings could be imposed, one-half of which went to the Company and the remaining half to the Crown.

That the measures were not aimed at obscene books can be seen from the opening words of the charter: 'Know ye that we considering and manifestly perceiving that certain seditious and heretical books, rimes and treatises are daily published and printed by divers scandalous, malicious, schismatical and heretical persons . . . and wishing to provide a suitable remedy in this behalf', etc. The Marian censorship, as indeed the whole Tudor and Stuart censorship was religious and political, not moral.

In 1559 the charter was confirmed by Queen Elizabeth, after which she introduced by decree the first effective system of licensing books,

* 16 November 1538, S.T.C. 7790. The King was anxious that he should not be taken to have approved the *contents* of the book. The original decree is altered to this effect in what is thought to be the King's own hand. For a discussion of the decree see W. W. Greg, *The Library*: O.U.P., Vol. IX, No. 4, p. 242.

[7] Charter of the Stationers' Company. All references to the company in this chapter are taken from Arber, *Transcript of Stationers' Registers, 1554–1640* (London 1875).

which lasted until 1695. No book was to be printed unless first licensed by

> her maiestie by expresse wordes in writynge, or by vi of her priuy council or be perused and licensed by the archbysshops of Cantorbury and Yorke, the bishop of London, the chauncelours of both unyuersities, the bishop beying ordinary and the Archdeacon also of the place where any suche shalbe printed, or by two of them, whereof the ordinary of the place to be alwaies one.

The decrees provided for the punishment of offenders and were addressed to the Company, which as under Mary acted on behalf of the Crown. Licensing fees were paid to the Company and every book printed was entered in the Company's register, thus making it possible to trace the majority of books printed in the later Tudor and early Stuart periods. At the end of Queen Elizabeth's decree came an interesting provision: 'Prouyded that these orders do not extend to anye prophane [i.e. classical] aucthours and workes in any language that hath been heretofore commonly receyued or allowed in any the unyuersities or Scoles: But the same may be prynted and vsed, as by good order they are accustomed'. For once *The Decameron* had been granted a reprieve.[8]

The injunctions were as far as possible enforced and imprints such as 'seen and allowed' and 'set forth and allowed', according to the order appointed in the Queene Majestie's Injunctions, became common form. But even with the help of the Stationers' Company it was not easy to secure universal obedience to the decrees, and their constant re-issue by Star Chamber shows that they were avoided, and that much secret printing and smuggling of books went on. The Papists and later the Puritans were the quarries of the government. Fr. Persons set up a printing press on his arrival in England in June 1580, his printer being Brinkley, who was seized with the press in 1581. Robert Southwell, the Jesuit poet probably had his own private press, and James Duckett was a well-known printer executed for printing Catholic books.

Later the government turned against the Puritans. Whitgift had become Archbishop of Canterbury in 1583 and although staunchly anti-Roman he was also a militant anti-Puritan. In 1586 he secured an extension of the censorship powers from the Star Chamber. No printing was to take place except in London and at Oxford and Cambridge, and no new printing presses were to be set up without the permission of the Archbishop of Canterbury and the Bishop of London. In October 1588 came the first of the Marprelate tracts

[8] 'Injunctions geven by the Queenes Majestie printed by R. Jugge and J. Cawood 1559.'

attacking the bishops with a broad scurrility. 'Printed oversea, in Europe', proclaimed the tract, 'within two furlongs of a Bounsing Priest, at the cost and charge of M. Marprelate, gentleman.' Seven tracts were issued before the government finally put an end to them, but the identity of Martin was never discovered. The tracts were remarkable for their ribaldry and outspokenness and this is the more significant since they were issued in the Puritan interest. The graver Puritans disapproved, but English Puritanism was still far from the prudery it was to assume in a later age. The anti-Martinists were equally broad in their invective and a stream of scurrilous pamphlets came from their pens.

Star Chamber and the ecclesiastical licensers did not, however, interfere with literature, nor save in extreme cases did they withhold licences because books were obscene. Arber stresses this point as well as the active part taken by prelates such as Archbishop Parker in promoting learned works of every kind. Commenting on the Tudor censorship R. B. McKerrow writes that there is not a single instance 'of a work of literary importance having been lost to us through the refusal to license it: tho' of course we cannot say what might have been written had freer criticism of current affairs been permitted'. In the records of the Stationers' Company there are only a few isolated references to the censoring of books for obscenity. 'Lewd' books are frequently referred to, but in Elizabethan times the word had a variety of meanings and was not confined to obscenity, although it was sometimes used in this sense.* The wide meaning of 'lewd' is shown by the following letter from the Bishop of London written to Lord Burghley on 30 December 1579.

> I have found out the press of printing with one Carter, a very lewd fellow . . . who has been divers times to prison for printing of lewd pamphlets. But now in search of his house, amongst other naughty papisticall books we have found one . . . entitled 'The Innocency of the Scottish Queen' a very dangerous book. . . . I can get nothing on him for he did deny to answer upon his oath.†

Again the Stationers' records contain the following entry for 3 December 1595:

> Abel Jeffes. Whereas Abel Jeffes hathe disorderlie without Aucthoritie and contrarie to the Decrees of the starre chamber

* 'Lewd' originally meant 'lay' and thus a 'lewd frere' meant a lay brother and not a licentious friar! Chaucer, however, did use the word in the modern sense, 'Lat be thy lewed dronken harlotrye', as did Shakespeare, 'He is not lulling on a lewd day-bed'.[9]

[9] *Richard III*, III, vii, 72.

† In 1584 he was hanged, drawn and quartered at Tyburn.

> printed a lewde booke called the most strange prophecies of Doctor Cipriano etc and divers othere lewde ballades and thinges very offensive/Yt is therefore ordered at a court holden the Daye and yeere abouesaid, That his presse and letters and other printinge stuffe which were seized and broughte to the hall for the said offenses Viz, one presse/xij paire of Cases and certen fourmes of letters,/shalbe defaced and made unserviceable for printinge.

A copy of the *Strange Prophecie* may be seen at the British Museum, but it is very dull and contains no obscenities!

Popular literature was certainly registered, the following being a typical entry: 'Recevyd of William Coplande for his lysence for pryntinge of a ballett intituled "the lamentation of an olde man for maryinge of a yonge mayde etc."' [10] Stubbes thought that the licensers were lax and complained of the delays in licensing serious books 'whilst other bookes full of all filthines, scurrility, baudy, dissoluteness, cosinage, conycatching and the like . . . are either quickly licensed or at least easily tolerate'.[11] One of the very few references to censure for obscenity occurs on 7 March 1591 where the entry reads: 'Entred for his copie a ballad of a yonge man that went a wooying etc. Abel Jeffes to be his printer hereof PROVYDED ALWAYES that before the publishing hereof the undecentnes be reformed . . . vjd.' Thomas Gosson was the author, but apparently he did not reform the ballad as the entry is scored through with thick black lines and a note appended: 'cancelled out of the book for the undecentnes of it in Diuerse verses'. The only other action taken against books on the grounds of obscenity was the burning of Christopher Marlowe's translation of Ovid's elegies in Stationers' Hall in 1599 by order of the Archbishop of Canterbury. Various satires and controversial works by Gabriel Harvey and Tom Nash were burnt at the same time, and this may have been the real reason for the raid.*

The toleration of obscenity by the government was not surprising in view of contemporary standards of taste. The Elizabethans were not squeamish and the delight in coarse and robust humour was shared by all classes. Jest books and collections of riddles were very popular amongst the middle classes, and German books were translated to stimulate those for whom English coarseness was not

[10] Arber, Vol. I, p. 100b.

[11] *A Motive to Good Works* (1593).

* In any case the orders were only of transient force. The books are found re-entered in the registers at pp. 466, 533 and 581. See Arber, Vol. III, p. 13. Marlowe's elegies were bound in one volume with Davye's epigrams and it may have been the latter which caused offence. *The Fifteen Joys of Marriage* was also destroyed.

enough. Shakespeare's humour was broad and his audiences saw nothing shocking in dialogue such as that between Hamlet and Ophelia in the play scene, which a later age was to expurgate. Elizabethans, like the Georgians, enjoyed their horror. No one protested against the last act of *Edward II*, nor condemned the plays of Webster or the mutilation of *Lear*. In such an atmosphere it was unlikely that the licensers would even think in terms of obscenity.

By the middle and latter part of Elizabeth's reign, however, Puritanism was rising and becoming vocal, preparing the way for a change in taste.

Just as the activities of the Evangelicals at the close of the eighteenth century foreshadowed the emergence of the 'Victorian Conscience' so the Puritans in the later sixteenth century prepared the way for the 'rule of the saints'. Nothing illustrates the Puritan temper better than its attitude to the stage. The true Puritan rejects pleasure of any kind as sinful and immoral. Even in medieval times miracle plays had been challenged, and in the *Handlyng Synne* of Mannyng of Brunne, published between 1303 and 1338, with its condemnation of both tournaments and plays, one finds a curious although isolated anticipation of Puritanism. As in the nineteenth century many who rejected the extreme Puritan position were nevertheless influenced by it, and Roger Ascham was typical of the new seriousness which Puritanism had engendered. The leader of the first school of English literary criticism, he denounced *Le Morte D'Arthur* in his book *The Scholemaster* (1570) as a work 'the whole pleasure of which . . . standeth in two speciall poyntes, in open mans slaughter, and bold bawdrye'. A bitter attack on the stage and poetry as immoral and sinful came with Stephen Gosson's *School of Abuse*, published in 1579. Poets, players and jesters were castigated as 'caterpillers of a Commonwealth'. *Honest Excuses* written by Thomas Lodge the same year in reply was suppressed by the licensers. The players countered by producing some of Gosson's own plays written before his conversion! A further attack came out in 1580, published with the blessing of the Corporation of London, *A second and third blast of retrait from plaies and Theaters.*

Puritans would naturally disapprove of bawdy books, but their efforts were concentrated against the stage, and the Marprelate controversy absorbed much of their energies. Nevertheless, efforts were made to purge the country of obscene books. In 1580 W. Lambard published a corrected draft of 'an Act of Parliament for the Establishment of the Governors of the English Print'. Both Puritanism and private greed were behind this draft measure, since monopolies were not granted for the lighter and more popular literature, and the established printers were jealous of the profits being made by their younger brethren. The Act was entitled 'An acte to restraine the licentious printing selling and utterynge of unproffitable and hurtfull Inglishe bokes', and was designed to deal with

> poœsies, sundrie bookes, pamfletes, ditties, songes and other woorkes and wrytinges of many sortes and names serving (for a great parte of them) to none other ende (what titles soever they beare), but only to let in mayne Sea of wickednesse and to set vp an arte of making lasciuious vngodly love, to the highe displeasure of GOD, whose guiftes and graces bee pitiefully misused thearby to the manifest inurie and offence of the godly learned whose prayse woorthie endevours and wrytinges are thearefore the lesse read and regarded, to the intollerable corruption of common lyfe and manners, which pestilently invadeth the myndes of many that delight to heare or read the said wantone woorkes, and to no small or sufferable wast[e] of the treasure of this Realme which is thearby consumed and spent in paper, being of it selfe a forrein and chargeable comoditie.

Eight members of the Inns of Court were to be established as 'Governours of the Inglyshe Prynte', and no printing was to take place without their licence. Punishments for unlicensed printing were to be fines and exclusion from the trade. The 'Act' remained a dead letter and was never presented to parliament.

THE ECCLESIASTICAL COURTS

If the prerogative courts used their jurisdiction sparingly over obscene offences, the common law courts refused to recognise them at all. There is no mention of 'obscene libel' in Coke's report *De Libellis Famosis* of 1606,[12] nor does he mention the offence when he treats of libel in his Institutes. From 1640 until 1727 all obscene offences were treated as being under the jurisdiction of the ecclesiastical courts.

These courts, which had been separated from the lay courts by William I, could impose only spiritual penalties such as excommunication or some public humiliation, but their jurisdiction was wide and undefined and they punished anything which they regarded as openly immoral or sinful without reference to rule or precedent. There are few reported cases of punishment for obscenity and in those there is nearly always an element of defamation, which until the sixteenth century fell within the ecclesiastical jurisdiction.

A typical case is that of 1584 taken from the Act Book of the Archidiaconal Court Book of Essex. 'Contra Willielmum Trene et

[12] 5 Co. Rep. 125a; 77 E. R. 250.

Elizabetham ejus uxorem, parochie de Rayneham . . . Detected for that they have made a fylthie ryme of the moste parte of the inhabitantes of this parishe. (14th February. Quia contumaciter recusant peragere penitenciam dominus eos excommunicavit.)' Another case, rather later, in 1627, occurred at East Hanningfield.

> Wheras one Benjamine Morgan of East Hanningfeild hath come into our parishe of Westhaningfeild and there not onlye made a songe, most dissolute and ribbaldrye songe in the alehowse to the great scandall of all the parishe, and doth like in other townes etc. The scandalous words used in this songe are that for the greatest parte of all the wyves are whores and their husbands cuckolds. These scandalous rymes were songe on Tuesdaye the 12th of June.[13]

That the clergy themselves sometime descended to obscene language is shown by the following case, which cost Dr. Dennison his curacy at Katharine Cree church in London.

> A painted window representing Abraham sacrificing Isaac having been put up in the church Dr. Dennison said it was 'a whirligig, a crow's nest and more like the swaggering hangman cutting off St. John the Baptist's head'. He also in diverse sermons reviled some of his parishioners, comparing them to frogs, hogs, dogs and devils and called them by the name of knaves, villains, rascals, queans, she devils and pillory whores.[14]

THE STUART CENSORSHIP; THE COMMONWEALTH

Under the first two Stuarts the ecclesiastical censorship grew more severe, but the Stuarts like the Tudors left literature free. If anything, the government took less interest in literary works, and there was a falling off in the registration of ballads and lighter literature, as the Stationers' records show. This was partly due to the poverty of those who printed this type of literature, which made it difficult for them to pay the registration fees, but the principal reason for the change was that it was no longer thought worth registering. In 1623 a proclamation was issued alleging that the decree of 1586 was not being observed, and a further decree of Star Chamber in 1637, again commanded that 'no person is to print or import (if printed abroad) any book or copy which the Company of Stationers have the right solely to print'. Star Chamber's days were, however, numbered and in 1640 the court was abolished, never afterwards to be revived.

[13] Hale's Ecclesiastical precedents.
[14] *Calendar of State Papers*, D.S. 1633, 40, 35, 36, p. 105.

At the same time the ecclesiastical courts and the Court of High Commission * were done away with and printing enjoyed a brief period of liberty.

This freedom was of short duration. On 21 March 1642 parliament commanded that 'the abuses of printing be reformed', and licensing was reintroduced by a decree of the Long Parliament dated 13 June 1643. This was the decree which moved Milton to write his *Areopagitica*, in which he conceded that certain books should be proscribed but condemned a general censorship. The tract was ignored and the licensing system rigorously enforced. Until the end of the Commonwealth, parliament or the Lord Protector continued to issue decrees regulating the printing of books.[15]

In 1646 *The Women's Parliament* was suppressed, 'being very lewdly written and tending to corrupt youth'.[16] Three years earlier, however, parliament had authorised the printing of what would today be considered an obscene book, *The first century of scandalous, malignant priests*, an action which further illustrates the absence of any prudery in contemporary language. The invective and scurrilities were accepted as normal, and justified by the book's purpose of exposing the evils of episcopacy.

Puritan influence in the first half of the seventeenth century did, however, result in a new seriousness in literature. Although the piety of these years was due in part to Episcopalians and Roman Catholics, they had been influenced by Puritan zeal. Humanism persisted, although the first exuberance of the Renaissance was over, and exercised a powerful influence not only over the Cavalier lyric poets, but also over Milton, the outstanding Puritan poet of his time.

As in the previous century Puritans were bent on reforming the drama which was still the dominant literary form. In 1605 the courts of record at Westminster were empowered to try proceedings against actors for profanity on the stage. The actions could be started by common informers, but penalties were limited to fines of up to £10.[17]

* The Court of High Commission punished, amongst other things, offences by the clergy which sometimes included obscenity. Dr. Slater was brought before the Court in 1632 for adding a 'scandalous' table to the Psalms. The Bishop of London took a dislike to his attire saying, '"and therefore Dr. Slater that band is not fit for a minister, nor those ruffles up to your elbows almost." Dr. Slater excused himself saying that he was now in his riding clothes. The Bishop replyed that if he sawe him in the like hereafter he would looke out some canon or other to take hould of him.' *Reports of cases in Star Chamber and High Commission* (1886). Ed. S. R. Gardiner.

[15] For a list of these, see Catalogue of Thomason Tracts, British Museum (1908). They were issued in 1647, 1648, 1649 and 1655.

[16] Record of Stationers' Company, V, lvi.

[17] 3 Jac. 1, c. 21. Repealed by 6 & 7 Vict., c. 68, s. 1, 1843.

Actors received royal protection and James I took the companies under his direct patronage on his accession, but the Puritans appealed to parliament against this unholy alliance, and in 1625 *A short treatise against Stage Plays* was significantly addressed to parliament. The most violent attack came from Prynne, later to lose his ears for insulting the Queen, who presented his arguments and invective in the 1,100-page *Histriomastix*. Parliament was not appealed to in vain and in September 1642 abolished the play-houses.

THE RESTORATION

At the Restoration in 1660 not only the King but the play-houses came into their own. Charles authorised the creation of two companies of players, one by Thomas Killigrew (The King's) and the other by William D'Avenant (The Duke of York's), housed eventually in Drury Lane and Salisbury Court. After the Puritan excess of moral zeal and policies of repression, a reaction took place leading to a spirit of cynicism in morals and manners, which found fullest expression in the revived drama. Literature, both poetry and drama, mirrored the immorality of its aristocratic patrons who formed a brilliant intellectual and social circle around the court at Whitehall. The age of Dryden, Rochester and Sedley, and later Congreve, Vanbrugh and Farquhar, was not concerned with the repression of 'obscenity', although the line was drawn at *Sodom*, published in Antwerp in 1684, which was never given a performance on the public stage.*

If manners were liberal the old attitude to freedom of expression in political and religious matters persisted. Star Chamber could not be revived, but its place was adequately filled by the Licensing Act of 1662.[18] All printing without licence was forbidden: powers were given to search premises and to seize any unlicensed books that might be found there: the number of master printers was limited

[18] 13 & 14 Car. 2, c. 33.

* It is of interest to compare passages in *Sodom*, which was not performed, with those in *The Relapse*, which was.

The Relapse (Vanbrugh)

COUPLER: What mischief brings you home again? Ha! you young lascivious rogue, you. Let me put my hand into your bosom, sirrah.

FASHION: Stand off, old Sodom.

COUPLER: Nay, prithee now, don't be so coy.

FASHION: Keep your hands to yourself, you old dog, you, or I'll wring your nose off.

COUPLER: Hast thou been then a year in Italy, and brought home a fool at last? By my conscience, the young fellows of this age profit no more by their

to twenty. The religious and political purpose of the Act can be seen from the text of its first section:

> No person shall presume to print etc. any heretical, seditious, schismatical, or offensive books or pamphlets wherein any doctrine of opinion shall be asserted or maintained which is contrary to the Christian faith, or the doctrine and discipline of the Church of England, or which shall or may tend or be to the scandal of religion, or the Church, or the government or governors of the Church, State, or Commonwealth, or of any corporation or particular person or persons whatsoever.

Books were required to carry a certificate from the licenser and here a direct reference to manners does occur. The certificate had to state that the book contained nothing 'contrary to the Christian faith or the doctrine or discipline of the Church of England, or against the state and government of this realm, or CONTRARY TO GOOD LIFE OR GOOD MANNERS,* or otherwise as the nature and work of the subject shall require'. This phrase was, however, widely construed and the censorship was moral only in name. Chapbooks, the 'Penny Merriments' and 'Penny Godlinesses', which Pepys delighted in collecting, provided light reading for the populace. These coarse trifles, which by modern standards would be considered obscene, were apparently submitted to the censor, because the printed copies carry his imprimatur. He did not think it worth his while to reform their crudities. Chapbooks were sold in the London streets by 'flying stationers' and 'running booksellers', but they were also sold in the country districts by wandering chapmen and hawkers.

Naturally a reaction against the licentiousness of the Restoration

going abroad than they do by their going to church. Sirrah, sirrah, if you are . . .

FASHION: Sayest thou so, old Satan? Show me but that, and my soul is thine.

COUPLER: Pox o' thy soul! give me thy warm body sirrah; I shall have a substantial title to't, when I tell thee my project.

FASHION: Out with it, then, dear dad, and take possession as soon as thou wilt . . .
(Act I, Sc. iii, p. 306 of Moxon's edition (1840).)

Sodom †

I would advise you Sire to make a pass
Once more at Pocherello's Royal arse
Besides Sire Pin has such a gentle skin
'Twould tempt a Saint to thrust his pintle in.
Come my soft flesh of Sodom's dear delight
To honoured lust thou art betrayed tonight
Lust with thy beauty cannot brook delay
Between thy pretty haunches I will play.

* Author's capitals.

† Rochester has been credited with the authorship but this is much disputed.

period was bound to occur, and once the political issues had been finally settled in 1688 the middle classes began to turn their attention to public morals. Jeremy Collier's *Short View of the Immorality and Profaneness of the English Stage* met with considerable public support on its appearance in 1698. His principal targets were Congreve and Vanbrugh, who replied, and the inevitable pamphlet war ensued. Collier's real object was not to reform but to abolish the stage, as appeared from his subsequent pamphlet *Dissuasive from the Playhouse* (1703). A more ominous sign was the emergence of a society pledged to the reformation of manners. Founded in 1692 under royal patronage the society had a twofold purpose, to enforce the existing laws against vice and to persuade to virtue by the distribution of improving tracts. At first confined to London it soon spread to other cities, which set up their own organisations designed to encourage virtuous living. In 1694 the society published *Some Proposals for the National Reformation of Manners*, together with a black list of the names of several hundred people who had been prosecuted by the Society. The crimes included whoring, drunkenness, and sabbath breaking, but there was no mention of 'obscenity'.

The puritanism, that is never far from the surface of English life, was to grow in strength during the following century. For the first half-century literary standards were not radically affected, but by the close of the eighteenth century the foundations of the self-imposed Victorian censorship had been laid. Not only had there been a revolution in manners, but in recognising the new crime of 'obscene libel' the courts had given the censors a powerful weapon, which when the time came they were not reluctant to use.

CHAPTER II

THE EIGHTEENTH CENTURY

THE NEW READING PUBLIC

DURING the eighteenth century a 'literary' reading public emerged and replaced the private patron as the arbiter of taste. Reading had become more common, leisure had increased, and the novel replaced the drama as the dominant literary form. Those to whom poetry made little appeal found a welcome form of relaxation and entertainment in novel reading. Subscription libraries sprang up to satisfy the new demand for books. In 1740 London's first circulating library was founded and was followed by others in provincial cities such as Bristol, where a public subscription library was formed in 1773.*

Literary periodicals had been unknown in the seventeenth century, but *The Tatler* (1709) and *The Spectator* (1711) started a new vogue. These magazines were of general rather than specifically literary interest, but they were followed by others such as *The Gentleman's Magazine* (1731) and the *London Magazine* (1732), which devoted much of their space to literary matters. *The Museum* (1746) was primarily a literary journal and was followed by the *Monthly Review* in 1749, edited by the Whig, Ralph Griffiths. Tory rivals were the *Critical Review* (1756), the *London Review* (1775) and the *British Critic* (1793). As yet these reviews occupied a subsidiary position,

* These libraries were viewed by some with disfavour. Cf. *The Rivals* (1774), Act I, Sc. ii.

SIR ANTHONY ABSOLUTE: In my way hither, Mrs. Malaprop, I observed your niece's maid coming forth from a circulating library!—She had a book in each hand—they were half-bound volumes with marble covers!—From that moment I guessed how full of duty I should see her mistress!

MRS. MALAPROP: Those are vile places indeed!

SIR ANTHONY: Madam, a circulating library in a town is an evergreen tree of diabolical knowledge! It blossoms throughout the year!—and depend on it, Mrs. Malaprop, that they who are so fond of handling the leaves will long for the fruit at last.

but they foreshadowed the great weeklies and reviews which were to exercise a dominant influence in the nineteenth century.

The eighteenth-century public was broadminded and although 'Old England' thought Fielding's *Tom Jones* 'a motley history of bastardom, fornication and adultery', the majority did not object. The *London Magazine* went so far as to produce an approving leading article (February 1749). In *Tom Jones* both narrative and conversation are frank and uninhibited. The following is a typical passage:

> 'I thought', said the parson, 'he had never been at the university.' 'Yes, Yes, he was', says the squire; 'and many a wench have we two had together. As arrant a whoremaster as any within five miles o' un. . . . Ask Sophy there—You have not the worse opinion of a young fellow for getting a bastard, have you, girl? No, No, the women will like un the better for 't!' [1]

In 1748 Smollett published his picaresque novel *The Adventures of Roderick Random* and by November of the following year had sold 6,500 copies. In spite of passages like the following, *Roderick Random* was even read aloud in drawing-rooms with women present:

> . . . mistaking one door for another, he entered Weasel's chamber and, without any hesitation, went to bed to his wife, who was fast asleep; the captain being at another end of the room, groping for some empty vessel, in lieu of his own chamber-pot, which was leaky; as he did not perceive Strap coming in, he went towards his own bed, after finding a convenience; but no sooner did he feel a rough head covered with a cotton night-cap, than it came into his mind that he had mistaken Miss Jenny's bed instead of his own and that the head he felt was that of some gallant, with whom she had made an assignation. Full of this conjecture, and scandalised at the prostitution of his apartment, he snatched up the vessel he had just before filled and emptied it at once on the astonished barber and his own wife, who, waking at that instant, broke forth into lamentable cries. . . . Poor Strap was so amazed and confounded that he could say nothing, but 'I take God to witness she's a virgin for me!' [2]

Fanny Boscawen wrote to the Admiral in 1748 acknowledging her enjoyment of Smollett and admitting that she was indebted to him 'for many a horse laugh'.[3] And in 1750 Mrs. Delaney, wife of the Dean of Down, was writing to her friend Mrs. Dewes, 'I have

[1] Bohn edition (1840), p. 44.
[2] Bohn edition (1858), p. 21.
[3] Letter of 29 January 1748.

read (or rather heard read) the Man of Honour, Roderick Random, and the Sieges of Drogheda and Derry'.[4]

Sterne's *Tristram Shandy* with its bawdiness and suggestive indecency shocked Dr. Johnson, but not the majority of his contemporaries. The *Monthly Review* hailed Sterne as 'a writer infinitely more ingenious and entertaining than any of the present race of novelists',[5] and the *London Magazine* began its review with the invocation 'O rare Tristram Shandy . . . if thou publishest fifty volumes all abounding with the profitable and pleasant like these, we will venture to say thou wilt be read and admired'. (February 1760.)*

Even Richardson, who was writing with an express moral purpose, did not spare his readers detailed descriptions of Clarissa's sexual humiliations by Lovelace.†

Although readers were broadminded the middle classes continued to attempt the reform of public morals. In 1702 Queen Anne issued a proclamation against vice, denouncing blasphemy, swearing, drinking, dicing, and the selling of liquor in coffee houses. Attention was drawn to 'the sodomites who have been but rarely heard of in this nation till the last age' and 'the herds of lewd women continually soliciting of men to lewdness in the open streets', but there was no mention of peddling 'lewd' books. Down to 1725 the Society for the Reformation of Manners had procured 91,899 arrests, and although it went out of existence in 1738 it was revived in 1757 with the blessing of John Wesley.

[4] *Correspondence of Mrs. Delaney*, Ed. S. C. Woolsey, Boston (1879), p. 375.

[5] December 1759.

* The following passage from *Tristram Shandy* illustrates Sterne's methods admirably: ' . . . the Homunculus is created by the same hand, engendered in the same course of nature, endowed by the same locomotive powers and faculties with us . . . is a being of as much activity, and in all senses of the word, as much and as truly our fellow creature as the Lord Chancellor of England. . . . Now, dear sir, what if any accident had befallen him in his way alone! or through terror of it, natural to so young a traveller, my little gentleman had got to his journey's end miserably spent; his muscular strength and virility worn down to a thread, his own animal spirits ruffled beyond description, and that, in this sad disordered state of nerves, he had lain down a prey to sudden starts, or a series of melancholy dreams and fancies for nine long months together. . . . "But alas!" continued he (my father) shaking his head a second time and wiping away a tear which was trickling down his cheek, "My Tristram's misfortunes began nine months before ever he came into the world." My mother who was sitting by, looked up; but she knew no more than her backside what my father meant, but my uncle, Mr. Toby Shandy, who had been often informed of the affair, understood him very well.' (*Tristram Shandy*, pp. 1, 2.)

† Walter Allen has described these passages as pornography, 'compared with which the obscenity of Smollett and the indecency of Sterne so often rebuked by the righteous appear innocent.' (*The English Novel* (1954, p. 46).)

THE STAGE

Attempts were also made to reform the immorality of the stage. Congreve and Vanbrugh were still performed, but only in expurgated versions and several prosecutions were brought for the speaking of obscene or profane words on the stage. In 1702 a group of actors were charged with acting Jonson's *Volpone* and Crowne's *Sir Courtly Nice*, and for speaking objectionable words, but all were found 'not guilty'.[6] In the same year another group of actors were charged with performing Congreve's *Love for Love*, *The Anatomist*, and Vanbrugh's *The Provoked Wife*, and with speaking obscene and profane words. One of the passages objected to in *Love for Love* was Sir Sampson's remark: 'I have known an astrologer made a cuckold in the twinkling of a star; and seen a conjuror, that could not keep the devil out of his wife's circle'.[7] No verdict appears to have been recorded.[8]*

Defoe attacked the theatres in 1705 in verse remarkable for its unrestrained invective:

> Here whores in hogstyes vilely blended lay,
> Just as in boxes at our lewder play;
> The stables have been cleans'd, the jakes made clear
> Herculean labours n'er will purge us here.
> Some call this metamorphosis a jest,
> And say we're but a dunghill still at best.[9]

Immorality and obscenity were charges which continued to be levelled against the stage, but when it was finally brought under governmental control, the reasons were political not moral. Fielding had attacked Walpole viciously in both *Pasquin* (1736) and the *Historical Register for 1736*, and the government retaliated by passing the Licensing Act of 1737.[9a] The Act provided that seven days before the performance in public of any play, it should be submitted for a licence to the Lord Chamberlain. Fielding turned from the drama to the novel, a symbolic change, because henceforward the lead in creative entertainment passed from the stage to prose fiction.

One result of the increased popularity of reading was a lowering

[6] Powell and others. *Coram Rege Roll*, Mich. 13 Wm. 3 (Public Record Office 2147), *Rex Roll*, r. 8.

[7] Cumberland's edition (1817), p. 24.

[8] (1702), Betterton. *Coram Rege Roll*, Mich. 13 Wm. 3 (Public Record Office 2147), Rex Roll, r. 9.

* In 1725 a further prosecution was brought against Harper and others for acting and for speaking obscene and profane words. Harper: *Crown Roll*, Mich. 12 Geo. 1 (Public Record Office 95), r. 51.

[9] 'On the New Playhouse in the Haymarket.' *Review II*, 3 May 1705, 103.

[9a] 10 Geo. 2, c. 19.

of literary standards and the creation of a new class of hack writers. The Licensing Act after repeated renewals (1664, 1685, 1692) finally expired in the spring of 1695, when parliament refused to extend it. This change was not due to liberalism but to the general conviction that the Act was unenforceable. New bills were introduced, the last in 1702, but they were all rejected, and the government turned to stamp duties [10] as a means of controlling journals and the Press. With the end of licensing the Stationers' Company lost its remaining importance, since it was no longer necessary to enter books in the register of the Company. Whatever the shortcomings of the licensing system it had restrained the printing and distribution of pornographic books and pamphlets to some degree. When the system was discontinued the underworld of letters, authors and booksellers who thought of nothing but a quick return for their money for the minimum of labour, flourished. A typical example of this class of publisher was Edmund Curl, the doyen of Grub Street. He is described by Amory [11] as 'very tall and thin an ungainly awkward, white faced man. His eyes were a light grey, large projecting, goggle and purblind. He was splay footed and baker kneed'. His business was founded principally on plagiary and pornography. Elizabeth Montagu wrote in November 1739:

> I got at last this morning the poems just published under Prior's name, brought them home under my arm, locked my door, sat me down by the fireside and opened the book with great expectation, but to my disappointment found it to be the most wretched trumpery that you can conceive, the production of the meanest of Curl's band of scribblers'.[12]

Again, Richard Savage under the name of Iscariot Hackney in *The Author to be Let* confessed: ''Twas in his Curll's service that I wrote obscenity and profaneness under the names of Pope and Swift. Sometimes I was Mr. Joseph Gay and at others theory Burnet or Addison.'

OBSCENE LIBEL RECOGNISED AT COMMON LAW

The activities of Curl and similar Grub Street writers were responsible for the creation of the new offence of 'obscene libel' at Common Law. Once the Licensing Act had expired the increase in importance of the libel law was inevitable, and the creation of the new

[10] Stamp Acts, 1712, 1725, 1743, 1757.
[11] *Life of John Buncle* (1825), Vol. III, p. 262.
[12] Quoted in Climenson, E. J., *Life of Elizabeth Montagu* (1906), Vol. I, p. 38.

misdemeanour was merely an example of the general expansion of the Common Law at this period. An unsuccessful attempt to establish the new offence had been made in 1708 in Read's case.[13] Read had printed a pornographic book *The Fifteen Pleagues of a Maidenhead* and was indicted. Mr. Justice Powell dismissed the case in these words: 'This is for printing bawdy stuff, but reflects on no person or persons or against the Government. It is stuff not fit to be mentioned publicly; if there should be no remedy in the Spiritual Court, it does not follow there must be a remedy here. There is no law, to punish it. I wish there were but we cannot make law.' Twenty years later, however, in Curl's case (1727)[14] this case was overruled and the jurisdiction taken over from the ecclesiastical courts. Curl had overreached himself in publishing a pornographic book *Venus in the Cloister or the Nun in her Smock*, and was brought into Court. Counsel for the defence argued strongly against this extension of jurisdiction and quoted Read's case in his support. For the prosecution the Attorney-General put forward a sweeping argument:

> What I insist upon is that this is an offence at common law as it tends to corrupt the morals of the King's subjects and is against the peace of the King. Peace includes good order and government and that peace may be broken in many instances without an actual force: (1) if it be an act against the constitution of civil government, (2) if it be against religion, (3) if against morality. I do not insist that every immoral act is indictable such as telling a lie or the like, but if it is destructive of morality in general, if it does or may affect all the King's subjects, then it is an offence of a publick nature. And upon this distinction it is, that particular acts of fornication are not punishable in the Temporal courts and bawdy houses are.

This argument was accepted by the court but not without hesitation, especially on the part of Mr. Justice Fortescue, who said: 'To make it indictable there should be a breach of the peace or something tending to it of which there is nothing in this case', and distinguished Sidley's case tentatively: 'And in Sir Charles Sidley's case there was a force in throwing out bottles upon the people's heads'. The report of that case is worth quoting:

> He was fined 2,000 mark, committed without bail for a week and bound to his good behaviour for a year, on his confession of information against him for shewing himself naked in a balcony and throwing down bottles (pist in) *vi et armis* among the people

[13] 11 Mod. Rep. 142; Fortescue, 98, 100.

[14] (1727), 2 Stra. 788.

> in Covent Garden, *contra pacem* and to the scandal of the government.[15]

Anthony Wood also gives an account of the trial, but as usual is inaccurate:

> In the month of June 1663 this our author Sir Charles Sedley, Charles Lord Buckhurst (afterwards Earl of Middlesex, Sir Thomas Ogilvie etc. were at a cook's house at the sign of the Cock in Bow Street near Covent Garden within the liberty of Westminster, and being inflamed with strong liquors they went into the balcony belonging to that house and putting down their breeches they excrementised in the street: which being done Sedley stripped himself naked and with eloquence preached blasphemy to the people.

At the trial he quotes Sir Charles as commenting on his fine of £500 that 'he thought he was the first man that paid £500 for ——'.[16]

Despite the doubts as to whether there had been any 'breach of the peace', Curl was condemned, the essential in Sidley's case being held not the force, but the assertion of jurisdiction as 'censor morum'. Thus the misdemeanour of 'obscene libel' entered the law and has never since been seriously challenged. 'Libel' here has no real connection with its popular meaning, but is an example of its original meaning, derived from 'libellus', a diminutive of 'liber'; literally it means 'a little book'.

Although condemned to the pillory Curl got the better of the judges. The State Trials record:

> This Edmund Curll stood in the pillory at Charing Cross, but was not pelted or used ill, for being an artful, cunning (though wicked) fellow, he had contrived to have printed papers dispersed all about Charing Cross, telling the people he stood there for vindicating the memory of Queen Anne: which had such an effect on the mob that it would have been dangerous even to have spoken against him: and when he was taken down out of the pillory, the mob carried him off as it were in triumph to a neighbouring tavern.[17]

Curl was condemned for publishing a pornographic book, not a work of literature, and throughout the eighteenth century no attempt was made to prosecute publishers of books of literary merit. The only approach to such action was the unsuccessful attempt to arrest the circulation of Matthew Lewis's *The Monk*, by means of an injunction. Neither are there any reported cases of prosecutions for

[15] (1663), 1 Sid. 168.
[16] *Athenæ Oxonienses* (1813–20), Vol. IV, p. 73.
[17] 17 St. Tr. 153.

pornography. It is true that Wilkes was prosecuted in 1763 for an obscene poem *Essay on Woman*, but this was only in name a prosecution for obscenity, the real purpose being political. Unfortunately, the case is only reported on certain technical points, and not on the issue of fact, whether or not the poem could be considered obscene. However, Lord Sandwich is reported as having read extracts to the House of Lords with evident relish. Lord Lyttelton demanded that he should cease but his protest was drowned by the cries of the other lords to 'go on!' *

PORNOGRAPHY

During the eighteenth century pornographic works circulated freely. John Cleland's *Fanny Hill or the Memoirs of a Woman of Pleasure* was written in 1748, and although he was summoned before the Privy Council he was granted a pension of £100 by Lord Granville on condition that he abstained from such writing in the future.†

As late as 1780 Harris's *List of Covent Garden Ladies*, a publication made up of erotic descriptions of various whores, who used it to advertise their charms, was generally available. In 1795 a new magazine, *Rangers*, was founded, which combined a directory of prostitutes with ribald stories of seduction and other frolics, together with a great number of bawdy anecdotes.[18]

CHANGING TASTE

By the latter part of the eighteenth century, however, taste was rapidly changing. A delight in the picaresque was replaced by an enjoyment of the sentimental. One reason for this was the increased number of women readers: 'All our ladies read now', said Dr. Johnson in 1788.[19] And ladies were not only reading, they were writing. In 1778 Fanny Burney published *Evelina*, a social comedy, which limited its range and avoided the coarseness and brutality of earlier writers. Its success was immediate and showed that readers were growing tired of the violent and the picaresque. Another book popular at this period and a good example of the 'sentimental' novel was Henry Brooke's *Fool of Quality*. John Wesley approved

* A copy of the poem is at the British Museum. It is much disputed whether Wilkes even wrote the poem. See E. R. Watson, *Notes and Queries*, 11th series, Vol. IX (14 February 1914). For the legal points see *R.* v. *Wilkes* (1770), 4 Burr. 2527.

† The British Museum has a copy of this book published in Paris in 1890. Cleland made £10,000 profit from the sales.

[18] Francis Place, B.M. Add. MS. 27, 825, s. 17.

[19] Boswell, *Life of Johnson*, Vol. III, p. 333.

it highly and having secured the author's permission to abridge it to a third of the original length, published it under a new title for use among the Methodists. Henry Mackenzie's *The Man of Feeling* (1771) was a further indication of the change in taste brought about by the cult of 'sensibility'

THE HORROR NOVEL

In contrast to this new refinement was the delight in horror that characterised the last quarter of the eighteenth century and is not without interest today, when 'horror comics' are apparently so popular and have caused great anxiety. Contemporary denunciation of these comics was paralleled in the late eighteenth century by a similar outcry against 'horror novels', the only difference being in the class of persons who read them. Horace Walpole inaugurated 'the literary reign of terror' [20] in 1764 when he published *The Castle of Otranto*, and in 1773 two essays appeared *On the Pleasure derived from Objects of Terror* and *An Enquiry into those kinds of Distress which excite Agreeable Sensations*. Walpole was followed by the more restrained Clara Reeve who wrote *The Old English Baron*, and then by Anne Radcliffe whose best-known work *The Mysteries of Udolpho* came out in 1794. In 1775 the Minerva Press had been set up in Leadenhall Street by William Lane and poured out a stream of horror for public delight.[21] Palates soon became jaded and grosser horrors were continuously demanded. A new point of ghastliness was reached in 1795 when Matthew Lewis published *The Monk*, which he had written in ten weeks. This was too much for the critics and it was widely attacked, and even more widely read. The *London Review* was scathing. 'This singular composition which has neither originality, morals nor probability to recommend it, has excited and will continue to excite the curiosity of the public'.[22] Lewis's biographer writes: 'So generally was the attention of all classes directed towards *The Monk* and so extensively was it read that serious apprehensions were excited in the minds of benevolent persons lest the work should contaminate the public morals'.[23] The 'benevolent persons' in the shape of one of the anti-vice societies instructed the Attorney-General to move for an injunction to restrain its sale. A rule *nisi* was obtained, the author showing no cause against it, but it was never made absolute and the proceedings were dropped. Lewis had been momentarily affected by the outcry. He wrote a penitent letter to his

[20] S. D. Neill, *History of the English Novel*, London (1951), p. 92.

[21] *Bibliography of Publications 1790–1820. 'The Minerva Press'*, Blakey. The Bibliographical Society (1939).

[22] February 1797, Vol. XXXI, p. 3.

[23] *Life of M. G. Lewis*, 1839.

father and personally expurgated the second edition, but, warns his anonymous biographer, 'even in its improved state the work is still unfit for general perusal'. Despite these setbacks the book brought Lewis great esteem, he was lionised by society, and even changed his name from 'Matthew' to 'Monk'. The *Monthly Mirror* published a favourable article, 'An apology for the Monk', and in 1798 there was even a poem, 'An epistle in rhyme to M. G. Lewis'. After *The Monk* the flood-gates of 'horror' opened, the most popular books being translations of German 'romances', or those which masqueraded as such. These lurid publications revelled in ghouls, vampires, pacts with the devil, poisons, murders and horrors of every kind. Many of them were frankly sadistic and voluptuous and these were the elements which caused the moralists alarm. By the first decade of the nineteenth century the force of 'horror' was spent and when the classic of the type, *Melmoth the Wanderer* by Charles Maturin, appeared in 1820, it aroused little attention and was rapidly forgotten.

Today, legislation is the panacea advocated to check the taste for horror, but the eighteenth-century experience throws some doubt on both the wisdom and the necessity for such action. 'The reign of terror' passed, and although the dominance of horror is clearly unhealthy, an element may well be necessary in the present conventional and highly organised society. That the horror comic is the successor of the Gothic novel can scarcely be doubted. As Michael Sadleir has written in *Things Past*:

> The Gothic novel crashed and became the vulgar 'blood'. But if the once despot of the boudoir became the servant of the chapmaker in the slums of Seven Dials; if the 'Children of the Abbey', 'The Romance of the Pyrenees', 'The Bravo of Bohemia' and all the rest sank from the drawing-room floor to the sourest recesses of the basement—the spirit of melodrama and terror (which is only in rousing guise the spirit of escape) persisted unsubdued and persists to this day.

'Horror novels' ceased to be written, not through legal action, but because of a change in public taste. In a sense they were bound to fail: they contained within themselves the seeds of their own destruction: sooner or later readers immunised by constant inoculation would fail to respond. Critics and satirists hastened this process. William Beckford, Thomas Love Peacock and E. S. Barrett mercilessly parodied their follies. Jane Austen's satire in *Northanger Abbey*, although more gentle was as devastating. Scott summed up the general feeling in the *Quarterly* (1810) when he wrote 'spirits and patience may be as completely exhausted in perusing trifles as in following algebraic calculations'. But the horror novel ultimately failed because better books were written, which people preferred to read. Scott was the principal architect of their destruction. When *Waverley* was published John Murray wrote to his wife, 'Pray read *Waverley*, it is excellent. No dark passages: no secret chambers: no wind howling in long galleries.' On a lower level novelists such as Mary Meeke provided 'simple narratives founded on events within the bounds of probability'. In 1802 the Minerva Press which had fallen on evil days published her *Midnight Wedding* and its prosperity revived. In this approach of providing better books and comics lies perhaps the best answer to contemporary problems of 'horror'.

The eighteenth century, which had inherited the coarseness and brutality of the preceding age, ended with a refinement in manners and a delicacy in literary expression new to English life. The way had been prepared for the acceptance of the Victorian code of manners which raised etiquette to the level of ethics and confounded cleanliness with godliness. In 1738 John Wesley had started the evangelical revival and its influence, although at first confined to the lower classes, was eventually to permeate the whole of English society. The role of the evangelicals in the formation of the Victorian conscience will be considered in the following chapter, but a preliminary quotation from Wesley's *Collection of Moral and Sacred Poems*, published at Bristol in 1744, will suffice to show that the mid-Victorian attitude to literature had an eighteenth-century foundation.

> It has been a common remark for many years [wrote Wesley] that poetry which might answer the noblest purposes has been prostituted to the vilest, even to confound the distinction between virtue and vice, good and evil. And that to such a degree, that among the numerous poems now extant in our language there is an exceedingly small portion which does not more or less fall under this heavy censure, so that a great difficulty lies on those who are not willing on the one hand to be deprived of an elegant amusement nor on the other to purchase it at the hazard of innocence and virtue.

CHAPTER III

THE VICTORIAN CONSCIENCE

TO generalise about the Victorians is to mislead as much as to illuminate: the period possessed no natural unity—it was one of ceaseless change, each thesis faithfully reproducing its antithesis so that one emerges from its study with a sense of escape from an Hegelian nightmare. But when this has been said, one characteristic quality can be detached which binds together figures as diverse as those of William Wilberforce, Carlyle, Tennyson and Arnold, and to which Halevy attributed the stability of an age of doubt and revolution, namely an intense moral seriousness. The criticism of life from a moral standpoint was as typical of the great Victorian agnostics as of those who remained in or later embraced orthodoxy. All George Eliot's work, despite the irregularity of her private life, bears the stamp of the twin ideas of moral responsibility and retribution, and it was John Morley, an agnostic, who led the attack on Swinburne in the 'sixties of the century.

Nothing illustrates this moral austerity better than the Victorian attitude to sex. An ever-widening toleration of the expression of heterodox opinion in religion and politics was matched by a fierce intolerance of free discussion about sexual relationships and morality. At first these seem contradictory attitudes, but in a sense they are complementary, restriction in one sphere compensating for freedom in the other. John Chapman, a contemporary publisher wrote in his diary for 1851:

> Received and read through one of Miss L.'s 'proofs' of a love scene which is warmly and vividly depicted, with a tone and tendency which I entirely disapprove. . . . I said that such passages were addressed [to] and excited the sensual nature and were therefore injurious;—and that as I am the publisher of works notable for the[ir] intellectual freedom it behoves me to be exceedingly careful of the MORAL tendency of all I issue.[1]

[1] From G. Haight's *George Eliot and John Chapman* (1940), p. 130–1. Quoted by K. Tillotson, *Novelists of the 1840's* (1954), p. 62.

This attitude is reflected in the literature of the period, both poetry and prose, but especially in the contemporary novel. Coarseness was frowned upon and the confusion of morals with manners resulted in a spinsterish verbal prudery. In his introduction to the 1841 edition of *Oliver Twist* Dickens proudly proclaimed that he had 'banished from the lips of the lowest character I introduced any expression that could by possibility offend'. A more serious blemish was the false picture of sexual life given by Victorian novelists, of which *Oliver Twist* again provides an example. In his book *The Dickens World* Humphry House wrote of the Victorian underworld as 'drenched in sex', but one would never guess this from reading *Oliver Twist*. The whole character of Nancy is falsified so as not to offend the susceptibilities of readers, and for the same reason her relations with Bill Sykes are only vaguely hinted at. 'Podsnappery', the avoidance of topics that 'would bring a blush to the cheek of a young person', was the distortion of what had originally claimed to be a decent reticence.

It is too often assumed that Queen Victoria was the creator of this attitude, whereas the essentials of 'Victorianism' were dominant years before her reign. In his essay on *The Age of Tennyson* G. M. Young pointed out that as early as 1805 the Germans had coined a word 'Engländerie' to convey the same meaning as our own 'Victorianism', while much of the unpopularity of George IV and William IV can be attributed to their survival as unwelcome Georgian relics into an age where a revolution in manners had already been brought about. Queen Victoria's accession was confirmation not cause of the movement which bears her name.

THE EVANGELICALS

The Victorian conscience was forged in the fires of evangelical enthusiasm. Although dating from 1738 the evangelical movement did not become powerful until the close of the century. By 1780 there were still only 44,000 Arminian Methodists, although a smaller group of Calvinist Methodists existed and the Methodists had many sympathisers within the establishment. From that date, however, expansion was continuous and rapid. The strength of evangelical Christianity was shown by the passing in 1781 of Bishop Porteous's Act [2] prohibiting Sunday evening amusements. Four years later the Sunday School Society was founded and the custom of holding Sunday schools for children spread all over the country. The Industrial Revolution with its accompanying rapid shift of classes also increased Methodist influence. Many of the new rich were Methodists

[2] 21 Geo. 3, c. 49.

who kept their principles, despite the change in their social position. They were supported by a strong, respectable lower middle class, also the product of industrialisation, factory foremen, clerks and skilled workers, who kept themselves distinct from the lower-paid workers by the strictness and respectability of their lives.

Fear of revolution combined with the example of evangelical earnestness and piety to bring about a counter reformation within the Church of England. 'It was a wonder', noted the *Annual Register* for 1798, 'to the lower orders throughout all parts of England to see the avenues to the churches filled with carriages. This novel appearance prompted the simple country people to enquire what was the matter.' From 1792 the Clapham sect had been active within the Church of England and under the leadership of William Wilberforce helped to spread evangelical ideals. Churchmen avoided evangelical excesses, but became imbued with an evangelical seriousness in their approach to religious and social affairs. Besides stirring-up Anglicans the Methodists aroused the sects such as the Baptists, the Congregationalists and the Presbyterians to new activities. As a result by the second decade of the nineteenth century the evangelicals were a powerful influence in the national life, reaching the peak of their influence before the accession of Queen Victoria.

Evangelical views showed a marked kinship to those of the early Puritans, but where Puritans had attacked the stage, Evangelicals denounced the novel. 'Novels', proclaimed the *Evangelical Magazine* in 1793, 'generally speaking are instruments of abomination and ruin'.[3] After reading a novel Arthur Young wrote in his autobiography: 'It has unhinged my mind and broken my attention to better things which shows how strongly pernicious this reading is and what a powerful temptation to vice such productions are sure to prove. Oh the number of miserables that novels have sent to perdition!' In 1800 Joshua Collins in an address to parents and guardians solemnly announced: 'It is much to be questioned whether any sort of fictitious representation of life and manners ought to be put into the hands of youth'. An interesting diagram, 'the spiritual barometer', appearing in the *Evangelical Magazine* in 1800, aptly illustrates the evangelical view of novels. Forty degrees above zero represents 'the love of God and frequent approach to the Lord's Table', while the equivalent forty degrees below is 'love of novels: scepticism: and neglect of private prayer'. Adultery comes only ten degrees lower, while 'love of wine' comes ten degrees higher than the addiction to novels.[4]

The stage, of course, was not exempt from evangelical attack.

[3] August 1793, Vol. I, pp. 78, 79.

[4] Reproduced in *Victorian Prelude*, M. J. Quinlan (1941).

The 'Spiritual Barometer' puts 'the theatre' thirty degrees below zero, and in 1806 John Styles wrote a strongly worded essay attacking the stage. Rowland Hill's views, although extreme, were not untypical: 'A young fellow clasps a young girl in his arms before all the spectators; what folly not to suppose that every impure passion is not immediately excited by such scenes as these'.[5]

Such absurdities were not generally accepted but their constant repetition did create the view that literature was a threat to integrity unless kept within strict limits, and was only to be tolerated if it served a wider moral purpose. The change in public taste brought about by evangelical influence is amusingly illustrated by an anecdote preserved by Lockhart in his biography of Sir Walter Scott. Scott's aunt was deeply shocked by a re-reading in the 'twenties of Aphra Behn's novels which had been the delight of her youth. She noted that at that time 'they were read aloud for the amusement of large circles consisting of the first and most creditable society in London'. Aphra Behn was not the only novelist to incur displeasure and both Smollett and Fielding were banished to the upper shelves.

BENTHAMISM

Evangelical distrust of literature was reinforced by the other great seminal movement of the period, Benthamism. The rise of evangelical piety was paralleled by the growth of utilitarian ideals in politics, and although separated on doctrinal grounds they had many practical points in common. As Dicey has shown[6] they were both individualist, humanitarian and anti-traditionalist. Above all, they both propagated a constricted view of life, whether the achievement of spiritual salvation or material happiness, to the attainment of which literature and the arts were equally irrelevant. Benthamite views on literature were expressed in the *Westminster Review*, founded in 1824, and their spirit is epitomised in Mill's reproach of Hume for allowing himself to become 'enslaved by literature . . . which without regard for truth or utility seeks only to arouse emotion'.

BOWDLER AND PLUMPTRE

An immediate result of the evangelical outlook was the expurgation of Shakespeare. In 1784 William Richardson voiced the growing distaste for Shakespeare in his essay *On Faults of Shakespeare*, in which he criticised him for his coarseness. In 1806 John Styles was sweeping in his condemnation: 'Barefaced obscenities, low vulgarities

[5] Expostulatory Letter, London (1795), p. 32.
[6] Dicey: *Law and Opinion in England*, pp. 397–404.

and nauseous vice so frequently figure and pollute his pages that we cannot but regret the luckless hour in which he became a writer for the stage'.[7] Even Coleridge succumbed to the fever, writing: 'Shakespeare's words are too indecent to be translated. . . . His gentlefolk's talk is full of coarse allusions such as nowadays you could hear only in the meanest tavern'.[8]

In 1807 an edition of Shakespeare was published by a relative of Bowdler and this was followed in 1818 by an expurgated text of all the plays. The Editor summed up his intention in the preface—to exclude 'whatever is unfit to be read by a gentleman in the company of ladies'. *Othello*, however, was too much for even Bowdler's cleansing activities and he advised 'the transferring of it from the parlour to the cabinet'. In 1822 Pitman's grasped the nettle and their school edition of that year purged *Othello*, the character of Bianca being excluded from the play.

Bowdler had been anticipated in his task by Plumptre who had in 1805 published an expurgated song-book containing Shakespeare songs. His aims were stated clearly. They were to make literature serve a definite moral purpose; to remove objectionable ideas and situations; and to delete all expressions which were in any way gross or impious. Romantic love scenes were banned, since he feared they might have the effect of forcing young people into unhappy unions. In accordance with these principles Plumptre introduced changes such as the following:

> Under the Greenwood Tree
> Who loves to lie with me

became

> Under the Greenwood Tree
> Who loves to work with me

while the burden of the musician's song in *Cymbeline*,

> With everything that pretty is
> My lady sweet arise;
> Arise, arise!

was changed into the improving

> With everything that pretty is
> For shame thou sluggard rise!

Strangely enough no comment came from the reviewers about these monstrosities, but the Evangelicals bestowed unstinted praise.[9]*

[7] *Essay on the Stage*. [8] *On Shakespeare* (1815).

[9] *British Critic*, Vol. XXX, August 1807, p. 194; *Anti-Jacobin*, Vol. XXII, October 1805, p. 167.

* Plumptre even included lyrics of his own such as the improving ode to the onion intended to reconcile the poor man to the meagreness of his diet. Its

Critics have sometimes treated Bowdler and Plumptre with too much harshness, since their work had its uses. 'He [Bowdler] is also too commonly seen as a mere censor', writes Kathleen Tillotson, 'whereas he was rather a populariser'.[10] Swinburne paid him an unlikely tribute: 'More nauseous and more foolish cant was never chattered than that which would deride the memory or depreciate the merits of Bowdler. No man ever did better service to Shakespeare than the man who made it possible to put him into the hands of intelligent and imaginative children.' Unhappily, the Evangelicals did not limit their concern to the minds and morals of children.

THE VICE SOCIETIES

Their anxiety for the consciences of adults was shown by the revival of the 'vice societies'. These societies, as has been indicated were in existence before the Evangelicals, but they revived them. In 1787 George III followed the example of Queen Anne and issued a proclamation against vice, but unlike the earlier proclamation it contained a direct reference to obscene books. The public were exhorted to 'suppress all loose and licentious prints, books, and publications, dispensing poison to the minds of the young and unwary, and to punish the publishers and the vendors thereof'. Wilberforce formed the Proclamation Society to enforce the King's injunctions. Its first president was the Duke of Montagu and besides many peers it was supported by seventeen bishops and the Archbishops of Canterbury and York. Its report for 1800 stated explicitly: 'The publication of obscene books and prints is an offence which attracted the society's earliest attention: and to which as an object of the first importance it has uniformly continued to direct its regard'. A more formidable society, which eventually absorbed the Proclamation Society was the 'Society for the Suppression of Vice', founded in 1802. John Bowdler was an original subscriber. At first the Society was confined to London, but it soon spread to other cities, and branches were set

inclusion is one of the many indications of the connection at this time between political conservatism and the reform of manners.

A plant there's in my garden grows
In all my tastes a sharer.
Its scent to me outvies the rose.
The lily is not fairer.
My food, my physic, my delight,
No longer for to fun ye on,
My rhyme and reason shall unite,
In praising of the onion.

[10] *Op. cit.*, p. 54.

up amongst other places at Bath, Hull and York.* The Society had a variety of purposes. It was to prevent the profanation of the Lord's Day, prosecute blasphemy and suppress blasphemous publications, bring the trade in obscene books to a halt, close disorderly houses, and suppress fortune tellers.[11] 'Infidelity and insubordination fostered by the licentiousness of the press', said the official address in 1803, 'have raised into existence a pestilent swarm of blasphemous, licentious, and obscene books and prints which are insinuating their way into the recesses of private life to the destruction of all purity of sentiment and all correctness of principle.'[12]

These activities did not go unchallenged. Many felt that the Society was nothing better than a group of busybodies interfering in matters which were not its concern. Sydney Smith dubbed it 'a society for suppressing the vices of persons whose incomes do not exceed £500 p.a.'[13] When the secretary appeared before the House of Commons Police Committee in 1817 much of the questioning was hostile.

> Much prejudice has prevailed against the Society [said the secretary] which I think is to be ascribed to the utter falsehoods and gross misrepresentations which have appeared from time to time in many of the public journals frequently throwing ridicule on the society by exhibiting it as at issue with low and insignificant individuals such as the keepers of green and fruitstalls, barbers, etc.[14]

Most of the Society's unpopularity was incurred by its campaign of prosecutions for blasphemy, which was waged most thoroughly between 1819 and 1823. Its earlier efforts had been concentrated against obscene books and strangely enough these incurred no censure. Richard Carlile, who himself had been a victim of the society's activities,† even commended the prosecutions: 'The first object of your society was to seek out the persons who were instrumental in disseminating obscene books and prints. Had you confined yourself to this no honest or moral man would have complained

* The report of the Society for 1812 included an account of the Oxford branch of the Society but this never existed. Shortly after publication the Oxford branch was discovered to have been an undergraduate hoax.

[11] *Report of Society, 1825.* London.

[12] *Part the First of an Address to the Public from the Society for the Suppression of Vice* (London 1803).

[13] *Edinburgh Review*, Vol. XXVI, January 1809.

[14] *1817 Report*, H. of C., p. 391.

† Richard Carlile was prosecuted in 1819 for publishing Paine's *Age of Reason.* He was sentenced to two years' imprisonment and fined £1,000. The Society set prosecutions going all over the country, and filed twenty-five informations against ten newsvendors in London alone.

or objected to your conduct as a society'.[15] Again Joseph Hume attacked the society for its prosecution of blasphemous offences, but commended its work in suppressing obscene books. Francis Place also expressed approval of the destruction of bawdy ballads.

Two explanations of this attitude may be put forward. First the trade in obscene books and prints had increased greatly during the last years of the eighteenth century and by 1802 had become a public menace. Between 1780 and 1830 the reading public had greatly expanded and undoubtedly the new class of inexperienced readers was being exploited. Secondly, the Society dealt almost exclusively with what we should describe as 'pornographic' books and pictures. Its one attempt to control serious literature was unsuccessful. In 1822 it prosecuted a bookseller Benbow * for publication of certain love stories and pictures and also for the issue of a French novel in sixpenny parts. Benbow who had already been ten months in prison after a prosecution by the Constitutional Association † proved that the novel had been translated into English thirty years before, and was obtainable from all the great circulating libraries. The Chairman of the Sessions told the jury that they were the sole judges of the case, and they immediately gave a verdict of 'not guilty'.[16]

Prosecutions for pornography originated with the Society. 'The Society', stated the secretary before the House of Commons Committee in 1817, 'first entered upon investigation into the state of the trade in 1802: at which period prosecutions for such offences being unknown, so little disguise and concealment were used by dealers of this class that with no great difficulty important discoveries were soon made as to its nature and extent'. Prosecution, however, drove the trade underground and in 1825 the Society was complaining:

> Experience only could convey any adequate idea of the systematic manner in which the base traffic is conducted or of its various forms and great extent, yet from its nature it courts concealment, and therefore it requires no little assiduity to discover the noxious vermin by whom it is carried on and to suppress their pernicious practices.

Much of the trade was carried on by foreigners who employed hundreds of English as well as foreign agents. The secretary gave

[15] *The Republican*, Vol. II, 25 February 1820, p. 182.

* Benbow had a shop in Castle Street, Leicester Square. Southey referred to it as 'one of those preparatory schools for the brothel and the gallows where obscenity, sedition and blasphemy are retailed in drams for the vulgar'.

† The Constitutional Association was founded in 1820 to prosecute seditious works. The Duke of Wellington and six bishops supported it, but by 1823 it was extinct.

[16] See *Rambler's Magazine*.

evidence of 'thirty Italians' who acted as hawkers.[17] These hawkers and others covered cities and towns from York to Maidstone, while Norfolk and Suffolk were centres of the trade. Pornography was sold by ballad stall-holders, by booksellers and even by 'opulent tradesmen'. The magnitude of the trade is shown by the Society's report of an individual case where 1,200 obscene prints were seized from one man. Foreign manufacturers may have dominated the market, but there were also domestic sources of supply as is shown by a letter written on 6 December 1808 to George Prichard, the Society's secretary. John Birtill visited Stapleton prison and was scandalised when the prisoners tried to sell him obscene wares.

> Inclosed are some of the drawings which I purchased in what they call their market without the least privacy on their part or mine: they wished to obtrude on me a variety of devices in bone and wood of the most obscene kind, particularly those representing a crime which ought not to be named among Christians which they termed 'the new fashion'. I purchased a few but they are too bulky for a letter, yet I will forward them if you wish. Straw platt was tendered me by at least thirty of the prisoners who carry it about with them.

Unhappily there is no record of what constituted 'the new fashion' and one is left to one's own speculations.

Undergraduates at Oxford and Cambridge were keen buyers of pornography, especially in the form of snuff boxes, in which there was a flourishing trade. These also found their way into boarding schools for young ladies. James Price was apprehended in September 1816 for selling snuff boxes without a licence.

> The defendant now pleaded great poverty and said he was ignorant that the license had expired and the magistrate was about to discharge him when upon further investigation it was discovered that many of the snuff boxes had indecent and obscene engravings and pictures upon them: some of them very highly finished and on being closely interrogated by the worthy magistrate in consequence of some information conveyed to him, the defendant was obliged to confess that he was in the habit of exposing these boxes to sale at Ladies' boarding schools and of disposing many of them to the young pupils.[18]

The Society took prompt action to end this iniquity, as the secretary informed the Commons Committee:

[17] Police Committee of the House of Commons, 1 May 1817.
[18] Police Committee of the House of Commons, 1817.

> Having obtained undoubted evidence of the practices I have before detailed they immediately sent cautionary letters to almost all the schools for female education in and about the metropolis and to the Head Masters of different public schools.

The offending snuff boxes were even exposed in shop windows, but the Society put an end to that. Within twelve months they brought five prosecutions 'which have greatly tended to the removal of that indecent display by which the public eye hath of late been much offended'.

Between 1802 and 1807 thirty to forty prosecutions were brought and convictions were recorded in every case. Magistrates were sympathetic. As one put it: 'The mischief done to the community by such offences greatly exceeds that done by murder, for in the latter case the mischief has some bounds, but no bounds can be set to the pernicious consequences of a crime which tends to the entire corruption of morals'.[19] Up to a point the Society was successful and in 1811 the *Christian Observer* congratulated the members on their zeal without which 'many of those polluting publications which are now only sold by stealth and with peril to the vendor might have been seen a few years ago exhibited in the shops of respectable booksellers'.[20] Such complacency was premature, since the ending of the war with France meant a renewed influx of obscenities from the Continent. Between 1817 and 1825 twenty prosecutions were brought and the tide was again turned back. The Society itself destroyed many publications, but certain specimens were saved for subsequent use as evidence. No chances were taken even with the Society's staff: 'These specimens are kept in a tin box secured by three different locks: one of the keys of which is kept by the treasurer, one by a member of the committee and one by the secretary; so that the box can at no time be opened but with the concurrence of these three persons'.[21]

Besides enforcing the existing law by bringing prosecutions the Society made its provisions widely known by special legal publications. In 1810 *An abstract of the Laws against vice and immorality* was published, and by 1832 *The Constable's Assistant: a compendium of the duties and powers of constables and other peace officers* had reached four editions. The Society was also instrumental in the passing of the Vagrancy Act of 1824 which punished public exhibitions of indecent prints with not less than three months' hard labour.[22]

[19] Police Committee of the House of Commons, 1817.
[20] Vol. X, March 1811, p. 184.
[21] Police Committee of the House of Commons, 1817.
[22] 5 Geo. 4, c. 83.

PORNOGRAPHY

Undoubtedly the Society kept pornography in check, but its flow continued throughout Victorian times and caused constant anxiety. The nineteenth century in England was the great period for pornography of every kind, from highly priced erotica designed for bibliophiles to the cheap trash intended for the general public. Up to 1845 for example there had been twenty editions of *The Memoirs of a Woman of Pleasure*. William Dugdale published many pornographic books, a typical title being *Love: How to raise love or the art of making love in more ways than one, being the voluptuous history and secret correspondence of two young ladies* (*cousins*) *handsome and accomplished, minutely detailing their first sexual emotions, their feelings at its introduction and their delicious enjoyment of the enchanting revelries of love.*[23] Apart from books there were a considerable number of periodical publications, explicitly pornographic in character such as *The Exquisite* (1842–4), *The Cremorne* (1851), *The Boudoir* (1860) and *The Pearl* (1879), as well as the long-established *Rambler's Magazine*. A pornographic magazine with a deceptively innocent title was *The Englishwoman's Domestic Magazine* (1868–70). Literature detailing the delights of flagellation was very popular, a genre which reached its peak with the publication in 1888 of *The Whippingham Papers* to which Swinburne contributed. In *Letters from a Friend in Paris* (1874) one may find detailed descriptions of buggery, *fellatio*, etc., while other popular erotica were Edward Sellon's *The New Epicurean* (1865) and *The Romance of Lust* (1873). (For further information see the relevant bibliographies cited on page 49.) Such was the extent of the trade that in 1857 Lord Campbell's Act was passed in a vain attempt finally to suppress it.

The existence and extent of this underworld literature severely restricted the freedom of serious novelists, who had to be vigilant to keep their own work distinct from the obscene species. In October 1851 a contributor to *Fraser's Magazine* commented on the impossibility of an English novelist writing on themes such as those chosen by George Sand for *Lelia* or *Indiana*. Such a novel, he wrote, 'would sink at once to Holywell Street [The centre of the pornographic book trade] and contempt'. 'With the Victorian underworld what it was', writes Kathleen Tillotson, 'it is hard to see how the innocent tyranny of the Young Person could have been avoided, though it might have been attended with less hypocrisy'.[24] This somewhat overstates the case, but it does indicate that there were reasonable

[23] Published 1860–5, at 3 gns. [24] *Op. cit.*, p. 63.

grounds for the tenderness of the Victorian conscience on matters connected with sex. When the extent of Victorian pornography and prostitution is taken into account, it is possible to interpret the conventions about sex as a necessary means of self-defence, adopted to prevent subjugation by the underworld. Equally, 'respectability' when considered against the actual background of social conditions loses much of its stuffiness and hypocrisy and can be reappraised as a valuable and even a moral social ideal. 'Respectability' not only protected middle-class standards, but enabled the skilled worker to rise above and keep himself distinct from the amorphous mass of the industrial proletariat.

FAMILY LITERATURE

Both evangelical religion and fear of the underworld contributed to the formation of the Victorian conscience, and these two forces combined to bring about the cult of the family. Evangelicalism may have had its platform triumphs, but above all it was the religion of the home. To paraphrase Augustine Birrell, it was not the Mass but family prayers that mattered. As for the underworld the family, and the larger the better, stood as a bulwark against it, and of this ideal the Royal Family provided a splendid example.* The family cult led to family literature, reviewers reflecting with satisfaction that whereas in France novels were written for adults, in England they were written for the family. This had a further restricting effect on English writers, which was intensified by the widespread habit of reading aloud to a family gathering. In a letter to her sister Cassandra Jane Austen writes: 'My father reads Cowper to us in the mornings to which I listen when I can', and she goes on to comment on *Alphonsine* by Madame de Genlis: 'We were disgusted in twenty pages as independent of a bad translation it has indelicacies which disgrace a pen hitherto so pure; and we changed it for the female Quixote which now makes our evening's amusement to me a very high one, as I find the work quite unequal to what I remember of it'. Thomas Moore also illustrates the habit: 'I pass my day in my study or in the fields, after dinner I read to Bessy for a couple of hours and we are at present (in this way) going through Miss Edgeworth's works'. It must be remembered that the middle-class dining hour

* Thus Disraeli in a speech at Manchester, 3 April 1872: 'The influence of the Crown is not confined merely to political affairs. England is a domestic country. Here the home is revered and the hearth sacred. The nation is represented by a family—the Royal Family; and if that family is educated with a sense of responsibility and a sentiment of public duty, it is difficult to exaggerate the salutary influence they may exercise over a nation.'

was between six and seven, and this gave time for a long period of reading before the family retired to bed. The court dined at eight, but this did not become fashionable until later in the century. Inevitably, the criterion of a good book became its fitness to be read aloud in the family circle. Thus the test of what could be inserted in a novel became what a parent could read aloud to his own children in the sanctity of his own home. It is not surprising that writers were reticent.

The delicacy of the Victorian conscience can then to some extent be rationally explained, but its dictates could hardly have been enforced had it not been for the close relationship between author and reader and the dominant influence exercised by the great reviews and magazines. Readers by present-day standards were few, but they formed a single unified public. Novels, and to a lesser extent poetry, were read by all who were able to read. Thackeray, for example, may not have commanded a wide public but he commanded all of it, the essential consideration being wholeness not breadth. Most of the great novels of early and mid-Victorian times were best-sellers, and were read not only by the educated middle classes, but by those working men who were aspiring to a culture denied to the majority of their fellows. This unity enabled critical standards to be set and maintained, and the close contact with his readers was fruitful for the writer, as long as he shared the assumptions of the majority of his readers. Dickens is the best example of an author whose work benefited by close contact with his public: in one way he needed to feel his readers' presence in order to produce his best work. Dickens, however, was pre-eminently a product of his own age, and when he criticised it his criticisms were those which his readers instinctively felt but were unable to express. Thackeray found the conventions of his public cramping, but was skilful enough to exploit them for his own ends. He did not however deceive Walter Bagehot.

> He never [wrote Bagehot] violates a single conventional rule; but at the same time the shadow of the immorality that is not seen is scarcely ever wanting to his delineation of the society that is seen. Everyone may perceive what is passing in his fancy. Mr. Dickens is chargeable with no such defect—he does not seem to feel the temptation.[25]

To later writers like Hardy, who were writing not with but against their age, the conventions became a tyranny which threatened to stifle their creative work.

[25] *Literary Studies*, Vol. II, pp. 187–8.

PUBLISHING METHODS

Publishing methods in Victorian times brought writer and reader closer together. Novels were published in volume form, but usually in three volumes at the high price of one and a half guineas. When the higher money values of the period are taken into account as well as the perennial dislike of buying fiction, it can be seen that circulation in this form was unlikely to be high. Publishers in the 'thirties resorted to publication in parts in order to increase their sales. Issued monthly in paper wrappers they sold for as little as a shilling and had the immediate effect of increasing novel readers, since many who would have been deterred by the outlay of thirty shillings thought little about the expenditure of a monthly shilling. 'Hire-purchase' in fiction proved an immediate commercial success, but it had other consequences which its inventors had not foreseen. A novel issued in this form might take as long as eighteen months before it was completely in the hands of the public, and the writer could gauge the reaction of his public by their reception of each instalment. Many readers wrote after the receipt of a new instalment to express their views: 'Oh my dear dear Dickens!', wrote Lord Jeffrey, who was reading *Dombey and Son*, with eager interest, 'what a No. 5 you have given us! I have so cried and sobbed over it last night and again this morning; and felt my heart purified by those tears'.[26] With the artistic limitations that this method of publication imposed we are not concerned, but it intensified the feeling of communion between writer and reader. Thackeray referred to it in his preface to *Pendennis*:

> In his constant communication with the reader the writer is forced into frankness of expression and to speak out his own mind and feelings as they urge him. Many a slip of the pen and the printer, many a word spoken in haste, he sees and would recall as he looks over his volume. It is a sort of confidential talk between writer and reader which must often be dull, must often flag.

This intense consciousness of his readers is further illustrated by his frequently irritating habit of addressing them direct in the course of his narratives.

Another popular method of publication was the magazine serial. Amongst novels published in this form in the 'thirties and 'forties were Thackeray's *Catherine*, Dickens's *Oliver Twist* and Kingsley's *Yeast*. Although magazine serials had preceded part publications they also outlived them and their increasing popularity in the late

[26] Cockburn, *Life of Lord Jeffrey* (1852), Vol. II, pp. 406–7.

'fifties led eventually to the latter's discontinuance. In 1859 and 1860 *Macmillan's Magazine* and the *Cornhill* were founded and sold for only a shilling, their cheapness making them formidable rivals. While publication in serial form continued to foster the relationship which had been established between writer and reader it added a further threat to the author's independence in the person of the Editor whose eye was perpetually on his readers. Thackeray himself, when Editor of the *Cornhill*, rejected Trollope's story *Mrs. General Talboys* because it might offend the susceptibilities of his readers. Hardy is perhaps the most celebrated example of an author falling foul of the magazine editors, and his experiences with *Macmillan's* and *The Graphic* will be recounted later.*

THE LIBRARIES

Not all novels were published in part or serial form, however, and for these as well as for later reprints the Victorians made use of the circulating libraries, which became one of the most potent instruments of censorship. The basis of their power was the expensive three-volume novel—they frequently bought up seventy-five per cent. of an issue—and as long as this form persisted they could exercise a widespread censorship by the simple expedient of declining to stock a book of which they disapproved. In the 'eighties George Moore clashed with the libraries,† but his publication of *A Mummer's Wife* in one volume at six shillings foreshadowed the end of their reign. Up to that date, however, their influence was unchecked, the widest powers being wielded by Mudie, who later shared his kingdom with W. H. Smith. Mudie founded his library in the 'forties in King Street, Bloomsbury, and began business by lending books to the impecunious students of London University, which had recently been established in the neighbourhood. Mudie was a dissenter and although his business made it impossible for him to adopt the full evangelical doctrine on novels, he made up for it by drawing a sharp distinction between those which were 'good' and those which were 'bad'. His trade name of 'Mudie's SELECT Library' suitably reflected this classification. By 1852 his business had become so profitable that he was able to move to New Oxford Street, where his emporium soon became a fashionable centre. In 1861 he had 800,000 books in stock and it was estimated that 10,000 people passed in and out every day. Moral standards were strict and became stricter; offending books were rigorously excluded, and an attitude fostered which Edmund Gosse dubbed 'Mudieitis'. Mudie's influence

* See page 76. † See page 75.

in the capital was paramount and he also drew subscribers from every part of the country. A writer's future might depend on his being found acceptable by Mudie. Mrs. Oliphant wrote: 'My own first production was so honoured and I confess it seemed to me in those days that the patronage of Mudie was a sort of recognition from heaven'. Celestial principles did, however, occasionally come into conflict with the commercial necessity and Mudie admitted *Ruth* and *Adam Bede* and in 1863 Ouida's *Held in Bondage*, when the public demand for these books was high, despite the critics' denunciation. Equally commercially successful and no less high-minded was W. H. Smith, who conceived the idea of railway book-stalls. In 1851 he gained a monopoly of bookstalls on the London and North-Western Railway and ten years later his bookstalls were to be found on all the principal railway systems. A book could be borrowed and a deposit paid at the station of departure and was returnable by the traveller when he reached his destination. The deposit less a small deduction was then repaid. W. H. Smith was a zealot for the moral welfare of his readers and earned for himself the titles of 'The North-Western Missionary' and 'Old Morality'. In 1857 during the debate on the Obscene Publications Act, Lord Shaftesbury referred appreciatively to the work of Mr. Smith in disseminating 'an immense body of the purest literature', and described him as 'a truly Christian gentleman utterly incapable of doing an unworthy act'.

THE REVIEWS

Powerful as the libraries were, their influence came second to that of the reviews, which throughout the Victorian period maintained and elevated public standards of taste. Their history, as has been noted, stretched back into the eighteenth century, but their dominance was of later date. In 1802 *The Edinburgh Review* was founded to express Liberal views and was followed in 1809 by its Tory rival *The Quarterly*. Weekly reviews flourished, each adopting a particular standpoint; the *Athenæum* (1828) devoted much of its space to literature; the *Spectator*, founded in the same year, expressed the opinions of educated radicalism; and the *Saturday Review* (1855) made public morality its principal concern. Magazines were also widely read and published poetry and serialised novels as well as book reviews. *Blackwood's* was founded in 1817: a new *London Magazine* in 1820 and *Fraser's* in 1830. *Fraser's* reviewed many novels, George Henry Lewes, who also reviewed for the Benthamite *Westminster* (1824), being one of its principal contributors. The 'sixties saw a new crop of periodicals, amongst them the *Fortnightly* (1865) and the

Contemporary (1866), both monthlies, and new weeklies such as the *Academy* (1869). At a period when much time was spent in the home free from the distractions of radio and television, and newspapers were few, their influence was considerable, each new edition being eagerly awaited and on arrival conscientiously read.

The reviews and magazines faithfully reflected the views of the rising middle class who had gained a measure of political power by the Reform Acts and whose social influence was widespread. Like all those new to power the middle class was intolerant especially in moral matters, and laid down rigid standards which literature was required to follow. This austere morality characterised all the great critics of the time. Victorian criticism of the arts was moral rather than æsthetic, the artist being expected to edify as well as to delight. Not until Pater was autonomy claimed for art and æsthetic experience, and even he suppressed his conclusion to 'Studies in the History of the Renaissance for 15 years', as he feared it 'might possibly mislead some of the young men into whose hands it might fall'. In any event æstheticism was a late bloom of ephemeral hothouse growth, and did not flower until the Victorian age was already on the wane, its influence never extending outside a coterie. Carlyle was the dominant critic of the period, and expressed the views of his contemporaries when he wrote: 'The fine arts too like the coarse, and every art of man's God given faculty, are to understand that they are sent hither not to fib and dance but to speak and work'. Ruskin subscribed to this thesis: 'The arts have had, and can have but three principal directions of purpose: first that of enforcing the religion of men: secondly that of perfecting their ethical state: thirdly that of doing them material service'. He defined the standard of perfect taste in art as 'the faculty for receiving the greatest possible pleasure from those material sources which are attractive to our moral nature in its purity and perfection'. Arnold, too, who elevated culture into a religion, was imbued with this moral sense, stating in his critical essays that 'a poetry of revolt against moral ideas is a poetry of revolt against life: a poetry of indifference towards moral ideas is a poetry of indifference towards life'.

Such views can be defended, but unhappily they lend themselves to distortion and moral austerity can easily degenerate into prudery. Ruskin himself illustrated this tendency and one has only to consider his announcement in 1872 when Professor of Fine Art at Oxford that 'the representation of the nude in art has been essentially destructive to every school of art in which it has been practised', and his denunciation of the study of anatomy by art students as 'not only a hindrance but a degradation', to see to what follies the moral view of art could lead. With the example of such a mentor it is not surprising that the lesser lights of the reviews should confound purity and prudery and distort morality into an excessive squeamishness.[27]

KEATS, BYRON AND SHELLEY

The first of the long series of outcries by the critics against immoral poetry or novels came in 1818 when Keats published his poem 'Endymion'. *Blackwood's* reproached him for his pruriency, and the *British Critic* announced:

> Not all the flimsy veil of words in which he would involve immoral images can atone for the impurity and we will not disgust our readers by relating to them the artifices of vicious refinement by which under the semblance of 'slippery blisses, twinkling eyes, soft completion of faces, and smooth excess of hands' he would palm upon the unsuspicious and the innocent, imaginations better adapted to the stews.

This, however, was only a curtain raiser for the howl of execration that arose when Byron published the first two cantos of 'Don Juan' in the following year. The attack on Byron is of interest as it shows clearly the connection between anti-Jacobinism and the new moral orthodoxy.

Murray was reluctant to publish at all, and did his best to dissuade Byron from his purpose. In a letter of 1 February 1819 Byron wrote that 'his cursed puritanical committee' had thrown 'milk and water on the first canto'.

> If they had told me the poetry was bad I would have acquiesced but they say the contrary . . . and then talk about morality . . . the first time I ever heard the word from anybody who was not a rascal that used it for a purpose. I maintain that it is the most moral of poems, but if people won't discover the moral that is their fault not mine.

Murray even feared a prosecution, and insisted on the poems being published anonymously at the high price of a guinea and a half. His fears of legal intervention were not fulfilled but the reviews were vigorous in their denunciation. The *British Critic* branded the poem as 'a narrative of degrading debauchery in doggerel rhyme', and declined to conduct its readers 'through the shameless indecency which characterises the first cantos'. Objection was taken to both the treatment and the theme: 'The adventures which it recounts are

[27] For a full treatment of this point, see H. Ladd, *The Victorian Morality of Art* (New York 1932).

of such a nature and described in such language as to forbid its entrance within the doors of any modest woman or decent man. Nor is it a history only but a manual of profligacy. Its tendency is not only to excite the passions but to point out the readiest means of their indulgence.' The *Monthly Review* on the other hand praised the poem and was not blind to its beauties, but included a warning to its author: 'We trust however and we believe that the noble author will pay sufficient deference to the public morals and to that public voice which we doubt not will in this instance call on him to abstain from pursuing a design which may indeed add to his poetic reputation but can never procure for him any moral fame'. *Blackwood's Magazine* for August 1819 also declared that its 'indignation in regard to the morality of the poem has not blinded us to its manifold beauties', but the indignation was considerable. 'This miserable man . . . a cool unconcerned fiend laughing with a detestable glee over the whole of the better and worse elements of which human life is composed', and the writer went on to attack him for his ill usage of his wife! The next three cantos were treated more kindly by *Blackwood's*. Harry Franklin wrote a light boisterous review:

> In the particular descriptions they are not quite so naughty as their predecessors: indeed his lordship has been so pretty and well behaved on the present occasion that I should not be surprised to hear of his work being detected among the thread cases, flower pots and cheap tracts that litter the drawing room tables of some of the best regulated families.

The *Monthly Review* was also more balanced although it continued to ask 'what benefit can accrue to the reader from a series of love intrigues?' The *British Critic* remained implacable:

> The poem before us is one of those hole and corner deposits not only begotten but spawned in filth and darkness. Every accoucheur of literature has refused his obstetric aid to the obscure and ditch delivered foundling: and even its father though he has unblushingly stamped upon it an image of himself which cannot be mistaken, forbears to give it the full title of allowed legitimacy.

'Cain' on its publication in 1821 also aroused the ire of the reviewers, but more for blasphemy than for obscenity. An anonymous 'Remonstrance' was written addressed to Murray and a spate of pamphlets followed. 'The very highest in the land' (i.e. King George IV) according to the *Examiner*, 'had expressed his disapprobation of the blasphemy and licentiousness of Lord Byron's writings.' This disapprobation was to lead to John Hunt's prosecution in 1822 for publishing Byron's 'Vision of Judgment', but here again the cause was not obscenity but defamation.* Looking back at the contemporary attitude to one of its greatest poets one is inclined to agree with Macaulay in his essay on Byron when he wrote: 'We know of no spectacle so ridiculous as the British public in one of its periodical fits of morality'.

Shelley incurred the same critical disfavour. Harris the manager of Covent Garden turned down the *Cenci* when offered to him for public performance as he thought the subject too horrible for contemporary audiences.† Shelley published the play in 1820 and was widely denounced. *The Literary Gazette* ended a blistering review with the words 'We now most gladly take leave of the work and sincerely hope that should we continue our literary pursuits for fifty years we shall never need again to look into one so stamped with pollution, impiousness and infamy'. Other periodicals referred to their 'sentiments of horror and disgust' and 'the radical foulness of moral composition'. The *London Magazine* had, however, to admit the beauty of the poetry: 'But in the midst of these disgraceful passages there are beauties of such exquisite, such redeeming qualities that we adore while we pity—we admire while we execrate'.

Execration was also the meed of 'Queen Mab' which appeared in a pirated edition in 1822. The prosecution brought by the Society for the Suppression of Vice was for blasphemy, and Clarke the publisher was sent to prison for four months.‡ When Shelley had written the work in 1813 and published it in a limited edition he had prophesied that 'the iron souled attorney general would never dare to attack',[28] but the Vice Society was made of even sterner mettle and its counsels prevailed.

These prosecutions cannot be defended, but perhaps something can be said for the critics despite the violence of their views. In the early nineteenth century it could still be maintained that poetry was

* Byron described the arrival of George III at the celestial city and the comments of St. Peter on hearing of his attitude to Catholic emancipation. Hunt was convicted in 1824, and *The Times* poured scorn on the proceedings. Carlile at once brought out the poem for 6*d*. for purchasers of Volume X of *The Republican*.

† The play was not performed until 10 March 1866 when the Shelley Society having been refused a licence for a public performance gave a 'private' production at the Grand Theatre, Islington, attended by 3,000 people. The first public performance was in November 1922 at the New Theatre. Four matinées were given with Miss Sybil Thorndike taking the part of Beatrice.

‡ For further details see H. B. Forman, *The Vicissitudes of Shelley's Queen Mab*. The irrepressible Carlile produced at 5*s*. what Clarke had been imprisoned for publishing at 12*s*. 6*d*. Carlile himself was in prison but on release he produced a vest-pocket edition at 2*s*. 6*d*. These were pirated editions, since Lord Eldon declined to grant injunctions to arrest the pirating of blasphemous works. *Southey* v. *Sherwood* (1817) 2 Mer. 435.

[28] Letter to Hookham, 18 August 1812.

a social force and should, therefore, be subjected to social and moral criticism. Critical excesses are indefensible, but the assumption of the value and relevance of poetry to the life of the community which determined their approach was sound.

THE 'FORTIES

Such rancorous outbursts were characteristic of the earlier years of the century, but their tone was muted in the 'thirties and 'forties, and it was not until the 'fifties and 'sixties that similar outcries were heard. One can only speculate on the reasons for this change, but some tentative explanations may be put forward. Evangelical influence had passed its zenith and with the passing of foreign revolutionary fears and the end of the period of reaction, public opinion had become more liberal. Fewer pornographic books were published, as a study of the relevant bibliographies shows, and the vice societies were not pursuing their crusade against impure literature with their former vigour.[29] Perhaps the best explanation is that the writers of these decades accepted the conventions of the age in which they lived. Novelists, for instance, such as Frances Trollope, Susan Ferrier, Harrison Ainsworth and Frederick Marryat, all popular in the 'thirties, were not likely to violate prevailing standards of good taste either in their choice of subject or its treatment. The same broadly speaking is true of the novelists of the 'forties. Kathleen Tillotson writes of this period:

> With very few exceptions novelists were contented with such limitations as existed, and moved freely within them, or figure skated along the edge. There was no fatal discrepancy between what the writer wished to say and what his public was willing to let him say; and it is that discrepancy, not limitation in itself, which is damaging to the novel, as Hardy and Henry James were to find.[30]

This rather than any fundamental change in the manners of the time is perhaps the best explanation of the apparent liberality of the period. Later Victorians who were more outspoken or who extended the range of their enquiries into the forbidden area of sex relations were not treated with much indulgence.

An examination of the reception given to the Brontë novels published in the 'forties might be expected to throw some light on this

[29] See P. Fraxi (H. S. Ashbee), *Index Librorum Prohibitorum* (1877); *Centuria Librorum Absconditorum* (1879); *Catena Librorum Tacendorum* (1885). Also R. S. Reade (A. Rose), *Registrum Librorum Eroticorum* (1936). The infamous *Maria Monk* was however published in 1837.

[30] *Op. cit.*, p. 64.

perplexing problem, but the results yielded are inconclusive. *Jane Eyre* was first published in 1847 and on the whole met with a favourable reception: there was certainly no general outcry. The *Westminster Review* said forthrightly that it was 'the best novel of the season' and *Fraser's* commented 'almost all that we require in a novelist the writer has'. *The Spectator*, however, stressed its 'low tone of behaviour' and the criticisms constrained the author to add a preface to her second edition published in 1848. 'Conventionality', she wrote, 'is not morality. Self righteousness is not religion. To attack the first is not to assail the last. To pluck the mask from the face of the Pharisee is not to lift an impious hand to the crown of thorns.' That these criticisms were religious rather than moral can be seen from the subject-matter of her preface, as also from the attack launched on the book by Lady Eastlake in the *Quarterly Review.*[31] She reproached the book mainly for its Jacobinism and only incidentally for its 'horrid taste'. 'Nor is she even a Pamela adopted and refined to modern notions', wrote Lady Eastlake, 'for though the story is conducted without those derelictions of decorum which we are to believe had their excuse in the manners of Richardson's time, yet it is stamped with a coarseness of language and laxity of tone which have certainly no excuse in ours.' For good measure she added the reproach that the author had committed 'the highest moral offence a writer can commit, that of making an unworthy character interesting in the eyes of the reader'. In the same article Lady Eastlake reviewed the annual report of the Governesses' Benevolent Institution and *Vanity Fair*. She had only praise for the latter, and the subtleties of Thackeray's revelations had clearly not been comprehended: 'Considering Becky in her human character we know of none which so thoroughly satisfies our highest beau ideal of feminine wickedness with so slight a shock to our feelings and proprieties'. Thackeray had clearly 'figure skated' an eight.

Anne Brontë's *The Tenant of Wildfell Hall* described realistically the effect of dipsomania on married life, yet passed almost unscathed through the ranks of the reviewers. G. H. Lewes in *Fraser's* even justified its coarseness.[32] But again the reviews conflict, and *The Spectator* in 1848 reproached her with a 'morbid love for the coarse not to say the brutal'. *Wuthering Heights*, published in the same year as *Jane Eyre*, might have illuminated the problem, but as usual it is an exception to every rule, and its publication passed almost unnoticed, being dismissed as an immature effort of Currer Bell or not reviewed at all. The *Athenæum*, however, thought it a 'disagreeable story' and reproached the Bells because they 'did not turn away

[31] December 1848, Vol. LXXXIV. [32] April 1849.

from dwelling upon those physical acts of cruelty which we know to have their warrant in the real annals of crime and suffering but which true taste rejects'.[33]

The Brontës, despite criticism, were able to speak their minds. 'When I feel it my duty to speak an unpalatable truth, with the help of God, I WILL speak it', wrote Anne in the preface to the second edition of her book. Thackeray, however, was not so courageous and his continual complaints about the restrictions imposed by convention testify to their continued efficacy. In reviewing *Jack Sheppard* in *Fraser's* in 1840 he lamented 'the refinements of society which will not allow us to call things by their right names'.[34] Again, writing in *The Times*, he complained that 'Fielding's men and Hogarth's are Dickens' and Cruickshanks' drawn with ten times more skill and force, only the latter humorists dare not talk of what the elders discussed honestly'.[35] In his preface to *Pendennis* (1848) he expressed himself even more forcefully: 'Since the author of Tom Jones was buried no writer of fiction among us has been permitted to depict to his utmost power a MAN. We must drape him and give him a certain conventional simper. Society will not tolerate the natural in our art.' He goes on to apologise in advance to his readers because 'a little more frankness than is customary has been attempted in this story; with no bad desire on the writer's part it is hoped and with no ill consequences to any reader'.

In the 1840's Moxon brought out unexpurgated editions of many of the Elizabethan and Restoration dramatists.* In 1840 he published the *Dramatic Works of Wycherley, Congreve, Vanbrugh and Farquhar*, edited by Leigh Hunt, who added bibliographical and critical notes. His attitude can be contrasted with that of Plumptre and Bowdler earlier in the century, but it would be unsafe to draw too decisive a conclusion as his edition was attacked and suppression suggested. Macaulay opposed this with vigour:

> The whole liberal education of our countrymen is conducted on the principle that no book which is valuable either by reason of the excellence of its style or by reason of the light which it throws on the history, polity and manners of nations should be withheld from the student on account of its impurity. . . . We find it difficult to believe [he added] that in a world so full of temptations as this, any gentleman whose life would have been virtuous if he had not read Aristophanes and Juvenal will be made vicious by reading them. A man who exposed to all the influences of such a state

[33] December 1847. [34] February 1840. [35] 2 September 1840.

* Moxon published Ben Jonson's works in 1846. Previous to this, in 1840, H. G. Bohn published the works of Fielding.

of society as that in which we live is yet afraid of exposing himself to the influence of a few Greek or Latin verses acts we think much like the felon who begged the sheriffs to let him have an umbrella held over his head from the door of Newgate to the gallows because it was a drizzling morning and he was apt to take cold. . . . We are therefore [he concluded] by no means disposed to condemn this publication though we certainly cannot recommend the handsome volume before us as an appropriate Christmas present for young ladies.[36]

The attitude of the reviewers to French novels of the period is of interest as it indicates that no great change in taste had taken place. The *Quarterly* in 1836 did not mince its words in referring to Balzac: 'A baser, meaner, filthier scoundrel never polluted society than Monsieur de Balzac's standard of "public morals", nor one who better exemplified the divine warning—"Do men gather grapes of thorns or figs of thistles"'.[37] *Blackwood's* announced in November 1849 that it would review no more French novels 'until a manifest improvement takes place'.

POPULAR LITERATURE

The period also saw a great increase in the more popular forms of literature. *The Penny Magazine*, *The Saturday Magazine* and *Chambers's Journal* enjoyed in 1836 a circulation of 360,000 copies and they were followed by *The Family Herald* and *The People's Police Gazette*.* A witness before the Select Committee on Arts and Principles of Design (1836) reflected with satisfaction on the high circulation of the first three claiming that they diffused 'science and good taste and good feeling without one sentence of an immoral tendency in the whole'. Such complacency did not extend to the *Police Gazette*, which exploited the taste of ill-educated readers for bloodcurdling stories, and reported the grosser metropolitan crimes. In 1843 Lloyd first published the *Weekly Penny Miscellany*, which was packed with horror stories of the 'Gothic' romance type. This fiction was dubbed 'The Salisbury Square School' from the situation of Lloyd's offices and aroused the anxiety of the upper classes. A witness before the Libraries Committee of 1849 blamed the low tax of a penny on newspapers for the prevalence of this fiction, since it 'makes the cost of a good thing dear and adds facility to the cheap

[36] *Critical and Historical Essays* (1843), Vol. III, p. 256.
[37] *French Novels*, Vol. LVI, April, p. 69.
* The most recent publication on reading matter of the working class is R. K. Webb's *The British Working Class Reader, 1790–1848*. Allen & Unwin, 1955. See especially Chapter I.

people to circulate trash to an extent which is almost incredible; the rubbish issued every Saturday is very great indeed'. Others thought that the publications were 'replete with moral contamination'. William Lovett said that they had 'an immoral and anti-social character'. Lloyd on the other hand made sweeping moral claims:

> We shall make it our study [he announced in the preface to the first volume of his *Penny Miscellany*] to maintain the high majesty of virtue over the turbulence of vice, and to make our pages while they glow with the romantic and the chivalrous so replete with true nobility of sentiment, that we shall, as hitherto, find our way and maintain our place, among the young and pure of heart. . . . We paint temptation—we paint virtue—we describe how it is oppressed and borne down by the wicked, and then we show how, like a spring of tempered steel, the rebound of its energies places it on a higher pinnacle of excellence than it before affected, while the wild turbulence of vice has brought forth nothing but evil fruits and deep vexation of spirit.

Such claims may legitimately be doubted, but he was on firmer ground when he wrote that he was 'laying before a large and intelligent class of readers, at a charge comparatively insignificant, those same pleasures of the imagination which have hitherto to a great extent only graced the polished leisure of the wealthy'. Lloyd felt with some justification that the poor should not be denied their share of 'horror'.

One final point must be noted in the 'forties, the Theatres Act of 1843.[39] The provisions of this Act still govern public theatrical performances today. The Act required all theatres to be licensed by letters patent or by justices of the peace; conferred on them powers to close any theatre which abused its position, and required every NEW play to be submitted to the Lord Chamberlain seven days before the date fixed for a public performance. Power was given to the Lord Chamberlain to prohibit the performance of such plays should he be of the opinion 'that it is fitting for the preservation of good manners decorum or public peace, so to do'. Plays written before 1843 are exempted from the operation of the Act.

THE 'FIFTIES AND 'SIXTIES

Whatever doubts may be entertained about standards of taste in the 'forties, they do not extend to the following decades, which in their strictness were reminiscent of the early years of the century.

[39] 6 & 7 Vict., c. 68.

Pornography once again had become a pressing social problem, and armed with the powers conferred by Lord Campbell's Act the police were able to carry out a full-scale assault on Holywell Street. Any descent into coarseness or voluptuousness was vigorously rebuked by the reviews, and writers who strayed into the forbidden pastures of sexual relations were scathingly denounced. Robert Buchanan typified the views of his contemporaries (in an article in the *Fortnightly*), when he wrote:

> If an Englishman of today were to write like Catullus or Herrick or to tell such tales as 'La Berceau' of La Fontaine, or the 'Carpenter's Wife' of Chaucer, we should hound him from our libraries and justly: because no Englishman in the presence of our civilisation with the advantages of our decisive finalities as to the decencies of language could say to his conscience 'I have a right to say these things'.[40]

MRS. GASKELL

Mrs. Gaskell committed not only a tactical error but a mortal sin when she dared to make a heroine of a 'fallen woman', *Ruth*, in 1853. Her mentors were none too gentle in leading her back into the ways of righteousness, and she wrote pathetically to her sister-in-law Mrs. Nancy Robeson: 'I had a terrible fit of crying all Saturday night at the unkind things people were saying, but I have now promised William that I will think of it as little as ever I can help. Only don't fancy me overwhelmed with letters and congratulations.' She added significantly: 'Of course it is a prohibited book in THIS as in many other households; not a book for the young people unless read with someone older'. In another letter to Miss Fox written at the same time she noted: 'About "Ruth" one of your London libraries (Bell I believe) has had to withdraw it from circulation on account of "it being unfit for family reading" and Spectator, Literary Gazette, Sharpe's Magazine, Colborn have all abused it as roundly as may be.' Some voices were, however, raised in her defence and it might have been a consolation to her had she heard Archdeacon Hare's reply to his wife when she informed him approvingly that *Ruth* had been burnt—'Well, the Bible has been burnt'.

GEORGE ELIOT

George Eliot, stern moralist though she was, also aroused opposition. The *Saturday Review* deplored her realism:

> The author of *Adam Bede* has given his adhesion to a very curious practice that is now becoming common amongst novelists and

[40] 15 September 1866, Vol. VI, p. 297.

> it is a practice that we consider most objectionable. It is that of dating and discussing the several stages that precede the birth of a child. We seem to be threatened with a literature of pregnancy. . . . Let us copy the old masters of the art who if they gave us a baby gave it us all at once. A decent author and a decent public may surely take the premonitory symptoms for granted.[41]

The *Saturday's* comments on *The Mill on the Floss* are worth quoting at length because they illustrate so aptly the prudery which was by this time rampant.

> Currer Bell and George Eliot and we may add George Sand all like to dwell on love as a strange overmastering force which through the senses captivates and enthralls the soul. They linger on the description of the physical sensations that accompany the meeting of hearts in love. Curiously too they like to describe these sensations as they conceive them to exist in men. We are bound to say that their conceptions are true and adequate. But we are not so sure that it is quite consistent with feminine delicacy to lay so much stress on the bodily feelings of the other sex . . . she [George Eliot] lets her fancy run on things which are not wrong but are better omitted from the scope of female meditation. The heroine for example is in love with a man who passionately loves her, but as each is pre-engaged they are separated by duty and honour. All goes very well until one day the lover, when alone with the heroine, takes to watching her arm. Its beauties are minutely described as well as the effect gradually produced on him. At last in a transport of passion he rushes forward, seizes on the lovely arm and covers it with kisses. There is nothing wrong in writing about such an act, and it is the sort of thing that does happen in real life; but we cannot think that the conflict of sensation and principle raised in a man's mind by gazing at a woman's arm is a theme that a female novelist can touch on without leaving behind a feeling of hesitation if not repulsion in the reader.[42]

MEREDITH

George Meredith whose poem 'Modern Love' was later to be subjected to widespread attack was another of the *Saturday's* targets. Referring to *The Ordeal of Richard Feverel* the reviewer wrote: 'To show that an absurd and imaginary system of education breaks down under very powerful temptations is much too useless an errand

[41] *Saturday Review*, 26 February 1859, Vol. VII, p. 250.
[42] *Ibid.*, 14 April 1860, Vol. IX, pp. 470–1.

to warrant the introduction of some of the most unflinching sketches of immorality that the pen of a modern Englishman has ventured to draw.[43] *

CHARLES READE

When Charles Reade published *Griffith Gaunt* in 1866 in book form the outcry started on the further side of the Atlantic, but was soon taken up in London. The *London Review* republished the strictures of the *Round Table* which had called the book indecent and immoral and opined that 'the modesty and purity of women could not survive its persual'. Unwisely, the accusation that the book was plagiary was repeated, and Reade decided to start a legal action. Matthew Arnold and Wilkie Collins consented to appear as literary 'experts' but Dickens declined. A letter on the matter which he wrote to Wilkie Collins is of great interest since it reveals not only the mind of Dickens but also one of the reasons for the increased prudery of the 'sixties. It must be remembered that both the *Cornhill* and *Macmillan's*, recently founded and selling at a shilling, had greatly extended family reading, and it is these readers who were Dickens' chief concern.

> I have read Charles Reade's book [he wrote] and here follows my state of mind—as a witness respecting it. I have read it with the strongest interest and admiration. I regard it as the work of a highly accomplished writer and a good man; a writer with a brilliant fancy and a graceful and tender imagination. I could name no other living writer who could in my opinion write such a story nearly so well. As regards a so-called critic who should decry such a book as Holywell Street literature and the like I should have merely to say of him that I could desire no stronger proof of his incapacity in and his unfitness for the post to which he has elected himself. . . . But if I were reminded (as I probably should be supposing the evidence to be allowed at all) that I was the editor of a periodical of large circulation in which the plaintiff himself had written, and if I had read to me in court those passages about Gaunt's going up to his wife's bed drunk and that last child's being conceived, and was asked whether as Editor I would have passed those passages whether written by the plaintiff or anybody else, I should be obliged to reply No. Asked why? I should say

[43] 9 July 1859, Vol. VIII, pp. 48–49.

* Another book attacked at this period was W. Winwood Reade's *Liberty Hall Oxon*, branded by the *Saturday* as 'the filthiest book that has been issued by a respectable English publisher during the lifetime of the present generation' (*Saturday Review*, 21 January 1860, Vol. IX, p. 84.)

> that what was pure to an artist might be impurely suggestive to inferior minds (of which there must necessarily be many among a large mass of readers) and that I should have called the writer's attention to the likelihood of those passages being perverted in such quarters.[44]

Reade won his action without the assistance of Dickens, but was awarded derisory damages. His pocket did not benefit by the action but he assuaged the bitter feelings which he had expressed earlier in *The Prurient Prude*, condemning his detractors.*

Dickens was certainly not temperamentally inclined to rebel against Victorian conventions, and as can be seen from his letter was not unwilling to see them enforced, but the prudishness of the 'sixties was too much even for him and in his novel *Our Mutual Friend* (1864) he poked fun at them by introducing Mr. Podsnap with his perpetual concern for the cheeks of young persons. Such a corrective was badly needed but it had little effect. In 1866 the *Contemporary* was reproaching Trollope's *The Belton Estate* for the coarseness of its ending: 'The end of the book too is deadly coarse. It is a poor inelegant device to give Captain Aylmer a wife with a red nose.' [45]

FRENCH NOVELS

The reviews continued to protest against French novels which they feared would sully the minds of English readers. In France itself, under Napoleon III's clerical empire, some of its most distinguished authors were brought before the criminal courts. In 1857 an unsuccessful prosecution was brought against Flaubert for writing *Madame*

[44] 20 February 1867. *Letters of Charles Dickens to Wilkie Collins* (London 1892).

* *The Prurient Prude* was written in the form of an open letter and was reproduced by Chatto and Windus in *Readiana* (1883). 'Dear Sir', it begins, 'there is a kind of hypocrite that has never been effectually exposed, for want of an expressive name. I beg to supply that defect in our language and introduce to mankind the PRURIENT PRUDE.

'Modesty in man or woman shows itself by a certain slowness to put a foul construction on things, and also by unobtrusively shunning indelicate matters and discussions. The PRURIENT PRUDE, on the contrary, itches to attract attention by a parade of modesty (which is the mild form of the disease), or even by rashly accusing others of immodesty (and this is the noxious form).

'"Dr. Johnson", said a lady, "what I admire in your dictionary is that you have inserted no improper words."

'"What! you looked for them, madam?" said the Doctor.

'Here was a PRURIENT PRUDE that would have taken in an ordinary lexicographer.'

[45] October 1866, Vol. III, p. 301.

Bovary, while Baudelaire was convicted in the same year for publishing *Les Fleurs du Mal.** In 1851 R. W. Sibthorpe was warning fathers to 'take care of your wives and daughters', when the foreigners arrived for the Great Exhibition,† and his distrust of continentals seemed justified by the licentiousness of French novels. T. C. Sanders branded Xavier de Montepin's *Les Filles de Platre* as an 'infamous book' and maintained that 'vice as such has no place in the creations of the novelist'.[46] Fitzjames Stephen reviewed *Madame Bovary* in 1857 and found her character 'one of the most essentially disgusting that we ever happened to meet with'. Stephen, however, saw the dangers of an emasculated literature and in the same review he raised a disturbing question which he made no attempt to answer. Referring to the writers of light fiction he wrote:

> Many of them seem to think that the highest function of the poet is the amusement of children; but we are by no means prepared to say that in literature emasculation produces purity. Our statistical returns, the nightly appearance of our streets, and those verbatim reports of trials which are so disgusting that the papers which publish them advocate the repeal of the laws, which as they affect to think necessitate their publication, surely teach us that we are not so very immaculate. Whether a light literature entirely based on love and absolutely and systematically silent as to one most important side of it may not have some tendency to stimulate passions to which it is far too proper even to allude is a question which we should do well to take into serious consideration before we preach the doctrine that the contemporaries of Mr. Dickens have made a vast step in advance of the contemporaries of Fielding.[47]

Such self-questioning was foreign, however, to most reviewers, and when in a review of Eugène Sue's *Les Fils de Famille* the writer pointed out that 'in England novels nowadays are written for families—in France they are written for men', the remark was congratulatory not reproachful.[48] The realism of English writers was compared favourably with that of the French: 'Mr. Patmore's realism is as thoroughgoing as if he had studied in the school of

* On 31 May 1949 the conviction of Baudelaire and his publishers was reversed under a law of 1946 allowing such cases to be reheard. See appendix on French Law, p. 246.

† The Surrey magistrates wished to provide the statues with aprons. (*Hansard*, 1857, Vol. CXLVII.)

[46] *Saturday Review*, 5 April 1856, Vol. I, p. 461.

[47] *Ibid.*, 11 July 1857, Vol. IV, p. 40.

[48] *Ibid.*, 15 August 1857, Vol. IV, p. 160.

Balzac, although he occupies himself solely with those human relations which French novelists habitually exclude from their conception of love'.[49]

POETRY

Similar standards of propriety were invoked in judging poetry, and even Tennyson failed always to come up to the mark. Much of the criticism of 'Maud' (1855) was for its political doctrine, but it was also criticised for its tone 'of extravagant sensibility'. One reviewer suggested leaving out either of the vowels from the title—which one, it didn't matter. Another wrote: 'If an author pipe of adultery, fornication, murder and suicide set him down as the practiser of those crimes'. To which Tennyson not unreasonably replied: 'Adulterer I may be, fornicator I may be, murderer I may be, suicide I am not yet'.[50] *Macmillan's Magazine* praised 'The Idylls of the King' in 1859, but as if anticipating attack qualified its view: 'the subject is revolting we admit it'.

If Tennyson was censured there was little chance for Whitman who was described as 'exceedingly obscene'. 'If the "Leaves of Grass" should come into anybody's possession our advice is to throw them immediately behind the fire', said the *Saturday Review*.[51] And when a second edition was published it wondered at the popularity of such a poet 'in a country where piano legs wear frilled trousers, where slices are cut from turkey's bosoms and where the male of the gallinaceous tribe is called "a rooster"'.[52] *

Meredith put forward the idea of sex equality in his poem *Modern Love* (1862) and was bitterly reproached. *The Spectator* referred to its 'clever, meretricious, turbid pictures' and accused him 'of meddling causelessly and somewhat pruriently with a deep and painful subject on which he has no convictions to express'. The *Saturday Review* anticipated and demolished his defence:

> The writer's apology for his choice of subject would probably be the same that he has put into the mouth of one of his characters:
>
> These things are life
> And life they say is worthy of the muse.

[49] Review of *The Victories of Love*, *Saturday Review*, 5 December 1863, Vol. XVI, p. 729.
[50] *Alfred Tennyson*, by Charles Tennyson (London 1950), p. 286.
[51] March 1856, Vol. I, p. 393.
[52] July 1860, Vol. X, p. 19.
* The United States reviewers repaid the compliment of the attack on Whitman by condemning Elizabeth Barrett Browning's *Aurora Leigh* as 'the hysterical indecencies of an erotic mind'. (Boston 1857.) See A. L. Haight's *Banned Books*, Allen & Unwin (London 1955).

> A more flimsy sophism could hardly be devised. . . . So far from a condition of doubt and uncertainty on the general tone of matrimonial morality being in any sense an interesting and attractive thing, it is one of the most disastrous calamities that can befall a nation. To write of the rotten places of our social system as if they were fitting subjects for the Muse is just as reasonable as it would be to compose a sonnet to the gout or an ode on the smallpox.[53]

Meredith himself witnesses to his contemporary reputation. In a letter to Augustus Jessopp he wrote 'Does she (Pallas) know that my literary reputation is as tabooed as worse than libertine in certain virtuous societies? . . . that there have been meetings to banish me from book clubs? And that paterfamilias has given Mr. Mudie a very large bit of his petticoated mind concerning me.' [54]

SWINBURNE

All these attacks, however, pale into charitable mildness when one considers the reception given to Swinburne's *Poems and Ballads* on publication in 1866. John Morley's review in its hysterical frenzy carried moral invective to a point which no other English critic has surpassed. Its tone is all the more amazing when one considers Morley's breadth of mind and culture.* He began by pointing out the uselessness of scolding Swinburne 'for grovelling down among the nameless, shameless, abominations which inspire him with such frenzied delight'. Undeterred by this utilitarian consideration he proceeded to pour out the vials of his wrath upon the unfortunate poet's head.

> It is not merely the noble, the nude, the antique, which he strives to reproduce. If he were a rebel against the fat headed Philistines and poor blooded Puritans who insist that all poetry should be such as may be wisely placed in the hands of a girl of eighteen, and is fit for the use of Sunday schools, he would have all wise and enlarged readers on his side. But there is an enormous difference between an attempt to revivify amongst us the grand old pagan conceptions of joy and an attempt to glorify all the bestial delights that the subtleties of Greek depravity was able to contrive. It is a

[53] 24 October 1863, Vol. XVI, p. 562.

[54] *Letters of G. Meredith* (London 1912), p. 159.

* It is worth noting that Morley later changed his mind about Swinburne. Edmund Gosse revealed this in a letter to the *Times Literary Supplement*. He quoted Morley: 'Although I was perfectly sincere when I wrote it, I changed my mind, grew to value and admire Swinburne exceedingly and (in short) it is an incident which I regret'. (20 October 1923, p. 86.)

good thing to vindicate passion and the strong and rightful pleasures of sense, against the narrow and inhuman tyranny of shrivelled anchorites. It is a very bad and silly thing to try to set up the pleasures of sense in the seat of the reason they have dethroned. And no language is too strong to condemn the mixed vileness and childishness of depicting the spurious passion of a putrescent imagination, of the unnamed lusts of sated wantons, as if they were the crown of character and their enjoyment the great glory of human life.

Swinburne was 'an unclean fiery imp from the pit'; 'the libidinous laureate of a pack of satyrs', with a mind 'aflame with the feverish carnality of a schoolboy over the dirtiest pages of Lemprière'.[55] *

On 5 August it was announced that Moxon's had withdrawn the volume from circulation and Rossetti accompanied by Sandys went to interview Payne. They found him trembling with fear of a prosecution and full of memories of the Shelley prosecution of thirty years before. He had been told that Dallas had written a review for *The Times* demanding a prosecution and refused to take any further risks. Swinburne was not deterred and took the poems to Hotten, a disreputable publisher, who, reassured by a guarantee in writing from a police magistrate that they were not indictable, agreed to publish. In November the poems made a second appearance.

Meanwhile he had aroused a fierce debate. The *Athenæum*, the *Pall Mall Gazette*, and *The Spectator* condemned, and *Punch* went so far as to refer to their author as 'Mr. Swineborne'. Beresford Hope wrote to a friend who disapproved of the outcry: 'I don't at all agree with you in your condemnation of the review of Swinburne. Such a brute as he is both as author and man had to be squelched and you can't squelch a toad with rosewater.'[56] This letter shows that the attacks were not entirely disinterested, and supports the view put forward by some writers that they reflected a personal vendetta.[57]

[55] *Saturday Review*, 4 August 1866, Vol. XXII, pp. 145–7.

* A verse is here quoted to remind readers of what aroused Morley's fury.

> Ah that my lips were tuneless lips, but pressed
> To the bruised blossom of thy scourged white breast!
> Ah that my mouth for Muses' milk were fed
> On the sweet blood thy sweet small wounds had bled!
> That with my tongue I felt them and could taste
> The faint flakes from thy bosom to the waist!
> That I could drink thy veins as wine, and eat
> Thy breasts like honey! that from face to feet
> Thy body were abolished and consumed,
> And in my flesh thy very flesh entombed.

[56] Law, *The Book of the Beresford Hopes*, p. 225.

[57] See Lafourcade, *Swinburne*, p. 136.

The *Sunday Times* on the other hand approved of the poems as did the *Examiner*, which published an enthusiastic article. At Cambridge the poems were the subject of a debate and added to the Union library list. From Dublin came an anonymous letter threatening castration, but to set against this was Ruskin's private approval: 'All I can say of you or them . . . is that God made you and that you are very wonderful and beautiful'.

Swinburne like Reade was not a man to be cowed: the toad was only 'scotched' not 'squelched': and he hit back at his detractors by publishing the same year his *Notes on Poems and Reviews*, a work now forgotten but which bears comparison with Milton's *Areopagitica.*

> The virtue of our critical journals [he wrote] is a dowager of somewhat dubious antecedents: every day that thins and shrivels her cheek hardens and thickens the paint on it: she consumes more chalk and ceruse than would serve a whole courtful of crones. 'It is to be presumed' certainly that in her case 'all is not sweet, all is not sound'. The taint on her fly blown reputation is hard to overcome by patches and perfumery . . . if literature is not to deal with the full life of man and the whole nature of things let it be cast aside with the rods and rattles of childhood. Whether it affect to teach or to amuse it is equally trivial and contemptible to us: only less so than the charge of immorality. Against how few really great names has not this small and dirt encrusted pebble been thrown. A reputation seems imperfect without this tribute also: one jewel is wanting to the crown. If it is good to be praised by those whom all men should praise; it is better to be reviled by those whom all men should scorn.

To the reviewers he addressed some contemptuous verses:

> Why grudge them lotus leaf and laurel
> O toothless mouth or swinish maw
> Who never grudged you bells and coral
> Who never grudged you troughs and straw?
>
> Lie still in kennel, sleek in stable
> Good creatures of the stall or sty,
> Shove snouts for crumbs below the table
> Lie still: and rise not up to lie.

He dealt at greater length, but even more effectively with the reviewer's stock character 'the eighteen-year-old daughter'.

> I have overlooked the evidence which every day makes clearer that our time has room only for such as are content to write for

children and girls. But this oversight is the sum of my offence. It would seem indeed as though to publish a book were equivalent to thrusting it with violence into the hands of every mother and nurse in the kingdom as fit and necessary food for female infancy. Happily there is no fear that the supply of milk for babes will fall short of the demand for some time yet. There are moral milkmen enough in all conscience crying their wares about the street and by-ways; fresh or stale, sour or sweet, the requisite fluid runs from a sufficiently copious issue. In due time perhaps the critical doctors may prescribe a stronger diet for their hypochondriac patient; the reading world; or that gigantic *malade imaginaire* called the public may rebel against the weekly draught or the daily drug of MM. Purgon and Diafonus. We meanwhile who profess to deal neither in poison nor in pap may not unwillingly stand aside. Let those read who will and let those who will, abstain from reading. No one wishes to force men's food down the throats of babes and sucklings.

He concluded by looking forward to a more liberal age.

When England has again such a school of poetry, so headed and so followed, as she has had at least twice before or as France has now; when all higher forms of the various arts are included within the larger limits of a stronger race; then if such a day should ever rise or return upon us, it will be once more remembered that the office of adult art is neither puerile nor feminine, but virile; that its purity is not that of the cloister or the harem; that all things are good in its sight out of which good work may be produced. Then the press will be as impotent as the public to dictate the laws and remove the landmarks of art, and those will be laughed at who demand from one thing the qualities of another, who seek for sermons in sonnets and morality in music. Then all accepted work will be noble and chaste in the wider masculine sense, not truncated and curtailed but outspoken and full grown; art will be pure by instinct and fruitful by nature, no clipped and forced growth of unhealthy heat and unnatural air; all baseness and triviality will fall off from it and be forgotten; and no one will then need to assert in defence of work done for the work's sake, the simple laws of his art which no one will then be permitted to impugn.

THE FLESHLY SCHOOL

These exhortations fell on deaf ears and five years later the attack on the early æsthetes was continued by the publication of Robert Buchanan's article 'The Fleshly School of Poetry' in the

Contemporary Review.[58] * Compared with Swinburne, Rossetti was a conventional figure, and indeed had taken the strongest exception to Swinburne's naked descents of the banisters at Cheyne Walk, but he was too closely associated with Swinburne in the public mind to escape attack. As the elder of the two he was especially vulnerable, as it might be inferred that he had encouraged Swinburne in his outrages, the truth being that he had tried unsuccessfully to restrain him. Swinburne had written an enthusiastic but indiscreet review of Rossetti's poems in the *Fortnightly* and this contributed to provoking the attack. 'No nakedness', he had written, 'could be more harmonious, more consummate in its fleshly sculpture than the imperial array and ornament of his august poetry.' [59] Buchanan castigated Rossetti as 'a fleshly person with nothing particular to tell us or teach us' and as a man 'fleshly all over from the roots of his hair to the tips of his toes—never spiritual, never tender, always self-conscious and æsthetic'. The *Quarterly* joined in the attack with references to 'emasculate obscenity' and accused Rossetti of 'the deification of the animal instincts'.[60] This attack was serious for Rossetti, since it might well have cost him many patrons, and he replied trenchantly in his article 'The Stealthy School of Criticism',[61] the title being a reference to Robert Buchanan's use of the pseudonym 'Thomas Maitland'. 'All the passionate and just delights of the body are declared—somewhat figuratively it is true, but unmistakably—to be as naught if not ennobled by the concurrence of the soul at all times.' Swinburne also defended Rossetti in a pamphlet *Under the Microscope*, many copies of which were bought by German scientists under the impression that it was a scientific monograph. Buchanan, whose identity had by this time been revealed, published a further pamphlet in May widening the scope of his attack. He complained about the shopwindows of the capital being filled with 'photographs of nude, indecent and hideous harlots in every possible attitude that vice can devise'. He even indicted the sweetshops because they exhibited 'models of the female leg, the whole definite and elegant article as far as the thigh, with a fringe of paper cut in imitation of the female drawers and embroidered in the female fashion'. The controversy dragged on with Buchanan becoming more violent, but he was definitely worsted. Rossetti had many

[58] October 1871, Vol. XXVIII, p. 334.

* The pre-Raphælites had already been censured for the 1850 Royal Academy Exhibition. The *Athenæum* spoke of 'the disgusting incidents of unwashed bodies' and the presentation in 'loathsome reality' of 'flesh with its accidents of putridity'.

[59] May 1870.

[60] Vol. CXXXII, pp. 59–84.

[61] *Athenæum*, December 1871.

friends and they remained vocal when illness withdrew him from the dispute. Like John Morley Buchanan later recanted, writing in the *Academy* for 1 July 1882 that Rossetti 'never was a Fleshly poet at all'. The vigour with which Rossetti was defended showed that the foundations of the later æsthetic movement had been securely laid.

CHAPTER IV

THE LAW INTERVENES

LORD CAMPBELL'S ACT

IF standards of taste had become stricter the law had kept pace by growing more severe. The Customs Consolidation Act of 1853 [1] contained the first express prohibition intended to ban the importation of pornography: 'Indecent or obscene prints, paintings, books, cards, lithographic or other engravings, or any other indecent or obscene articles' were to be seized by the customs authorities. The legislature then turned from continental to domestic sources of supply and in 1857 Lord Campbell's Act [2] was passed. This Act created no new criminal offence, but gave magistrates the power to order the destruction of books and prints if in their opinion their publication would amount to a 'misdemeanour proper to be prosecuted as such'. To enforce the provisions of the Act magistrates were empowered to grant warrants to the police to search suspected premises. Lord Campbell had raised the question of pornography when speaking of the effects of a recent Act to control the sale of poisonous drugs.

> He was happy to say that he believed the administration of poison by design had received a check. But from a trial which had taken place before him on Saturday, he had learned with horror and alarm that a sale of poison more deadly than prussic acid, strychnine or arsenic—the sale of obscene publications and indecent books was going on.[3]

To check this trade he proposed to introduce a Bill, and in the debates which followed he gave evidence of its extent which he claimed made legislation urgent. In fifty-five years the Society for the Suppression of Vice had brought 159 prosecutions, securing convictions in all save five cases. The average sentence had been

[1] 16 & 17 Vict., c. 107. [2] 20 & 21 Vict., c. 83.
[3] *Hansard*, April 1857, Vol. CXLV, p. 102.

eight months' imprisonment, but sentences had varied from anything from fourteen days to two years. He gave one specific instance of a dealer convicted in 1845 from whom 12,346 prints, 393 books, 351 copper plates, 188 lithographic stones and 33½ cwts. of letterpress had been seized! As a result of the Society's activities between 1834 and 1857 the number of shops dealing in this sort of literature had been reduced from fifty-seven to twenty.

Despite his advocacy the Bill met with lively opposition. Its leading opponent was Lord Lyndhurst, who was actuated partly by motives of personal pique since Campbell had referred to him slightingly in his *Lives of Lord Chancellors*, and tactlessly presented him with the relevant volume. Lord Lyndhurst asked how a work of art like Correggio's 'Jupiter and Antiope' was to be distinguished under the Bill from a pornographic print. Rochester's poems would certainly come within its scope and in the same way 'the dramatists of the Restoration, Wycherley, Congreve and the rest of them; there is not a page in any one of them which might not be seized under this Bill'. As for Ovid not a single volume would be safe. Lord Lyndhurst thought the existing law adequate, all that was required was its vigorous enforcement. Lord Brougham also opposed the Bill on similar grounds. To these critics Lord Campbell replied that

> He had not the most distant contemplation of including in the Bill the class of works to which the noble and learned lords referred. The measure was intended to apply exclusively to works written for the single purpose of corrupting the morals of youth and of a nature calculated to shock the common feelings of decency in a well regulated mind. Bales of publications of that description were manufactured in Paris and imported into this country. He was ready to make what was indictable under the present law a test of obscenity.[4]

Later he reiterated that

> He had no desire whatever to interfere by legislation with books or pictures or prints such as were described to their Lordships the other evening as being endangered by this measure. The keeping or the reading or the delighting in such things must be left to taste and was not a subject for legal interference, but when there were people who designedly and industriously manufactured books and prints with the intention of corrupting morals and when they succeeded in their infamous purpose, he thought it was necessary for the legislature to interpose and to save the public from the contamination to which they would otherwise be exposed.

[4] 146 *Hansard Parl. Debs.* (3rd series 1857), pp. 327 *et seq.*

Lord Lyndhurst's comment on this was prescient: 'Why it is not what the Chief Justice means, but what is the construction of an Act of Parliament'. The subsequent uses to which the Act has been put would seem to have justified his forebodings.

In the Commons the Bill also met with opposition. Lord Campbell appeared in the gallery and the Speaker sent a message of protest: 'He had appeared in the House to overawe their deliberations like Cardinal Wolsey and Charles I and that it would become his duty to protest against such an unconstitutional proceeding'. A Scottish member, Roebuck, declared that 'a more preposterous Bill had never been sent down from the House of Lords and that was saying a great deal. It was an attempt to make people virtuous by Act of Parliament. A man who had a taste for the class of prints and publications referred to in the Bill would get them in spite of all the laws they could pass.' [5]

Monckton Milnes was also numbered amongst the Bill's opponents. The Commons amended the Bill extensively; a power of appeal to Quarter Sessions was conferred; an actual sale was required before the procedure could come into operation; and Scotland was exempted from its provisions. Scotland's laws were said to be adequate and Lord Campbell turned the point to his own advantage: 'He might be permitted to say that perhaps the existence of those powers had contributed to the greater morality which was allowed to exist in the northern part of the kingdom'. These amendments were accepted by the Lords and the Bill was eventually passed without a division, Lord Campbell expressing the hope 'that the time would soon come when Holywell Street would become the abode of honest, industrious, handicraftsmen and a thoroughfare through which any modest woman might pass'.* Lord Campbell may not have succeeded in extending the perambulations of 'modest women', but he had no doubt about the success of his Act. Some time later he noted in his diary:

> Its success has been most brilliant. Holywell Street which had long set law and decency at defiance has capitulated after several assaults. Half the shops are shut up and the remainder deal in nothing but moral and religious books. Under the Bill similar

[5] *Hansard*, 12 August 1857, Vol. CXLVII, p. 1475.

* On the report stage of the Bill Lord Campbell produced a copy of *The Lady of the Camellias* to press home his point. *La Traviata*, based on the book, was being given at Covent Garden but a note on the programme informed patrons that 'no English translation of the libretto' was available. Lord Campbell produced the book merely as a general illustration: 'He did not wish to create a category of offences in which this book might be included although it was certainly of a polluting character'.

abominations have been cleared away in Dublin. Even in Paris its influence has been felt, for the French police roused by the accounts of what we are now doing have been energetically employed in purifying the Palais Royal and the Rue Vivienne.

THE HICKLIN CASE

Ten years later in 1868 Sir Alexander Cockburn made the second great contribution to the law of obscene libel when he formulated the test of obscenity in the Hicklin case.[6] This was not a prosecution, but was a case brought under Lord Campbell's Act, against Henry Scott, a Wolverhampton metalbroker who had sold copies of a pamphlet published by a militant Protestant society with the flamboyant title: *The Confessional Unmasked: shewing the depravity of the Roman Priesthood, the iniquity of the Confessional and the questions put to females in confession.* The British Museum possesses a copy of the second edition of this pamphlet, expurgated and amended, and published in January 1869 at a shilling, under the title: *The Morality of Romish Devotion or the Confessional Unmasked.* Its bright green cover has a picture of Britannia being eyed by the Pope who is about to let a dragon out of a cage. Even in this edition much of the content is obscene. Its tone can be gauged from the following extract:

> The prudent confessor will endeavour as much as possible to induce his confidence by kind words and then proceed from general to particular questions, from less shameful to more shameful things. . . . Has not the penitent been troubled with improper cogitations? Of what kind was the thought indulged? Did he experience any unlawful sensations? etc.

This is allegedly an extract from a Catholic manual of moral theology. Other passages deal with the seduction of penitents by confessors *et al.*

The first half of the pamphlet related to controversial questions, but the remainder was made up of obscene extracts all allegedly taken from Roman Catholic devotional and theological publications. Scott was a zealot for the Protestant cause and sold the pamphlets at cost price without making any personal profit, but those who bought the publications may not have been inspired by similar high motives. The Wolverhampton magistrates seized 252 of the pamphlets and made an order for their destruction. Scott appealed against this decision to Quarter Sessions, and the Recorder, holding that Scott's purpose had been not to corrupt public morals but to expose the Church of Rome, revoked the

[6] (1868), L. R. 3 Q. B. 360.

destruction order. A further appeal brought the case before the Court of Queen's Bench presided over by Chief Justice Cockburn who reversed the decision of the Recorder and restored the destruction order. Sir Alexander Cockburn in the course of his judgment laid down the test for obscenity: 'The test of obscenity is whether the tendency of the matter charged as obscenity is to deprave and corrupt those whose minds are open to such immoral influences and into whose hands a publication of this sort may fall'.*

This test has ever since been accepted by the judges as an accurate statement of English law. The Protestant Electoral Union which had published the pamphlet however did not do so:

> Whence originate prosecutions at the hands of magistrates? [it asked] Whereto are we to ascribe false verdicts passed by judges and courts of law? . . . We answer directly to the Romish priests and indirectly to the mighty influence exercised by the Popish faction in parliament, whereby the priests are enabled to intimidate and coerce when they cannot bribe magistrates, judges and other officials.[7]

A further change was made in the law in 1870 by the Post Office Act,[8] which empowered the Postmaster-General to make regulations for preventing the sending or delivery by post of 'any indecent or obscene books, prints, engravings, cards, or postcards etc., having on the covers thereof any words, marks or designs of an indecent, obscene, libellous or grossly offensive character'. No power was given, however, to open letters or packets.

THE BRADLAUGH CASE

In 1877 the scope of the law was further extended when Charles Bradlaugh and Annie Besant were prosecuted for publishing Charles Knowlton's *Fruits of Philosophy*, a pamphlet advocating birth control. Hitherto prosecutions had been confined to pornographic books, attacked for their language rather than their theme. The Bradlaugh case was the first of a series of prosecutions still continuing for the publication of what may be described as 'sex manuals'.† The case really began in 1876 with the prosecution of a Bristol bookseller for selling the book, which had been freely available in England for

* For a full discussion of the meaning of this formula and the effects of the case, see p. 126.

[7] Preface to the *Morality of Romish Devotion* (1869).

[8] 33 & 34 Vict., c. 79.

† Books are not considered 'obscene' today for the mere advocacy of birth control. 'It cannot be assumed', said the Home Secretary in answer to a question in the House of Commons in 1922, 'that a court would hold a book to be obscene merely because it deals with the subject referred to'.

forty years. He pleaded guilty and was bound over.* Charles Bradlaugh and Annie Besant, who had formed the 'Free Thought Publishing Company', decided to republish the book in London without the illustrations which had been added without authorisation, and which may have prompted the original prosecution. They announced that they would personally sell the books themselves at their own premises in Stonecutter Street on 23 March. At the appointed hour the street was filled with an eager throng of purchasers and sightseers including policemen and detectives. A brisk sale ensued and a few days later they were both arrested on a warrant.

The case was remanded until 17 April when the couple appeared at the Guildhall. An offer was made to drop the charges against Mrs. Besant, but she preferred to stand trial with Bradlaugh. Both were then liberated on their own recognisances. On 7 May they were charged before a grand jury who were directed by the Recorder to

> consider the general nature of the work and whether, whatever might have been the object of the publisher, it was calculated to excite to filthy acts and to deprave and debauch the minds of its readers. If they were of the opinion that it was indecent and obscene they would have to consider the circumstances in which publication had been made and see whether they were such as to afford justification to the publisher. There were undoubtedly circumstances which would justify the publication of what they would not hesitate to describe as highly indecent works. Take for instance that which might be lawfully published in a medical lecture room as being necessary to give the requisite instruction to students. Yet if that work, with the illustrations that might be necessary to qualify students for the exercise of their professions, were to be scattered broadcast through the land, the justification would not exist and the publisher would be liable to indictment.

The grand jury presented the accused, and on the application of Bradlaugh the case was removed by certiorari from the Old Bailey to the Queen's Bench Division where it was tried before a judge and special jury. The judge was once again Chief Justice Cockburn.

The trial which opened on 18 June aroused great public interest and continued for nearly a week. The origin of the prosecution was never revealed, but the Solicitor-General, Sir Hardinge Giffard (later Lord Halsbury) appeared for the prosecution. The defendants conducted their own defence.

> You [said the Solicitor-General, addressing the jury], are the guardians of public morals. You the jury are to determine a

* C. Watts, who at Bradlaugh's instigation had declared himself to be responsible for the publishing, was also tried. He pleaded guilty.

question of this sort. Every man's own feelings must tell him whether such matters as these are not obscene. And if they are then there is no excuse for the general publication of such matters. Don't tell me about doctors who it is said have published similar matters. Whoever chooses to circulate the publication of such filth—for I do not hesitate to call it filth—must justify it by some principle of law.[9]

Mrs. Besant then began her address. She spoke for many hours and for much of the time was addressing the public on the laws of Malthus and the necessity for birth control, rather then defending herself against the obscene libel charge. 'Better not to produce children than to produce them only to be destroyed by starvation, disease and death', she declared at the end of the first day of the trial and at this point the court adjourned. *The Times* wearily commented: 'Mrs. Besant intimated (though she had spoken several hours) that she had not yet nearly finished her address and when she has concluded Mr. Bradlaugh is to follow'. She spoke all the following day and again at the end of her trial. Her final speech to the jury ended with a rousing peroration:

Will you convict me of indecency? Will you send me to prison to herd with poor degraded creatures, contact with whom would be agony to me? Think what such a verdict would mean to me. A verdict of guilty—you cannot give it. If you believe in truth, in justice, in innocence itself, you cannot give it; and if you did so it would be a sad miscarriage of justice against which I should appeal to posterity who would assuredly reverse your verdict.

Bradlaugh made a more closely reasoned defence. At the end of the third day both he and Mrs. Besant were loudly cheered, and throughout the trial Sir Alexander Cockburn had shown himself markedly favourable to the defence. At one point he complimented Mrs. Besant, and after the jury had given their verdict congratulated Bradlaugh on his straightforward conduct. Opening his summing-up he said that there was one point on which all were agreed:

A more ill advised and more injudicious prosecution never was instituted. Here is a work which has been published for more than forty years and which appears never to have got into general circulation and which by these injudicious proceedings has got into large circulation so that the sale has suddenly risen by thousands.

His interpretation of the law was however strict:

The charge in the indictment is: 'That the defendants unlawfully and wickedly devising and intending to vitiate and corrupt the

[9] *The Times*, 19 June 1877.

morals of youth and of others, and to bring them into a state of wickedness, lewdness, and debauchery, unlawfully and wickedly and designedly did publish a certain lewd, filthy and obscene book i.e. a book called the *Fruits of Philosophy*, thereby contaminating and vitiating and corrupting the morals of youth and of others'. Such is the charge and here again I agree that if the effect is as here described the defendants as they certainly published the book advisedly and intentionally and well aware of its character must abide the result, however strange and anomalous it may seem that while it is admitted that they were acting in the belief that they were doing what was right, they are to be held responsible, and it must be found against them that they published the book intended to corrupt and vitiate the morals of the people.

The jury then retired and were out for one and a half hours. So loud was their discussion that people in the corridor outside could hear every word they said, and much of the time was being spent in debating Bradlaugh's atheism! When they did return they gave an extraordinary verdict: 'We find that the book is calculated to corrupt public morals, but we entirely exonerate the defendants from any corrupt motives in publishing it'. 'That', said the Chief Justice firmly, 'is a verdict of guilty.' This decision caused confusion. After the trial two jurymen sent a guinea towards the costs of the defence, and another wrote saying that he had not agreed with a verdict of guilty and that it had been agreed that should the judge reject their special plea, they were to retire again.

On the next day the defendants moved a motion in arrest of judgment, Mrs. Besant claiming that the verdict was one of acquittal, and Bradlaugh maintaining that the indictment was bad, since the book had not been set out in full in the indictment. The judge decided against them on both points. He was about to discharge them without any sentence, when a dramatic new point was raised by the prosecution. Annie Besant's fluency had proved fatal. After the verdict of the jury she had apparently addressed a packed meeting of 600 people, declared that she would go on with publication, sold copies of the book, and said that 'one of the most highly trained intellects in England the Chief Justice was on their side'. Bradlaugh had also been present. Sir Alexander Cockburn, unmollified by the references to his intellect, rebuked the defendants for their conduct, and sentenced them to six months' imprisonment, imposing in addition a fine of £200 on each.

The drama, however, was not over. 'Would your lordship entertain an application to stay the execution of the sentence?' asked Bradlaugh. 'Certainly not', was the reply. Bradlaugh turned and had reached the door of the court when the judge called him back. He consented to a stay of execution, provided that Bradlaugh would give an undertaking not to sell any more copies of the book until the issue had been finally settled. Bradlaugh agreed and the defendants were then liberated on bail. He then moved for a writ of error on the grounds that the indictment was bad for setting out only the title and not the whole book. This point was sustained by the High Court and the conviction was quashed, as was the order for destruction of the pamphlets.[10] Over a thousand pounds was raised in public subscriptions for the defence, and the only result of the prolonged proceedings was that the circulation of *The Fruits of Philosophy* rose from a few hundred a year to one hundred and twenty thousand.

THE LITERARY REVOLT

The last quarter of the nineteenth century saw the open emergence of the revolt which had been foreshadowed in the poetry of Swinburne and Rossetti. Writers as varied as Henry James, Thomas Hardy, George Moore and Oscar Wilde rejected the conventions which previous writers, although finding irksome, had on the whole accepted. Public opinion remained intransigent, but the assumptions on which it was based were crumbling: the end of the tyranny of the reviews was at least in sight. Neither Henry James nor Thomas Hardy can strictly be included in the movement of 'art for art's sake', but they approved of many of its doctrines. Gautier had early proclaimed the new gospel in France, remarking acidly: 'un drame n'est pas un chemin de fer', but it took time for the ideas expressed in his epigram to establish themselves in England. Pater had first published his *Renaissance* in 1873 and attracted much hostile criticism. Four years later Mallock wrote *The New Republic* satirising him, and the new edition published the same year omitted the offending 'Conclusion' which did not reappear until 1888 and then in a slightly modified form. The final lines of the 'Conclusion' summed up Pater's philosophy and outraged contemporaries:

> Well, we are all condamnés, as Victor Hugo says: les hommes sont tous condamnés à mort avec des sursis indefinis: we have an interval and then our place knows us no more. Some spend this interval in listlessness, some in high passions, the wisest in art and song. For our one chance is in expanding that interval, in

[10] *Bradlaugh* v. *R.* (1878), 3 Q. B. D. 607. The only proceedings reported in the *Law Reports* are those on the final point of the validity of the indictment. Passages, etc., quoted above are taken from: *The Times*, June 1877; *The Queen* v. *Charles Bradlaugh and Annie Besant*—a verbatim report of the trial by Bonner and Forder; and Vol. II of Hypatia Bonner's *Charles Bradlaugh* (1894).

> getting as many pulsations as possible into the given time. High passions give one this quickened sense of life, ecstasy and sorrow of love, political or religious enthusiasm, or the 'enthusiasm of humanity'. Only, be sure it is passion, that it does yield you this fruit of a quickened, multiplied consciousness. Of this wisdom, the poetic passion, the desire for beauty, the love of art for art's sake has most; for art comes to you professing frankly to give nothing but the highest quality to your moments as they pass, and simply for those moments' sake.

Alfred Douglas put the point more crudely in a later sonnet:

> Tell me not of Philosophies
> Of morals, ethics, laws of life

and Wilde was equally emphatic in his preface to *The Picture of Dorian Gray*: 'There is no such thing as a moral or an immoral book. Books are well written or badly written. That is all'. By this time, however, æstheticism had become inextricably confused with decadence, and the creed suffered in consequence.

Henry James stated the doctrine less flamboyantly in a passage on the modern novel. He pointed out that the English novel was always addressed to 'young unmarried ladies'.

> This fact to a French story teller appears of course a damnable restriction and Monsieur Zola would probably decline to take as serious any work produced under such unnatural conditions. Half of life is a sealed book to young unmarried ladies and how can a novel be worth anything that deals only with half of life? How can a portrait be painted (in any way to be recognisable) of half a face? It is not in one eye but in the two eyes together that the expression resides and it is the combination of features that constitutes human identity. These objections are perfectly valid and it may be said that our English system is a good thing for virgins and boys and a bad thing for the novel itself, when the novel is regarded as something more than a simple *jeu d'esprit* and is considered as a composition that treats of life and helps us to KNOW.

THE CIRCULATING LIBRARIES

Such arguments did not appeal to the circulating libraries, who continued their old policy of repression. In 1883 George Moore published *A Modern Lover*, which dealt unusually frankly with a painter's sexual life in London and Paris. On the whole, reviews were laudatory and he was contrasted favourably with Zola by *The Spectator*.[11]

[11] 18 August 1883.

Mudie's, however, refused to take it, and Smith's declined to renew their original order.

On hearing of this Moore jumped into a cab and drove to Smith's head office himself. He was told: 'Your book was considered immoral, two ladies from the country wrote to me objecting to the scene in which the girl sat to the artist. After that I naturally refused to circulate the book unless a customer said he wanted particularly to read Mr. Moore's novel.'

A similar fate overtook *A Mummer's Wife* in 1884, and besides producing a cheap edition Moore countered by writing a blistering attack on the libraries, entitled *Literature at Nurse or Circulating Morals* (1885).

> The librarian [he wrote] rules the roost; he crows and every chanticleer pitches his note in the same key. He, not the ladies and gentlemen who place their names on the title pages is the author of modern English fiction. He models it, fashions it to suit his purpose, and the artistic individualities of his employees count for as little as that of the makers of the pill boxes in which are sold certain well known and mildly purgative medicines. And in accordance with his wishes English fiction now consists of either a sentimental misunderstanding which is happily cleared up in the end, or of singular escapes over the edges of precipices, and miraculous recoveries of one or more of the senses of which the hero was deprived, until the time has come for the author to bring his tale to a close. The novel of observation, of analysis, exists no longer among us. Why? Because the librarian does not feel as safe in circulating a study of life and manners as a tale concerning a lost will. . . . Let us renounce [he went on] the effort to reconcile these two irreconcilable things—art and young girls. That these young people should be provided with a literature suited to their age and taste, no artist will deny: all I ask is that some means may be devised by which the novelist will be allowed to describe the moral and religious feeling of his day as he perceives it to exist, and to be forced no longer to write with a view of helping parents and guardians to bring up their charges in all the traditional beliefs.

Despite this pamphlet neither Mudie's nor Smith's would take in *Esther Waters* on publication in 1894. They thought the book immoral as it dealt with the life of an unmarried mother, and outraged decency to the extent of including a scene in a maternity hospital.

Hardy's struggle on the other hand was waged not with the libraries but with the magazines. *Tess of the d'Urbervilles* was submitted to *Murray's* in October 1889, but they refused it, fearing that it would offend their readers. *Macmillan's* took the same attitude and finally it appeared expurgated in *The Graphic* in 1891. A mock marriage was substituted for the seduction, and since the Editor objected to the scene in which Clare carries the dairymaids across the flooded lane, Hardy obligingly introduced a wheelbarrow. 'I'll wheel you through the pool—all of you—with pleasure if you'll wait till I get a barrow—there's a barrow in that shed yonder.' * Hardy's plan was to publish the expurgated chapters in serial form; to publish the expurgations elsewhere as episodic adventures; and finally to bring them together in volume form. He put this plan into operation and published the full volume in 1891, adding after the title the words 'A Pure Woman'. An immediate outcry followed, but sales were high and Edmund Gosse wrote counselling him not to mind 'what the *Saturday's* ape leading and shrivelled spinster said or thought'. 'Let them', he said, 'rave!'

Jude the Obscure was published in volume form in 1895 and was viciously attacked on both sides of the Atlantic. Hardy had attempted to forestall criticism by stating in the preface that the story was 'addressed by a man to men and women of full age', but such prevarications did not save him. In the *New York World* Jeanette Gilder wrote:

> Thomas Hardy has scandalised the critics and shocked his friends. What has gone wrong with the hand that wrote *Far from the Madding Crowd.* I am shocked, appalled by this story . . . no wonder that *Harper's* magazine could not print it all. The only wonder is that it could print any of it . . . aside from its immorality there is coarseness which is beyond belief . . . Mr. Hardy's mind seems to be grovelling all through the story. When I finished the story I opened the window and let in the fresh air.[12]

In *Blackwood's* Mrs. Oliphant accused Hardy of founding 'an anti-marriage league'; the *Bookman* thought it 'a novel of lubricity'; and in the *Critic* Professor Thurston Peck described it as 'one of the most objectionable books he had ever read'. A lecturer at Liverpool thought the author had 'a curious mania for exploring sewers: filth and defilement he faces with the calm, unshrinking, countenance of a Local Board labourer'. The Bishop of Wakefield threw *Jude* in the fire and at his instigation Smith's withdrew it from circulation.

* Cf. a reviewer's objection to *Tom Brown at Oxford.* Tom carried a girl who had broken an ankle: 'If this be muscular Christianity, the less we have of it the better'. *Athenæum,* 30 November 1861.

[12] 8 December 1895.

Almost alone Havelock Ellis raised a dissentient voice in *The Savoy* (1896) and hailed it as 'the greatest novel written in England for many years'. He did not confine himself to the book but discussed some wider issues.

> It seems indeed on a review of all the facts that the surer a novel is of a certain immortality the surer it is also to be regarded at first, as indecent, as subversive of public morality. So that when as in the present case charges are recklessly flung about in all the most influential quarters we are simply called upon to accept them placidly as necessary incidents in the career of a great novel.

Ellis also raised the question of the relation between novelists and morals.

> A few persons have incautiously asserted that the novelist has nothing to do with morals. That we cannot assert: the utmost that can be asserted is that the novelist should never allow himself to be made the tool of a merely moral or immoral purpose. For the fact is that so far as the moralist deals with life at all, morals is part of the very stuff of his art. That is to say that his art lies in drawing the sinuous woof of human nature between the rigid warp of morals.

IBSEN

Sharing the honours of battle with Moore and Hardy during the 'nineties was Ibsen whose plays had been introduced into England by Gosse and Archer and which were being performed before an unappreciative public. *Ghosts* was first produced in 1891 and was greeted with a volley of abusive epithets. 'Noisome corruption', said *Stage*; 'garbage and offal', suggested *Truth*; 'foul and filthy', ventured *Era*; 'repulsive and degrading', commented *The Queen.* Some years later Queen Victoria attended a performance. The reviewers, however, were not disarmed by even royal patronage, and further outbursts against Ibsen occurred in 1893 and 1896. Bernard Shaw's *Mrs. Warren's Profession* was refused a licence in the 'nineties and when it was finally performed privately in 1902 was roundly abused by the Press.* Other plays refused licences were Wilde's *Salome*; Fagan's *The Earth*; and *Waste* by Granville Barker.

ZOLA AND THE VIZETELLY PROSECUTION

Hardy, Moore and Ibsen may have been censured by public opinion but they fared no worse. Zola was less fortunate, his books in the

* No public performance was given until 1925.

'eighties twice being subjected to criminal prosecution. These prosecutions are of the greatest interest, since they provide the first examples of the law being invoked successfully against works of literary merit. Hitherto, its scope had been limited to the suppression of pornography. The prosecutions marked a definite change of policy in administering the law. Some attempt must be made to explain this change. The immediate cause was the intervention of Kensit's National Vigilance Association and it may well have been encouraged in its efforts by the 'Maiden Tribute' scandal of three years before. Stead had exposed the extent of London's prostitution in a series of articles in the *Pall Mall Gazette* (1885) and these articles had done much to create feelings of anxiety about the general state of moral welfare. Stead himself, after release from prison, where his activities had landed him, conducted a campaign against pernicious literature, and a motion was passed in parliament calling for an enforcement and, if necessary, a strengthening of the relevant laws. These explanations, however, will not suffice, since prosecutions of literary works continued after 1888, and, indeed, have been continuous if sporadic up to the present time. An explanation may perhaps be found in the great increase in literacy which took place in the last decades of the nineteenth century. Forster's Education Act, the first attempt to provide a universal system of elementary education, had been passed in 1870, but it was some years before its effects were fully felt, especially as school attendance had not been made compulsory until 1880. In 1861 the illiteracy figures were as high as 25 per cent. for males and 35 per cent. for females but by 1893 these had fallen to 5 per cent. and 5·7 per cent. respectively.[13] Doubtless it was felt that at a time when Victorian standards were crumbling this great new semi-literate public needed legal protection. As has been seen, the Victorian synthesis was coming to an end, and the breakdown of accepted literary standards was hastened by the influx of new readers. As long as the reading public remained roughly unified the censorship imposed by the reviews and libraries made legal intervention superfluous. Publication of novels in cheap one-volume form greatly reduced the librarians' powers and at the same time the emergence of autonomous groups of readers lessened the influence of the reviews. This stratification of fiction primarily affected authors, but it also had the subsidiary result of fragmenting criticism, and thus making it a less effective means of control. It is not too fanciful to see in the 'literary' prosecutions an attempt to substitute legal sanctions for the increasingly ineffective anathemas of reviewers and librarians in upholding public standards of taste.

[13] Figures taken from Graham Balfour's *Educational Systems of Great Britain and Ireland.*

The prosecution of Vizetelly for publishing Zola's works was the climax of the long campaign which had been waged against the French naturalists. The clergy, the reviews, and the Press had for long been pressing these attacks. Typical of this attitude was a review in the *Temple Bar* in 1886 which contrasted Balzac with Zola.

> In his most outspoken passages the former maintains a certain decent reserve, which the latter and his followers—those shameless purveyors of hideous garbage—have set aside . . . this new school has imagined the impossible. Hyenas delighting in carrion they have lost touch with humanity, and the contrast between their corrupting imaginations and the searching analysis of Balzac is as great as that between the obscene ravings of delirium and the quiet dignity of a clerical demonstration.* [14]

L'Assommoir had been earlier subjected to attack, and amongst the hostile critics one finds the unlikely figure of Swinburne, now under the tutelage of the virtuous Watts-Dunton. In a letter to the *Athenæum* he recommended the same treatment for Zola's books as that given to sordid police court proceedings: 'The further details . . . were too revolting for publication in our columns.' [15] In similar vein is a later notice appearing in *The Scottish Review*: 'It is certainly coarse almost beyond expression and contains one description which should never have been written by man born of woman'.[16] Even Tennyson joined in the attack and included the following lines in his disillusioned 'Locksley Hall—Sixty Years After':

> Rip your brother's vices open, strip your own foul passions bare
> Down with Reticence, down with reverence—forward—naked—
>   let them stare.
> Feed the budding rose of boyhood with the drainage of your
>   sewer;
> Send the drain into the fountain, lest the stream should issue pure.
> Set the maiden fancies wallowing in the troughs of Zolaism
> Forward, forward, ay and backward, downward too into the
>   abysm.

Russian realism was contrasted with French naturalism, and the execration of the one was matched by adulation for the other. Tolstoy's moral and spiritual qualities appealed to the Victorians, and they turned thankfully away from Zola to the pages of his novels.

* It is of interest to contrast this view of Balzac with that current earlier in the century (see p. 52).

[14] October 1886, Vol. LXXVIII, p. 199.

[15] June 1877, p. 767.

[16] September 1883, Vol. XXXV, p. 301.

> It is refreshing [said the *Westminster Review*] in these degenerate days of the modern novel to turn away from the inane indelicacies of fashionable fiction, from the hysterical emanations of the unhealthy imagination of the New Woman and the vapid outpourings of 'fin de siècle' young man to the luminous pages of a literature that has in it all the life of true realism, whilst it does not flaunt in our faces those lower phases of human nature which are best left to the imagination.[17]

This constant stream of vituperation prepared the public for a prosecution which had in fact been demanded by the *Whitehall Review*. Samuel Smith referring to Zola's novels in the House of Commons described them as 'diabolical . . . fit only for swine' and warned the public that if they read them they would 'turn their minds into cesspools', but the government took no action and it was left to the Vigilance Association to bring the proceedings.*

Vizetelly, the accused, was a publisher of the highest repute with a keen interest in foreign literature. He had early given the public the *Tales* of Edgar Allan Poe, as well as Harriet Beecher Stowe's *Uncle Tom's Cabin.* He specialised in French literature and had published the works of Sand, Daudet, and Merimée, as well as those of Balzac and Flaubert. Zola had begun his great series of novels dealing with the Rougon-Macquart family in 1871 with *La Fortune des Rougons*, but it was not until 1884 that Vizetelly began to publish them in translations, executed by his son. *L'Assommoir* and *Nana* were the first to be published and these were followed by sixteen others, *La Terre* being published in 1884.

Vizetelly never published the complete text of the novels, but expurgated them to make them more suitable for an English audience. He had, however, miscalculated, and, on Wednesday, 31 October 1888, was brought to trial. Among the books mentioned in the indictment were *La Terre*, *Madame Bovary*, Daudet's *Sappho*, Maupassant's *Bel Ami*, and Gautier's *Mme de Maupin*, a rich harvest for a single trial. The prosecution was, however, directed against Zola. Twenty-one objectionable passages had been selected from *La Terre* by counsel for the prosecution, who said he did not believe 'there was ever collected between the covers of a book so much bestial obscenity as was found in the pages of this book . . . there was not a passage in it which contained any literary genius or the expression of any elevated thought'. Counsel for the defence reminded the court that the works were the works of a great French author.

[17] December 1895, Vol. CXLIV, p. 539.

* They were then taken over by the Crown.

SOLICITOR-GENERAL: 'A voluminous French author.'

THE RECORDER: 'A popular French author.'

COUNSEL: 'An author who ranks high among the literary men of France.'[18]

A juryman then objected to the passages being read aloud in court, and at this point Vizetelly gave up the struggle and changed his plea to guilty. On giving an undertaking to withdraw all of Zola's books from circulation he was discharged. *The Times* produced an approving leading article:

> Between prudency and pruriency in such matters there is a wide debatable ground and it is not always easy to draw the line which separates what is permissible from what is not. But if the line is not to be drawn so as to exclude translations of such works as *La Terre* and *Pot Bouille* it is plain that it cannot be drawn at all.[19]

Meanwhile, Vizetelly had sent the Attorney-General a copy of a book specially compiled from the English classics, and containing extracts 'showing that the legal suppression of M. Zola's novels would logically involve the bowdlerising of some of the greatest works in English Literature'. Authors from Shakespeare to Swinburne were included, and Vizetelly showed both courage and enterprise in producing the book.* In his preface Vizetelly pointed to the injustice of prosecuting a book which had been freely available for four years, and stressed that 'the government has thought proper to throw its weight into the scale with the view of suppressing a class of books which the law has never previously interfered with'. He reiterated the pleas of Swinburne, James and Moore: 'Is actual life to be no longer described in fiction simply because the withdrawing of the veil that shrouds it displays a state of things unadapted to the contemplation—not of grown-up men and women, but of the "young person of fifteen" who has the work of all Mr. Mudie's novelists to feast upon?' He referred to a recent unsuccessful attempt to suppress *The Decameron* and went on:

> It requires no particular foresight to predict that a couple of generations hence—when the tribe of prejudiced scribes who ignorant for the most part of their own country's literature, now join in the hue and cry against Mr. Zola—are relegated to their proper obscurity, the works of the author of the Rougon-Macquart family, spite of

[18] *The Times*, 1 November 1888. [19] 1 November 1888.

* In 1877 Annie Besant had produced a similar book made up of extracts from the Bible showing that it also should logically be suppressed. But the English, as has been noted, are not a logical nation.

their admitted coarseness, will take rank as classics among the productions of the great writers of the past.*

Vizetelly relapsed into his old bad habits, and in 1889 was once again in the courts for publishing French novels. On this occasion, although an old man of sixty-nine, he was sentenced to three months' imprisonment. He died in 1894, his death hastened by the hardships of prison life.† Edmund Gosse organised a petition for his release and it was signed by many leading men of letters, including Leslie Stephen, George Moore, Arthur Symons and Pinero. An unexpected champion was Robert Buchanan who addressed a wordy epistle to Henry Matthews, then Home Secretary, entitled 'On Descending into Hell'. He appealed to him to intervene and thus put the Catholic Church—Matthews was a Roman Catholic—on the side of the angels. He admitted that Zola had a mind devoted to examination of 'social sewage', but it was 'one thing to dislike the obtrusion of things unsavoury and abominable and quite another to regard any allusion to them as positively criminal'.

HAVELOCK ELLIS: 'SEXUAL INVERSION'

The second famous prosecution was that of the bookseller Bedborough in 1898 for selling Havelock Ellis's psychological classic *Sexual Inversion*, one of the first studies of homosexuality to be published in England.‡ In 1875 Ellis had resolved to devote his life to an exploration of sexual problems and *Sexual Inversion* was the first volume of his series 'Studies in the Psychology of Sex'. It first appeared in England in 1897, but a German translation had previously been published in Leipzig. Ellis's English publisher carried the curious name of the 'Watford University Press', and, in fact, this masked the identity of an extraordinary character 'De Villiers', whose real name was George Ferdinand Springmuhl von Weissenfeld, the son of an eminent German judge. De Villiers had a taste for luxurious living, but, unfortunately, lacked the necessary means to support life in a grand style. He made up for this by indulging in a

* *La Terre* was not republished in English until 1954 (Elek, 15*s*.).
Cyril Connolly commented in the *Sunday Times* (8 August 1954): 'It is excellent that such a book should have at last been translated for the English public'. The public had, however, been deprived of it for over sixty years.

† Two years after Vizetelly's death Zola was fêted by literary London. Three weeks before the first English prosecution Zola had been awarded the Legion of Honour by the French government.

‡ Edward Carpenter had done some work in this field in *Love's Coming of Age* (1896), but could find no publisher and eventually published the book himself.

series of swindles, confidence tricks, and promotions of false companies. He had so many aliases and false banking accounts that he had compiled his own 'Who's Who', which he carried with him for his private use. His business activities centred on London, but his residence was at Cambridge and would not have been out of place in the pages of Mrs. Radcliffe. The house was bounded by four roads leading to which were four underground passages by means of which in an emergency an escape could be made. But when the emergency arose they remained unused and De Villiers was apprehended in the house. He had been engaging in large-scale trade in pornographic books, and after seizing two tons of these from an agent in London, the police obtained a warrant for De Villier's arrest. When the police arrived at De Villier's house there was no sign of him, but a constable was certain that he entered it a few minutes before. After a search the police were about to leave, when they heard a movement in the roof and discovered De Villiers hiding in a secret chamber of his own construction. He put up a fierce struggle but was overpowered and taken to the police station. Inspector Drew told thc parliamentary committee of 1908, which was investigating the trade in obscene books, that at the police station he was seized with apoplexy and died. This was not correct. De Villiers remained a 'Gothic' character to the end, and committed suicide by a poison ring which he wore on his left hand.[20]

Apart from the shadiness of his publisher Ellis was handicapped by his bookseller, who was the secretary of the 'Legitimation League', which was concerned with securing rights for illegitimate children, and was disapproved of by the police. In prosecuting Bedborough they were also attempting to put an end to the League. A further disadvantage was the Wilde trials (1895), memories of which were still in people's minds, which did not dispose them to a rational consideration of inversion.

Nevertheless, Ellis resolved to fight the case. Horace Avory was briefed for the defence, and a team of experts assembled to give evidence of the scientific value of the book. To the consternation of everybody, Bedborough, when it came to the trial, pleaded guilty. Ellis and the lawyers were helpless, and had to stand by while the book was condemned with no word being said in its defence. The Recorder, Sir Charles Hall, however, approved his action.

> You have acted wisely [he said] for it would have been impossible for you to have contended with any possibility whatever of being able to persuade anybody that this book, this lecture and this

[20] Statement of Bedborough, 1 December 1925. See Goldberg, *Havelock Ellis* (London 1926).

magazine were not filthy and obscene works. . . . I am willing to believe that in acting as you did, you might at the first outset perhaps have been gulled into the belief that somebody might say that this was a scientific work. But it is impossible for anybody with a head on his shoulders to open the book without seeing that it is a pretence and a sham, and that it is merely entered into for the purpose of selling this obscene publication.' [21]

Bedborough earned the reward of his pliancy and was bound over.

Ellis was understandably bitter about the prosecution and published the remaining volumes in the United States, where they received gentler treatment. About the trial he wrote:

It must be remembered that so far as an author is concerned the injury done by such a prosecution is done in the act of bringing it. . . . The anxiety and uncertainty produced by so infamous a charge on a man and those who belong to him, the risk of loss of friends, the pecuniary damages, the proclamation to the world at large which has never known and will never know the grounds on which the accusation is made, that an author is to be classed with the purveyors of literary garbage—this power is put into the hands of any meddlesome member of that sad clan against which they themselves are powerless.[22]

His attitude mellowed later and in his autobiography he spoke not only for himself but for all those writers who had suffered at the hands of the Victorian censors, literary and legal, when he wrote:

The Law and the Press were indeed well matched and between them they thought they had dismissed me and my book from the world. Yet I—rather the spirit of Man I chanced to embody—have overcome the world. My 'filthy' and 'worthless' and 'morbid' book has been translated into all the greatest living languages to reach people who could not say what a Recorder is, nor read the *Daily Chronicle*, even if they saw it. Unto this day it continues to bring me from many lands the reverent and grateful words of strangers, whose praise keeps me humble in the face of the supreme mystery of life.

[21] *The Times*, 1 November 1898.
[22] *A Note on the Bedborough Trial* (London 1898).

CHAPTER V

THE TWENTIETH CENTURY

FOR a decade before the Queen's death 'Victorianism' had been in decline, but although its moral ideas were rejected by an ever-widening circle, its influence remained strong in the years preceding the outbreak of the Great War. A revolution in manners and social customs had long been foreshadowed, but without the war, it would have taken much longer to accomplish. Today, vestiges of 'Victorianism' still remain—the word 'immoral' in English usage still has only one unmistakable meaning—and in so far as puritanism represents a perennial element in the national character, the continuance of this attitude to sexual matters in one form or another can be safely prophesied. The 'reviews' and periodicals which had for so long dictated standards of taste continued to lose both circulation and influence and one by one they either amalgamated or went out of existence. A significant portent of change had been the founding in 1901 of *The Times Literary Supplement*, but the newspapers although they became dominant only partially filled the place occupied by the old 'reviews'. Nevertheless, it is possible to see in James Douglas and John Gordon the modern descendants of the moral pundits of the *Saturday Review*, breathing anathemas with an equal zest and ferocity.

After the success of the 'Vizetelly' prosecution the law continued to intervene sporadically in its new rôle of arbiter of public taste. As sanctions the authorities used both the criminal law and the destruction order, but pursued no coherent policy, the operation of the law being essentially spasmodic. A puritanical Home Secretary; a newspaper outcry; a question in parliament; a protest from the Public Morality Council; all these at different times have set the law in motion. Haphazard prosecutions are preferred by authors and publishers to a consistent policy of restraint, and such action is justified by the authorities on the grounds that it does little harm, and is useful in keeping venturesome publishers within bounds, causing them to be more careful.

As in the late nineteenth century so in the early years of its successor, pornography continued a vexing problem. The Society for the Suppression of Vice was dead, but its campaign against 'indecent literature' was continued by the National Vigilance Association, a Low Church body, and the Public Morality Council (1899), which included members of the main religious denominations under the presidency of the Bishop of London. In 1902 the Council was campaigning against the 'metascope', recently invented, which was being used to display 'abominable' scenes, and in the same year a deputation headed by Lord Kinnaird met the Home Secretary, to request that Lord Campbell's Act be made more stringent.[1] In 1903 the Headmasters' Conference appealed for a suppression of the pornography circulating in their schools and the Council set up a committee to investigate. The committee found that

> Publications of a most disgraceful character were offered for sale in thousands of newsagents' shops. Demoralising newspapers were sold to boys and girls at railway bookstalls. Lewd illustrated postcards were to be seen in hundreds of shop windows. Such publications were a direct incentive to vice. One of our judges in charging a jury said that 40,000 copies of these pernicious publications were issued in the country every week. It has also been stated that three tons of a single vile newspaper had been exported weekly to the colonies.[2]

In 1907 the Council was busy trying to suppress displays of 'living statuary' in the music halls, and secured the passage of a condemnatory resolution by the London County Council. The following year a conference on 'indecent literature' was held at the Caxton Hall, and as a result a committee of peers and members of parliament was formed to prepare new legislation, and magistrates were petitioned to apply severer penalties.

JOINT COMMITTEE OF BOTH HOUSES

The Government was not unaware of the problem, and in 1908 a Joint Select Committee of both Houses of Parliament was appointed to investigate 'lotteries and indecent advertisements'. The Committee recommended the repeal of the numerous statutes dealing with pornography, and the enactment of a comprehensive amending and consolidating Act, making all offences summary and providing a uniform mode of procedure. Penalties for a first offence were to be a fine of £30 or one month's imprisonment, but in the case of a

[1] *Annual Report of the Council for 1902.*
[2] *Annual Report of the Council for 1903.*

second offence or sale to a young person under sixteen this was to be increased to £100 or six months in prison.

> A provision [recommended the Committee] should also be inserted to exempt from operation of the Act any book of literary merit or reputation or any genuine work of art. The Committee think it would be almost impossible to devise any definition that would cover this exception. In their opinion the decision in such cases should be left to the magistrate, but they believe that if a provision such as they recommend were inserted in the Act, a magistrate would be enabled to take into consideration all the circumstances of the case and would be free from a supposed obligation to decide upon the decency or indecency of the particular literary or artistic work brought to its notice.[3]

These recommendations were never implemented, although when a deputation from the Public Morality Council met the Home Secretary in 1911 he assured them that a Bill embodying the proposals had been drafted, but the session was too crowded for its introduction.[4] With the outbreak of war the Bill was shelved and until recently the Committee and its proposals had been forgotten.

One recommendation of the Committee was, however, acted upon, that to tackle the problem internationally. In 1910 by French initiative a conference was held in Paris to draw up an international agreement to check the sale and distribution of pornography. Great Britain, France, Germany, Austria-Hungary, Russia and the United States were represented. A Convention was signed, and the countries present undertook to establish central authorities which would collect and exchange information about the traffic in obscene publications.[5]

H. G. WELLS

Meanwhile the old game of denouncing books as immoral continued, H. G. Wells being selected to fill the place of Zola, who by this time had become generally accepted. *In the Days of the Comet* was published in 1906, and caused an outcry because of its attack on the conventional marriage bond and its advocacy of free love. Some newspapers in attacking the book were clearly not concerned with its morality, but used it as a weapon to discredit Socialism. They seized triumphantly on the point that Socialism would inevitably lead to the breakdown of family life. On 15 September the *Daily*

[3] *Report of Joint Select Committee on Lotteries and Indecent Advertisements* (1908), Stationery Office, p. 275.

[4] *Annual Report of the Council for 1911.*

[5] 1910 Convention. Records of 3rd Assembly League of Nations, 1922. 5th Committee. Annex 19.

Express carried a leading article which attacked Socialism, the Trade Unions, Free Love and Wells, without clearly distinguishing between any of them. On the 19th a reply from Wells was published repudiating the charge that he was advocating promiscuity. Referring to *The Comet*, he wrote:

> The people in this exalted world, in this kingdom of heaven on earth, become communists—as the early Christians did—and just as in the Christian Utopia there is neither 'marrying nor giving in marriage' among them. If the suggestion in my book is 'horrible' to the Reverend Lenthal Davids, equally 'horrible' must be that teaching of the Founder of the religion he has undertaken to represent.

This defence did not impress the *Express*, which replied with a further denunciatory leader, or *The Spectator* which published an article 'Socialism and Sex Relations.' 'We may feel certain that the triumph of Socialism must mean the overthrow of the Christian moral code in regard to marriage and the relations of the sexes, and must end in free love and promiscuity.[6]

In 1909 Wells published *Ann Veronica* and aroused even more vehement protests. 'Mr. Wells', said *The Sphere*, 'has not ceased to be interesting but he has ceased to be an artist . . . his book is not only defective as a novel, being here rather good journalism than good literature, but it will be actually pernicious in its influence. In any case there is a strain of vulgarity.' [7] 'Ought Mr. Wells to have written this book?' asked William Barry in *The Bookman*.[8] 'I think *Ann Veronica* imperfect as a work of art, though picturesque and exciting, persuasive against the great human law which bridles passion, and therefore dangerous to every woman into whose hands it is likely to fall. I wish Mr. Wells had not written it.'

The Spectator headed its review 'A Poisonous Book.' [9] The reviewer had no quarrel with its language 'there is not a coarse word in it', but feared for the effects of its theme:

> It is a book capable of poisoning the minds of those who read it. . . . The loathing and the indignation which the book inspires in us are due to the effect it is likely to have in undermining that sense of continence and self-control in the individual which is essential to a sound and healthy state. . . . His [went on the reviewer] is a community of scuffling stoats and ferrets unenlightened by a ray of duty or abnegation.

[6] *The Spectator*, 19 October 1907, Vol. XCIX, p. 558.
[7] *The Sphere*, 9 October 1909.
[8] November 1909, Vol. XXXIII, p. 89.
[9] 20 November 1909, Vol. CIII, p. 846.

On 4 December Wells replied:

> My book was written primarily to express the resentment and distress which many women feel nowadays at their unavoidable practical dependence upon some individual man not of their deliberate choice, and in full sympathy with the natural but perhaps anarchistic and anti-social idea that it is intolerable for a woman to have sexual relations with a man with whom she is not in love, and natural and desirable and admirable for her to want them, and still more so to want children by a man of her own selection.

Ann Veronica brought to a head the agitation against immoral novels which had been going on for some time. The journals of the period were filled with articles attacking contemporary fiction as well as reports of denunciations from the pulpit and at public meetings.* The Rev. H. Bull wrote to *The Spectator* and opened a fund for the financing of prosecutions and received support in a leading article. *The Spectator* recommended the setting up of a committee 'to take action in regard to what we believe is only a passing phase in fiction and to deal with books which are now finding their way into places where a few years ago works of their kind would never have been published or sold'. This committee which would initiate prosecutions should consist of 'men of the world, the kind of men who get returned to parliament by the best type of constituency. They should certainly number among them one or two lawyers of distinction.' [10] This committee was never set up although the Reverend Bull reported in a later issue that he had collected £305 in cash and promises.

A more important repercussion was the publication in *The Spectator* of 4 December 1909 of a letter from the circulating libraries. Mudie's, Smith's, Boots', *The Times*, and Days, had formed a libraries association to censor impure literature. 'We have decided in future that we will not place in circulation any book which by reason of the personally scandalous, libellous, immoral or otherwise disagreeable nature of its contents is in our opinion likely to prove offensive to any considerable section of our subscribers.' A committee was to be set up to enforce this policy, and publishers were asked to send a copy of any novel to the committee at least a week before publication date. This proposal caused a bitter controversy. Edmund Gosse attacked it in the *English Review*: 'Let us take our

* These continued e.g.: A meeting in London of the National Purity Crusade where John Murray read a paper on how to control noxious literature (1910); 'Undesirable Fiction', 'Notable Protest against Present Day Fiction', *The Birmingham Daily Mail*, 22 March 1911; 'Pernicious Literature' by H. D. Rawnsley in the *Hibbert Journal*, January 1912.

[10] *The Spectator*, 27 November 1909.

courage in both hands and say that we would rather see English Literature free than decent.[11] Throughout January the columns of the *Observer* were filled with letters of protest from authors and others. *The New Age* also attacked the proposed censorship, and the Chief Librarian of the Times Book Club, Janet Hogarth, resigned in protest. In *The Times* itself Anthony Hope and Edmund Gosse published a letter of protest. A supporter of the new policy was William Barry.

> We may grant [he wrote in *The Bookman*] in old and famous writings a freedom which present everyday stories, put into general circulation, ought not to be allowed. The reason is plain. Old classics are read by students, not by the man or woman in search of amusement. They exact an attention to their language and peculiarities which blunts the edge of appetite. And they have lost the novelty which they had in their day. . . . In a civilised Christian society books which undermine its moral foundations have not any valid claims to exist. They spread the plague: they should be stamped out like the yellow fever and the sleeping sickness.[12]

The proposed censorship came to nothing, but until the outbreak of the war denunciations of contemporary fiction continued. Thus in 1912 at Edinburgh the Archbishop of York expressed himself, 'sick of this hot, panting, blear eyed fiction of the present day. This twentieth century fiction is obsessed with the sex problem and that not in its oldest, simplest, happiest or most tragic form, but simply in its relation to sexual passion'.

In the same year Canon Rawnsley wrote an article on 'pernicious literature' in the *Hibbert Journal*.

> The chief degraders today are the nasty novelists . . . this erotic contemptible trash has great vogue with the idle classes, and, though it cannot be obtained at our free libraries is found upon the top shelf literature of many small lending libraries . . . these corrosive novels are flaunted beneath the eyes of a passing public in the most seductive guise. One of the worst of them a year or two ago, which under threat of prosecution was withdrawn from circulation came out magnificently apparelled in royal purple and coroneted. A lady found it on a railway bookstall which she believed was impeccable, and because she had just re-papered her bedrooms with the same royal purple, purchased five of the beastly books right off and put one in each said bedroom. Again a young

[11] March 1910, Vol. IV, p. 616.
[12] *The Cleansing of Fiction*, January 1910, Vol. XXXVII, p. 178.

Eton boy purchased another of these abominations to give to his mother as they travelled together to Eton, because it was such a pretty book.[13]

THE STAGE

The strictness of stage censorship continued, although opposition to the Censor grew steadily more vocal. By the turn of the century Ibsen was accepted, although it was not until 1914 that *Ghosts* was given a licence for a public performance. Shaw's plays *The Shewing Up of Blanco Posnet* and *Mrs. Warren's Profession* remained banned, the latter being greeted with abuse and consternation when it was given a private performance in 1902.* *Salome* despite repeated applications for a licence was not performed until 1931. In 1902 Maeterlinck's *Monna Vanna* was refused a licence, as was *Œdipus Rex* until 1911. Edward Garnett's *The Breaking Point* was banned, as was *Waste*, by Granville Barker. *The Times* comment on *Waste* is an interesting reflection of contemporary opinion:

> The play is a work of extraordinary power dealing with some of the most fundamental facts of human life with an unflinching truthfulness, and at the same time blending these facts with certainly the most vivid, and probably the most authentic presentation we have yet had on the English stage of great social and political questions, that come home to all Englishmen's homes and bosoms. But this is not the end of the matter. For our part we have no hesitation in approving the censor's decision. The subject matter of *Waste*, together with the sincere realism with which it is treated, makes it in our judgment wholly unfit for performance, under ordinary conditions, before a miscellaneous public of various ages, moods and standards of intelligence. Questions of art are one thing and questions of public policy and public expediency are another thing.[14]

In 1907 a deputation of seven authors including Barrie, Galsworthy and Yeats was received by the Prime Minister, Herbert Asquith, who discussed with them the subject of stage censorship. As a result of their efforts and those of Robert Harcourt, a playwright who had been elected to the House of Commons, a Joint Committee of both Houses of Parliament was appointed to study the problem. The Committee recommended the abolition of the existing licensing system, and its replacement by a voluntary system.

[13] Vol. X, p. 462 (1912).
* It was not given a public performance until 1925.
[14] Quoted by Edward Garnett in an article in the *Fortnightly*, 'The Censorship Public Opinion', July 1909, Vol. CXI, p. 137.

The Committee concluded that licensing was harmful to the theatre, and considered the law of 'obscene libel' sufficient to keep indecency in check.[14a] Like the recommendations of the Committee on 'Indecent Advertisements' of the previous year, these proposals have never been implemented.

THE CINEMA

A new problem was created by the invention of the cinematograph. In 1909 the Cinematograph Act [15] forbade the showing of inflammable films unless the premises where they were shown had been duly licensed, power to grant licences being conferred on the local authorities.* Each local authority imposed its own conditions and the result was chaos. To remedy this the Association of Kinematograph Manufacturers set up their own Board of Censorship in 1912 with premises at 77 Shaftesbury Avenue. This censorship has never had any legal authority, but local authorities when granting licences for cinemas invariably insist that no films shall be shown unless they carry the certificate of the Censorship Board. In 1916 Herbert Samuel proposed an official censorship, but this met with little support and today the film censorship is entirely voluntary.

'THE RAINBOW'

During the First World War publication was restricted in certain ways and a new category of press offences was created, but this was for security reasons and was not concerned with public morals. Postal correspondence was subject to certain restrictions and a censorship operated in the case of forces on active service.[16]

From the point of view of literary censorship the war years were uneventful save for the destruction of D. H. Lawrence's *The Rainbow* in 1915. Lawrence had spent three years in writing this novel, but it was unfavourably received, being denounced by some reviewers as 'immoral'. Robert Lynd reviewed it scathingly in the *Daily News*, heading his notice 'The Downfall'. He described the book as 'a monotonous wilderness of phallicism', and added:

> If Mr. Lawrence had written the *Iliad* there would have been nothing in it but Paris and Helen and they would have been simply a pair of furious animals. . . . It is not chiefly that the book will offend the general sense of decency, many an indecent

[14a] Verbatim report of the proceedings, and text of recommendations: *The Stage*, (London 1910).

[15] 9 Edw. 7, c. 30.

* No licence is required in the case of trade shows, performances in private houses or in the open air.

[16] See *Defence of the Realm Manual* (1917), pp. 88, 150. Also *Fox* v. *Spicer*, 33 T. L. R. 172. For the postal restrictions see regulation 24B.

> book is none the less fine literature by reason of its humanity, its imaginative intensity or its humour. *The Rainbow* though it contains intense passages lacks the marks of good literature.[17]

James Douglas and Clement Shorter also attacked the book, but mainly on the grounds of indecency.

On 14 November Methuen's, the publishers, were summoned to Bow Street to show cause why one thousand copies of the book seized by the police should not be destroyed. H. Muskett appeared for the police and maintained that the book was 'a mass of obscenity of thought, idea and action throughout, wrapped up in language which he supposed would be regarded in some quarters as artistic and intellectual effort, and he was at a loss to understand how Messrs. Methuen had come to lend their name to its publication.'[18] Methuen's neither informed Lawrence of the proceedings nor defended the book, but expressed regret that they had published it. They pointed out that they had sent the manuscript back for alteration in July 1914 and returned it once again in its amended form. Lawrence, however, had refused to make any further alterations. Sir John Dickinson when ordering the book's destruction regretted 'that a firm of such high repute should have allowed their reputation to be soiled as it had been by the publication of this work', and rebuked them for not suppressing it when it had been criticised by the Press. On 18 November Philip Morrell, a Liberal and husband of Lady Ottoline Morrell, raised the question in the House of Commons but nothing was done. Of this incident Richard Aldington wrote:

> Lawrence was left owing his publishers the advance: he lost all chance of earning anything for three years of work; he lost his copyright; he was publicly stigmatised as obscene: and his name was made so notorious that publishers and periodicals for a long time avoided using his work. When he did a book on European History for the Oxford University Press it was published under a pseudonym.[19]

Lawrence's comment was bitter: 'I am not very much moved: I am beyond that by now. I only curse them all, body and soul, root, branch and leaf to eternal damnation'.*

The First World War destroyed many of the conventions about sex which had been accepted by previous generations as fundamental moral truths. This change was reflected in literature where sexual attitudes and problems which had previously been ignored or treated

[17] *Daily News*, 5 October 1915, p. 6.
[18] *The Times*, 15 November 1915.
[19] Richard Aldington, *D. H. Lawrence* (1950).
* In 1949 *The Rainbow* was published in a Penguin edition.

with reticence were openly and fully discussed. The old pattern of outcry and legal suppression continued, but the protests were less frequent and the opposition to legal intervention grew more widespread. More and more the protests were confined to the popular Press, the serious reviews, formerly the champions of orthodoxy, having grown more tolerant. This division of opinion further illustrates the fragmentation of the reading public and hence of criticism, which has already been mentioned, and is exemplified in the reaction to James Joyce's *Ulysses* on publication in 1922.

'ULYSSES'

Writing in the *Observer* Sisley Huddleston commented: 'There is one chapter devoted to the revery of a woman, and her *monologue intérieur* is I imagine—and am bound in all honesty to say—the vilest according to ordinary standards in all literature. And yet its very obscenity is somehow beautiful and wrings the soul to pity. Is that not high art?' [20] Middleton Murry thought Joyce 'a genius of the very highest order', and compared him to Goethe, while Arnold Bennett wrote that he had never read anything to surpass it: 'The book is not pornographic but it is more indecent, obscene, scatalogical and licentious than the majority of professedly pornographic books'.[21] With these opinions can be contrasted that of James Douglas in the *Sunday Express*:

> I have read it and I say deliberately that it is the most infamously obscene book in ancient or in modern literature. The obscenity of Rabelais is innocent compared with its leprous and scabrous horrors. All the secret sewers of vice are canalised in its flood of unimaginable thoughts, images and pornographic words. And its unclean lunacies are larded with appalling and revolting blasphemies directed against the Christian religion and against the holy name of Christ—blasphemies hitherto associated with the most degraded orgies of Satanism and the Black Mass.[22] *

As the book had not been published in England no legal action was possible, but the authorities shared the views of James Douglas.

[20] The *Observer*, 5 March 1922. [21] *The Outlook*, 29 April 1922.
[22] 28 May 1922.
* For a full discussion of the reviews see *James Joyce*, by Herbert Gorman, Chapter 10 (London 1941). Catholic opposition to the book was strong. Thus the *Dublin Review*: 'Having tasted and rejected the devilish drench we most earnestly hope that this book be placed not only on the *index expurgatorius*, but that its reading and communication be made a reserved case'. So also Shane Leslie in the *Quarterly*: 'From any Christian point of view this book must be proclaimed anathema'. (October 1922.)

In January 1923 a consignment of 500 copies, comprising an entire edition, was intercepted by the Customs at Folkestone and all but one burnt. In this the British Customs officials were following the example of their American colleagues who had taken similar action the year before. In January 1924 an unlimited edition was published in Paris, but no publisher in either England or America dared to publish the book until the 'thirties. In 1933 the United States ban on *Ulysses* was lifted by Judge Woolsey * and in the following year Random House published an unlimited edition. In 1936 John Lane brought out an edition limited to one thousand copies and followed this in 1937 with the first unlimited English edition, which has been three times reprinted.

THE GENEVA CONFERENCE

While the Customs men were burning *Ulysses* in Folkestone preparations were being made in Geneva to hold the second International Conference to discuss the traffic in obscene publications. Mrs. Coombe-Tenant, one of the British delegates, had made it clear that the Conference was not concerned with prescribing standards of artistic and literary propriety.

> The trade which I have had in mind . . . is that which is concerned with the production and distribution of articles such as photographs of the grossest character dealing with sexual relationships, which are intended merely to gratify the passions of depraved persons or to spread corruption amongst others, especially young men and women.

Mr. Castorkis of Greece by defining obscenity also indicated the limited purpose of the Conference. 'It was', he said, 'the deliberate exhibition of subjects, drawings, and pictures of situations which were calculated directly to evoke in the imagination the presence of unhealthy ideas, and which denoted in the author the perverse intention of addressing himself principally to the spirit of debauchery.' [23]

Over the means to be employed for suppressing the international trade in pornography the French and British delegates were divided. The French delegate wished participation in the trade to be made an international offence, justiciable in the courts of any country taking part in the conference; while the British delegate Sir Archibald Bodkin, maintained the principle of territorial jurisdiction, namely that criminals should only be tried in the country where their offence had been committed. After prolonged debate the British view pre-

* See page 162. [23] League of Nations, 20 and 22 September 1922.

vailed. No attempt was made to define 'obscenity', this being considered a question of fact to be decided by the courts of individual countries. The French wished a ban to be imposed on propaganda advocating contraception, but this was defeated principally through the opposition of Great Britain.

On 12 September 1923 over forty states signed the Convention and undertook to bring their national law into conformity with its provisions.* The states agreed to make trade in obscene publications a punishable offence, and to exchange information on every aspect of the problem. Whenever obscene publications were seized on importation they undertook to give immediate information of all the circumstances to the authorities of the exporting state.[24] †

'JIX'

In England the signing of the Convention was the signal for a new domestic drive against pornography. But when Sir William Joynson-Hicks became Home Secretary in the following year (1924) the campaign was extended to cover serious works to which the Convention was never intended to apply.

Such a policy aroused widespread opposition and in 1929 he was pilloried in a political satire *Policeman of the Lord* written by P. R. Stephensen and illustrated by Beresford Egan. The following are typical verses:

> Twinkle, twinkle little Jix
> What a bag of monkey tricks
> Up above the clouds so high
> Playing pleeceman in the sky.

* The United Kingdom seems to be in breach of the Convention because Article 1 makes it an offence to 'have in possession' obscene publications for purposes of trade. This is not an offence under English law.

[24] See *International Convention for the Suppression of the Circulation of and Traffic in Obscene Publications*. Stationery Office, London. Treaty Series No. 1 (1926), Cmd. 2575. Also *Protocol*, etc. Stationery Office. Treaty Series No. 2 (1952), Cmd. 8438.

† On 12 November 1947 the League of Nations Convention and the earlier agreement of 1910 were taken over by the United Nations.

On 28 August 1924 it was agreed by the World Postal Convention that the sending of 'obscene or immoral' objects by post should be forbidden. It was further agreed that: 'explosives, inflammable, or dangerous substances, and obscene or immoral objects are not to be returned to the office of origin, but they are to be destroyed on the spot by the postal authorities who detect their presence'. (Art. 41/1/f.)

In 1926 the General Assembly of the International Conference of Police meeting at Vienna passed a resolution condemning the international trade in pornography.

Leave the Well alone
The Old Prayer Book will do
Little Bo-Peep has lost her sheep
And doesn't know where to look
Leave them alone and they'll come home
Reading a naughty book.

'Jix' defended himself in a pamphlet *Do we need a censor?*, to which he gave an affirmative answer. He explained his actions in these enigmatic words: 'The practice and policy during my term of office may be summarised in this way: the Home Secretary never moved against other than admittedly pornographic productions of his own volition'. The 'Jix' period clearly illustrates the weakness of the law: its scope is so wide that it is only made tolerable when administered with moderation and restraint. Ultimately everything depends on executive discretion.

'THE WELL OF LONELINESS'

'Jix' caused the greatest resentment by his suppression of Radclyffe Hall's *The Well of Loneliness*, a case which has bestowed on him a vicarious immortality. The book deals with sexual relations between women and is a passionate over-written plea for more toleration and understanding. Its heroine Stephen Gordon is an invert from birth, and after various unfortunate amatory adventures falls in love with Mary Llewellyn with whom she lives in Paris. Finally she sacrifices her own happiness to that of Mary by giving her up to an old lover (male) who is in love with Mary and wishes to marry her. Much of the writing is florid and the book is too unrestrained to be a work of art, but it is redeemed by the passionate sincerity of the authoress and there can be no doubt of her serious purpose. Jonathan Cape published it in July 1928 and nearly all reviewers were favourable. The conservative *Daily Telegraph* praised it highly:

> This is a truly remarkable book. It is remarkable in the first place as a work of art finely conceived and finely written. Secondly it is remarkable as dealing with an aspect of abnormal life seldom or never presented in English fiction—certainly never with such unreserved frankness. As in all works of true art, subject and treatment are inseparably bound together in this book; it would be a mistake to compliment Miss Hall on her style, on her marvellously just selection of words, and on her burning sincerity, while at the same time condemning her choice of subject and accusing her of lack of restraint. Her book must be accepted as a whole, and so accepted it is likely to excite two directly opposite opinions,

> according as the reader admits or denies the subjects as legitimate material for art.[25]

This judgement was generally supported. *The Times Literary Supplement* described it as 'sincere, courageous, high minded and often beautifully expressed'.[26] The *Sunday Times* was equally enthusiastic, but added ominously: 'If it is reviewed as it was written it will be something of a landmark in the history of human development'. Arnold Bennett praised her work: 'It is honest, convincing and extremely courageous'. Even the *Saturday Review* was disarmed: 'Her appeal is a powerful one and is supported by passages of great force and beauty'.

All appeared to be going well, when on 19 August a sensational article by James Douglas appeared in the *Sunday Express.*

> I am well aware [he wrote] that sexual inversion and perversion are horrors which exist amongst us today. They flaunt themselves in public places with increasing effrontery and more insolently provocative bravado. The decadent apostles of the most hideous and loathsome vices no longer conceal their degeneracy and degradation. . . . This novel forces upon our society a disagreeable task which it has hitherto shirked, the task of cleaning itself from the leprosy of these lepers and making the air clean and wholesome once more. . . . It is a seductive and insidious piece of special pleading designed to display perverted decadence as a martyrdom inflicted upon those outcasts by a cruel society. It flings a veil of sentiment over their depravity. It even suggests that their self-made debasement is unavoidable because they cannot save themselves.

In a celebrated passage he added: 'I would rather put a phial of prussic acid in the hands of a healthy girl or boy than the book in question . . . What then is to be done? the book must be at once withdrawn'. Douglas was supported in his stand by the *Sunday Chronicle*; while *Truth*, although it condemned the legal action, approved of the book's withdrawal. 'There are certain evils in the world which as they cannot be cured must be endured.'

Alarmed by the violence of this onslaught and fearing prosecution Cape's communicated with the Home Secretary and offered to withdraw the book. Joynson-Hicks counselled withdrawal as the best course and Cape's acted accordingly. Over this step a renewed controversy broke out. The *Daily Herald* carried on a campaign against the government, claiming that a secret censorship was being organised and printing many protests. Bernard Shaw wrote: 'I read

[25] 7 August 1928. [26] 28 July 1928.

it and read it carefully and I repeat that it ought not to have been withdrawn.[27] He was supported by H. G. Wells and many others. *The Spectator* on the other hand, approved of the book's withdrawal:

> When we received the review we decided not to publish it because we thought that the subject of sexual perversion is one which is better ignored unless there is some overwhelming justification for dragging it into the full light of day. . . . We think that the Home Secretary acted wisely in asking Mr. Cape to withdraw the book and we congratulate the publisher on complying with the request so promptly.

Meanwhile Radclyffe Hall had not been silent and had issued a series of protests.

> I wrote the book [she said] from a deep sense of duty. Had I refrained through a lack of courage from fulfilling my duty, then I should not have deserved the respect or the support of my public. I am proud indeed to have taken up my pen in defence of those who are utterly defenceless, who being from birth a people set apart in accordance with some hidden scheme of Nature, need all the help that society can give them.[28]

A further sensation occurred when it was learnt in late September that a new edition of the book was being printed in Paris for the English market. Many people received circulars informing them that they could buy the book—in which not one word had been altered—for twenty-five shillings plus elevenpence postage. On 5 October the first consignment of copies arrived at Dover and was immediately seized by the Customs. Again there was an outcry, the left-wing press in particular attacking the government. The culminating point of the controversy was reached on 9 November when the government applied at Bow Street for a destruction order under Lord Campbell's Act.

Eustace Fulton and Vincent Evans appeared for the Crown and Norman Birkett, K.C., with Herbert Metcalfe, K.C., for Jonathan Cape. J. B. Melville represented the Pegasus Press of Paris who had reprinted the book. As these were proceedings for a destruction order, and not a criminal prosecution, Radclyffe Hall was unable to appear although she was present in court. Sir Chartres Biron presided. First witness for the prosecution was Chief Inspector Prothero who had bought a copy of the book. He considered the whole theme offensive, because it dealt with physical passion: the book was

[27] *Daily Herald*, 6 October 1928.
[28] *Reynolds Illustrated News*, 6 August 1928.

indecent because it dealt with an indecent subject. Norman Birkett then spoke in defence of the book:

> Nowhere is there an obscene word or a lascivious passage. It is a sombre, sad, tragic, artistic revelation of that which is an undoubted fact in this world. It is the result of years of labour by one of the most distinguished novelists alive, and it is a sincere and high minded effort to make the world more tolerable for those who have to bear the tragic consequences of what they are not to blame for at all. In the course of the case I hope to be allowed to quote the views of critics in various reviews and newspapers, which constitute a chorus of praise from those well qualified to speak upon matters affecting literature in general. Further than that, there are in court people of every walk of life who desire to go into the witness box and to testify that this book is not obscene, and that it is a misuse of words for the prosecution to describe it as such.

At this point he was interrupted by the magistrate: 'The test is whether it is likely to deprave or corrupt those into whose hands it is likely to fall. How can the opinion of a number of people be evidence?'

NORMAN BIRKETT: 'I want to call evidence from every conceivable walk of life which bears on the test whether the tendency of this book was to deprave and corrupt. A more distinguished body of witnesses has never before been called in a court of justice.'

THE MAGISTRATE: 'I have the greatest doubt whether the evidence is admissible.'

NORMAN BIRKETT: 'If I am not allowed to call evidence it means that a magistrate is virtually a censor of literature.'

THE MAGISTRATE: 'I don't think people are entitled to express an opinion upon a matter which is for the decision of the court.'

Mr. Desmond MacCarthy, then editor of 'Life and Letters', went into the box and replying to Mr. Birkett said he had read the book.

NORMAN BIRKETT: 'In your view is it obscene?'

THE MAGISTRATE: 'No I shall disallow that. It is quite clear that the evidence is not admissible. A book may be a fine piece of literature and yet obscene. Art and Obscenity are not disassociated at all. There is a room at Naples to which visitors are not admitted as a rule, which contains fine bronzes and statues, all admirable works of art, but all grossly obscene. It does not follow that because a book is a work of art it is not obscene. I shall not admit the evidence.'

NORMAN BIRKETT: 'I formally tender thirty-nine other witnesses. The evidence which a number of them would have given is identical with that of Mr. MacCarthy. In a second category are distinguished authors and authoresses who would have said that they had read the book and in their view it was not obscene. Other witnesses include booksellers, ministers of religion, social workers, magistrates, biologists, including Professor Julian Huxley, educationists, including the Registrar of Durham University, medical men and representatives of the London libraries.'

THE MAGISTRATE: 'I reject them all.'

After the luncheon interval Norman Birkett requested the magistrate to state a case for a higher court on the question of the admissibility of the expert evidence which he wished to tender, but the request was refused.

Sir Chartres then made an order for the destruction of the book. In the course of his judgement he said:

> With regard to the point that the book is well written and therefore should not be subjected to these proceedings, that is an entirely untenable position. I agree that the book has some literary merits, but the very fact that the book is well written can be no answer to these proceedings because otherwise we should be in the preposterous position that the most obscene books would be free from stricture. It must appear to anyone of intelligence that the better an obscene book is written the greater the public to whom it is likely to appeal. The mere fact that the book deals with unnatural offences between women does not make it obscene. It might even have a strong moral influence. But in the present case there is not one word which suggests that anyone with the horrible tendencies described is in the least degree blameworthy. All the characters are presented as attractive people and put forward with admiration. What is even more serious is that certain acts are described in alluring terms.

Sir Chartres went on to deal with the passages concerning the ambulance drivers at the front who engaged in homosexual practices, but this was too much for Miss Hall who was sitting at her solicitor's table. 'I protest', she cried, 'I emphatically protest'.

SIR CHARTRES: 'I must ask you to be quiet.'
MISS HALL: 'I am the author of this book.'
SIR CHARTRES: 'If you cannot behave yourself in court I shall have to have you removed.
MISS HALL: 'Shame!'

On 14 December an appeal was made to Quarter Sessions and on this occasion Sir Thomas Inskip appeared for the Crown. 'The whole book', he said, 'as to ninety-nine hundredths of it may be beyond criticism, yet one passage may make it a work which ought to be destroyed as obscene.' The presiding magistrate, Charles Read, upheld the decision of Sir Chartres, describing the book as 'most dangerous and corrupting'.[29]

After the trial there was an outburst of protest. Forty-five authors including T. S. Eliot, A. P. Herbert, Virginia Woolf, Desmond MacCarthy and E. M. Forster signed a letter criticising the law, which was published in the *Daily Telegraph.* Another eminent protest bearing the names of Bernard Shaw, Laurence Housman, Rose Macaulay, John Buchan, Arnold Bennett, Lytton Strachey, Sheila Kaye-Smith, and Laurence Binyon appeared in the *Manchester Guardian.*[30] In *The Times* Cyril Asquith called for a reform of the law. These protests, however, achieved nothing, and it was not until 1949 that the book was republished in England. No action has been taken against it and today it is freely available at its original price of fifteen shillings.*

'THE SLEEVELESS ERRAND'

In the following year, 1929, another novel of considerable merit, *The Sleeveless Errand*, by Norah James was destroyed. The writer had clearly been greatly influenced by James Joyce, and her novel took the form of a conversation extending over two days in which the characters revealed their most intimate thoughts. In applying for a destruction order, Percival Clarke, who appeared for the Director of Public Prosecutions, stressed that it not only tolerated but advocated adultery. He drew attention to the number of times the name of 'God' or 'Christ' was mentioned and gave as an example of 'shocking depravity' the words of one drunken character: 'For Christ's sake give me a drink'. For the defence it was pleaded that although there were many horrible things in the book, its object was to portray and condemn the mode of life and language of a certain section of the community. This argument was not accepted by the magistrate Mr. Graham Campbell: 'I am certain that the book in question would suggest to the minds of the young of either sex, even to persons of more advanced years, thoughts of a most impure

[29] The information about *The Well of Loneliness* trial and the reconstructed speeches have been taken from newspaper reports of the time, especially the *Daily Telegraph* and *The Times* for 10 November 1928, and *The Times* for 14 December 1928.

[30] 22 November 1928.

* The trial inspired another lampoon illustrated by Beresford Egan, *The Sink of Solitude.* Chief targets were Douglas and Joynson-Hicks, but Radclyffe Hall was also satirised. A copy may be seen at the British Museum.

character. I cannot accept the view that the book in its result is not obscene if the passages referred to are not held up to glorification.'[31]

Sir Joynson-Hicks was subjected to hostile questioning in the House as to the part he had played in bringing about the proceedings. He denied that he had ordered the book to be seized: 'I thought it was a proper case to be sent to the Director of Public Prosecutions which I did and there my responsibility ceased'.[32] The day following the destruction of *The Sleeveless Errand* he addressed a deputation from the Public Morality Council and was warmly cheered. Archibald Allen, the Chairman of the Council, gave examples of books which should be destroyed, including all manuals on birth control and translations of *The Decameron.* The Council pressed the Home Secretary to introduce legislation making it a summary offence punishable with imprisonment to sell obscene books to those under eighteen years of age, but he declined, maintaining that the existing law adequately fulfilled its purpose.[33]

LAWRENCE AGAIN

The year 1929 also saw further legal attacks on D. H. Lawrence.* In the previous year he had published *Lady Chatterley's Lover* in Florence,† and although not published in England copies reached many reviewers. They were unanimous in their condemnation. 'Most evil outpourings—sewers of French pornography—beastliness—muddy minded pervert—diseased mind—literary cesspool—shameful inspiration—this bearded satyr—book snapped up by degenerate booksellers and British decadents—the foulest book in English literature—poisoned genius' were only some of the epithets.[34] *John Bull* hoped that Lawrence would be 'ostracised by all except the most degenerate coteries' and regretted that there was 'no law at the present under which he may be ostracised more completely for a good stiff spell'. No legal action could, however, be taken against the author or publisher since they were out of the country, and only

[31] For a report of the case see *The Times*, 5 March 1929.

[32] *The Times*, 1 March 1929.

[33] *Ibid.*, 5 March 1929.

* In May 1921 Martin Secker had published *Women in Love. John Bull* denounced it in an article headed 'A Book the Police should ban: Loathsome Study of Sex Depravity—Misleading Youth to Unspeakable Disaster'. By the end of the year Bottomley, the editor, was himself on trial for fraud.

† Lawrence published the book himself with the help of Orioli. The first edition of 1000 was sold to subscribers at 2 gns. a copy.

[34] Taken from Richard Aldington on D. H. Lawrence, *Portrait of a Genius But.* Heinemann (1950), p. 338.

a few copies penetrated the customs barrier. Indeed, an unexpurgated edition of *Lady Chatterley's Lover* has never been published in England.

The first act of legal intervention was the seizure by the Post Office in January 1929 of the manuscript of his poems *Pansies.** A week later the Introduction to his Volume of Paintings was also seized by the Post Office. Questioned in the House of Commons Sir Joynson-Hicks denied that he had ordered their seizure and pointed out that a sealed postal packet could only be opened under the warrant of a Secretary of State. The postal authorities had discovered the manuscripts in the course of a routine investigation of the 'open book post' and they had been sent to the Home Office. As there was no doubt that they were indecent he had sent them to the Director of Public Prosecutions, but there were to be no proceedings until the author had had an opportunity to establish their decency.[35] No further action was, in fact, taken, the manuscripts being sent to the publishers with a recommendation that fourteen of the poems, should be omitted. Martin Secker complied and the remaining poems were published in 1929.

A more serious attack was the raiding by the police in July 1929 of Lawrence's picture exhibition at the Warren Galleries. A number of pictures was seized, including it is said, a folio of Blake, for which the initial application for destruction was withdrawn. On 8 August the police applied for a destruction order at Marlborough Street Magistrate's Court for thirteen of the twenty-five pictures originally exhibited. Mr. Muskett appeared for the Crown and St. John Hutchinson and John Maude for the defendants, Mr. and Mrs. Philip Trotter, lessees of the gallery. St. John Hutchinson maintained that the pictures were works of art. To prove this he hoped to call Sir William Orpen, Mr. Augustus John, Mr. G. Philpot, and possibly Mr. Agnew, Professor Blair, Professor Gleadowe and Mr. Rothenstein. Like Sir Chartres, Mr. Mead, the magistrate, aged eighty-two, was not impressed by the distinction of these potential witnesses and excluded them from the court. 'It is utterly immaterial', he said, 'whether they are works of art. That is a collateral question which I have not to decide. The most splendidly painted picture in the Universe might be obscene.' On the defendants promising to close the exhibition the case was dismissed with five guineas costs being awarded against them. They replaced the Lawrence pictures by an exhibition of 'Art Forms in Nature taken from Vegetable Growths'. This caused less offence.[36] Lawrence felt this incident keenly. He

* 'Jix' was not responsible. He was out of office, succeeded by a Labour Home Secretary, J. R. Clynes.

[35] *The Times*, 1 March 1929. [36] *Ibid.*, 9 August 1929.

wrote a little-known poem about it which is here reproduced, more remarkable for its quality of naked feeling than its poetic value.

> Give me a sponge and some clear clean water
> and leave me alone awhile
> with my thirteen sorry pictures that have just been rescued
> from durance vile.
>
> Leave me alone now for my soul is burning
> as it feels the slimy taint
> of all those nasty police-eyes like snail tracks smearing
> the gentle souls that figure in the paint.
>
> Ah my nice pictures they are fouled they are dirtied
> not by time, but by unclean breath and eyes
> of all the sordid people that have stared at them uncleanly
> looking dirt on them, and breathing on them lies.
>
> Ah my nice pictures, let me sponge you very gently
> to sponge away the slime
> that ancient eyes have left on you, where obscene eyes have
> crawled
> leaving nasty films upon you every time.
>
> Ah the clean waters of the sky. Ah can you wash
> away the evil starings and the breath
> Of the foul ones from my pictures? Oh purify
> them now from all this touch of tainted death.

DE MONTALK'S CASE

The pattern of prosecution and suppression continued in the 'thirties, but despite the protests of authors and publishers neither the administration nor the substance of the law was changed. In 1932 Count Potocki de Montalk was sent to prison for publishing obscene poems, the actual publication being technical since he had left the poems with the printer who thereupon placed them in the hands of the police. De Montalk was a bizarre and eccentric figure, and was one of the sights of London as he strode through the streets clad in purple robes, his long hair streaming behind him. In politics he was an extreme royalist, being editor of *The Right Review*, in which he maintained his own claims to the throne of Poland. He was not the type of man to appeal to Sir Ernest Wild who tried him at the Old Bailey, and perhaps some personal antipathy accounts for the savagery of a prison sentence for what was only a technical offence. Summing up Sir Ernest Wild pointed out: 'A man must not say he was a poet and be filthy. He has to obey the law just the same as ordinary citizens, and the sooner the highbrow school learns that, the better for the morality of the country.' The following extraordinary dialogue followed:

SIR ERNEST WILD: 'Can't you suggest what punishment you think you deserve.'

DE MONTALK: 'Yes, my lord. I think I deserve to be sentenced to several years in Buckingham Palace.'

The Recorder, however, decided in favour of six months at Wormwood Scrubs and despite an appeal the sentence stood.[37]

Books destroyed in the 'thirties ranged from Huysman's *La Bas* [38] to James Hanley's *Boy*.[39] On 10 October 1934, at Westminster Police Court, Mr. Rowland Powell ordered the destruction of three books by Pierre Louys including his *Aphrodite* and *Les chansons de Bilitis* as well the *Satyricon* of Petronius and an anthology of Greek poetry and prose. Magistrates, however, were more concerned with the modern novel than translations of the classics and two notable novels condemned were *Boy* and Wallace Smith's *Bessie Cotter*.

'BOY'

Boy had first been published in 1931 and had been favourably reviewed. The *New Statesman* described it as 'a brutal, pitiful, impossible book: one that demands to be read and makes the reader sick with apprehension and disgust and indignation . . . the book has art but Mr. Hanley is not fair to his own considerable talents'.[40] The subject-matter and language of the book is certainly startling. Fearon, the hero, is a working-class boy who is brutally treated by his parents and workmates, and runs away to sea. On board he is raped and criminally assaulted and after contracting syphilis in Alexandria is murdered by his captain. The book shocks, but it is not pornographic, its most prominent characteristic being the serious purpose of its author. Four years after publication the police brought a prosecution against the publishers, Boriswoode Ltd., who pleaded guilty. The company was fined £250 and the two directors £50 each. A curious point about the case was the lapse of time between

[37] See *R.* v. *De Montalk* (1932), 23 Cr. App. R. 182.
[38] 10 October 1934, at Westminster Police Court.
[39] 20 March 1935, at Manchester Assizes.
[40] 14 November 1931, N.S. Lit. Supp., p. xxii.

publication and prosecution, but an explanation may perhaps be found in the publication in 1934 of the first cheap edition at three shillings and sixpence.*

'BESSIE COTTER'

Bessie Cotter which was published in 1935 by Heinemann tells in a realistic way the story of life in an American brothel.† The *Manchester Evening News* thought it a 'brilliant and appalling novel', adding: 'If you feel it is one of those subjects which an enlightened community would at least wish to understand and not merely to condemn by taboo, here is a brilliantly etched picture'.[41] The *Sunday Dispatch*, however, thought it 'should never have been printed', a view shared by the police.[42] Sir Thomas Inskip appeared for the Crown when the case came on at Bow Street on 10 April 1935 and Sir Patrick Hastings for the publishers. Sir Patrick Hastings pointed out that had the publishers been given any intimation that the police objected to the book it would at once have been withdrawn. Heinemann pleaded guilty and were fined one hundred pounds with one hundred guineas costs.

'THE SEXUAL IMPULSE'

In October 1935 Boriswoode Ltd. were again in court, this time to defend *The Sexual Impulse*, by Edward Charles. The book had first been submitted by the publishers to their medical reader, Dr. Jensen of Westminster Hospital, who had written a favourable report. Subsequently the book was set up in type and proofs submitted to Professor Julian Huxley, who wrote the foreword, and also to Lord Horder and Mrs. Janet Chance. At the hearing both Professor Huxley and Dr. Maude Royden of Eccleston Square Church gave evidence of the medical and psychological value of the book, but the magistrate Mr. Rowland Powell thought their evidence of little importance. He was of the opinion that the book was not 'fit and decent for people of the working class to read'. 'I have not to decide' he said, when ordering the book to be destroyed

> whether it is of any medical or psychological value. The only thing for me to decide is as to whether it comes under the heading

* E. M. Forster protested about this case at the International Conference of Authors, Paris, June 1935.

† The book bears comparison with De Maupassant's *Le Maison Tellier*. It is worth noting that Alberto Moravia's *The Woman of Rome*, which presents the life of a prostitute in a similar amoral way was published in a Penguin edition in 1952.

[41] 17 January 1935. [42] 13 January 1935.

of an obscene book. . . . It is quite clear to my mind that one chapter is written carelessly and consciously reckless of desirable convention. Some of the poems are absolutely unnecessary and gross and repulsive. The author is sneering at the pre-nuptial chastity of women.[43]

WAR-TIME CENSORSHIP

When the Second World War broke out in 1939 Defence Regulation 39B made it an offence to make use of any false statement, document or report in such a way that the defence of the country might be endangered or the prosecution of the war impeded. Originally, the Regulation gave power to establish a censorship of the Press, but this was later modified so that power of suppression was limited to publication of articles which might prejudice foreign relations. In 1940 Defence Regulation 2D gave power to suppress newspapers which systematically pursued a policy encouraging opposition to the successful prosecution of the war.* These regulations were concerned with the defence of the country and were neither intended nor used to establish a censorship of morals. Prosecutions for 'obscene libel' were brought from time to time, the best known being that of James Hadley Chase in 1942 for publishing *Miss Callaghan comes to Grief*. The book was suppressed. In the same year Dr. Chesser and his publishers were acquitted on a charge of publishing an obscene libel *Love Without Fear*.

'THE NAKED AND THE DEAD'

After the war the campaign against pornography continued,† but it was not until the 'fifties that reputable publishers were subjected to criminal prosecution. An attempt to invoke the law to suppress

[43] *The Times*, 3 and 17 October 1935.

* In 1941 the *Daily Worker* was suppressed and in 1942 the *Daily Mirror* was warned that this power might be invoked if it pursued its policy.

† A number of pornographic publishers and booksellers were prosecuted in the 'fifties. e. g. Bernard and Alfred Kaye were sent to prison for publishing books such as *Shameless*; *Soho Street Girl*; *Academy of Love*; *Big Sin*, etc. (*The Times*, 25 September 1954).

The Leeds Stipendiary Magistrate made an order for the destruction of 108,000 copies of a monthly publication *A Basinful of Fun* (*The Times*, 12 October 1954).

Fifty-two destruction orders were made against Hank Janson books of which five million copies had been sold in three years at two shillings each (*News Chronicle*, 20 January 1954). In February 1955 the author, D. F. Crawley, was brought to trial for writing seven of them, but was acquitted when it was proved that he had not written these particular books, having sold his pen-name some years before (*Manchester Guardian*, 12 February 1955).

Norman Mailer's book on American service life, *The Naked and the Dead*, had been made in 1949, but the Attorney-General refused to take any action. The campaign against the book started in the *Sunday Times* on 1 May 1949. An article signed by the Editor called for the immediate withdrawal of the book. 'Mr. Mailer', wrote the Editor, 'is a writer of exceptional gifts and much of the book has real value but large parts of it are so grossly obscene that it is quite unfit for circulation. No decent man could leave it lying about the house, or know without shame that his womenfolk were reading it.' The language of the book was described as 'incredibly foul and beastly'. The publishers defended the book and refused to withdraw it and on 8 May the *Sunday Times* returned to the charge: 'The *Sunday Times* is opposed to nearly all forms of censorship and particularly to the censorship of opinion. But it holds that in extreme cases of obscenity—and this is an extreme case—it is wholly against the public interest that beastliness should be offered for sale.'

The *Evening Standard* did not agree with the *Sunday Times*' view:

> If any adult reads *The Naked and the Dead* seeking pornography he is likely to be bored and disappointed. What he will find (apart from language he may hear any day if he wishes) is a picture of war as dreadful and lurid, as real and terrifying as an etching by Goya. If that misguided adult persists to the end (which is improbable) he is more likely to emerge a better man than a worse one.[44]

The publishers Allan Wingate Ltd. issued a statement in reply to the *Sunday Times*' attack: 'It is our moral and literary duty to publish it. It presents a true picture of the way soldiers talked and behaved during the war and American reviewers have compared it with Stendhal and Tolstoy.'[45]

On 23 May the Attorney-General, Sir Hartley Shawcross, explained government policy in answer to questions in the House of Commons.

> In cases of the kind involved here [said Sir Hartley] there are two public interests to which I must have regard. It is important that no publisher should be permitted to deprave or corrupt morals, to exalt vice or to encourage its commission. It is also important that there should be the least possible interference with the freedom of publication, and that the Attorney-General should not seek to make the criminal law a vehicle for imposing a censorship on the frank discussion or portrayal of sordid and unedifying

[44] 3 May 1949. [45] *News Chronicle*, 2 May 1949.

aspects of life simply on the grounds of offence against taste or manners. While there is much in this most tedious and lengthy book which is foul, lewd and revolting, looking at it as a whole I do not think that its intent is to corrupt or deprave or that it is likely to lead to any other result other than disgust at its contents.

THE 'FIFTIES

In 1954 this policy was changed and, for the first time since the period of Joynson-Hicks at the Home Office, a full-scale campaign of prosecutions was opened against publishers who were admitted by all parties to be of the highest standing and repute. The origin of this campaign remains obscure, but some tentative suggestions may be put forward. As in the case of the Joynson-Hicks campaign of the 'thirties an international conference on suppressing the trade in obscene publications immediately preceded the outbreak of the prosecutions. In September 1953 this had been the principal topic discussed at the Oslo conference of the International Criminal Police Commission. The Conference had concluded that the reading of obscene literature was an important contributory cause of the increase in sexual offences since the war, and recommended that its members should take the strongest measures against this trade. This may well have prompted the British police to take firm action.[46]

It has been suggested that the campaign was undertaken at the wish of the Home Secretary, then Sir David Maxwell Fyfe, with the support of the Director of Public Prosecutions, Sir Theobald Mathew, as part of an effort to reform public morals. Yet another explanation traced the origins of the campaign to the Lord Chief Justice, who commented unfavourably on certain books offered in evidence at earlier obscenity trials, as books which were being freely circulated. Some of the books subsequently prosecuted were among those offered in evidence.[47]

Whatever the origin of the prosecutions they were to have far-reaching results, since they led to a demand for a change in the law, and the introduction of a reforming Bill into the House of Commons. In all, five publishers were prosecuted: Werner Laurie for *Julia* (convicted); Secker and Warburg for *The Philanderer* (acquitted); Hutchinson for *September in Quinze* (convicted); Heinemann for *The Image and the Search* (two juries failed to agree and formal acquittal followed), and Arthur Barker for *The Man in Control*

[46] Commission Internationale de Police Criminelle. XXIIe Assemblé Generale, Oslo, 24 au 29 juin 1953. Rapport présenté par M. A. Amstein. No. 6.
[47] See *R.* v. *Reiter*, [1954], 2 Q. B. 16.

(acquitted). In the same year the Swindon magistrates caused indignation by their condemnation of *The Decameron* as obscene, but their order for destruction was quashed on appeal.*

'THE PHILANDERER'

The Philanderer had been published by Secker and Warburg in April 1953. In the previous year it had been published in the United States and had been favourably reviewed. The hero of the book is Russel Conrad, a lecherous publicity man working in New York and happily married to an attractive girl. Despite this, Conrad is unable to resist temptation, and the book traces his progress from one unsatisfactory love affair to another, ending as it opens with the hero embarking on yet another amorous adventure. On publication the book caused little stir, the reviews being favourable, although not especially enthusiastic. Writing in the *New Statesman* Walter Allen drew attention to its moral attitude.

> What is interesting in this novel is the rendering of the moral struggle. Conrad is a 'case', and might have been treated solely in case-book terms. But, a man of intelligence and sensitivity and with the passionate interest in morals that only the self-conscious sinner can have, he realises that the psychological causes of his addiction do not in fact explain it; the problem remains obstinately at the moral level, even though, in the course of Conrad's rigorous self-analysis, we get as devastating a criticism as any I've read of the consequences of the tradition of American adolescent competition in sexual experience that we have already had described for us by Dr. Margaret Mead and Mr. Gorer.[48]

Marghanita Laski writing in *The Spectator* also praised the book.[49]

In September 1953 the law intervened and Boots were prosecuted in the Isle of Man for circulating the book in their libraries. *Julia* by Margot Bland was also named in the indictment and later was the first of the five to be tried in England. In a reserved judgement the High Bailiff said that he was bound by the law to find the books obscene, but he did so only with reluctance. He held that the question of intent was irrelevant, and that the only question he had to decide was whether the books contained passages which might tend to deprave and corrupt those into whose hands they might fall. Although the public might regard modern books with a different eye from their

* *The Decameron* had been destroyed several times before without arousing any protest, e.g. 1951 (twice); 1952 (3); 1953 (2). In at least one case the edition destroyed was the same as that cleared on appeal.

[48] 25 April 1953. [49] 10 April 1955.

fathers, the law had not altered correspondingly, and he was bound by the law. As a mark of his reluctance, however, the High Bailiff imposed only nominal fines of £1 in each case.

The two books were, however, to be prosecuted again, this time in England. Werner Laurie pleaded guilty to the charge of publishing an obscene libel and were fined the modest sum of £30 and 10 gns. costs. The Chairman of Secker and Warburg, Fredric Warburg, decided to fight the case and after a preliminary appearance at Clerkenwell Police Court on 26 May, elected to go for trial. The importance of this decision cannot be overestimated, since it enabled Mr. Justice Stable to deliver his now famous summing-up, and was the first step in the campaign for a change in the law.*

On 29 June the trial opened at the Old Bailey. Mr. Griffith-Jones appeared for the prosecution, Mr. Rodger Winn for Fredric Warburg, and Mr. Maxwell Turner for the company, Martin Secker and Warburg Ltd., as well as the printers, The Camelot Press Ltd. The defendants pleaded not guilty and the jury were sent home by the judge, Mr. Justice Stable, to read the book.† He instructed them to read the book as a whole: 'Do not pick out the highlights. Read it as a book and we will come back here on Friday and proceed with the case'.[50] ‡

When the court reassembled on 2 July the prosecution conceded that the publishers were of the highest repute, but maintained that the novel might well corrupt the young into whose hands it might fall. Mr. Justice Stable summed up strongly in favour of the defendants. He warned the jury of the importance of their task: 'Your verdict will have a great bearing upon where the line is drawn between liberty and that freedom to read and think as the spirit moves us, on the one hand, and, on the other, a license that is an affront to the society of which each of us is a member. The discharge

* Michael Foot speaking in the debate on the 'Harmful Publications' Bill, designed to bring 'horror comics' under control, referred to the debt which English freedom owed to Fredric Warburg. See *Hansard*, Vol. DXXXVII, No. 38, Cl. 1108, 22 February 1955.

† Mr. Justice Stable requested the defendant to leave the dock and sit by his solicitor, stating that in his view the dock was not a suitable place for the prisoner to occupy in a trial of this sort.

[50] *The Times*, 30 June 1954.

‡ The judge said: 'Will you take that book home and would you mind reading it, as I said, from cover to cover. Read it as a book. Do you follow? Not picking out bits that you think have, shall we say, a tendency here or there, or picking out bits that you think have a sort of immoral tendency, but read it as a book.' Taken from the shorthand note of the trial. Old Bailey, 29 June 1954. Note taken by Messrs. G. Walpole and Co. (shorthand writers to the court), Cheshire House, Cheshire Court, 142 Fleet Street, E.C.4. Copy in possession of Secker and Warburg Ltd.

of this important duty rests fairly and squarely upon your shoulders.' The judge laid down the test of obscenity as that adopted in the Hicklin case, but added this rider:

> Remember the charge is a charge that the tendency of the book is to corrupt and deprave. The charge is not that the tendency of the book is either to shock or to disgust. That is not a criminal offence. Then you say: 'Well, corrupt or deprave whom?' and again the test: those whose minds are open to such immoral influences and into whose hands a publication of this sort may fall. What exactly does that mean? Are we to take our literary standards as being the level of something that is suitable for a fourteen-year-old school girl? Or do we go even further back than that, and are we to be reduced to the sort of books that one reads as a child in the nursery? The answer to that is: Of course not. A mass of literature, great literature, from many angles is wholly unsuitable for reading by the adolescent, but that does not mean that the publisher is guilty of a criminal offence for making those works available to the general public.
>
> You have heard a good deal about the putting of ideas into young heads. But is it really books that put ideas into young heads, or is it nature? When a child be it boy or girl, passing from a state of blissful ignorance, reaches that most perilous part of life's journey which we call 'adolescence', and finds itself traversing an unknown country without a map, without a compass, and sometimes, I am afraid, from a bad home, without a guide, it is this natural change from childhood to maturity, that puts ideas into its young head. It is the business of parents and teachers and the environment of society, so far as is possible, to see that those ideas are wisely and naturally directed to the ultimate fulfilment of a balanced individual life. . . .
>
> This is an American novel written by an American, published originally in New York and purporting to depict the lives of people living today in New York, to portray their speech and attitude in general towards this particular aspect of life. If we are going to read novels about how things go on in New York, it would not be of much assistance, would it, if, contrary to the fact, we were led to suppose that in New York no unmarried woman of teenage has disabused her mind of the idea that babies are brought by storks or are sometimes found in cabbage plots or under gooseberry bushes?
>
> You may think that this is a very crude work; but that it is not, perhaps altogether an exaggerated picture of the approach that is being made in America towards this great problem of sex. You

may think that if this does reflect the approach on that side of the Atlantic towards this great question, it is just as well that we should know it and that we must not close our eyes or our minds to the truth because it might conceivably corrupt or deprave any somewhat puerile young mind.

The judge outlined the plot of the novel and went on:

So far as his amatory adventures are concerned, the book does, with candour or, if you prefer it, crudity, deal with the realities of human love and intercourse. There is no getting away from that, and the Crown say: 'Well, that is sheer filth'. Is the act of sexual passion sheer filth? It may be an error of taste to write about it. It may be a matter in which some, perhaps old fashioned, people would prefer that reticence continued to be observed as it was yesterday. But is it sheer filth? That is a matter which you have to consider and ultimately to decide.

I do not suppose there is a decent man or woman in this court who does not wholeheartedly believe that pornography, the filthy bawdy muck that is just filth for filth's sake, ought to be stamped out and suppressed. Such books are not literature. They have got no message; they have got no inspiration; they have got no thought. They have got nothing. They are just filth and ought to be stamped out. But in our desire for a healthy society, if we drive the criminal law too far, further than it ought to go, is there not a risk that there will be a revolt, a demand for a change in the law, and that the pendulum may swing too far the other way and allow to creep in things that at the moment we can exclude and keep out?

That is all I have to say to you. Remember what I said when I began. You are dealing with a criminal charge. This is not a question or a case of what you think is a desirable book to read. It is a criminal charge of publishing a work with tendency to deprave and corrupt those to whom it may fall. Before you can return a verdict of 'Guilty' on that charge you have to be satisfied, and each one of you has to be satisfied, that that charge has been proved. If it is anything short of that the accused are entitled to a verdict at your hands of 'Not Guilty'.[51] *

The jury of nine men and three women then retired and within a short time brought in a verdict of 'not guilty' for all the defendants.

Mr. Justice Stable's summing-up was hailed by most of the Press as the greatest pronouncement on the law of obscene libel since the

[51] *R.* v. *Martin Secker & Warburg*, [1954] W. L. R. 1138.

* Mr. Justice Stable's summing-up has been published in full as a pamphlet (price 1*s.*) by Secker and Warburg. It is also printed in the latest edition of *The Philanderer*.

Hicklin judgement. Newspapers from *The Times* to the *Church of England Newspaper* published approving leading articles, but few of the leader writers noticed that the judge had left the law as formulated in the Hicklin case practically unchanged.[52] What he had done was to give a common-sense view of the contemporary meaning of the word 'obscene', and indicated that in applying the law contemporary not Victorian standards were to be applied. This interpretation was, however, a personal one, and it became apparent in the *September in Quinze* case which followed some months afterwards that the law could be interpreted in a very different way.

'SEPTEMBER IN QUINZE'

Hutchinson Ltd. and Mrs. Katherine Webb were tried at the Old Bailey on Friday, 17 September, for publishing Vivian Connell's *September in Quinze.** Mr. Griffith-Jones prosecuted and Mr. Fearnley-Whittingstall, Q.C., defended both Mrs. Webb and the company. In his speech for the defence Mr. Fearnley-Whittingstall quoted liberally from *The Philanderer* judgement, but this did not impress the Recorder, Sir Gerald Dodson, who summed up for a conviction and expressly contradicted the standards laid down by Mr. Justice Stable. 'A book', he said, 'which would not influence the mind of an Archbishop might influence the minds of a callow youth or a girl just budding into womanhood. Sex is a thing, members of the jury, which you may think has to be protected and even sanctified, as indeed it is by the marriage service and not dragged in the mud.' The jury brought in a verdict of 'guilty' and the defendants were fined five hundred pounds each.

> I should have thought [said the Recorder] any reader, however inexperienced, would have been repelled by a book of this sort, which is repugnant to every decent emotion which ever concerned man or woman . . . it is a very comforting thought that juries from time to time take a very solid stand against this sort of thing and realise how important it is for the youth of this country to be protected and that the fountain of our national blood should not be polluted at its source.[53]

'THE IMAGE AND THE SEARCH'

The three books so far considered had each been disposed of at a single trial, but *The Image and the Search* was to be the subject of

[52] *The Times*, 3 July 1954; *Church of England Newspaper*, 9 July 1954.
* The author was not indicted as he was out of the country.
[53] *Manchester Guardian*, 18 September 1954; *Smith's Trade News*, 25 September 1954, p. 8.

three trials before its author and publisher were finally acquitted. The book had been published by Heinemann in 1953 and had met with a mixed reception from the Press. The *Sunday Times* described it as 'a bald and graceless narrative',[54]: *Time and Tide* dubbed it 'the trashiest kind of woman's serial',[55] *The Sphere* on the other hand called it 'an amazing book, with moments of beauty, moments of shock, and through it all a vein of deep human compassion [56]; while E. M. Forster in a private letter to the publisher wrote: 'This serious and beautiful book is bound to make a deep impression, even upon those who do not share its underlying philosophy'. By 7 March 1954 the *Sunday Express* had discovered the book and attacked it in a leading article. Referring to the heroine the leader writer wrote:

> Her erotic odyssey takes her from England to France, Spain, India and is persistently described in language abhorrent to a civilised palate. And every amorous experience is analysed by the author with tearful and treacly sympathy. This is the wickedest thing about this piece of rubbish which Mr. Forster sees fit to praise. We are supposed to be sorry for the lady.

The *Sunday Express* demanded the book's immediate withdrawal.

The book which deals with the adventures of a nymphomaniac is in no way pornographic, although it does contain obscene and outspoken passages. There can be no doubt that its author Walter Baxter wrote it with a serious purpose and in some ways the novel is a religious one.* On his first appearance at Bow Street Magistrate's Court on 8 October 1954, when he was jointly charged with Mr. Frere, the company chairman, and Heinemann's, with publishing an obscene libel, the author had this to say: 'In writing my book my object was a serious portrayal of the vulnerability to evil of any egocentred personality, and the disintegrating effect of sin on such a personality'. Mr. Frere also made a statement:

> I personally was alone responsible for the decision of my company to publish this book. I read it and considered that it merited publication, though its literary quality was not comparable with that of the author's first book, which was very widely and highly praised. I regard Walter Baxter as one of the most gifted writers of this generation, whose powers are not yet fully developed. I feel that publishers owe a duty to such writers, and to the public,

[54] 20 October 1953. [55] 7 November 1953. [56] 31 October 1953.

* Walter Baxter had previously published in 1951 his first novel *Look Down in Mercy*. This book which is a study of the moral disintegration brought about by the war in the jungle, also deals with a homosexual problem and was universally praised on its publication. It has never been subjected to legal action.

> to ensure that their creative work is not stillborn, if it has value and is not deleterious to potential readers. I was, and am, myself satisfied that this book will not harm any reader.[57]

The magistrate, Mr. Robey, accepted the pleas of 'not guilty' and committed the defendants for trial at the Old Bailey, releasing them meanwhile on bail.*

Later in the month the first trial opened at the Old Bailey before Mr. Justice Devlin. Mr. Griffith-Jones again appeared for the prosecution and Mr. Rodger Winn for the defence, and as in *The Philanderer* case the jury was sent away to read the book as a whole. On 18 October the case was continued, Mr. Griffith-Jones describing the book as 'pornography dressed up as a twelve-and-sixpenny novel', and Mr. Winn maintaining that the only real criticism of the book was that 'it might tend to frighten susceptible and only partly developed minds and make a young girl, ready to be a bride, timid about embarking on sex'. In his summing-up Mr. Justice Devlin confined himself to a straightforward exposition of the law, but the jury after retiring for three hours returned to say, that they could reach no agreement. After retiring again they still could not agree and the judge then discharged them from further service.

On 24 November the case was opened once again at the Old Bailey. The judge this time was Mr. Justice Lynskey; Mr. Griffith-Jones appeared for the prosecution, and Mr. Gerald Gardiner, Q.C., replaced Mr. Winn, who had been appointed a Treasury Counsel, for the defence. On 30 November the jury who had retired to read the book, returned to the Old Bailey and the case was continued. In his final speech for the defence Mr. Gardiner described the book as

> a story of a soul and its development until there rose a beginning of the acceptance of God. This is a book which plainly says rightly or wrongly that all our very fine modern ideas of sexual license are getting us absolutely nowhere extremely fast. If you apply the test—namely of whether this book tends to deprave or corrupt—I suggest it is far from having that tendency on anyone but would have exactly the opposite tendency.[58]

The judge then began his summing-up.

> Members of the jury [he said] the matter is a serious one. It is a serious one not only for the defendants: it is a serious one also for

[57] See *Smith's Trade News*, 16 October 1954, and *The Times*, 9 October 1954. These statements were also read at the trials.

* At the magistrate's court Detective-Sergeant Kirk gave evidence that 8,300 copies of the book had been sold.

[58] *The Times*, 31 November 1954.

> the general public. You have only got to look at my list at this Assize to see the kind of immorality of a criminal character that exists in this country—case after case of buggery, case after case of incest and case after case of abortion. So you will realise this is not an evil lightly to be brushed aside; it is an evil, if it exists that has got to be cleaned up.

The judge did not finish his summing-up on the first day, but the following morning he modified his remarks.

> Members of the jury, when we adjourned last evening I had endeavoured to explain to you what was the offence of publishing an obscene libel, and I had endeavoured to point out to you the importance of this case from the point of view of each of the defendants, or all the defendants, and also from the point of view of the general public, and I did refer, you may remember, to the type of cases I have had to try during this session. Well, I did not want to suggest to you—did not even want to hint to you that this book had had anything whatever to do with those cases. It is perhaps a possible inference you might have drawn. Please do not. There is not a single scintilla of evidence that any one of those people with whom I have had to deal has ever read the book or seen it or heard of it.

After the judge had concluded the jury retired for two hours when they returned to announce that they could not agree.

MR. JUSTICE LYNSKEY: 'Is there anything I can add to help you in any way, or anything I can clear up for you?'

THE FOREMAN: 'Speaking on behalf of the jury, I do not think so. We understood your summing-up completely, including the definition of the word "obscene", etc., and we are in disagreement. It is not a majority verdict you want?'

MR. JUSTICE LYNSKEY: 'No. It must be a unanimous verdict. You think there is no hope at all?'

THE FOREMAN: 'No hope. If we were to stay here for a few hours or a few days I do not think we should get any further. I am sorry my Lord.'

The jury were then discharged and Mr. Griffith-Jones announced that it was not the intention of the Director of Public Prosecutions to proceed with the case. On 2 December a third jury returned a formal verdict of 'not guilty', no evidence being offered by the prosecution, and the defendants were discharged.[59]

[59] Taken from the transcript of the shorthand note of Messrs. G. Walpole and Co., Cheshire House, 142 Fleet Street, London, E.C.4, in the possession of Messrs. Secker and Warburg.

'THE MAN IN CONTROL'

While Heinemann's were being acquitted in one court of the Old Bailey, Arthur Barker was being indicted in another for publishing Charles McGraw's book *The Man in Control.** Mr. Griffith-Jones who prosecuted said that the story concerned Lesbians and a young girl corrupted at seventeen by a confirmed Lesbian. It was not suggested that the whole or greater part of the book was obscene but the jury might feel that 'the smell of the book was directly obscene, but for the opening pages'. After Judge Aarvold had summed-up the jury retired, and after thirteen minutes brought in a verdict of 'not guilty': the defendant was discharged.

So ended the five prosecutions which marked a new stage in the administration of the law of obscene libel. But if the cases themselves were over, their effects continued to be felt and of these some account must now be given. The prosecutions aroused lively public interest in the law of obscene libel which was discussed in newspapers and periodicals and on the radio.[60]

On 5 June 1954 a correspondence in *The Times* on 'Literature and the Law' was opened by Grahame Greene who expressed fears for the freedom of writers, and attacked the prosecutions as 'Manichean nonsense', warning against an attitude which would condemn any description of man's sexual nature as though sex in itself were ugly. A second correspondence on 'Freedom of the Pen' opened on 27 October with a letter signed by Bertrand Russell, Harold Nicolson, Compton Mackenzie, J. B. Priestley, H. E. Bates, W. Somerset Maugham and Philip Gibbs. They thought the prosecutions were an attempt to establish a police censorship to deny authors the right of describing 'the realities of life, freely and fearlessly for adult minds'.

* The author was not prosecuted, being dead. H. van Thal, a director of the firm, was also tried.

[60] The articles are too numerous to be listed in full, but the following are of particular interest. *New Statesman*, 10 July, 2 October, 9 October, 30 October, 4 December 1954; 6 November 1954, article by Fredric Warburg. *The Spectator*: 4 September 1954, article by Compton Mackenzie; 21 January 1955, C. S. Lewis; 4 February 1955, Norman St. John-Stevas. *Criminal Law Review*: November 1954, Norman St. John-Stevas. *The Tablet*: 5 February 1955, Christopher Hollis. *The Listener*: 7 October and 14 October 1954. Two broadcast talks by F. J. Odgers. A discussion on Obscenity was also broadcast on 24 February 1955. Those taking part were Noël Annan, Rupert Hart-Davis, F. J. Odgers and Norman St. John-Stevas. The *Observer*: 26 September 1954 and 27 February 1955, Roy Jenkins, M.P. *Sunday Times*: 1 August and 5 December 1954, two leading articles. *The Times*: 5 June 1954 and 3 February 1955, two leading articles. *Time and Tide*: 4 December 1954, Lord Justice Birkett. *Punch*: 20 October 1954, A. P. Herbert, 'Misleading Cases'. *The Times Literary Supplement*: 29 April 1955, leading article. *Illustrated*: 9 April 1955, A. P. Herbert. *The Author*: March 1955, Norman St. John-Stevas.

It would be disastrous to English literature if authors had to write under the shadow of the Old Bailey if they failed to produce works suitable for the teenager, and if publishers were forced to reject books which however serious in intent and however lit by genius, contained passages which might be blue-pencilled by a police sergeant or common informer.

THE HERBERT COMMITTEE

In November the Society of Authors set up a Committee presided over by Sir Alan Herbert to examine the existing law of obscene libel and to recommend reforms. The Committee which included authors, publishers, printers, critics, lawyers and a Member of Parliament, drafted a Bill embodying proposed changes in the law and also two memorandums, one historical, the other legal. These documents were sent to the Home Secretary, Mr. Lloyd George, who had earlier expressed great interest in the Committee's work.*

On 3 February 1955 the Committee's proposals were made public. The principal reform proposed was to make the state of mind of the accused person an essential element in the offence, thus shifting the emphasis from 'tendency' to 'intention'. The Bill made no attempt to define obscenity, but instructed juries and magistrates to take into account literary or artistic merit in all cases of obscene publication. On this point the Bill provided for the admission of expert evidence. The Bill repealed all existing obscenity statutes, but re-enacted the provisions of the Obscene Publications Act of 1857 with certain important modifications. Authors, publishers and printers were given a *locus standi* in the court to enable them to give and call evidence, and proceedings under the Act were speeded up. Destruction of obscene publications by the customs authorities was made dependent on the issuing of a destruction order by a magistrate, and uniformity in administration of the law was provided for by making all proceedings subject to the consent of the Attorney-General.

On publication the Committee's proposals met with the approval of almost the entire Press.[61] In a leading article headed 'Reform Overdue', *The Times* called for the implementation of the

* The Committee was presided over first by Sir Alan Herbert and later by Sir Gerald Barry. Other members were Walter Allen, H. E. Bates, David Carver, Professor Guy Chapman, W. B. Clowes, W. A. R. Collins, Joseph Compton, Rupert Hart-Davis, C. R. Hewitt, Roy Jenkins, M.P., Denys Kilham Roberts, A. D. Peters, V. S. Pritchett, John Pudney, Sir Herbert Read, Norman St. John-Stevas, and W. E. Williams. For a full account of the Committee's work see *The Spectator*, 4 February 1955 and *The Author*, March 1955.

[61] See *The Times*, 3 February 1955; *Manchester Guardian*, 5 February 1955; *Time and Tide* and the *New Statesman*, 5 February 1955.

Committee's recommendations, and described the Bill as a 'valuable work', 'a blue print on which a long overdue reform can and should be based'.

On 15 March 1955 the Bill was introduced into the House of Commons by Roy Jenkins under the ten-minute rule and given an unopposed first reading. After summing-up the anomalies of the existing law Mr. Jenkins said that they made it necessary 'to introduce a clarifying and if possible, a liberalising measure to give greater security to works of good intent. That is the purpose of the Bill which was produced and submitted to the Home Secretary before Christmas, and it is the Bill which I am seeking leave to introduce this afternoon'.[62]

HORROR COMICS

The Herbert Committee Bill also contained a clause designed to cover the problem of horror comics. The clause extended the meaning of the word 'obscene' to include publications that 'unduly exploit horror cruelty and violence'. Horror comics, mainly imported from the United States, had for some time caused concern in England because of the sadistic and horrific nature of many of their illustrations. In the United States Dr. Wertham had long been campaigning against the comics,[63] stating that the portrayal of violence had become a new form of pornography, seriously harming American children. As early as 1951 the Public Morality Council had drawn attention to the problem in England but the Home Office declined to take any action.[64] It was not until 1954 that the English public became seriously alarmed about 'horror comics' and their effect on children, and a demand arose for their suppression. Agitation against the comics had arisen earlier in the Dominions and legislation banning them was passed in Canada in 1949 and in Australia and New Zealand in 1954. In 1954 a Comics Campaign Council was formed to protect children and the campaign was carried further by a remarkable article of Kingsley Martin's, 'Sadism for Kids', which appeared in the *New Statesman* in September.[65]

[62] *Hansard, House of Commons, Official Report,* Vol. DXXXVIII, No. 53, Col. 1133, 15 March 1955.

[63] See *Seduction of the Innocent*, Frederick Wertham, Rinehart (New York). English Edition (1955), Museum Press. See also Geoffrey Wagner's study of the portrayal of violence in American comics and films, *Parade of Pleasure*, Verschoyle (London 1954).

[64] *Annual Report for 1951.*

[65] The article was a review of Dr. Wertham's book *Seduction of the Innocent*, *New Statesman*, 25 September 1954.

On 11 November the National Union of Teachers opened a display of 'horror comics' in London in order to create greater public interest. The Council of the Union was against the introduction of legislation, preferring to deal with the problem by means of an aroused public opinion, and was supported in this view by *The Times*.[66] The following day a deputation from the Church of England Education Council led by the Archbishop of Canterbury was received by the Home Secretary and requested the introduction of legislation banning the comics.[67] The Government took the view that only legislation could deal effectively with the problem and on 11 February 1955 published its proposals in the form of a Bill.*

The Government proposals were criticised by both *The Times* and the *Manchester Guardian* on 12 February and later in the week by the *Sunday Times*. Chief criticism was of the drafting of the Bill and in particular its definition clause which the *Manchester Guardian* pointed out was wide enough to include a reputable magazine such as *Picture Post* if it published an illustrated article on, for example, napalm bombing. The *Sunday Times* condemned the Bill as an attempt to deal in a patchwork way with the obscene libel law, when what was needed was a new and carefully drafted code dealing with the whole subject.[68] These criticisms were forcefully repeated in the House of Commons when the Government introduced the Bill on 22 February.[69] The opposition to the Bill was led by two Labour Members, Roy Jenkins and Michael Foot, but they were supported by Members from both sides of the House. They pointed out that to introduce a minor amending Bill when the Home Office had under consideration the Herbert Committee's Bill dealing comprehensively with the whole obscenity problem was to miss an

[66] 11 November 1954. First leader entitled 'A Horrible Trade'. See also a letter from Marghanita Laski, *New Statesman*, 13 November 1954.

[67] *The Times*, 13 November 1954.

* The Bill proposed to prohibit the importation or sale of harmful publications, punishing offences with imprisonment for not more than four months or a fine of not more than one hundred pounds or both. 'Harmful publications' were defined in the Bill as 'any book, magazine or other like work which consists wholly or mainly of stories told in pictures (with or without the addition of written matter), being stories portraying—

(*a*) the commission of crimes; or

(*b*) acts of violence or cruelty; or

(*c*) incidents of a repulsive or horrible nature;

in such a way that the work as a whole would tend to corrupt a child or young person in whose hands it might fall (whether by inciting or encouraging him to commit crimes or acts of violence or cruelty or in any other way whatsoever)'.

[68] See the correspondence in *The Times* during February and March, especially the letter from A. P. Herbert, 21 February 1955. See also leading articles 22 February and 24 March 1955.

[69] For debate, see *Hansard*, Vol. DXXXVII, No. 38.

opportunity for a general reform of the law. They also criticised the adoption by the Government of the Hicklin rule of 'tendency to corrupt', which the Herbert Committee Bill was intended to abolish. The Bill was given an unopposed second reading, but only on the understanding that it was to be committed to a Committee of the whole House, where there would be opportunity for amendment.

The Committee stage of the Bill opened on 24 March and ended on 29 March.[70] Numerous amendments were moved by Mr. Jenkins and others, but only two were accepted by the Government. The first made all proceedings under the Bill subject to the consent of the Attorney-General, the second limited the duration of the Bill to ten years. When the Bill reached the House of Lords the Government had further amended it by including a special defence for anyone prosecuted who could prove 'that he had not examined the contents of the work and had no reasonable cause to suspect that it was one to which this Act applies'. Another amendment limiting the Act's operation to publications 'of a kind likely to fall into the hands of children or young persons' was moved by Lord Jowitt and accepted by the Government.[71] The Bill [72] was criticised both in Parliament and the Press as an attempt to deal piecemeal with a problem which the Herbert Committee Bill treated as a whole. *The Times* expressed this view on 24 March in a leading article entitled 'The Wrong Measure'. Meanwhile the Herbert Committee Bill awaits a Member lucky in the ballot and willing to introduce it as a Private Member's Bill.

[70] See *Hansard, House of Commons, Official Report,* Vol. DXXXVIII, Nos. 60, 61, 62, 63.

[71] *Hansard,* Vol. CXCII, No. 48, 27 April 1955, Col. 617.

[72] Now the Act 3 & 4 Eliz. 2, c. 28.

CHAPTER VI

PROBLEMS OF THE ENGLISH LAW

PUBLICATION of obscene matter is punishable in English law under the common law or by statute. The assumption of jurisdiction by the common law courts has already been described * and the common law offence must now be examined in greater detail.

THE MISDEMEANOUR

The two essentials of the misdemeanour are publication and obscenity. It is no offence to write an obscene book, only to 'publish' it. Publication is used in its legal, not its colloquial sense, and means in effect the showing of the obscene matter to any other person. Thus in Carlile's case (1845) [1] there was held to be sufficient publication when an officer of the Society for the Suppression of Vice went to the prisoner's shop and asked to see some obscene prints. He was shown several in a back room and bought two in order to found the prosecution. The interpretation of 'publication' was even wider in De Montalk's case (1932),[2] where the mere handing of De Montalk's poems to the printer was held to be a sufficient act of publication. Thus publisher, author, printer, literary agent, and bookseller are all equally liable and so presumably is a private individual who passes on an obscene book to a friend.† In practice however, the bookseller is rarely prosecuted, author, publisher and printer being jointly indicted.‡

* *Ante*, p. 22. [1] (1845), 1 Cox C. C. 229. [2] (1932), 23 Cr. App. Rep. 182.

† Authors and printers, etc., are indicted as principals even if they have only 'aided and abetted', there being no degrees of guilt in a misdemeanour. See Accessories and Abettors Act, 1861 (24 & 25 Vict., c. 94). Thus in *R.* v. *De Marny*, [1907] 1 K. B. 388, C. C. R. a man was convicted of causing obscene books to be sent through the post when he had inserted advertisements in a magazine, which although not obscene related as he knew to the sale of obscene books. 'In misdemeanours', said the judge, 'persons who "aid, abet, counsel or procure" the commission of an offence are themselves principal offenders.'

‡ It is no offence to have obscene matter in one's possession with intent to publish it. Campbell, C.J., 'The mere intent cannot constitute a misdemeanour when unaccompanied with any act'. (*Dugdale* v. *R.* (1853), 1 E. & B. 435.) Thus

OBSCENITY DEFINED

As for obscenity no attempt was made to give a legal definition until 1868 when in Hicklin's case (1868) [3] Chief Justice Cockburn laid down his famous test: 'The test of obscenity is this, whether the tendency of the matter charged as obscenity is to deprave and corrupt those whose minds are open to such immoral influences and into whose hands a publication of this sort may fall'. These words have always been followed by the courts and in 1954 they were expressly approved by Lord Goddard in the Reiter case (1954): [4] 'The learned recorder said, and this court entirely agrees with him, that the law is the same now as it was in 1868'. Lord Goddard did add later: 'I can well understand that, nowadays, novelists and other writers mention things which they would not have mentioned in the reign of Queen Victoria, but it is one thing to discuss a subject and quite another to discuss it and write about it in the way in which these books deal with it'. The Lord Chief Justice did not say that the standards to be applied in judging books were those prevailing in 1868, but that the law had not changed since that date. 'Tendency' is thus the essence of the common law offence, and it follows that if the necessary effect of a publication is to corrupt, then the motive of the defendant in publishing the obscene matter is not material.

The meaning of Lord Cockburn's formula is however by no means clear, especially that of the two words 'deprave and corrupt'. One point seems evident, that a book which shocks or disgusts by the offensiveness of its language does not come within the scope of the test. 'Deprave' and 'corrupt' are both strong words, and cannot be equated in meaning with writing that is merely offensive or shocking.* The words can have any or all of three meanings. First, they can mean that the tendency of the book is to arouse impure thoughts in the mind of the reader or viewer. Secondly, they can mean that such a person would be encouraged to commit impure actions. Thirdly, they can mean that the reading of the book or looking at the picture would endanger the prevailing standards of public morals. The courts have used the words in all three senses.

Great Britain appears to be in breach of the Convention of 1923, which laid down that such possession should be punishable. The signatory states undertook to bring their law into conformity with the convention. See articles 1 and 4. On the other hand, it is an offence to 'procure obscene matter with intent to publish', the distinction being that in this case there has been an overt act towards publication, while in the first, intention only is present. (*R.* v. *Roberts* (1855), Dears. 539; 169 E. R. 836.) This followed the case of *R.* v. *Rosenstein* (1826), 2 C. & P. 414, where a count of having 'an obscene snuff box in possession with intent to publish it' was struck out of the indictment at the judge's suggestion.

[3] (1868), L. R. 3 Q. B. 360.
[4] [1954] 2 Q. B. 16, 19.

* Cf. Stable, J., in *The Philanderer* case (1954), see p. 114.

In the Hicklin case, Chief Justice Cockburn emphasised the tendency of the book to arouse libidinous thoughts. He pointed out that the indiscriminate sale of the pamphlet had exposed the 'minds' of those previously pure to the danger of contamination and pollution. It would 'suggest to the minds of the young of either sex or even persons of more advanced years, thoughts of a most impure and libidinous character'. Again in the second *Image and the Search* trial Mr. Justice Lynskey referred to the minds of the readers in clear language:

> You will note the phrase 'corrupt and deprave the minds of those whose minds are open to such immoral influences'. What you have got to ask yourselves is, are there those—not an isolated case—but are there those of a class into whose hands this book may fall who when reading that book might suffer in their moral outlook; might be depraved as a result of that book; might be induced to have impure and lascivious thoughts, and might have desires started in their minds which would make them the more anxious to indulge in some of the things which are described in that book?'[5]

It seems clear that the law takes into consideration the thoughts which a book might arouse in the mind of a reader, and that it is not sufficient for these thoughts to be of a sexual nature, but they must be of an impure or lecherous kind. If the words involve the arousing of lecherous thoughts it is obvious that they apply equally to books which arouse or incite sexually impure actions. American cases have laid more stress on impure actions than thoughts. The point was succinctly put by a Massachusetts judge when dismissing a charge against the book *Forever Amber*: 'While conducive to sleep it is not conducive to sleep with a member of the opposite sex'.[6]

The words, however, have also been interpreted to apply to books which do not arouse erotic thoughts in the minds of the reader, but which challenge conventional moral standards. The words were used in this sense by Chief Justice Cockburn in the Bradlaugh case. 'The difficulty in a case of this kind', he said, 'is in determining whether the publication is calculated to corrupt public morals or is allowable in the discussion of a public question.' The pamphlet was a straightforward exposition of birth-control methods and was in no sense an erotic book. Again *The Well of Loneliness* contained no obscene passages, the nearest approach being 'that night they were not divided'. Sir Chartres Biron condemned the book because the

[5] Taken from G. Walpole's shorthand note of the trial. Note that the learned judge has misquoted the Hicklin judgement, inserting the word 'minds' where this does not occur in the original.

[6] *Cw.* v. *Forever Amber*, 32 Mass. L. Q., No. 2, 79 (Mass. Superior Court, 1947).

authoress condoned the practice of sexual relations between women: 'In the present case there is not one word which suggests that anyone with the horrible tendencies described is in the least degree blameworthy'.[7] *

WHO IS CORRUPTED?

A further question which must be answered is to whom do the words 'corrupt and deprave' apply? The answer may be normal adults, abnormal adults, normal children, or abnormal children. The English law has always stressed the importance of protecting the young. Thus the old form of indictment contained an averment about the 'morals of youth', and Lord Campbell stated that he had the youth of the nation in mind when he introduced his Obscene Publications Act in 1857. In the Hicklin judgement the words occur 'whose minds are open to such immoral influences and into whose hands a publication of this sort may fall'. Chief Justice Cockburn specifically mentioned youth in his judgement and the protection of the young seems to have been uppermost in the minds of most judges and counsel who have taken part in obscenity trials. In *The Philanderer* case, however, Mr. Justice Stable rejected the youth criterion. 'A mass of literature', he said 'great literature, from many angles is wholly unsuitable for reading by adolescents, but that does not mean that the publisher is guilty of a criminal offence for making those works available to the general public.'

CIRCUMSTANCES OF PUBLICATION

Whether or not youth is to be considered in every case there can be no doubt that the courts will take into consideration the mode and circumstances of publication. The point is illustrated by two passages in the Hicklin case.

KYDD (for the appellant): 'What can be more obscene than many pictures publicly exhibited, as the Venus in the Dulwich gallery?'

LUSH, J.: 'It does not follow that because such a picture is exhibited in a public gallery, that photographs of it might be sold in the streets with impunity.'

[7] *The Times*, 17 November 1928.

* Cf. the U.S. law, where in 1944 *Lady Chatterley's Lover* was held obscene because of its central theme: namely 'It is dangerous to the physical and mental health of a young woman to remain continent and that the most important thing in her life, more important than any rule of law or morals is the gratification of her sexual desires'. (*People* v. *Dial Press*, 182 Misc. 416; 48 N.Y.S., 2d, 480 (1944).)

And later:

COCKBURN, C.J.: 'A medical treatise, with illustrations necessary for the information of those for whose education or information the work is intended, may, in a certain sense, be obscene, and yet not the subject for indictment; but it can never be that these prints may be exhibited for anyone, boys or girls, to see as they pass. The immunity must depend on the circumstances of the publication.'

In Thomson's case in 1900 the Common Serjeant in his direction to the jury pointed out that no one would think of destroying the indecent pictures discovered in the ruins of Roman towns, 'but to sell photographs of them in the streets of London would be an indictable offence'.[8] Again in 1954 the stipendiary magistrate at Leeds said: 'A work of art like *The Decameron* is not considered obscene, but if it was sold at sixpence halfpenny on a bookstall to attract customers it could well be so.'[9] Similar arguments were advanced by counsel for the Crown in the Swindon *Decameron* case on 15 September 1954. He contended that it was right that the book should be available to students of Italian social history, but when it was put into the setting of this newsagent and bookseller's shop in the Commercial Road, Swindon, its purpose was to excite all those persons likely to be corrupted. The magistrates rejected these arguments, which would be more convincing if 'intention' was treated as part of the misdemeanour.[10]

PUNISHMENT

Since the misdemeanour of publishing an obscene libel is a common law crime there is no limit to the punishment which may be imposed.* It is clearly undesirable that penalties should be left to the sole discretion of the judge or magistrates, and an improvement in the law would be the fixing of a maximum penalty.

STATUTE LAW: THE 1857 ACT

Statute has modified the common law, but it is interesting to note that the principal statute, the Obscene Publications Act of 1857,[11] which gave rise to the Hicklin case leaves the common law misde-

[8] (1900), 64 J. P. 456. [9] *The Times*, 12 October 1954.

[10] *Criminal Law Review*, November 1954, p. 868. [11] 20 & 21 Vict., c. 83.

* The point that a common law misdemeanour carries an unlimited penalty has been decisively established by four recent cases: *Morris*, [1951] 1 K. B. 394; *Higgins*, [1951] 2 All E. R. 758; *Pearce*, [1952] 2 All E. R. 718; *Bryan* (1951), 35 Cr. App. Rep. 121.

The Criminal Procedure Act, 1851, (14 & 15 Vict., c. 100) gave statutory recognition to the common law misdemeanour but this was only to enable 'hard labour' to be imposed as an additional penalty. Since 'hard labour' has now been abolished this section of the statute has no further relevance.

meanour intact. It creates no new punishable offence and its preventive machinery of seizure only comes into operation if the magistrates are convinced that the publication of the obscene matter seized would amount to a misdemeanour, 'proper to be prosecuted as such'. The Act does not lay down any penalties except the destruction of the obscene matter, and the ordinary criminal procedure is not followed since the Act is a complete code in itself. Under the Act any person can lay an information on oath before a stipendiary magistrate or two justices, that he believes that obscene matter is being kept in premises within the jurisdiction for the purpose of sale or distribution, and that an actual sale has occurred. The magistrates, if they are satisfied that there is a satisfactory case for taking action,* may issue a warrant giving authority for the premises to be entered by a police officer and the obscene matter to be seized. The magistrates, when the seized articles have been brought before them, must issue a summons calling upon the occupier to appear within seven days to show cause why the matter seized should not be destroyed. They may order matter so seized to be destroyed immediately after the expiration of the seven days allowed for appeal.†

In *Cox* v. *Stinton* (1951) [12] Lord Goddard stressed that the 1857 Act provided its own procedure, but this procedure is in many ways anomalous. When books are seized the only person who has a right to show cause in court why they should not be destroyed is the occupier of the premises in which they were seized. Neither author nor publisher has any right to give or call evidence in the court. The magistrates are not bound to make any finding of obscenity based on evidence given in court, nor need the prosecution make out a *primâ facie* case of obscenity or indicate in what respects they consider a book obscene. This point was established by Lord Goddard in *Thomson* v. *Chain Libraries Ltd.* (1954).[13] 'It is not for the prosecution', said Lord Goddard, 'to read out particular paragraphs unless the justices ask the prosecution to address them or point out some particular thing. It is for the justices to look at the publications for themselves.' Mr. Justice Hilbery added that the justices were not required to go through the books in the court at the hearing of the summons.

> If they have already read them—the books having been brought into court—and they say, as they said here, that they have read

* i.e. that publication of the matter would amount to a misdemeanour 'proper to be prosecuted as such'. For discussion of the meaning of this phase see p. 152.

† Appeal under the Act is to the Appeal Committee of Quarter Sessions and from there it may go by way of case stated—on a point of law only—to a Divisional Court of the Queen's Bench Division.

[12] [1951] 2 K. B. 1021; 2 All E. R. 637.

[13] [1954] 1 W. L. R. 999; 2 All E. R. 616.

> them and are ready to proceed, as they are the persons to decide whether the publications are obscene or not, they have done all that is necessary as the preliminary which has to be observed before the occupier of the premises discharges the burden which is then put on him, viz. to show cause why the publications should not be destroyed.

This interpretation of the Act obviously makes it very difficult for the occupier to make an adequate defence since he does not know whether it is the whole of the book, or parts, or even an isolated passage to which objection has been taken.

Another anomaly is the absence of any time limit within which proceedings under the Act must be taken. Thus when obscene matter has been seized under the Act the police could theoretically hold it indefinitely, without bringing it before the magistrate for a destruction order. In *Cox* v. *Stinton* (1951), Mr. Justice Devlin stated that application for a destruction order should be made within a reasonable time, but this was not the point before the court, and his remark must be treated as *obiter*. In fact in Cox's case there was a gap of nine months between the seizure of the articles and the application for the destruction order.*

TEN ACTS

Apart from the Obscene Publications Act there are ten other public Acts dealing with obscene offences, as well as many local Acts and by-laws. The Vagrancy Acts of 1824 (s. 4) and 1838 (s. 2) [14] make it a summary offence to hold indecent exhibitions.† In 1889 the Indecent Advertisements Act [15] created a further summary offence of indecent advertising punishable by a fine of forty shillings or a month's imprisonment. The Act was intended to cover cases such

* Cox's case also decided the following points: s. 11 of the 1848 Summary Jurisdiction Act (11 & 12 Vict., c. 43), now repealed by the Magistrates' Courts Act, 1952 (15 & 16 Geo. 6 & 1 Eliz. 2, c. 55), see s. 104, sch. 6, requiring a complaint to be made within six months of the time when the offence arose does not apply to the 1857 Act. *Per curiam*: under the 1857 Act only one complaint need be made, i.e. that made to support the application for a warrant to enter and search. There is no need for a further complaint to be laid as a preliminary to issuing a summons to show cause why the matter seized should not be destroyed. The case also decided that negatives not intended for sale, were, in fact, published by the publication of the positives, and were therefore liable to seizure.

† The 1824 Act punishes the holding of an indecent exhibition in a public place with not more than three months' imprisonment. Doubt arose as to whether the Act covered exhibitions in shop windows and the 1838 Act was passed to make the point clear.

[14] 5 Geo. 4, c. 83 and 1 & 2 Vict., c. 38.

[15] 52 & 53 Vict., c. 18.

as the pasting up of indecent posters in public places.* The Indecent Advertisements Act dealt expressly with posters about venereal diseases and in 1917 the Venereal Disease Act [16] was passed making it an offence, subject to certain exceptions, to offer by public advertisement to treat any person for venereal disease or to give any advice in that connection.†

Newspapers had long been accustomed to report the sensational details of murder and divorce cases and to check this the Judicial Proceedings (Regulation of Reports) Act [17] was passed in 1926, making it an offence punishable with four months' imprisonment and/or a fine of five hundred pounds, 'to print or publish or cause or procure to be printed or published in relation to any judicial proceedings any indecent medical, surgical, or physiological details, being details the publication of which would be calculated to injure public morals'. This Act accords with the common law view. At common law the provisions relating to fair comment, privilege and justification, applicable to defamatory libel do not extend to libels of an obscene character. Thus publication of indecent matter is not protected by proof that it is a fair and accurate report of the proceedings of a court of justice.[18] A further summary offence of publicly offering obscene books or articles for sale or distribution or exhibiting them to the public view was created by the Metropolitan Police Act of 1839,[19] and this was extended to other towns by the Town Police Clauses Act, 1847.[20] ‡

CUSTOMS

Importation of obscene matter is now an offence under the Customs Acts of 1876 and 1952.[21] Section 42 of the Customs Act of 1876 for-

* Section 4 of the Act provides a greater penalty of a five-pound fine or up to three months' imprisonment for any person who gives such a poster to another with intent that he shall display it in a public place.

[16] 7 & 8 Geo. 5, c. 21.

† The Act does not apply to advertisements receiving the sanction of local authorities or the Ministry of Health.

[17] 16 & 17 Geo. 5, c. 61.

[18] See *R.* v. *Carlile* (1819); 3 B. & Ald. 161; *R.* v. *Creevey* (1813), 1 M. & S. 273; *Steele* v. *Brannan* (1872), L. R. 7 C. P. 261. *Bona fide* reports intended for the use of the legal profession are exempted from the Act.

The Law of Libel Amendment Act, 1888, s. 8 (51 & 52 Vict., c. 64), makes an order of a judge in chambers necessary before the prosecution of a proprietor or editor of a newspaper. See s. 3 as to indecent matter and Defamation Act, 1951–2 (15 & 16 Geo. 6 & 1 Eliz. 2, c. 66), s. 7 (3) and s. 9 (2).

[19] 2 & 3 Vict., c. 47. This Act does not extend to London City and Liberties, for which corresponding provision was made in 2–3 V. c. xciv (Loc.).

[20] 10 & 11 Vict., c. 89.

‡ The Act also punishes the singing of obscene or profane songs and ballads.

[21] 39 & 40 Vict., c. 36 and 15 & 16 Geo. 6 & 1 Eliz. 2, c. 44.

bids the importation of 'indecent or obscene prints, paintings, photographs, books, cards, or other engravings or any other indecent or obscene articles'. Under s. 45 of the Customs Act, 1952, if such articles are imported with an intent to avoid the prohibition, the importer is liable to a fine of up to one hundred pounds and may also be sentenced to a maximum of five years' imprisonment. Apart from the penalties the articles may be seized and destroyed. If the seizure is not from the owner the Customs authorities must give him notice of the seizure in writing, and he may then make a claim—also in writing—for the return of his goods. If such a claim is made the Customs authorities must take the seized articles before the courts for a finding on their obscene character, or in default of such action return them to the owner. The provision for intervention by the courts is a necessary one, but it places the onus of invoking the courts' jurisdiction on the owner. A more desirable provision would be to make an application to the courts by the Customs authorities obligatory from the first. This would ensure a uniform standard in the application of the law, and be in accord with the rules of natural justice.*

POST OFFICE

The Post Office Act, 1953,[22] replacing similar provisions in the Post Office Act, 1908,[23] makes it an offence to send indecent books or prints through the post, punishable on indictment by a maximum of twelve months' imprisonment or on summary conviction by a fine of ten pounds. The Act covers any indecent designs or words on the outside of the 'packet', as well as obscene enclosures, and it is under this section of the Act that those who send vulgar post-cards through the post are prosecuted.[24]

A further statutory change is embodied in the Magistrates' Courts Act of 1952.[25] If the accused is over seventeen and gives his consent, and the court is of the opinion that the offence is not a

* Schedule VII of the 1952 Customs and Excise Act contains the above provisions. There is no obligation to serve personal notice on an owner resident abroad and, since the goods can be destroyed within a month of notice in the *Gazette*, they may have been destroyed before the owner knows they have been seized.

[22] 1 & 2 Eliz. 2, c. 36 (1953). [23] 8 Edw. 7, c. 48.

[24] Section 11 (1) (*b*), (*c*), replacing the Post Office Act, 1908, s. 63 (1) (*b*). Section 17 gives the Post Office power to detain any postal packet 'suspected to contain' obscene articles. The Post Office may open such packets but must first give notice to the consignee so that if he wishes he may be present at the opening. The Post Office may detain any obscene articles found. Section 58 declares the power of the Post Office to open packets under the express warrant of a Secretary of State given in writing.

[25] 15 & 16 Geo. 6 & 1 Eliz. 2, c. 55.

serious one, then the common law misdemeanour may be tried summarily, the maximum penalty being a fine of one hundred pounds and six months' imprisonment. This provision is subject to the general rule that in any case which involves the Director of Public Prosecutions, the Director's consent to summary trial must also be obtained.[26]

The common law and statutory positions have now been outlined, but on a number of important questions the law is uncertain and these must now be discussed.

ISOLATED PASSAGES OR DOMINANT EFFECT

The first point in doubt is whether the test of a book's obscenity is an isolated passage or passages, or the character of the book as a whole. The origin of the 'isolated passages' test can be traced to the necessity in the general law of libel to specify the passages complained of in the indictment. This practice was followed in the law of obscene libel and so gave rise to the 'isolated passages' test. It is submitted that the answer to the problem will depend on the form of the indictment.* If the indictment specifies certain passages then the book will be judged on those passages: if a copy of the book is submitted with the indictment then the book will be judged as a whole.† In practice, one of these courses must be followed, and the Bradlaugh conviction was quashed because the indictment merely set out the title of the book without submitting the book or setting out the objectionable passages.

The Hicklin case is frequently referred to as authority for the 'isolated passages' test, but an examination of the actual report gives no support to this view. It was found as a fact by the Recorder and accepted by the Queen's Bench court that half the book was obscene and that the other half dealt with controversial questions. The question of 'isolated passages' was not raised in any of the judgements delivered. Again, in *Steele* v. *Brannan* (1872) where a

[26] *Olim* Criminal Justice Act, 1925, schedule II (15 & 16 Geo. 5, c. 86).

* See the form of indictment in *Archbold*, pp. 1400, 1401, Indictment Rules, 1915, r. 8—*Archbold*, 1948.

† *R.* v. *Bradlaugh* (1878), 3 Q. B. D. 607. 'In an indictment for publishing an obscene book it is not sufficient to describe the book by its title only, for the words thereof alleged to be obscene must be set out: and if they are omitted the defect will not be cured by a verdict of guilty and the indictment will be bad either upon arrest of judgement or upon error.' At first instance, Cockburn, C.J., laid down that where passages as distinct from the whole book were objected to, then they must be set out. In *Robinson's case* (1843), 1 Broun 590, 643, a Scottish case, this view was slightly modified. The court held it was not necessary to quote offensive passages but special reference should be made to the works themselves by line and page and copies should be lodged with the clerk of the court.

revised edition of the same pamphlet was considered, Bovill, C.J., stated that despite the expurgations 'no inconsiderable portion of its contents is of a most shockingly filthy description'. In the Bradlaugh case Chief Justice Cockburn again presided and interpreted his own test in terms of considering the book as a whole.

MRS. BESANT: 'Could it be said to be obscene if the preface was not obscene? If not so the jury must acquit the defendant.'

COCKBURN, C.J.: 'No. The book must be looked at as a whole and if its effects as a whole are to produce obscenity it is not the less so because particular passages were not so.'

Presumably this argument must apply *mutatis mutandis.*

Present-day practice supports the test of reading the book as a whole.* In all five of the 1954 prosecutions already referred to, the juries were sent away to read the entire book, but it must be remembered that in all these cases the whole book was the subject of the indictment. Thus in *The Philanderer* case Mr. Justice Stable, sustaining counsel's objection, would not allow the Prosecution to mark selected passages until the jury had read the book as a whole, 'without picking out its highlights'. In the first *Image and the Search* trial, Mr. Winn, counsel for the Defence, again objected to the proposal to give the jury a list of page numbers.

> The jury ought to read that book, my Lord [he said] as though they themselves had just bought it. Where the defence are prohibited from calling any evidence of opinion, it is only fair that the prosecution should be prohibited, too. Handing the jury a list of page numbers is simply expressing an opinion that those pages contain obscene passages; and the jury are supposed to be considering whether the book, as a whole, is obscene.

Mr. Justice Devlin agreed: 'No doubt', he said, 'the Prosecution must indicate to the jury at some time what passages are complained of in particular, but it is obviously best that they should read it without that guidance in the first place.'[27]

* Such practice is a return to the traditional common law view. Thus when Stockdale was tried in 1789 for libelling the House of Commons over the conduct of the Warren Hastings trial, Lord Kenyon told the jury: 'I admit also that in forming your opinion you are not bound to confine your inquiry to those detached passages which the Attorney-General has selected as offensive matter and the subject of the prosecution . . . you have a right to look at all the context; you have a right to look at the whole book; and if you find it has been garbled and that the passages selected by the Attorney-General do not bear the sense imputed to them: the man has a right to be acquitted and God forbid that he should be convicted'. Verdict: 'Not guilty'. (Trial of John Stockdale, 22 St. Tr. 237, at p. 292.)

[27] *Smith's Trade News*, 16 October 1954, 'A Book on Trial', by C. H. Rolph.

In the second *Image and the Search* trial, Mr. Justice Lynskey was equally explicit on the point of reading the book as a whole.

> What you have got to ask yourselves [he said] is ... are you satisfied in your minds that this particular book read as a whole—not passages you think objectionable read out of their context, but anybody reading the book as a whole—are you satisfied that the matter in it would tend to deprave and corrupt those whose minds were open to such immoral influences and into whose hands a publication of this sort may fall? [28]

The same point was made by Judge Aarvold in the Arthur Barker prosecution:

> The tendency, of course, first of all, is only judged by the book as a whole; it cannot be judged by small parts of the book. There are little passages that might be one side or other of the borderline of decency. The tendency is not judged by that sort of passage; it is judged by a consideration of the book as a whole and not part of it. [29]

The practice of indicting the whole book and the consequent reading of it as a whole seem now well established under the prosecution procedure, but when the Obscene Publications Act is invoked a different test appears to apply. Thus in *Paget* v. *Watson* (1952) [30] the magistrate found that only the covers of a book were obscene, but, nevertheless, held that he had jurisdiction under the Act to order the book's destruction. Lord Goddard upheld him and pronounced the point unarguable. 'It is not necessary', he said, 'to show that a publication is obscene on every page.' He did not explicitly discuss the question of 'isolated passages', but his words would seem to support that test. His judgement may, however, have been influenced by his own view, stated in court, that had he to decide the question of the obscenity of the rest of the book, he would have differed from the magistrate. In Thomson's case (1954) Lord Goddard also mentioned the possibility of the marking of obscene passages by the police for magistrates acting under Lord Campbell's Act. He in no way disapproved of the practice.

INTENTION

The second legal point in doubt, and this is of much greater complexity, is whether it is necessary to establish a criminal intention

[28] Transcript of George Walpole's shorthand note of the trial.
[29] George Walpole's shorthand note of the trial, Old Bailey, 2 December 1954.
[30] [1952] 1 All E. R. 1256.

to secure a conviction for publishing an obscene libel? There can be no doubt that today the courts act on the assumption that proof of such an intention is unnecessary. This view is not only undesirable on general grounds of social utility, but is in conflict with the general principles and decided cases of the common law. Given that the purpose of the law is to suppress pornography, but not to censor literature, then intention becomes of paramount importance, since it is only by considering the intention or purpose of the author or publisher that the two can be distinguished. A serious or artistic purpose on the author's part distinguishes *The Decameron*, for instance, from a book like *The Romance of Lust*, whose only purpose is to arouse erotic thoughts or desires. This is not to say that the sale of *The Decameron* in any circumstances could not make its seller guilty of the crime of publishing an obscene libel. In the case of the publisher all would depend on the circumstances of the publication, and the selling of the book in a sixpenny edition outside a children's school would clearly be an offence. It is not 'obscenity' itself which the law is punishing, but the distribution of obscene matter in a manner calculated to deprave and corrupt. Whether such an offence has been committed depends logically on the intention of the accused person. It is thus quite possible that in the case of a book objectively obscene one person might be convicted of an offence, while the other might be acquitted. If this were not the case the librarian of the British Museum would be as guilty as a pornographic bookseller if he allowed a reader to see an obscene book.

Before embarking on a discussion of the common law position, however, one must be clear as to the exact meaning in law of the word 'intention'. The general legal rule may be briefly stated: the law will take 'intention' into account but will not concern itself with a person's 'motive'.* What is the difference between the two? The distinction was first clearly made by Bentham. Intention concerns an act and its consequences. To establish criminal liability the act must be intentional, that is it must be a voluntary action of the accused person, not an involuntary one, such as a sudden unpremeditated muscular contraction. Hence, if a man when holding a gun is seized by a spasm and unintentionally squeezes the trigger and the gun goes off he will not be held liable if the shot kills someone. Thus in the law of obscene libel there must be an intentional act of publication. Intention, however, concerns the consequences of an act as well as the Act itself. An Act may have a variety of consequences, some lawful, others unlawful. The law selects certain

* There are certain exceptions to this rule, e.g. a malicious motive may negative the defence of qualified privilege in a defamation case and motive is relevant in establishing the tort of malicious prosecution.

consequences of an action and makes them unlawful. Thus in the crime of murder it is not the firing of the gun that is the guilty act, but the victim's death, which is the result of the gun being fired. To found criminal liability the prosecution must establish that the accused intended the unlawful consequences. 'Intention' in this respect is equated with foresight. The prosecution must show that the accused foresaw and desired the consequence of his action, or that he foresaw it and did not care whether it took place or not. This latter state of mind is known as 'recklessness', namely foresight without desire.[31]

The point was summed-up by Lord Kenyon when he said: 'It is a principle of natural justice and our law that "actus non facit reum, nisi mens sit rea".* The intent and the act must both concur to constitute the crime'.[32] † The requirement of a subjective guilty state of mind is the principal distinction between civil and criminal law. The normal standard in the law of torts, for example, is that of the reasonable man. Here the question asked is not 'Did X foresee the harmful results of his conduct?' but 'Would a reasonable man have foreseen these consequences?' This standard, that of negligence, is not, however, appropriate to criminal law.

[31] For a full treatment of this concept see *The Mental Element in Crimes at Common Law*, by J. W. C. Turner. Chapter XIII of *The Modern Approach to Criminal Law* (Macmillan, 1948). Also *Kenny's Outlines of Criminal Law* (Cambridge University Press), 16th edition (1952), Chapter II. See also Glanville Williams, *The Criminal Law, the General Part* (1953), paras. 22, 27, 29 and 228.

[32] *Fowler* v. *Padget* (1798), 7 T. R. 509, 514.

* This is the most honoured maxim of the common law. Thus Stephen, J.: 'The full definition of every crime contains expressly or by implication a proposition as to a state of mind' (*R.* v. *Tolson* (1889), 23 Q. B. D. 168, at p. 187).

The requirement is much more ancient than this, however. Thus Coke: 'If one shoot at any wild fowl upon a tree and the arrow killeth any reasonable creature afar off, without any evil intent in him, this is *per infortunium*' (*Institutes*, Vol. III, p. 56).

Again, Blackstone writes: 'And as a vicious will without a vicious act is no civil crime, so on the other hand an unwarrantable act without a vicious will is no crime at all. So that to constitute a crime against human laws there must first be a vicious will, and secondly an unlawful act consequent upon such vicious will (*Commentaries*, 2nd edition, Vol. IV, Bk. 6; *Of Crimes*, p. 98).

† The only exceptions to this rule at common law are the offences of 'non repair of highways' and 'public nuisance'. Statutory crimes may not require *mens rea*, but there is a judicial presumption that they do, unless the requirement is expressly excluded by the statute creating the crime. Certain statutes such as the Offences against the Person Act, 1861, (24 & 25 Vict., c. 100) create crimes requiring a specific intent, e.g. s. 20 which creates the offence of wounding with intent to commit grievous bodily harm. In such cases it is not enough to prove foresight, desire must also be proved.

MOTIVE

'Motive' was distinguished by Bentham from 'intention', as the desire prompting an act, a state of mind which the law cannot take into account.* The point will be made clearer by an example. X fires a gun and kills Y. His intention in firing the gun is to bring about the death of Y. His motive may be to inherit Y's fortune, marry Y's wife, or merely hatred of Y. Motive is thus the reason which leads X to form his intention of killing Y. Whether this motive is good or bad is irrelevant as far as the law is concerned, although it may well be relevant for the moralist.

With these distinctions in mind one can now approach the common law misdemeanour of publishing an obscene libel. The problem of intention in relation to publication of an obscene libel is more complicated than its relation, for instance, to the crime of murder by inflicting a deadly wound, for two reasons. First, there is no consequence of obvious primary importance flowing from the act of publication comparable to the death of the wounded person. When a book is published a number of consequences follow which may be of equal importance. Thus by publishing a book literature may be enriched, pleasure may be given to a group of people, the publisher may make money, and someone may be corrupted. The law, however, forbids only one of these consequences and that is the possible corruption of a person or a group. On the general common law principle, which has been outlined, the law having selected a consequence and forbidden it, must prove that the publisher of the book intended that consequence to be brought about. The fact that the publisher had other intentions, such as making money or benefiting literature, does not *ipso facto* exclude the intention to corrupt; a man can have as many intentions as there are consequences, but the existence of other intentions may be evidence that he had not that unlawful intention which the law requires.†

The second difficulty is that there is no such obvious causal connection between the corruption of a mind and the publication of a book as there is between the infliction of a deadly wound and the consequent death. This, of course, is true, but is a problem inherent in this branch of the law which is not solved but avoided by the exclusion of intention.

* See *Introduction to the Principles of Morals and Legislation* (Blackwell, 1948), edited by W. Harrison, Chapters VIII and X. Motive is defined as 'the internal perception of any individual lot of pleasure or pain, the expectation of which is looked upon as calculated to determine you to act in such and such a manner'.

† It should be remembered that once one has singled out a specific intention, intentions with regard to other consequences may become motives for that particular intention. Thus the intention to make money may be the motive for intending the corruption of others.

A WORKABLE TEST

An argument, which must be answered at this point, is that if the doctrine of intention were to be applied to obscene libel, then the law would become unworkable. It is impossible in practice, runs the argument, to prove any intention to corrupt. This objection, however, if it is raised at all, must be applied to the whole criminal law. It is not a novel argument: in 1477 Chief Justice Brian raised exactly this point: 'It is common knowledge', he said, 'that the intention of a man will not be probed, for the Devil does not know man's intention.' [33] The common law, however, has preferred Lord Justice Bowen's dictum that 'the state of a man's mind is as much a fact as the state of his digestion'. [34] The law, of course, must use external evidence from which to infer intention, but the two concepts of the 'intention' and the evidence by which it is proved must be kept distinct. The point has been well put by Sir William Holdsworth:

> We must adopt an external standard in adjudicating upon the weight of the evidence adduced to prove or disprove *mens rea.* That of course does not mean that the law bases criminal liability upon non-compliance with an external standard. So to argue is to confuse the evidence for a proposition with the proposition proved by that evidence.[35]

That 'intention' is a workable concept in the law of obscene libel may be illustrated by an example. X publishes a magazine made up of photographs of an obscene character showing men and women having sexual intercourse with one another. He is indicted for publishing an obscene libel with intent to corrupt. In the witness box he denies that he had any such intention. The jury have two pieces of evidence before them: the magazine and X's statement. No normal jury would have any difficulty in deciding that he had an intention to corrupt. Y on the other hand has published a novel containing obscene passages and is also indicted. He gives evidence that he published the novel with a serious purpose as a contribution to literature. Evidence is given as to the character of his business, which is of the highest, and he calls literary critics who give evidence of the literary quality of the book. The chances are that the jury would acquit the publisher in such a case. Of course, none of these things can happen under the present practice in the courts, and the legal justification for that practice must now be examined.

[33] *Y.B.*, 17 Edw. IV, fo. 2.
[34] *Edgington* v. *Fitzmaurice* (1885), L. R. 29 Ch. 459, 482.
[35] *History of English Law*, Vol. III, p. 374.

THE HICKLIN CASE

It has already been sufficiently shown that the exclusion of intention is contrary to common law doctrine, but its justification is said to be case law and especially the Hicklin case. One example of the citing of that case for a proposition which it cannot support has already been given (p. 134), but 'intention' provides a second. Neither Chief Justice Cockburn nor Mr. Justice Blackburn ever excluded intention from the crime.* Both judges did, however, state that the intention to corrupt must be inferred from the publication itself.

> I think [said Chief Justice Cockburn] that if there be an infraction of the law the intention to break the law must be inferred, and the criminal character of the publication is not affected or qualified by there being some ulterior object in view (which is the immediate and primary object of the parties) of a different and of an honest character.[36]

Mr. Justice Blackburn made the same point even more explicitly:

> I take the rule of law to be as stated by Lord Ellenborough in *Rex* v. *Dixon* [37] in the shortest and clearest manner: 'It is a universal principle that when a man is charged with doing an act' (that is, a wrongful act without any legal justification) 'of which the probable consequence may be highly injurious, the intention is an inference of law resulting from the doing the act'. And although the appellant may have had another object in view, he must be taken to have intended that which is the natural consequence of the act.[38]

A PRESUMPTION OF FACT

The Hicklin case does not then exclude intention, but makes it a matter of construction to be inferred from the actual publication, achieving this end by the use of a presumption. The nature of this presumption of 'intending natural consequences' was for some time in doubt and judges in the past have used it as though it were an irrebuttable presumption of law.[39] There has, however, always been

* Much of the confusion has arisen from the Chief Justice's use of the words 'motive' and 'intention' as though they were synonyms, when they are, in fact, distinct. See pp. 370–2 of the case.

[36] p. 370. [37] (1814), 3 M. & S. 11. [38] p. 375.

[39] So Brett, J., in *R.* v. *Prince* (1875), L. R. 2 C. C. R. 154. His remarks on obscene libel were, however, *obiter*.

a strong body of judicial opinion which has regarded it as a presumption of law or even of fact, open to rebuttal by the introduction of evidence to the contrary. Thus in 1823 in Harvey's case,[40] a prosecution for libel for imputing insanity to King George III, the jury asked Chief Justice Abbot whether there should be a malicious intention to constitute a libel. The Chief Justice replied: 'The man who publishes slanderous matter in its nature calculated to vilify and defame another, must be presumed to have intended to do that which the publication is calculated to bring about, UNLESS he can show the contrary and it is for him to show the contrary'.* Again in Sullivan's case in 1868 [41] Mr. Justice Fitzgerald stated that 'the intentions of men are inferences of reason from their actions when the action can flow but from one motive and be the reasonable result of but one intention'.[42] The same point was made by Stephen in his *History of the Criminal Law.*[43]

> This account of the nature of intention [he wrote] explains the common maxim which is sometimes stated as if it were a positive rule of law, that a man must be held to intend the natural consequences of his act. I do not think that the rule in question is really a rule of law, further or otherwise than it is a rule of common sense. The only possible way of discovering a man's intention is by looking at what he actually did and by considering what must have appeared to him at the time the natural consequence of his conduct.

Stephen's view of the presumption has been adopted by judges in recent cases and the view that the presumption is rebuttable seems now firmly established. Thus in Steane's case (1947) where a man was charged with doing an act with intent to assist the enemy, namely broadcasting on their behalf, he was able to rebut the presumption by showing that he acted under duress.

> No doubt [said Lord Goddard] if the prosecution prove an act the natural consequence of which would be a certain result and no evidence or explanation is given, then a jury may on proper direction, find that the prisoner is guilty of doing the act with the intent complained of, but if on the totality of the evidence there is room for more than one view as to the intent of the prisoner,

[40] 2 B. & C. 257.

* Bayley, J., also said: 'In the absence of any such evidence (i.e. rebutting) I think the intention was naturally and properly to be drawn from the libel itself'.

[41] 11 Cox C. C. 44, at p. 50.

[42] Cf. *Burn's case* (1886), 16 Cox C. C. 355, at pp. 364–5.

[43] 1883, Vol. II, p. 111.

the jury should be directed that it is for the prosecution to prove the intent to the jury's satisfaction.[44] *

Again Lord Justice Denning has said, in reference to the presumption: 'There is no "must" about it; it is only "may". The presumption of intention is not a proposition of law but a proposition of ordinary good sense.' [45] In Westall's case (1949) the Lord Justice dealt with the point at greater length:

> In cases of drunkenness, gambling, or crime, it is nothing to the point to say that a man must be taken to intend the natural consequences of his own acts. That has sometimes been referred to as if it were a proposition of law which introduced a conclusive presumption against a man. I beg leave to say that it is nothing of the kind. It is simply a proposition of ordinary good sense. It means this: that as a man is usually able to foresee what are the natural consequences of his act, so it is as a rule, reasonable to infer that he did foresee them and intend them. But while that is an inference which may be drawn it is not one which must be drawn. If on all the facts of the case it is not the correct inference then it should not be drawn.[46]

The presumption seems now to be treated as not of law at all but of fact.

It is submitted then, that, despite the confusion created by Hicklin's case, intention is an intrinsic part of the misdemeanour of publishing an obscene libel; that an objective 'natural consequences' test is applied; but that this presumption can be rebutted by proof of other circumstances, amongst which may be included evidence of a contrary intention.

THE OLD INDICTMENT

Support for the view that intent is a necessary part of the offence of publishing an obscene libel comes from the form of drafting employed

[44] [1947] K. B. 997, at p. 1004.

* This is in accord with Viscount Sankey's judgement in Woolmington's case: 'It is not till the end of the evidence that a verdict can properly be found . . . at the end of the evidence it is not for the prisoner to establish his innocence but for the prosecution to establish his guilt. . . . But while the prosecution must prove the guilt of the prisoner there is no such burden laid on the prisoner to prove his innocence and it is sufficient for him to raise a doubt as to his guilt. . . . No matter what the charge or where the trial, the principle that the prosecution must prove the guilt of the prisoner is part of the common law of England and no attempt to whittle it down can be entertained.' ([1935] A. C. 462; 25 Cr. App. Rep. 72.)

[45] *Hosegood* v. *Hosegood* (1950), 66 T. L. R., pt. 1, 735.

[46] *Westall* v. *Westall* (1949), 65 T. L. R. 337.

in the old indictment. The practice of alleging an intent to corrupt public morals prevailed until the Indictments Act of 1915 changed the form of the indictment. The following is a typical pre-1915 indictment:

> The jurors for our lord the king upon their oath present that X being a scandalous and evil disposed person and devising, contriving and intending the morals as well as of youth as of divers other liege subjects of our said lord the king to debauch and corrupt, and to raise and create in their minds inordinate and lustful desires, . . . in a certain open and public shop of him the said X there situate, unlawfully, wickedly, maliciously and scandalously did sell and publish to one Y a certain indecent, lewd, wicked, scandalous and obscene libel in the form of a book intituled ——, and containing divers lewd, impure, gross, bawdy and obscene matters, to the manifest corruption of the morals as well as of youth as of other liege subjects of our said lord the king.[47]

Although the new form of indictment omits the averment as to intention, the Act expressly provided that any change in form should have no effect on the substance of the law. Thus s. 8 enacts:

> Nothing in this Act or the rules thereunder shall affect the law or practice relating to the jurisdiction of a court or the place where an accused person can be tried, nor prejudice or diminish in any respect the obligation to establish by evidence according to law any acts, omissions or INTENTIONS which are legally necessary to constitute the offence with which the person accused is charged, nor otherwise affect the laws of evidence in criminal cases.[48]

In Thomson's case (1900) the Common Serjeant admitted evidence of other books sold by the defendant because 'it is some evidence to show that she sold this book with the intention alleged in the indictment and not accidentally'.[49] Again in Barraclough's case (1906) the Court for Crown Cases Reserved held that 'intent' was an essential part of the offence. 'There is no doubt', said Chief Justice Alverstone, 'that an indictment for obscene libel should be so drawn as to include the ordinary averment as to the corruption of public morals.' [50] Mr. Justice Darling agreed:

> It seems to me that if a thing which is properly called obscene is alleged to be unlawfully published, it follows that all the usual allegations in an indictment for obscene libel are included. Even

[47] Archbold, *Criminal Pleading and Practice* (1910).
[48] Indictments Act, 1915 (5 & 6 Geo. 5, c. 90).
[49] (1900), 64 J. P. 456.
[50] [1906] 1 K. B. 201, C.C.R.

in such an indictment as this, intent is I think part of the indictment. It is no doubt 'sous-entendu' and not set out with the wearisome reiteration to which we are accustomed in indictments, but it is still part of the charge or the publication would not have been unlawful.

The point was raised in the Bradlaugh case (1877) by Chief Justice Cockburn, himself the author of the judgement which is said to exclude intent.

SOLICITOR-GENERAL: 'As to the motive or intent of the publication it was quite immaterial, except so far as it was to be judged from the necessary tendency and effect of the book.'

COCKBURN, C.J.: 'But the indictment charges such an intent.'

SOLICITOR-GENERAL: 'Because by law a man is taken as intending the natural consequences of what he does.'

COCKBURN, C.J.: 'You seem to acquit them on one side while the indictment charges them with it on the other. It would be a strange and startling result if persons whom the prosecution acquit of any actual intent to corrupt public morals may nevertheless be convicted on an indictment that charges them with it.' [51] *

FOX'S LIBEL ACT, 1792

A further point supporting the relevance of intention, which has never been raised in the courts, is the effect of Fox's Libel Act, 1792,[52] on the law of obscene libel. Blasphemous, seditious, and obscene libel are the three branches of the law of public libel, which after the abolition of the Licensing Act grew steadily in importance as marking the limits of free speech and discussion. Libel as a criminal offence had been developed by the court of Star Chamber, but after its abolition the offence was taken over by the common law courts which developed its rules in detail during the seventeenth and eighteenth centuries. In Carr's case (1680) [53] where the defendant was accused of libelling Chief Justice Scroggs by imputing corruption to him in a paper entitled *The Weekly Packet of Advice from Rome*, the court held that the jury was competent to decide only one issue, the fact of publication. Whether the published material was libellous and whether it had been published with a malicious intent were matters of law for the judge. This ruling was followed in other

[51] *The Times*, 20 June 1877.

* The headnote to *De Montalk's case* (1932), 23 Cr. App. R. 182, states that intent is not part of the offence. This is erroneous since Lord Hewart in his very brief judgement made no reference to the point, although St. John Hutchinson had raised it for the appellant.

[52] 32 Geo. 3, c. 60.

[53] (1680) 7 St. Tr. 1111.

libel cases during the seventeenth century although when the Seven Bishops were tried in 1688, the whole matter in issue, including the questions of publication and libel, was left to the jury.*

In 1783 Erskine, the most famous advocate of his time, challenged this view of the law in Shipley's case.[54] Shipley, who was Dean of St. Asaph, had published a pamphlet, part of which could be interpreted as an incitement to rebellion, and consequently was prosecuted for publishing a seditious libel. The jury brought in a verdict of 'guilty of publishing ONLY' and the judge Mr. Justice Buller did not wish to record the 'only'. Erskine, however, insisted, and a lively dialogue followed in which Erskine was threatened with committal.

ERSKINE: 'Would you have the word "only" recorded.'
JURYMAN: 'Yes.'
ERSKINE: 'Then I insist that it shall be recorded.'
BULLER, J.: 'Mr. Erskine, sit down, or I shall be obliged to interpose in some other way.'
ERSKINE: 'Your lordship may interpose in any manner you think fit.' [55]

'The learned judge', wrote Campbell, 'took no notice of this reply and quailing under the rebuke of his pupil did not repeat the menace of commitment.' [56]

Erskine then moved for a new trial, and as a result of his submissions a full discussion of the law of libel took place among the judges. Erskine made five submissions maintaining that the jury were entitled on a plea of 'not guilty' to decide the whole issue, and could not be confined to decisions of particular questions selected by the judge. 'In all cases', he said 'where the mischievous intention (which is agreed to be the essence of the crime) cannot be collected by simple inference from the fact charged, because the defendant goes into evidence to rebut such inference, the intention becomes then a pure unmixed question of fact for the consideration of the jury.' [57] Lord Mansfield giving judgement rejected Erskine's arguments, saying: 'Such a judicial practice in the precise point from the

* (1688), 12 St. Tr. 183–521. This case is not a satisfactory legal authority as it was governed more by inflamed political passion than by considerations of law. In both Barnardiston's case ((1684), 9 St. Tr. 1334) and that of Samuel Johnson ((1686), 11 St. Tr. 1339), the Carr ruling was applied and the jury confined to the question of publication. For a detailed survey of this branch of the law see the judgement of Lord Mansfield in the Dean of St. Asaph's case ((1783), 21 St. Tr. 847, at p. 953). Also, Stephen, *History of the Criminal Law*, Vol. II (1883), Chap. XXIV.

[54] (1783), 21 St. Tr. 847.

[55] (1783), 21 St. Tr. at p. 953.

[56] Campbell's *Lives of the Lord Chancellors*, Vol. VIII, p. 277.

[57] (1783), 21 St. Tr. 847, at p. 966.

Revolution, as I think, down to the present day, is not to be shaken by arguments of general theory or popular declamation'.

This decision led nine years later to the passing of Fox's Libel Act, and while the Act was under consideration the House of Lords put seven questions to the judges on the existing state of the law. The judges unanimously upheld Lord Mansfield:

> The criminal intention charged upon the defendant in legal proceedings upon libel is generally matter of form, requiring no proof on the part of the prosecutor and admitting of no proof on the part of the defendant to rebut it. The crime consists in publishing a libel. A criminal intention in a writer is no part of the definition of libel at the common law. 'He who scattereth firebrands, arrows and death', which if not a definition, is a very intelligible description of a libel, is *ea ratione* criminal; it is not incumbent on the prosecutor to prove his intent, and on his part he shall not be heard to say, 'Am not I in sport?' [58]

To reform the law and reverse this opinion parliament passed the Libel Act, entitled, 'An Act to remove doubts respecting the functions of juries in cases of libel'.

> Whereas [says the Act] doubts have arisen whether, on the trial of an indictment or information for the making or publishing ANY* libel, where an issue or issues are joined between the King and the defendant or the defendants on the plea of not guilty pleaded, it be competent to the jury impanelled to try the same to give their verdict upon the whole matter in issue: Be it therefore declared and enacted by the King's most excellent Majesty, by and with the consent of the Lords spiritual and temporal, and Commons, in this present Parliament assembled, and by the authority of the same, that on every such trial the jury sworn to try the issue may give a general verdict of guilty or not guilty upon the whole matter put in issue upon such indictment and information; and shall not be required or directed by the court or judge before whom such indictment or information shall be tried to find the defendant or defendants guilty merely on the proof of the publication by such defendant or defendants of the paper charged to be a libel, and of the sense ascribed to the same in such indictment or information.

CRIMINAL LIBEL

Since the passing of the Act it has never been doubted that the law of criminal libel requires a criminal intention before a conviction

[58] Stephen, *Op. cit.*, p. 344. This is an abridged proposition taken from the answers to the questions which are set out in full at 22 St. Tr. 296–304.

* Author's capitals.

can take place. Such an intention was invariably averred in the old form of indictment in words such as these: 'Contriving and unlawfully, wickedly and maliciously intending to injure, vilify and prejudice one X and to deprive him of his good name, fame, credit and reputation, and to bring him into public contempt, scandal, infamy and disgrace.' [59] The intention may, of course, be inferred from the publication itself but such an inference is open to rebuttal. Thus Chief Justice Kenyon said in Lord Abingdon's case (1794):

> That in order to constitute a libel, the mind must be in fault and shew a malicious intention to defame, for, if published inadvertently it would not be a libel: but where a libellous publication appeared unexplained by any evidence, the jury should judge from the overt act and where the publication contained a charge slanderous in its nature should from thence infer that the intention was malicious . . . the intention may be collected from the libel unless the mode of publication or other circumstances explain it.[60]

Again in Munslow's case (1895), Baron Pollock held that although there was a presumption that a libel was published with a malicious intent the presumption could be displaced.[61] In civil cases of libel on the other hand no such intention is required since the standard is the normal civil standard of the inference a reasonable man would draw from reading the document concerned.*

ASSAULT

The difference between civil and criminal standards is illustrated by the analogous case of assault, which like libel is both a tort and a crime. A civil assault can be committed negligently,[62] but for a criminal prosecution there must be a criminal intention or at least recklessness.[63]

[59] Archbold, *Op. cit.* (1910). [60] (1794), 1 Esp. 226. [61] [1895] 1 Q. B. 758.

* Thus Lord Blackburn in *Capital and Counties Bank* v. *Henty* (1882), 7 A. C. 741 at p. 772: 'The question is not whether the defendant intended to convey that imputation, for if he without excuse or justification did what he knew or ought to have known was calculated to injure the plaintiff he must (at least civilly) be responsible for the consequences though his object might have been to injure another person than the plaintiff or though he may have written in levity only'. See also *Jones* v. *Hulton*, [1910] A. C. 20, and *Cassidy* v. *Daily Mirror*, [1929] 2 K. B. 331. Section 4 of the Defamation Act, 1952 (15 & 16 Geo. 6 & 1 Eliz. 2, c. 66), now provides a defence in such circumstances subject to certain conditions.

[62] *Weaver* v. *Ward* (1616), Hobart 134.

[63] *Ackroyd* v. *Barret* (1895), 11 T. L. R. 115.

SEDITIOUS LIBEL

Public criminal libel is made up of three branches, sedition, blasphemy and obscenity, and in the first two branches—since Fox's Act—a criminal intention has always been required. After discussing the offence of seditious libel Stephen sums up his conclusions in these words:

> The Libel Act must thus be regarded as having enlarged the old definition of a seditious libel by the addition of a reference to the specific intentions of the libeller—to the purpose for which he wrote. And a seditious libel might since the passing of that act be defined (in general terms) as blame of public men, laws, or institutions, published with an illegal intention on the part of the publisher. This was in practice an improvement upon the old law, which indeed was, as I have already pointed out, altogether inconsistent with serious political discussion.[64]

Accordingly, when in Burdett's case (1820), the judge directed the jury in this sense, in a seditious libel case, he was upheld by the whole court on appeal:

> With respect to whether this was a libel I told the jury that the question whether it was published with the intention alleged in the information was peculiarly for their consideration: but I added that this intention was to be collected from the paper itself, unless the import of the paper were explained by the mode of publication or any other circumstances.[65]

BLASPHEMOUS LIBEL

The requirement of criminal intention in blasphemous libel since the passing of Fox's Act is also upheld both by the text-books and the cases. Thus Starkie in his treatise on *Slander and Libel* (1869), has this to say of blasphemous libel.

> It is the mischievous abuse of this state of intellectual liberty which calls for penal censure. The law visits not the honest errors but the malice of mankind. A wilful intention to pervert, insult, and mislead others by means of licentious or contumelious abuse applied to sacred subjects or by wilful misrepresentations of artful sophistry, calculated to mislead the ignorant and unwary is the test of guilt. A malicious and mischievous intention or what is equivalent to such intention in law as well as in morals . . . a state of apathy and indifference to the interests of society is the broad boundary between right and wrong.' [66]

[64] Stephen, *Op. cit.*, p. 359. [65] (1820), 4 B. & A. 95. [66] p. 590.

During the nineteenth century the indictments for blasphemous libel always alleged a blasphemous intention, although it was not the same in every case, and a series of decided cases shows that these averments were treated as being of the greatest importance.[67]

If this be the law with regard to two branches of the crime of public libel, sedition and blasphemy, what grounds can there be for distinguishing between the effects of Fox's Act on these branches and that on the third, obscenity? The argument for the inclusion of 'intention' in the offence of publishing an obscene libel is finally established when one recalls the express words of Fox's Act stating that it is to apply to trials for 'any libel'.

TWO RECENT CASES

Hicklin's case cannot then be said to exclude intention, and indeed, in two recent cases the case has been explicitly followed while the judge held intention to be relevant. Thus in a recent Canadian case the judge applied the Hicklin rule, but held that since the intention of the accused was an artistic one there was no tendency to depravity within the meaning of the Hicklin case.* Again in *The Philanderer* case Mr. Justice Stable, having approved the Hicklin test, said:

> [The book] goes on to describe the pitfalls of slime and filth into which the unhappy adolescent, without knowledge or experience, without the map and the compass, and without the guiding hand of a wise parent or the example of a well-ordered, decent home, stumbles. You will have to consider whether in this the author was *pursuing an honest purpose* † and an honest thread of thought, or whether that was all just a bit of camouflage to render the crudity, the sex of the book, sufficiently wrapped up to pass the critical standard of the Director of Public Prosecutions.

Either this is a misdirection or the point of view put forward in this chapter represents the true state of the law.

DEFENCES

The third doubtful point concerns the defences that may be raised to a charge of obscene libel. It has been suggested that a plea of

[67] See *R. v. Eaton* (1812), 31 St. Tr. 927, at p. 950; *R.* v. *Hone* (1817), *The Three Trials of William Hone* (London 1818); *R.* v. *Carlile* (1819), 4 St. Tr. (N.S.) 1423, at p. 1425; 1 St. Tr. (N.S.) 1387, at p. 1390. The whole point *re* blasphemous libel is fully discussed in Nokes, *History of the Crime of Blasphemy*, pp. 79–82, 91–8 (Sweet and Maxwell, 1928).

* Lajure, J., of the Quebec Court, in *Conway* v. *The King*, [1944] 2 D. L. R. 530, a prosecution for staging a theatrical performance which had for its background actresses nude from the waist up who tried to create the impression of living statues.

† Author's italics.

publication for the public good would provide a defence to the charge. Such a plea may be regarded as merely another form of rebutting the presumption of intention or may be treated as a separate defence. Thus Mr. Justice Stephen wrote in his *Digest of the Criminal Law*:

> A person is justified in exhibiting disgusting objects, or publishing obscene books, papers, writings, prints, pictures, drawings or other representations, if their exhibition or publication is for the public good, as being necessary or advantageous to religion or morality, to the administration of justice, the pursuit of science, literature or art, or other objects of general interest; but the justification ceases if the publication is made in such circumstances as to exceed what the public good requires in regard to the particular matter published.[68] *

There is no decided case of a higher court for this view, but it was expressly approved by the recorder in his summing-up at the Central Criminal Court in De Montalk's case (1932) [69]:

> It would be a defence in this case [he said] if the thing was done for the public good, because although I am not sure that there has been any case upon it, I accept a submission by one of the most learned of our judges, Mr. Justice Stephen, in these words . . . therefore if you are of opinion that this can be for the public good as an advancement of literature, in my opinion that would be a defence.

The case eventually reached the Court of Criminal Appeal, but Lord Hewart made no comment on the point. Stephen's view was approved in 1953 in the first *Philanderer* case by the High Bailiff of the Isle of Man, although he held—as a question of fact—that *The Philanderer* did not fall within the exception.[70] As has already been mentioned the Joint Committee of both Houses recommended in 1908 that a similar defence should be included in their proposed consolidating Act.

* The Criminal Code Commissioners in their report of 1879 (Cmd. 2345) defined the offence of obscene libel in s. 147 and included a defence of publication for the public good. 'It shall be a question of law whether the occasion of the sale, publishing, or exhibition is such as might be for the public good, and whether there is evidence of excess beyond what the public good requires in the manner, extent or circumstances in, to, or under which the sale, publishing or exhibition is made, so as to afford a justification or excuse therefor, but it shall be a question of fact whether there is or is not such excess.' They added (p. 22 of the report), 'we believe that s. 147 as to obscene publications, expresses the existing law, but it puts it into a much more definite form than at present. We do not however think it desirable to attempt any definition of obscene libel other than that conveyed by the expression itself.'

[68] 9th edition, p. 173.

[69] (1932), 23 Cr. App. Rep. 182.

[70] *Manchester Guardian*, 19 September 1953.

In *The Well of Loneliness* case, however, Sir Chartres Biron rejected the Stephen view:

> With regard to the point that the book is well written and therefore should not be subjected to these proceedings [he said] that is an entirely untenable position. I agree that the book has some literary merits, but the very fact that the book is well written can be no answer to these proceedings, because otherwise we should be in the preposterous position that the most obscene books would be free from stricture. It must appear to everyone of intelligence that the better an obscene book is written the greater the public to whom it is likely to appeal.[71]

Again in the Warren Gallery case the magistrate, Mr. Mead, rejected the defence: 'It is utterly immaterial whether they are works of art. That is a collateral question which I have not to decide. The most splendidly painted picture in the Universe might be obscene.' [72]

The circumstances of publication may, however, provide a defence to the charge. Librarians presumably are not committing an offence when they lend obscene books to students of the subject, neither are law reporters when they report obscene details in publications intended for the use of the legal profession.

The drafters of the Obscene Publications Act, 1857, presumably had this point in mind when they limited magistrates' jurisdiction to cases where they considered a misdemeanour would be committed by publication, 'proper to be prosecuted as such'. This was the view of Mr. Justice Blackburn in the Hicklin case.

> I think [he said] with respect to the last clause, that the object of the legislature was to guard against the vexatious prosecutions of publishers of old and recognised standard works, in which there may be some obscene or mischievous matter. . . . In Moxon's case the publication of Shelley's *Queen Mab* was found by the jury to be an indictable offence; I hope I may not be understood to agree with what the jury found, that the publication of *Queen Mab* was sufficient to make it an indictable offence. I believe, as everybody knows, that it was a prosecution instituted merely for the purpose of vexation and annoyance. So whether the publication of the whole works of Dryden is or is not a misdemeanour, it would not be a case in which a prosecution would be proper; and I think that the legislature put in that provision in order to prevent proceedings in such cases.[73]

[71] *The Times*, 17 November 1928.
[72] *The Times*, 9 August 1929.
[73] *Hicklin's case*, p. 374.

EVIDENCE

Character

The fourth point of controversy concerns the evidence that is admissible in an obscene libel case. First can the accused call evidence of good character in such a case? Since the seventeenth century such evidence has been admissible and the principle is now established that in all criminal cases the accused may himself or through witnesses give evidence of good character.[74] Evidence of character must, of course, be relevant to the offence charged, hence evidence of a charitable disposition would be inadmissible in an obscene libel case. The accused could, however, give evidence as to his 'reputation' as a publisher and call witnesses to establish this. Evidence of good character is also admissible after the verdict, because it is relevant to the sentence which should be passed. Evidence as to bad character on the other hand is not normally admissible, but there are certain exceptions. Thus if the accused gives evidence of his own good character, or cross-examines the Prosecution's witnesses as to character, he is said 'to put his character in issue', and the prosecution may attack it. After the verdict, evidence of bad character and previous convictions is admissible to enable the court to pass an appropriate sentence.

Experts

The second doubtful evidence point is whether the accused can give or call evidence of a book's literary or artistic merit. If he is the author he is not allowed to give evidence of his purpose in writing the book although such purpose may be referred to by the prosecution. In the second *The Image and the Search* case Mr. Gerald Gardiner, Q.C., pointed out the inequity of this rule. Counsel for the Crown continually asked the following question: 'What possible purpose could be served, members of the jury, by dragging in that particular piece of indecency?' There could be no answer to this rhetorical question since the author was not allowed to give evidence on the point.[75]

Evidence of a book's literary merit is also excluded from the court, this practice being followed in both *The Well of Loneliness* and the *September in Quinze* cases.* The justification for this apart from its alleged irrelevancy is said to be the general rule excluding all evidence of opinion. This rule has received recent confirmation in the Court of Appeal.[76] The modern basis of the rule is that it is

[74] *R.* v. *Harris* (1680), 7 St. Tr. 925, at p. 929.
[75] See *New Statesman*, 4 December 1954.
* See p. 101.
[76] *Hollington* v. *Hewthorn and Co. Ltd.*, [1943] 1 K. B. 587, at p. 595.

for the court to draw conclusions from the facts proved and for a witness to do so would be to usurp the court's functions. To this rule there is one long established exception, admitting the evidence of experts on questions of science or art.* Thus in Whistler's case the opinions of artists, art critics and other experts were admitted as to the artistic merit of his painting.[77] Stephen in his *Digest* formulated the rule as follows: 'Where there is any question as to any point of science or art, the opinions upon that point of persons specially skilled in any such matter are deemed to be relevant facts. The words science or art include all subjects on which a course of special study is necessary to the formation of an opinion.' (Article 49.)

In obscene libel cases expert evidence of a book's scientific merit has always been admitted. Thus in the Bradlaugh case both Dr. Drysdale, senior physician to the Free Hospital, and a medical student Miss Vickery, gave evidence of the medical value of the book.

COCKBURN, C.J.: 'Does it appear to you that there is anything immodest or improper in the book?'

DR. DRYSDALE: 'Certainly not: in my opinion it is an excellent book.'

COCKBURN, C.J.: 'Is there anything in it calculated to excite sensual or libidinous feelings.'

DR. DRYSDALE: 'Certainly not. Indeed on me it had the contrary effect.' (Laughter.) [78]

Again, when in 1935 Boriswoode Ltd. were prosecuted for publishing *The Sexual Impulse*, by Edward Charles, the magistrate, Mr. Rowland Powell, allowed Professor Julian Huxley, Professor J. B. S. Haldane, and Dr. Maude Royden of Eccleston Square Church to give evidence of the book's scientific merit. Despite their evidence he held the book obscene, stating in his judgement that he had not to decide whether the book was of any medical or psychological value. 'The only thing for me to decide is whether it comes under the heading of an obscene book.' [79]

There seems to be no legal justification for distinguishing between 'literary' and 'scientific' experts, since expert evidence is admitted on any subject which requires special knowledge. Again a witness

* In the fourteenth century surgeons were allowed to give evidence as to whether an injury had resulted in mayhem. ((1354), 28 Lib. Ass. pl. 5.)

[77] *Whistler* v. *Ruskin* (1878), *The Times*, 26 November.

[78] *The Times*, 20 June 1877.

[79] *The Times*, 17 October 1935. Professor Malinowski of London University, author of *The Sexual Life of Savages*, also gave evidence.

coming forward as an expert need not be a professional specialist. Any person who is skilled in the relevant branch of knowledge is treated for legal purposes as an expert. If a general practitioner is allowed to give evidence on medical matters there seems no valid reason for excluding a literary critic or a professor of literature from testifying as to a book's literary merit. Of course, a tribunal is as free to reject the evidence of an expert as it is of any other witness: such evidence when admitted is never binding.*

Other Books

The final evidence point concerns the admissibility of books other than those made the subject of the indictment. Those accused of publishing obscene libels have frequently attempted to show that other books freely circulating were no worse than those being subject to prosecution. Thus in the Bradlaugh case Mrs. Besant attempted to put in a copy of *Tristram Shandy* as evidence. After consulting the other judges, Chief Justice Cockburn excluded the evidence. 'I am bound to reject every publication as evidence, but I can't prevent Mrs. Besant from committing a passage to memory and reciting it as part of her speech nor from reading from a book, as if reciting from memory, but the book is not evidence and need not be proved nor must it be handed to the jury.' [80]

The law on this point has recently been clarified by the Lord Chief Justice in his judgement in the Reiter case (1954).[81] Lord Goddard quoted with approval the judgement of the Lord Justice General in the Scottish case of *Galletly* v. *Laird* (1953),[82] commending the following passage:

> The magistrates disallowed cross-examination by the complainer's solicitor and positive evidence tendered for the defence designed to show that books other than those referred to in the complaint circulated freely in Paisley and were available in the local public library, the suggestion apparently being that these other books were not materially different in character from those complained of. I consider that the magistrate's ruling was right. The character of other books is a collateral issue, the exploration of which would be endless and futile. If the books produced by the prosecution are indecent or obscene, their quality in that respect cannot be made any better by examining other books or

* A possible explanation of the strictness of the rules of evidence in obscenity cases is that a sexual matter is concerned. Thus the admissibility of evidence as to unnatural offences is subject to special rules. See Article by P. B. Carter, *Law Quarterly Review*, April 1954, Vol. 70, at p. 231.

[80] *Queen* v. *Charles Bradlaugh and Annie Besant*. Bonner and Forder.

[81] [1954] 2 Q. B. 16.

[82] [1953] S. C. (J) 16.

listening to the opinions of other people with regard to these other books.

In these circumstances then, evidence of other books is excluded, but such books may still be put in as evidence of the character of the trade carried on in a particular shop. In Galletly's case itself such circumstances were held relevant. The prosecution, said the judge, must establish 'that such book or picture is being indiscriminately exhibited or circulated or offered for sale in such circumstances as to justify the inference that it is likely to fall, and perhaps *intended* * to fall into the hands of persons liable to be so corrupted'. If 'intention' is a part of the offence, evidence of other books sold will be even more relevant. Thus in Thomson's case (1900) the Common Serjeant said:

> Whilst the questions of the intention with which the book was sold is part of the indictment, it is impossible to say that the holding out and offering of other books may not bear on that intent. If the defendant sold other books whose titles go to suggest that they are indecent, it is some evidence to show that she sold the book with the intention alleged in the indictment and not accidentally. I cannot exclude the evidence.[83]

The points so far considered have been of general application but there are two problems of special application which must now be discussed, the position of the bookseller, and the responsibility of a master for the acts of his servants.

THE BOOKSELLER AND LIBRARIAN

The bookseller is in a different position from that of author, publisher and printer, for while they can be presumed to have knowledge of the contents of a book, a bookseller can only read a tiny fraction of the hundreds of books which pass through his hands. For the contents of most of the books he sells he must rely on the word of the publisher. Is a bookseller liable then for publishing an obscene libel when he knows nothing of the contents of the book in question? If intention is part of the offence he clearly is not because he can have formed no intention with regard to a book of which he knows nothing except the title. Even if intention is not part of the offence, it is submitted that in the absence of negligence, he will not be liable. The position of the innocent disseminator of a libel has been fully discussed in the cases, but they all deal with a civil libel. In *Emmens* v. *Pottle* (1885) [84] a newsvendor was held not to have

* Author's italics.

[83] (1900), 64 J. P. 456.

[84] (1885), 16 Q. B. D. 354; 2 T. L. R. 115.

published a libel of which he knew nothing. Lord Esher, Master of the Rolls, held that the newsvendors were *primâ facie* liable because they handed the paper containing a libel to a stranger and the burden of proof was thus on them to show that they had not 'published it'. Approving the judgement of the lower court, Lord Esher said:

> The charge against the defendants was that they disseminated the libel and so published it. But did they by disseminating it publish it? If the defendants had known the contents of the paper and disseminated it that would have been a publication; but here they did not know. The jury found that the defendants did not know and ought not to have known that the newspaper was one likely to contain libellous matter. They were therefore innocent disseminators of a paper containing a libel.

This case was followed in 1900 when Vizetelly brought an action against Mudie's Library for putting into circulation a book which contained a libel about him.[85] * The library was held to have been negligent in employing no reader and ignoring the notices about the libellous character of the book which had appeared in the trade papers.

In 1932 in the case of *Bottomley* v. *Woolworths*, the judge reviewed the authorities and laid down three propositions of law. To escape liability the defendant must prove: (1) that he was innocent of knowledge of the libel; (2) that nothing in the work or the circumstances in which it came to him ought to have led him to suppose that it contained a libel; (3) that when the work was disseminated by him it was not by any negligence on his part that he did not know that it contained a libel.[86] The criminal standard should certainly not be higher than the civil standard and if booksellers or librarians can prove that they were not negligent they should, even under present practice, escape liability.

Vicarious liability is not as a general rule a principle applied in the criminal law, since it offends against the rules of natural justice. At common law there have been only two exceptions to this rule public nuisance and criminal libel. The criminal libel rule applied only to newspapers, and newspaper proprietors were held liable for libels published by their servants.[87] Lord Campbell's Act of 1843,

[85] *Vizetelly* v. *Mudie's*, [1900] 2 Q. B. 170.

* Vizetelly had gone to Africa to search for Stanley. After their meeting he had sent letters to a London newspaper for which he was paid £2,000. The book suggested that Vizetelly was drunk at the time and had not written the letters himself. Constable sent the book to Vizetelly for review!

[86] (1932), 48 T. L. R. 521.

[87] *R.* v. *Walter* (1799), 3 Esp. 21. *The Times* was involved.

however, afforded them a defence if they could show that publication had taken place without 'authority, consent, or knowledge and that the said publication did not arise from want of due care. . . .[88] This provision apart, libel is not a crime of negligence, but always requires *mens rea*.

The liability of a bookseller for the acts of his assistants does not, of course, depend upon vicarious liability, but upon their position as innocent agents carrying out authorised acts. If the assistant knew of the obscene content of the book, he would also be liable for 'publishing' it, but not otherwise. If the assistant sold an obscene book without his master's authorisation, the master would not be liable.

ADMINISTRATION OF THE LAW

The principal legal problems have been discussed, but to complete the picture of English law, something must be said of the law's administration. It is still open to any private citizen to bring a prosecution for obscene libel, although in practice such prosecutions are rare. Most prosecutions are brought by the police and they are obliged under Regulations made in 1946 to consult the Director of Public Prosecutions before any action is taken.[89] They are not under any obligation to accept his advice but its rejection is unusual. No obligation to consult the Director exists when the police wish to use the procedure under the 1857 Act, but such consultation is usual in practice. The Customs authorities usually consult the Director although they are under no obligation to do so. Of Post Office practice no information is available.

In suitable cases the Director can take over a case from the police or private person and prosecute himself, or he may initiate a prosecution on his own behalf. Complaints about books by private individuals are frequently received by the Director's Office, as well as information sent by societies and organisations such as the Public Morality Council. The Director of Public Prosecutions is a permanent civil servant whose function it is to counsel and advise, but not to initiate policy. He acts under the general direction of the Attorney-General, who is responsible to parliament. A certain degree of uniformity in administering the law is obtained by the practice of consulting the Director on legal action, but an important reform of the law would be the abolition of all private prosecutions and making all proceedings involving obscenity, no matter what their character, subject to his or the Attorney-General's

[88] 6 & 7 Vict., c. 96, Section 7.

[89] Prosecution of Offences Regulations, 1946, S. R. & O. 1946, No. 1467/L. 17.

approval and consent. This would ensure a uniform standard of administration for the whole country.

No coherent policy can be detected behind the present administration of the law nor one which determines the choice between the use of the prosecution or the destruction order procedures. Serious novels containing obscene passages are a trifling problem when compared with the 'roneoed' pornographic sheets bearing no imprint which circulate in vast numbers and are constantly being destroyed. It is normal for the printer as well as the author and publisher to be prosecuted. Such a policy is undesirable since it leads to an unofficial censorship by printers who fear a prosecution. After the 1954 prosecutions many printers refused to print works of undoubted literary merit because they contained obscene passages. Were the intention or purpose of the printer to be taken into account and literary or artistic merit made relevant considerations, his position would be adequately safeguarded. In the case of serious books, booksellers are not often prosecuted, whereas the bookseller whose trade is mainly pornographic is frequently indicted. As has been pointed out in the historical chapters prosecutions are essentially sporadic, and it is not possible to generalise about the immediate cause of these activities.

CHAPTER VII

THE UNITED STATES EXPERIENCE

THE first reported prosecution for obscene literature in the United States was a Massachusetts case of 1821, in which the court held that obscene libel was a common law offence.[1] * The book attacked was entitled *Memoirs of a Woman of Pleasure*, and it was probably the famous *Fanny Hill*, by John Cleland, of which mention has already been made. Apart from this case there were very few obscenity prosecutions before the civil war, although American reviewers were no less censorious than their English contemporaries.† After the war, however, a puritan reaction took place against the general profligacy and laxity of moral standards, and it was against this background that Anthony Comstock began his forty-year campaign for decent literature, under the slogan 'Morals, Not Art or Literature'. In 1842 importation of obscene matter was forbidden and further amending legislation was passed in 1857.‡ In 1865 Congress forbade the use of the mails for despatching obscene goods and at the instigation of Comstock comprehensive legislation was passed in 1873.§ These are the only statutory federal obscene offences.

[1] *Cw.* v. *Holmes*, 17 Mass. 336 (1821).

* An earlier case was *Cw.* v. *Sharpless*, 2 S. & R. 91 (Pa. 1815). This, however, was not concerned with literature but painting. The defendants were convicted for exhibiting a painting: 'representing a man in an obscene, impudent and indecent posture with a woman'.

† Thus in 1851 Nathaniel Hawthorne's *The Scarlet Letter* was attacked on the grounds of indecency; A. C. Coxe in the *Church Review*, January 1851. The attacks on *Griffith Gaunt* started in the U.S.A.

‡ See U.S. Tariff Act, 1930, s. 305. The customs law is today contained in Title 19, 1305, of the U.S. Code. See also 18 U.S. Code 1462. This section also punishes those who convey obscene matter in interstate or foreign commerce by means of a common carrier. Contraceptives are covered by the section. Penalties are five thousand dollars fine or imprisonment for not more than five years or both.

§ Today mailing is covered by Title 18 of the U.S. Code 1461 and 1463. The wording of the section is similar to 1462 and the penalties are identical. In 1948 it was laid down that 'indecent' included matter of a character tending to incite

In 1879 the Hicklin ruling was accepted by the United States Courts and although constantly criticised was generally applied until the *Ulysses* case of 1933.[2] Judge Hand made a famous protest against the rule in 1913, but it had become so firmly established that he felt bound to follow it.

> I hope [he said] it is not improper for me to say that the rule as laid down, however consonant it may be with mid-Victorian morals, does not seem to me to answer to the understanding and morality of the present time. . . . I question whether in the end men will regard that as obscene which is honestly relevant to the adequate expression of innocent ideas, and whether they will not believe that truth and beauty are too precious to society at large to be mutilated in the interests of those most likely to pervert them to base uses. Indeed, it seems hardly likely that we are even today so lukewarm in our interest in letters or serious discussion as to be content to reduce our treatment of sex to the standard of a child's library in the supposed interest of a salacious few, or that shame will long prevent us from adequate portrayal of some of the most serious and beautiful sides of human nature. . . .
>
> Yet, if the time is not yet when men think innocent all that which is honestly germane to a pure subject, however little it may mince its words, still I scarcely think that they would forbid all which might corrupt the most corruptible, or that society is prepared to accept for its own limitations those which may perhaps be necessary to the weakest of its members. If there be no abstract definition, such as I have suggested, should not the word 'obscene' be allowed to indicate the present critical point in the compromise between candor and shame at which the community may have arrived here and now? . . . To put thought in leash to the average conscience of the time is perhaps tolerable, but to fetter it by the necessities of the lowest and least capable seems a fatal policy.[3]

The harshness of the Hicklin rule in practice was shown in 1930 when a Massachusetts court condemned Theodore Dreiser's *An American Tragedy* on the basis of objectionable passages. The judge refused to allow in evidence the two volumes of the book, and permitted the jury to consider only the passages and the pages or chapters

arson, murder, or assassination (c. 645, 62 St. 768). In March 1955 the Post Office seized a copy of *Lysistrata*, by Aristophanes, which had been sent from England, holding it obscene. On 18 March it was released. (*Daily Telegraph*, 19 March 1955.)

[2] *U.S.* v. *Bennet*, 24 Fed. Cas. 1093, No. 14,571. (C.C.S.D., N.Y.) (1879.) Adopted in the Court of Appeals, 1884. *People* v. *Muller*, 96 N. Y. 408 (1884).

[3] *U.S.* v. *Kennerley*, 209 Fed. 119. (S.D., N.Y.) (1913.)

in which they occurred. The Supreme Judicial Court upheld the trial judge's ruling:

> Even assuming great literary excellence, artistic worth and an impelling moral lesson in the story, there is nothing essential to the history of the life of its principal character that would be lost if these passages were omitted . . . the seller of a book which contains passages offensive to the statute has no right to assume that children to whom the book might come would not read the obnoxious passages or that if they should read them would continue to read on until the evil effects of the obscene passages were weakened or dissipated with the tragic dénouement of a tale.[4]

As a result of this case the relevant statute was altered. Previously it applied to books 'containing obscene, indecent or impure language, or manifestly tending to corrupt the morals of youth'. This became 'which is obscene indecent or impure etc.' [5]

THE 'ULYSSES' CASE

In 1933 Judge Woolsey lifted the ban on *Ulysses* and in so doing laid down a new test of obscenity in books.[6] The judge held that the first question to be decided was the intent with which the book was written. If that was pornographic then the book should be condemned, if not the court should go on to consider the book itself.

> The reputation of *Ulysses* in the literary world [said Judge Woolsey] warranted my taking such time as was necessary to enable me to satisfy myself as to the intent with which the book was written, for, of course, in any case where a book is claimed to be obscene it must first be determined, whether the intent with which it was written was what is called, according to the usual phrase, pornographic—that is written for the purpose of exploiting obscenity. If the conclusion is that the book is pornographic that is the end of the inquiry and forefeiture must follow. But in *Ulysses* in spite of its unusual frankness, I do not detect anywhere the leer of the sensualist. I hold therefore that it is not pornographic. . . . It is because Joyce has been loyal to his technique and has not funked its necessary implications, but has honestly attempted to tell fully what his characters think about, that he has been the subject of so many attacks and that his purpose has

[4] *Cw.* v. *Friede*, 271 Mass. 318; 171 N. E. 472 (1930).
[5] Mass. Acts, 1930, c. 162.
[6] *U.S.* v. *One Book Called* '*Ulysses*', 5 F. Supp. 182. (S.D., N.Y.) (1933.)

been so often misunderstood and misrepresented. For his attempt sincerely and honestly to realise his objective has required him incidentally to use certain words which are generally considered dirty words and has led at times to what many think is a too poignant preoccupation with sex in the thoughts of his characters. The words which are criticised as dirty are old Saxon words known to almost all men and, I venture, to many women, and are such words as would be naturally and habitually used, I believe, by the types of folk whose life, physical and mental, Joyce is seeking to describe. In respect of the recurrent emergence of the theme of sex in the minds of his characters, it must always be remembered that his locale was Celtic and his season Spring. Whether or not one enjoys such a technique as Joyce uses is a matter of taste on which disagreement or argument is futile, but to subject that technique to the standards of some other technique seems to me to be little short of absurd. Accordingly I hold that *Ulysses* is a sincere and honest book and I think that the criticisms of it are entirely disposed of by its rationale.

The judge having declared that he had found nothing which could be described as 'dirt for dirt's sake', went on to apply an objective test to decide whether the book should be considered obscene.

The meaning of the word obscene [he said] as legally defined by the courts is: tending to stir the sex impulses or to lead to sexually impure and lustful thoughts.[7] Whether a particular book would tend to excite such impulses and thoughts must be tested by the court's opinion as to its effect on a person with average sex instincts—what the French would call *l'homme moyen sensuel*—who plays in this branch of legal inquiry, the same rôle of hypothetical reagent as does the 'reasonable man' in the law of torts and 'the man learned in the art' on questions of invention in patent law. . . . It is only with the normal person that the law is concerned. Such a test as I have described, therefore, is the only proper test of obscenity in the case of a book like *Ulysses* which is a sincere and serious attempt to devise a new literary method for the observation and description of mankind. I am quite aware that owing to some of its scenes *Ulysses* is a rather strong draught to ask some sensitive, though normal, persons to take. But my considered opinion, after long reflection, is that whilst in many places the effect of *Ulysses* on the reader undoubtedly is somewhat emetic, nowhere does it tend to be an aphrodisiac. *Ulysses* may therefore be admitted into the United States.

[7] *Dunlop* v. *U.S.*, 165 U. S. 486, 501. *U.S.* v. *One Book Entitled 'Married Love'*, 48 F. (2d) 821, 824, etc. (S.D.N.Y.) (1933).

From this decision of the District Court the Attorney-General appealed and on 7 August 1934 the appeal was dismissed by the United States Court of Appeals.[8]

> That numerous long passages in *Ulysses* contain matter that is obscene under any fair definition of the word cannot be gainsaid, [said Judge Hand] yet they are relevant to the purpose of depicting the thoughts of the characters and are introduced to give meaning to the whole, rather than to promote lust or portray filth for its own sake. The net effect even of portions most open to attack, such as the closing monologue of the wife of Leopold Bloom, is pitiful and tragic, rather than lustful. . . . The book as a whole is not pornographic, and while in not a few spots it is coarse, blasphemous and obscene, it does not in our opinion, tend to promote lust. The erotic passages are submerged in the book as a whole and have little resultant effect.
>
> It is settled [he went on] at least so far as this court is concerned, that works of physiology, medicine, science, and sex instruction are not within the statute, though to some extent and among some persons they may tend to promote lustful thoughts.[9] We think the same immunity should apply to literature as to science where the presentation, when viewed objectively, is sincere and the erotic matter is not introduced to promote lust and does not furnish the dominant note of the publication. The question in each case is whether a publication taken as a whole has a libidinous effect. The book before us has such portentous length, is written with such evident truthfulness in its depiction of certain types of humanity, and is so little erotic in its resultant, that it does not fall within the forbidden class.

Judge Hand went on to approve the judgement of Judge Andrews in the New York Court of Appeals when he acquitted the seller of Gautier's *Mademoiselle de Maupin* and in particular his words:

> No work may be judged from a selection of such paragraphs alone. Printed by themselves they might, as a matter of law, come within the prohibition of the statute. So might a similar selection from Aristophanes or Chaucer or Boccaccio or even from the Bible. The book, however, must be considered broadly as a whole.
>
> We believe [concluded Judge Hand] that the proper test of whether a given book is obscene is its dominant effect. In applying this test, relevancy of the objectionable parts to the theme, the

[8] *U.S.* v. *One Book Entitled 'Ulysses'*, 72 F. (2d) 705 (2nd Cir.) (1934).
[9] *U.S.* v. *Dennet*, 39 Fed. (2d) 564 (2nd Cir.) (1930).

> established reputation of the work in the estimation of approved critics, if the book is modern, and the verdict of the past if it is ancient, are persuasive pieces of evidence, for works of art are not likely to sustain a high position with no better warrant for their existence than their obscene content. . . . We think that *Ulysses* is a book of originality and sincerity of treatment and that it has not the effect of promoting lust. Accordingly it does not fall within the statute, even though it justly may offend many.

Judge Manton dissented:

> The decision to be made is dependent entirely upon the reading matter found on the objectionable pages of the book. . . . Who can doubt the obscenity of this book after a reading of the pages referred to, which are too indecent to add as a footnote to this opinion? Its characterisation as obscene should be quite unanimous by all who read it. . . . No matter what may be said on the side of letters, the effect on the community can and must be the sole determining factor. . . . If we disregard the protection of the morals of the susceptible, are we to consider merely the benefits and pleasures derived from letters by those who pose as the more highly developed and intelligent? To do so would show an utter disregard for the standards of decency of the community as a whole and an utter disregard for the effect of the book upon the average less sophisticated member of society—not to mention the adolescent. The court cannot indulge any instinct it may have to foster letters. The statute is designed to protect society at large—of that there can be no dispute—notwithstanding the deprivation of benefits to a few, a work must be condemned if it has a depraving influence.

Certain propositions of law follow from the *Ulysses* case. First, the purpose of the author is a relevant factor in determining a book's obscenity although it is not the ultimate test. Secondly, the test of obscenity is a book's dominant effect and not the presence of isolated obscene passages. Thirdly, in considering the effect of the book, the court must take as its standard 'the reasonable man' and not an abnormal adult or a child.* Fourthly, in judging whether a book is obscene, literary or artistic merit should be weighed against incidental obscenity, and to assist the court in this assessment the opinions of literary critics are admissible evidence.

* This was not followed in *U.S.* v. *Levine*, 83 F. (2d) 156 (2nd Cir.) (1936), where the judge said: 'The standard must be the likelihood that the work will so much arouse the salacity of the reader to whom it is sent as to outweigh any literary, scientific or other merits it may have in that reader's hands'.

The *Ulysses* case applies principally to federal courts and although it has been followed in many state courts, in others the Hicklin rule is still applied.[10] Again certain states have modified the *Ulysses* judgement accepting some of the propositions but rejecting others. Thus in *Commonwealth* v. *Isenstadt* (1945), the Supreme Court of Massachusetts rejected as irrelevant the purpose of the author and did not accept the admission of book reviews as evidence.[11] Such evidence was also excluded in a Californian prosecution for publishing Henry Miller's *Tropic of Cancer* and *Tropic of Capricorn.*

> There is no direct authority [said the judge] for the proposition supported by claimant that the estimates or criticism of so-called literary experts are relevant. The Statements in the *Ulysses* case to this effect and in *U.S.* v. *Levine*[12] were purely dicta as in both cases all that was ever submitted to the lower court or before the higher court were the books themselves.[13]

Thus it must not be assumed that the *Ulysses* judgement is everywhere followed in the United States, nor that the Hicklin rule has been finally abolished.

'GOD'S LITTLE ACRE'

A similar judgement to that in the *Ulysses* case was delivered in New York in 1933 by magistrate Benjamin Greenspan, when he cleared Erskine Caldwell's *God's Little Acre* of a charge of being obscene.

> The author [said the magistrate] has set out to paint a realistic picture. Such pictures necessarily contain certain details. Because these details related to what is popularly called the sex side of life portrayed with brutal frankness, the court may not say that the picture should not have been created at all. The language too is undoubtedly coarse and vulgar. The court may not require the author to put refined language into the mouths of primitive people. The book as a whole is very clearly not a work of pornography. It is not necessary for the court to decide whether it

[10] For example: *U.S.* v. *Two Obscene Books*, 99 F. Supp. 760 (N.D. Calif.) (1951); *Hadley* v. *State*, 205 Ark. 1027, 172 S. W. (2d) 237 (1943); *King* v. *Commonwealth*, 313 Ky. 741, 233 S. W. (2d) 522 (1950); *Cw.* v. *Donaducy*, 167 Pa. Super 611, 76 A. (2d) 440 (1950).

[11] 318 Mass. 543, 62 N. E. (2d) 840 (1945). The latter point is academic since such evidence is now admitted by statute. Mass. Acts, 1945, c. 278, para. 28F.

[12] 83 F. (2d) 156 (2nd Cir.) (1936).

[13] *U.S.* v. *Two Obscene Books*, 92 F. S., 934, (U.S. Dis. Crt., N. California) (1950).

is an important work of literature. Its subject matter constitutes a legitimate field for literary effort and the treatment also is legitimate. The court must consider the book as a whole even though some paragraphs standing by themselves might be objectionable.[14]

Apart from this duality of standard, American law is further complicated by the existence in every state and territory—except New Mexico and Alaska—of special obscenity statutes. The language in these statutes varies, but all condemn 'the writing, composition, printing, publishing, sale, distribution, keeping for sale, giving, loan, or exhibition of any obscene writing, paper, book, picture, print, cast, figure, or the advertisement thereof'. Most of the statutes provide for heavier penalties where the obscene materials are distributed or sold to minors. In addition to the statutes there are innumerable city ordinances which punish the distribution or exhibition of obscene matter.

THE CONSTITUTIONAL ISSUE

The question whether statutes banning obscene books were unconstitutional was raised in 1948 in Doubleday's case.[15] * In 1946 Edmund Wilson, a leading American critic, published *Memoirs of Hecate County*. The book caused wide controversy, some critics dubbing it a 'pathological joke',[16] others hailing it as a 'literary event'.[17] † The New York Society for the Suppression of

[14] *People of State of N.Y.* v. *Viking Press Inc.*, 147 Misc. (N. Y.) 813, 264 N.Y. Supp. (534) (1933). Some cases where the *Ulysses* ruling has been applied are: *U.S.* v. *Levine*, 83 F. (2d) 156 (2nd Cir., 1936); *Parmelee* v. *U.S.*, 113 F. (2d) 729 (D.C. Cir.) (1940); *New American Lib. of World Lit.* v. *Allen*, 114 F. Supp. 823 (N.D. Ohio) (1953); *Bantam Books* v. *Melko*, 25 N. J. Super 292, 96 A. (2d) 47 (1953); *St. Paul* v. *Fredkove*, 38 Minn. Munic. 362 (Mun. Crt.) (1953).

[15] *Doubleday and Co.* v. *New York*, 335 U. S. 848 (1948).

* In 1954 the Supreme Court ruled unanimously that State Censorship Boards cannot ban films on grounds of immorality because to do so would infringe the 'freedom of speech' guaranteed by the constitution. (*The Times*, 19 January 1954.) *Commercial Pictures Corp.* v. *Regents of Univ. of N.Y.*, 346 U. S. 587 (1954).

[16] *Commonweal*, p. 660 (12 April 1946).

[17] 17 *Time* 102 (25 March 1946).

† The *New Republic's* comment is worth recording: 'The descriptions of love are so zoological, the narrator is so intent on making a safari through the bedroom with gun and microscope, that we find he is preserving only the stuffed and mounted hides of his love affairs: what has disappeared is simply their passion, the breath of their life. And the reader feels like those children in a very progressive school who went to their teacher with a question, "We know all about how babies come to be born," they said, "but what we can't understand is why people like to do it".' (25 March 1946.)

Vice denounced the book [18] and the publishers were charged with the publication of an obscene work.

The first trial took place before three judges in the New York Court of Special Sessions. Professor Lionel Trilling gave evidence as to the literary and moral quality of the book, but despite his intervention the book was condemned. 'The decision', commented *Time* magazine, 'made thousands of citizens more impatient than ever to get their morals ruined. It also proved again that finding a yardstick for proving a serious work indecent is as difficult as weighing a pound of waltzing mice.' [19] Meanwhile, the Defence had raised the constitutional question, claiming that the liberty of the Press under the New York Constitution and the XIVth amendment to the United States Constitution had been infringed. The XIVth Amendment (1868) states: 'No state shall make or enforce any law which shall abridge the privileges or immunities of citizens of the United States: nor shall any state deprive any person of life, liberty, or property, without due process of law; nor deny to any person within its jurisdiction the equal protection of the laws'. This was read by the Defence in relation to the 1st Amendment (1791): 'Congress shall make no law respecting an establishment of religion, or prohibiting the free exercise thereof; or abridging the freedom of speech, or of the press; or the right of the people peaceably to assemble, and to petition the government for a redress of grievances'.

Neither the Appellate Division of the Supreme Court of New York nor the Court of Appeals, both of which confirmed the decision, made any comment on the constitutional issue.[20] The case finally reached the United States Supreme Court, where the sole issue before the court was that of freedom of expression under the XIVth amendment. Counsel for the Defence claimed that works of literature dealing with sex were entitled to the same constitutional protection as any other literature and could only be suppressed if they constituted a 'clear and present danger' to some substantial interest of the state. On this point the court divided equally, four voting for the upholding of the conviction and four voting against.[21]

The constitutional argument was taken up and applied by Judge Bok in the Philadelphia case of *Commonwealth* v. *Gordon* in 1949.[22]

[18] 150 Publ. Wk. 287 (1946).

[19] 48 *Time* 23–5 (9 December 1946).

[20] 272 App Div. 799, 71 N. Y. S. (2d) 736 (1st Dep't) (1947); 297 N. Y. 687, 77 N. E. (2d) 6 (1947).

[21] *Doubleday and Co.* v. *New York*, 335 U. S. 848 (1948). Frankfurter, J., was absent. Jackson, J., commented: 'If the court decided constitutional issues on the merits of literary works it would become the High Court of Obscenity'.

[22] 66 Pa. D. and C. 101 (1949), affd. *sub nom. Cw.* v. *Feigenbaum*, 166 Pa. Super 120; 70 A. (2d) 389 (1950).

In March 1948 members of the vice squad of Philadelphia's police department began seizing books from publishers and booksellers. The latter struck back and commenced an action to restrain the police from making any further seizures. The police answer to this was to initiate criminal proceedings. Nine books were indicted including *Sanctuary* and *Wild Palms*, by William Faulkner, *The Studs Lonigan Trilogy* and *A world I never made*, by James Farrel, and *God's Little Acre*, by Erskine Caldwell. Judge Bok fully reviewed the social issues and the cases before laying down his new test of obscenity:

> It will be asked [said the judge] whether one would care to have one's young daughter read these books. I suppose that by the time she is old enough to wish to read them she will have learned the biologic facts of life and the words that go with them. There is something seriously wrong at home if those facts have not been met and faced and sorted by then: it is not children so much as parents that should receive our concern about this. I should prefer that my three daughters meet the facts of life and the literature of the world in my library, than behind a neighbour's barn for I can face the adversary there directly. If the young ladies are appalled by what they read they can close the book at the bottom of page one: if they read further they will learn what is the world and its people and no parents who have been discerning with their children need fear the outcome.

Judge Bok then formulated his new test.

> I hold that s. 524 may not constitutionally be applied to any writing unless it is sexually impure and pornographic. It may then be applied as an exercise of the police power, only where there is a reasonable and demonstrable cause to believe that a crime or misdemeanour has been committed or is about to be committed, as the perceptible result of the publication and distribution of the writing in question: the opinion of anyone that a tendency thereto exists or that such a result is self-evident is insufficient and irrelevant. The causal connection between the book and the criminal behaviour must appear beyond a reasonable doubt. The criminal law is not in my opinion the '*custos morum* of the king's subjects' as *Regina* v. *Hicklin* states: it is only the custodian of the peace and good order that free men and women need for the shaping of their common destiny. There is no such proof in the instant case.

'Sexual impurity' in literature was defined by Judge Bok as 'any writing whose dominant purpose and effect is erotic allurement—that is to say a calculated and effective incitement to sexual desire.

It is the effect that counts more than the desire and no indictment can stand unless it can be shown.' *

UNOFFICIAL CENSORSHIP

In the United States the law is supplemented in its work of suppressing obscene literature by both official and unofficial censorship bodies. The most active unofficial body is the National Organisation for Decent Literature which was founded in 1938 by the Roman Catholic hierarchy. Its purpose was 'to devise a plan for organising a systematic campaign in all dioceses of the United States against the publication and sale of lewd magazine and brochure literature'. [23] With the great increase in the number of paper-bound books, it brought these publications within the scope of its activities.† The N.O.D.L. pursues its aim by the following activities: (1) arousing public opinion against objectionable magazines, comics, and paper-bound books; (2) more rigorous enforcement of existing law controlling obscene literature; (3) promotion of stricter legislation to suppress obscenity; (4) the preparation of monthly lists of publications disapproved by the organisation ‡; and (5) the visiting of news-stands and stores to persuade the owners to remove objectionable literature. Since the Organisation can work through diocesan machinery in every part of the United States, its campaign has been effective and met with considerable success. At the present time it is continuing.

Encouraged by N.O.D.L. activities several states set up official censorship boards. Thus in Georgia a statute passed in 1953 created

* The Gathings Committee, 1952, noted the close connection of Judge Bok with the publishing trade through his grandfather Cyrus H. K. Curtis, his brother, and his mother Mrs. Efram Zimbalist, a director of Bantam Books Inc. 'It should definitely not be assumed that any question whatever has arisen in the course of the committee's inquiries or drawn from the fact of Judge Bok's relationship to those associated with the Curtis Publishing Co. which reflects in any way whatever upon Judge Curtis Bok's honesty or integrity as a judge. It is however reasonably possible that having been associated so closely with the publishing business that he became imbued with a liberal conception of the tradition founded upon constitutional provision guaranteeing the freedom of the press.'

[23] *Drive for Decency in Print*. Report of the Bishops' Committee (1939).

† The sale of paper-bound books in pocket form began in 1939, when 'Pocket Books' published thirty-four titles which sold 1,508,000 copies. In 1953 nearly 300 million copies of 1,200 titles were sold. Ten major publishers control the business. See Lewis, *Paper Bound Books in America* (1952); Waller, *Paper Bound Books and Censorship*, 47 A. L. A. Bull. 474 (November 1953); 48 *Fortune* 123 (September 1953).

‡ Among books disapproved are: Somerset Maugham's *The Painted Veil*, Zola's *Nana* and *Theresa*, William Faulkner's *Sanctuary* and *Pylon*, and Pierre Louys' *Collected Works*.

a State Literature Commission to prohibit the distribution of obscene literature and to recommend prosecutions.[24] Before deciding on a book's obscenity the commission asks the following questions: (1) What is the general and dominant theme? (2) What degree of sincerity of purpose is evident? (3) What is the literary or scientific worth? (4) What channels of distribution are employed? (5) What are the contemporary attitudes of reasonable men towards such matters? (6) What types of readers may be reasonably expected to peruse the publication? (7) Is there evidence of pornographic intent? (8) What impression will be created in the mind of the reader upon reading the work as a whole? Favourable replies to all these questions means that the book is cleared, otherwise it is classed as 'possibly obscene'. After a year of operation the commission had taken action against only four paper-bound books.

More stringent standards were applied by the Board of Review set up in St. Cloud, Minnesota, in 1950. The ordinance setting up the Board prohibited the sale of any book that

> prominently features an account of horrors, robberies, murders, arson, assault with caustic chemicals, assault with a deadly weapon, burglary, kidnapping, mayhem, rape, theft, voluntary manslaughter, ridicule of law enforcement or parental authority; or are obscene, immoral, lewd, or are suggestively obscene, immoral or lewd; or ridicules any person or persons by reason of race, creed, or color; or advocates un-American or subversive activities.

Reviewers were not required to read the whole book before placing it on the banned list.*

Other cities and states have no official boards, but the police have special bureaux for censoring books. The most important of these is the Detroit 'license and censor' bureau whose activities extend to all of Wayne County and indirectly to other parts of the country. Objectionable books are submitted to the County Prosecutor for an opinion and if he reports unfavourably the distributor of the book is warned. Monthly lists of obscene books are also sent to retailers, with a request to withdraw them from circulation. The Detroit bureau's influence is increased by the custom of some publishers of submitting books in manuscript before publication. Since it is not practicable to issue different editions of the same book for distribution in different parts of the country, the control exercised by Detroit is to some extent nation wide.[25]

[24] *Ga. Code Ann.*, para. 26—6301 (1953).

* The Board ceased operation in 1953 after 'banning' three hundred paper-bound books.

[25] *Minneapolis Star*, 11 February 1946.

THE GATHINGS COMMITTEE

In May 1952 the House of Representatives set up a Select Committee on Current Pornographic Materials, to investigate the extent of the obscene-book trade and to make recommendations for changes in the law. In December the Committee presented its report together with a minority report dissenting from the majority's conclusions.

> Pornography [said the report] is big business. The extent to which the profit motive has brushed aside all generally accepted standards of decency and good taste and substituted inferior moral standards has become not only a national disgrace, but a menace to our civic welfare as well. In addition to their other vices so called 'comics' for children are build ups for later sales to adults of low ethical standards. Cartoon comic books, a degenerate outgrowth of long established newspaper comic strips were 'bootlegged' when they first made their appearance, but are now flaunted openly in public markets. . . . What are known in the trade as 'art' or 'science' magazines are often pseudo art and science publications promoted by charlatans. They should not be confused with legitimate books containing charts and pictures designed to aid sincere students of the arts and sciences. Many go far beyond the bounds of decency in text, illustrations and advertisements. They are the products of commercial exploitation, devoid of literary merit and worthless as art or science. The so-called pocket-size books which originally started out as reprints of standard works have largely degenerated into media for the dissemination of artful appeals to sensuality, immorality, filth, perversion and degeneracy. The exaltation of passion above principle, and the identification of lust with love are so prevalent that the casual reader of such 'literature' might easily conclude that all married persons are habitually adulterous and all teen-agers completely devoid of any sex inhibitions.' [26]

The Committee divided pornography into three classes, pocket books, magazines and comics. No figures were given for the number of pornographic magazines in circulation, but the Committee did indicate the categories of magazines which they found most objectionable. The indiscriminate sale of 'cheesecake' magazines to children and adults was singled out: 'cheesecake', being a term of art, used in the trade to describe 'photographs of girls dressed in scanty attire, or partly clothed, or fully dressed but in revealing poses,

[26] Union Calendar 797. 82nd Congress, 2nd Session. *Report of Pornographic Materials*. House Report No. 2510.

but always emphasising shapeliness'. Nudist magazines and those which pandered to homosexuals by pictures of 'the male body beautiful' were also condemned. The Committee drew attention to the flourishing photographic trade built up in New York to supply pictures to the magazines, twelve firms keeping 'vast stockpiles' of 'cheesecake' pictures and others portraying deeds of 'incredible violence'.

HORROR COMICS

Much space in the report was devoted to the problem of criminal and horror comics, intended to be read by children. The 'horror comic' problem is now world-wide but it originated in the United States. Dr. Wertham in his book *Seduction of the Innocent* [27] pointed out that this trade was a postwar phenomenon. In 1937 only eighteen crime comic titles existed, but by 1948 one hundred and seven new titles had appeared. In 1947 such comics represented only one-tenth of the total comics available, but by 1954 they had become the vast majority.* Dr. Wertham emphasised the violence, horror, and sadism of these comics, claiming that they had become a new form of pornography. Of 'Jungle' comics, he wrote:

> Daggers, claws, guns, wild animals, well or over-developed girls in brassières and as little else as possible, dark 'natives', fires, stakes, posts, chains, ropes, big-chested and heavily muscled Nordic he-men dominate the stage. They contain such details as one girl squirting fiery 'radium dust' on the protruding breasts of another girl ('I think I've discovered your Achilles' heel, chum'); white men banging natives around; a close-up view of the branded breast of a girl; a girl about to be blinded. . . . While the white people in jungle books are blond and athletic and shapely, the idea conveyed about the natives is that they are fleeting transitions between apes and monkeys.

Developing this point elsewhere he wrote:

> There are two kinds of people, on the one hand is the tall, blond, regular-featured man sometimes disguised as superman, and the pretty, young, blonde girl with super breast. On the other hand are the inferior people: natives, primitives, savages, ape men, negroes, Jews, Indians, Italians, Slavs, Chinese and Japanese, immigrants

[27] Rinehart, New York (1953–4). Library of Congress, No. 54/5890.

* In 1954 the comics business in the U.S.A. was reported by the University of California as being worth 100 million dollars a year; more than that spent on the book supply of elementary and secondary schools. A survey showed that 25 per cent. of high school graduates read comics, 16 per cent. of adult college graduates and 12 per cent. of the nation's school teachers.

> of every description, people with irregular features, swarthy skins, physical deformities, oriental features. In some crime comics the first class sometimes wears some kind of superman uniform, while the second class is in mufti. The brunt of this imputed inferiority in whole groups of people is directed against coloured people and foreign born.

Thus the hero in one comic showing negroes and bombs being thrown from a plane, shouts: 'Bombs and bums away'.

One picture reproduced in the book suffices to indicate the nature of the 'comics'. Two men are tied by their feet to the rear bumper of a car and lie face down. One has his hands tied behind his back and the lower part of his face is dragging in the road. The other man's hands are not tied and his arms are stretched out. The three men in the car are talking. 'A couple more miles oughta do th' trick.' 'It better. These . . . gravel roads are tough on tyres.' 'But ya gotta admit there's nothing like them for ERASING FACES.' Next to the balloons containing this dialogue is a grinning face: 'Superb. Even Big Phil will admire this job . . . if he lives long enough to identify the meat.'

The estimated circulation of these comics in the United States is ninety million a month, a total higher than the combined circulation of books, magazines and periodicals. It is only exceeded by the circulation of the daily newspapers. The Committee condemned the comics as glorifying crime, and making a mockery of democratic living and respect for law and order.*

In 1948 an attempt to suppress the comics was made in New York under a statute forbidding the publication of stories 'principally made up of pictures or stories of deeds of bloodshed, lust or crime'.[28]

* One comic, selected at random, was analysed and the following table compiled:

1. Heads cut off by guillotine (3).
2. Heads cut off by bloody butcher cleaver (1).
3. Heads blown off by shotgun (1).
4. Woman being strangled (1).
5. Violent beatings (3).
6. Sleeping man about to be bludgeoned to death with sledgehammer (1).
7. Death sweat (1).
8. Piles of skulls and human bones (2).
9. Dead man in closet (naked) (1).
10. Bloody axes (1).
11. Men turned into worms (and stepped on) (11).
12. Bloody butcher cleaver (1).
13. Women being eaten alive by worms (1).
14. Scaly vampire (slimy variety) sucking blood (1).

The comic was entitled: *Journey into Fear*.

[28] *Winters* v. *New York*, 333 U. S. 507, 510 (1948).

The Supreme Court of the United States held the statute unconstitutional as being too vague and unclear. Mr. Justice Frankfurter dissented:

> We believe that the destructive and adventurous potentialities of boys and adolescents and of adults of weak character are often stimulated by collections of pictures and stories of criminal deeds of bloodshed or lust so massed as to incite to violent and depraved crimes against the person; and . . . we believe that such juveniles . . . do, in fact, commit such crimes at least partly because incited to do so by such publications . . . in any event there is nothing of any possible value to society in such publications so that there is no gain to the State, whether in edification or enlightenment or good of any kind . . . and the possibility of harm by restricting free utterance through harmless publications is too remote and too negligible a consequence of dealing with the evil publications, with which we are all concerned.

In 1951 the New York State Legislative Committee investigated the problem of children's comics and concluded that they 'impair the ethical development of children and are a contributing factor leading to juvenile delinquency'. A Bill to ban the comics was passed by both the Assembly and the Senate, but was vetoed by Governor Dewey.*

To deal with this threefold problem the Committee proposed certain minor changes in the Federal law. It suggested that the law prohibiting the transportation of obscene books should be extended to cover not only common carriers as under the existing law but also carriage by private transport. It further recommended that the Postmaster-General should be given power to impound mail addressed to a person carrying on an obscene-book trade through the post for purpose of gain and that the Post Office should be exempted from the Administrative Procedure Act.† Apart from these modifications the Committee recommended no changes in the law, but called upon the publishing trade to set its house in order.

> The Publishing Industry should recognise the growing public opposition to that proportion of its output which may be classified as 'border line' or 'objectionable' and take the steps necessary to its elimination on its own initiative, rather than allow this

* In 1955 a new Bill was drafted and approved by the legislature and the governor, Mr. Harriman.

† This Act contains certain safeguards, the operation of which delay the seizing of mail. A witness before the Committee testified that this rendered post office action nugatory in many cases.

opposition to increase to the point where the public will demand governmental action.

The minority report dissented vigorously from the majority conclusions and condemned the working methods of the Committee.* It accused the Committee of judging books by their covers and isolated passages without attempting to read them as a whole.† Furthermore, said the dissenters,

> There is a distinction between what may broadly be classified as obscene and what falls within the realm of free thought and creative expression, which is, perhaps, the most basic and fundamental principle in the free way of life. It is these distinctions that the Committee in its report and in its proceedings has clearly failed to recognise.

In March 1955 The Senate Committee on Juvenile Delinquency issued an interim report on comic books.[29] The report recommended against legislative action but advised the industry to reform itself. The report throws no new light on the connection between reading horror comics and the committing of delinquent acts.

* Signed by two of the nine members. One other member abstained.

† Thus the Committee condemned *Twilight Men*, by André Tellier, on the basis of the following passage. 'They embraced. We lie here like pagans rejoicing in a love that has been practised since the world began, but which is somehow struck off the white list of loves. In his heart he felt justified by instinct, by the mystic drawing within him. It is love, he reflected, with the boy's soft cheek pressing on his own. Men alone denied the holiness and saw shame and degradation in this one aspect of love . . . honour and nobility in the other. In spite of this the unknown law attracted and held and drew. They embraced. . . .'

[29] No. 62 of 1955.

CHAPTER VIII

THE IRISH CENSORSHIP: AN EXPERIMENT

ALONE amongst the English-speaking countries, with the exception of Queensland where a censorship board was established in 1954, Ireland possesses a full-scale administrative book censorship. Ireland's film censorship also differs from its English equivalent in being statutory and official, while for the Irish theatre there is no censorship of any kind.

THE STAGE

The Theatres Act of 1843 did not apply to Ireland, but this was not of importance until the revival of the Irish theatre in the early years of this century. It was not until 1904 that the Abbey Theatre opened, but the movement towards a national theatre had begun some years before. In 1899 the first performance of Yeats's *Countess Cathleen* was given in Dublin and aroused bitter controversy. This was theological not moral, the play being denounced as an insult to the Catholic faith. Its theme is the selling of men's souls to the devil, and the sacrifice which the Countess Cathleen makes in giving up her own soul for the redemption of her countrymen's. Before the first performance a pamphlet, *Souls for Gold*, had been circulated calling on Irishmen to protest against the 'insult to their faith', and the response was so overwhelming that the police had to be called to suppress a first-night riot. A further storm was occasioned by the production in 1903 of Synge's *Shadow of the Glen*, the insult this time being to Irish motherhood. Arthur Griffith had obtained a copy of the script in advance and used it to attack the play in the *United Irishman*. Again the attack was not primarily moral but nationalist, although one reviewer described it as 'A Boccaccio story masquerading as an Irish play'. In 1905 an outburst of abuse greeted Synge's new play, *The Well of the Saints*, but this and the other demonstrations were nothing compared to the hurricane of vilification which his later play, *The Playboy of the Western World* aroused, on its production in 1907.

Irish Puritanism is well illustrated by this outburst, since the objections centred on the use of the word 'shift' in the course of the play. The audience had been restive from the first, but the fighting only broke out when Christy, played by W. G. Fay, uttered the line: 'It's Pegeen I'm seeking only, and what'd I care if you brought me a drift of chosen females standing in their shifts itself, maybe from this place to the Eastern world'. This was too much for the susceptibilities of the audience; it turned them, in the words of Fay himself, into 'a veritable mob of howling devils'. Free-fights broke out in the stalls, the conductor, Mr. Hillis, was injured, and the stage narrowly escaped being stormed. This was on the Saturday, but by Monday, when the second performance was due, the opposition was even better organised. They made so much noise that the cast was compelled to go through the motions of the play without speaking a word. The uproar continued for the following performances, and was only quelled by lining the floor with felt to muffle the noise of stamping feet, and by calling in the police. An indignant letter signed 'Girl in the West', which appeared in a Dublin paper, typifies the popular reaction to the play: 'Every character', she wrote, 'uses coarse expressions and Miss Allgood (one of the most charming actresses I have ever seen) is forced to use a word indicating an essential item of female attire which the lady would probably never utter in ordinary circumstances even to herself.' [1] At the time and since, there have been various demands for the institution of a theatre censorship, but these have met with little response. As a result the Irish theatre has been considerably freer than the English, and when *The Showing Up of Blanco Posnet* was denied a licence by the Lord Chamberlain in 1909, Lady Gregory was able to produce it with impunity in Dublin.

FILM CENSORSHIP

Ireland's first censorship experiment was that for films, instituted in 1923. The Censorship of Films Act forbids any picture to be exhibited in public unless a certificate has first been obtained from the official censor, appointed by the government. From his decision an appeal lies to an Appeal Board of nine set up by the Act, whose decision is by majority vote. The Censor is obliged to grant a certificate for any film: 'unless he is of opinion that such picture or some part thereof is unfit for general exhibition in public by reason of its being indecent, obscene or blasphemous, or because the exhibition thereof in public would tend to inculcate principles contrary to

[1] Quoted in *The Fays of the Abbey Theatre*, W. G. Fay and C. Carswell (London 1935).

public morality or would be otherwise subversive of public morality'.[2]

Posters advertising films were not, however, subject to the Act, and in 1925 this loophole was closed by requiring all such advertisements to be first submitted to the Censor, and making it a criminal offence to exhibit them without his permission.[3] The Censor must forbid such exhibition if he finds that the advertisements are indecent or blasphemous or contrary to public morality. A defence is provided by the Act to those who show that they did not know or could not have reasonably known of the prohibition of the advertisements, or who were told by the supplier that no such prohibition existed. In 1930 the cinema legislation was further amended to cover talking films.[4]

On the whole this censorship has worked well and there has been little complaint. In 1952 nineteen films were banned and one hundred and ninety-six were cut. In five cases the decision of the censor was reversed by the Appeal Board.

THE 'EVIL LITERATURE' COMMITTEE

In 1926 the Dail appointed a committee to investigate the nature and extent of the trade in 'evil literature'. The Committee's terms of reference were: 'To consider and report whether it is necessary or advisable in the interests of public morality to extend the existing powers of the state to prohibit or restrict the sale and circulation of printed matter.' [5] The reasons for appointing this Committee are obscure, since there does not seem to have been an extensive trade in pornography. From 1922 to 1926 under the common law of 'obscene libel' there had been only five prosecutions, all resulting in convictions.[6]

In its report the Committee unanimously recommended the substitution of a preventive censorship for the sanctions of the criminal law. It advised that the proposed Board should ban 'books written with a corrupt intent or aiming at circulation by reason of their appeals to sensual or corrupt instincts and passions', but should discriminate between these and other books, 'having a purely literary aim in view, but which as part of their reflection of the world admit representation of the vices or the passions that exist'. The report

[2] Censorship of Films Act, 1923, No. 23.

[3] Censorship of Films (Amendment) Act, 1925, No. 21.

[4] Censorship of Films Act, 1930, No. 13.

[5] *Report of the Committee on Evil Literature* (1926). The Stationery Office, Dublin.

[6] *Dail Reports*, Vol. XXVII, p. 175. Answer of Minister of Justice.

went on to warn against a censorship designed exclusively for the protection of youth:

> The censorship that should protect the young from literary influences pernicious to the immature is the censorship exercised in the home and the school and through the spiritual director. But literature has never been restricted in any country to writings that meet the standard to be observed in works intended only for the youth and the maiden.

The Committee unanimously recommended that birth-control propaganda should be made illegal.

THE CENSORSHIP BOARD

In 1928 the government introduced a Bill to give effect to these proposals which became law in the following year. Subject to the amendments introduced by the Censorship Act of 1946, the 1929 Act governs the legal position today.* By it the Minister of Justice was empowered to set up a censorship board of five, who were to hold office for three years.† To ban a book there must be three affirmative votes, and not more than one dissentient. The Board can consider books or periodicals on its own initiative, but in practice the majority of books it considers are referred to it either by the Minister or the public. The censorship is moral not theological, no power being given to ban books hostile to the Catholic Church, unless they advocate 'the unnatural prevention of conception, or the procurement of abortion or miscarriage, or the use of any method, treatment or appliance for the purpose of such prevention or procurement'. 'Indecency' and 'obscenity' are the Board's quarries, 'indecency' being defined to include 'suggestive of, or inciting to, sexual immorality or unnatural vice or likely in any other similar way to deprave or corrupt'. Under the 1929 Act the Board had to find a book obscene in 'its general tendency', before issuing a ban, but these words were omitted in the 1946 legislation.

When judging books the Board is required to consider their 'general tenor'; their literary, artistic, scientific or historic merit; the language in which they are written; the nature and extent of their circulation; and the class of reader who may reasonably be expected to read them. Power is also given to the Board to communicate with the author or publisher of the book, and it may take into account any representation that either may wish to make.

* This power is confirmed by Article 40 of the 1937 Constitution: 'Publication or utterance of blasphemous, seditious, or indecent matter is an offence which shall be punishable in accordance with law'.

† Five years under the 1946 Act.

Customs officers may seize any banned books in the possession of travellers, but the travellers are not guilty of any offence if they were importing the books for their personal use. Customs officers may also seize books and refer them to the Board if they suspect them of being obscene, but not if the books are part of a traveller's personal luggage.

Periodicals which the Board considers have been 'usually or frequently' indecent or obscene, or which advocate birth control or abortion, or which 'have devoted an unduly large proportion of space to the publication of matter relating to crime', may be banned by the Board. The period for which they may be banned varies from one year to three months.*

The Board is under a duty to compile a list of banned books and periodicals and make it available for public inspection. Penalties for selling or distributing any book on this list are a fine of not more than one hundred pounds, or imprisonment up to six months, or both, as well as the forefeiture of the book in every case. The common law offence of publishing an obscene libel remains, but, in practice, prosecutions are seldom brought.

Until 1946 the decision of the Censorship Board had been final, but as a result of serious complaints about the working of the censorship an Appeal Board was then set up. The Board has five members, of whom the chairman must be either a judge or a practising barrister or solicitor of not less than seven years' standing. Author, editor, or publisher of any work banned by the Lower Board, or any five members of the Oireachtas † may within twelve months of the ban being imposed appeal to the Board. The Board may affirm, revoke, or vary the order, but no alteration is to be made unless at least three members are in favour of a change. Only one appeal is allowed in respect of each book, but if a new edition is published after the date of the ban a separate appeal may be brought.‡

* New bans may, however, be issued to run successively:

Periodicals, etc., banned have included: *Daily Worker* (eight years), *News of the World* (since 1930); *Razzle* (since 1935); *Sunday Pictorial* (since 1947); *Esquire* (since 1950); *Illustrated* (18 December 1953); *Sunday Express* (18 December 1953). Many English Sunday papers produce a special Irish edition substituting a serialised life of a saint for the lurid Sunday serial considered suitable for English readers.

† The Irish Parliament.

‡ The Appeal Board has much improved the working of the censorship and has met with general approval. Relations with the Lower Board have, however, been strained. In October 1948 the *Sunday Times* and *Observer* noted that the Censorship Board had revised its opinion about a book. On 8 October a letter from the Secretary of the Lower Board appeared in both papers. 'I am directed by the Censorship of Publications Board to inform you that this is incorrect. The ban on the book in question was removed by the Appeal Board and not by

When the Censorship Bill was debated in the Oireachtas during 1928 and 1929 it was criticised, but only by a minority. Professor Tierney feared 'that under the authority of the Dail a list of prohibited books will be produced which will make a laughing stock of this country', and Sir James Craig opposed the Bill because he objected to having his reading prescribed by 'four or five cranks'. These were isolated objections, and the principles of the Bill met with general approval. A stalwart opponent was, however, Yeats, himself a senator, but absent in England at the time.* He contented himself with writing a trenchant article in *The Spectator* [7]:

> The bill if it becomes law will give one man the Minister of Justice control over the substance of our thought, for its definition of indecency and such vague phrases as 'subversive of public morality', permit him to exclude the *Origin of Species*, Karl Marx's *Capital*, the novels of Flaubert, Balzac, Proust, all of which have been objected to somewhere on moral grounds, half the Greek and Roman classics, Anatole France, and everybody else on the Roman Index and all great love poetry. The government does not intend these things to happen, the holy gunmen and 'The Society of Angelic Welfare' do not intend these things to happen; but in legislation intention is nothing and the letter of the law is everything, and no government has the right whether to flatter fanatics or in mere vagueness of mind to forge an instrument of tyranny and say that it will never be used. Above all they have not the right to say it here in Ireland where until the other day the majority of children left school at twelve years old, and where even now according to its own inspectors, no primary schoolmaster opens a book after school hours.
>
> I know those reasonable committeemen who never served any cause but always make common cause against the solitary man of imagination or intellect. Had such a committee with even the two Protestant clergymen upon it somebody suggests, censored the stage a while back, my theatre, now the State theatre, would never have survived its first years. It now performs amid popular applause four plays of which two when first performed caused riots, three had to be protected by the police, while all four had to face the denunciations of press and public. Speaking from the

the Censorship Board which originally imposed the ban and has not changed its opinion of the book.' Such a letter opens interesting possibilities for English High Court judges overruled by the Court of Appeal!

Between 1946 and 1955, 250 appeals were brought of which 220 were successful. One hundred and thirteen of these occurred in the first year and many were for books long banned. A year was allowed for appeals concerning such books. Many English publishers do not bother to appeal as Irish sales are negligible.

* Yeats ceased to be a senator the same year.

[7] 29 September 1928.

stage I told the last rioters, today's newspaper burners, that they were not the first to rock the cradle of a man of genius.

To this an indignant Irishman replied, denouncing somewhat irrelevantly the portrayal of the nude in art. 'There are things', he wrote, 'higher than art or literature or science, namely the morals, the virtues, the chastity of a nation. It is these things that make a nation great and not the others . . . one saint is worth them all in lifting a nation out of the slough of sexual passion and making it clean and pure and chaste.' [8]

BANNED BOOKS

In practice the working of the Board has justified many of the fears of those who opposed it from the outset. Up to the present time over four thousand books and nearly four hundred periodicals have been banned. In the list of banned books titles like *Hot Dames on Cold Slabs* and *Gun Moll for Hire* are found side by side with Proust's *Remembrance of Things Past* and André Gide's *If It Die.* Four winners of the Nobel Prize for Literature, and nearly every Irish writer of distinction, including St. John Gogarty, Liam O'Flaherty, Kate O'Brien and Sean O'Faolain appear in the list, but strangely enough James Joyce's *Ulysses* has never been banned. Irishmen may not read Charles Morgan's *The Fountain*, Somerset Maugham's *The Painted Veil*, Aldous Huxley's *Point Counter Point* or George Orwell's *Nineteen-Eighty-Four.* Four novels of H. G. Wells are banned, two of Hugh Walpole, and three of Alberto Moravia. Explicitly Catholic writers such as Bruce Marshall have been banned, and until released by the Appeal Board Grahame Greene's novels *The Heart of the Matter* and *The End of the Affair* were forbidden to Irish readers. The British Government's *Report of the Royal Commission on Population* (1949) was placed on the list, because it advocated birth control, and the same fate overtook Halliday Sutherland's *Laws of Life* despite the fact that it carried the imprint of the Roman Catholic Censor of the Archdiocese of Westminster.*

[8] *The Spectator*, 6 October 1928.

* Other banned books include:

H. E. Bates, *Dear Life*; Pearl S. Buck, *Portrait of Marriage*, *The Patriot*; Erskine Caldwell, *God's Little Acre*; Joyce Cary, *Prisoner of Grace*, *The Horse's Mouth*; Warwick Deeping, *Reprieve*; Theodore Dreiser, *Dawn*; Daphne du Maurier, *I'll Never Be Young Again*; William Faulkner, *Sanctuary*; C. S. Forester, *The African Queen*; Ernest Hemingway, *Across the River and into the Trees*; Christopher Isherwood, *Goodbye to Berlin*; Naomi Jacobs, *Fade Out*; Arthur Koestler, *Arrow in the Blue*; Sinclair Lewis, *Cass Timberlaine*; Angus Wilson, *Hemlock and After*.

Between them forty-four Irish writers have had one hundred and seventy books banned.

Undoubtedly, the Board has succeeded in keeping out of Ireland a great mass of pornography of a filthy and corrupting kind, but this has only been achieved at the price of depriving Irish readers of many of the best works of contemporary literature. In a debate in the Senate on 14 November 1945 Senator Kingsmill Moore described the Board's list as 'Everyman's guide to the modern classics', and added that the working of the censorship 'had affronted the general opinion of decent and responsible men; the effect of it has been to impose the view of five persons as a kind of fetter upon the intellect and information of the nation'.

Today, the Board is presided over by a parish priest who acts as chairman, the other members being a District Justice, a business man, and two professors. All are Roman Catholics. Books about which complaints have been made are screened by the Secretary, who sends out selected volumes to members of the Board, marking any objectionable passages.* On average fifty books are dealt with each month, and of the total books sent into the Board about a third remain unbanned. The Board holds a monthly meeting to exchange views, and make orders for the banning of books.† No reasons are given for decisions, and although the Board has the power to consult author or publisher, this power has never been exercised.

THE BOARD'S METHODS

In 1937 a Protestant member of the Board, Mr. Lyn Doyle, resigned in protest against its working methods. In a letter to the *Irish Times*,[9] he stated:

> The books are sent to the Minister by private objectors in different parts of the country. A permanent official marks by writing folio numbers on a card, passages that he thinks come under the Act. The marked books are then sent to the members of the Board in turn. Now the Board is required to make recommendations according to the general tendency of the book. It is nearly impossible to report on a general tendency after reading the marked passages. Even when one reads the book through afterwards, one is under the influence of the markings. There is another reason. Here I speak

* This method was approved by a conference presided over by the Minister of Justice, 2 February 1930. But in the original debate on the Act the Minister, Fitzgerald-Kenney, had stated: 'A book can be fairly condemned only where in its whole course it makes for evil, when its tenor is bad, when in some important part of it, it is indecent, when, I might put it this way, it is systematically indecent'. (*Dail Debates*, Vol. XXVI, Col. 594, 18 October 1928.)

† Under the 1929 Act the Board submitted its list of books to the Minister with recommendations that they should be banned. The 1946 Act gave the Board power to ban the books themselves.

[9] February 1937. Reprinted *Irish Times*, 3 May 1954.

for myself only. It is so terribly easy to read merely the marked passages, so hard to wade through the whole book afterwards.

Mr. Doyle might have added that for even the most zealous it must be almost impossible to read fifty books a month, especially when all members of the Board are voluntary unpaid officials with other full-time occupations.

On 6 July 1949 Dr. Smyth, a Protestant fellow of Trinity College, also resigned from the Board after he had served for four months. In a letter to the *Irish Times*,[10] he complained:

On occasions I have been handed books of considerable length on which I was expected to form a judgment within a few hours, and indeed it is not at all unusual for books to be handed to members of the Board for the first time actually in the course of a meeting at which the fate of the books is being decided. In these circumstances my colleagues appear satisfied to proceed immediately to the banning of the books in question although nothing has been taken into account except a few marked passages. This is a state of affairs against which I protest most strongly. It has the effect of depriving the public of many works of literary, historical, artistic or scientific merit and in my opinion constitutes a maladministration of the Act.

Dr. Smyth also maintained that the Board paid little or no attention to a book's literary merit. He had always considered this an essential element to be taken into account when judging a book.

My colleagues on the other hand take the view that if a book contains passages which in their opinion are offensive it may be banned without reference to the other qualities referred to in the clause quoted above.* When I have protested against this proceeding the Secretary has referred me to a ruling which he says obliges the Board to attach more importance to the existence of offensive passages than to the general literary or artistic merits of the book in question.

On 14 July the Secretary of the Board, acting on its instructions, replied. He pointed out that the Minister had decreed that literary merit should not be a final consideration,[11] and had warned against the inclusion of anyone on the Board who 'thinks that nothing can ever be immoral in art and that anything which is artistic must be

[10] 6 July 1949.

* Section 6 (2) (a) of Censorship of Publications Act, 1946: 'When examining a book under this section, the Censorship Board shall have regard to the following matters: (*a*) The literary, artistic, scientific or historic merit or importance, and the general tenor of, the book'.

[11] *Dail Debates*, Vol. XXVIII, No. 2, Col. 503.

allowed into the country'.[12] 'It happens', wrote the Secretary, 'on occasion that some member has not had time to read a certain book, but he has the views of his colleagues to guide him, in addition to a quick examination during the meeting.' He defended the banning of a certain unread book on the grounds of its denunciation as indecent by the editor of a leading English Sunday newspaper, and added that in any case the Board was not bound to read all books before they were banned. In his support he quoted the Minister of Justice: 'There are books which are so blatantly indecent that it would be unnecessary for the members of the Board to read every line of them. Should the members of the Board, for instance, be compelled to read every line of *Ulysses*, a book which has been universally condemned?' [13]

Some years before Dr. Smyth's resignation Sir John Keane had moved in the Senate, a motion of 'No Confidence' in the Censors.[14] He pointed out that the *Laws of Life* approved of by the Archdiocese of Westminster had been condemned as 'indecent and obscene', and that Kate O'Brien's novel *Land of Spices* had been banned because of a single phrase about homosexuality. The novel is about a girl who had detected her fiancé in her father's arms and consequently had retired to a convent. There she made good and became mother-general of the order. On its appearance the book had been welcomed by the Irish Press, including the Church-inspired *Irish Independent*. 'It is a picture of rare fidelity and charm with the portrait of the reverend mother splendidly life-like in every line. But there is one single sentence in the book so repulsive that the book should not be left where it would fall into the hands of very young people.' [15] The *Irish Times* also welcomed the book as adding a new character 'to the saintly types in the Roman Catholic Church depicted in modern fiction'.[16] Sir John Keane's motion was overwhelmingly defeated, the Minister of Justice being warmly approved when he said in reference to *The Land of Spices*: 'Whether the Board was technically or legally correct, whether the book in its general tendency was indecent or obscene may be open to question, but on the ground that it was calculated to do untold harm I was perfectly satisfied that it should be banned'.*

[12] *Dail Debates*, Vol. XXVI, No. 7, Col. 837. See also *Seanad Debates*, Vol. XII, No. 1, Col. 50.

[13] *Dail Debates*, Vol. XXVIII, No. 2, Cols. 495 and 496.

[14] 18 November 1942. *Seanad Debates*, Vol. XXVII, Col. 16.

[15] *Irish Independent*, 11 March 1941.

[16] *Irish Times*, 8 March 1941.

* Mr. Goulding vindicated the Board during the debate in these words: 'I hold the Censorship Board is quite justified in banning a book if it contains one passage subversive of Christianity or morality'.

It thus appears that the Board includes not only treatment of a theme, but the theme itself within its definition of obscenity. Where 'unnatural vice' is concerned, the standard seems to be stricter than in other matters. Thus Walter Baxter's *Look Down in Mercy*, a book whose language is beyond reproach, and Radclyffe Hall's *The Well of Loneliness*, are both subject to a ban.

THE LIBRARY CENSORSHIP

As important as the official censorship, but less well known is the unofficial censorship exercised by the libraries. The following letter from Sean O'Faolain appeared in the *Irish Times* on 13 July 1949. 'Recently I wrote to my local librarian (Dun Laoghaire Corporation Public Library) to ask him why among other books he did not stock Mr. Grahame Greene's *The Power and the Glory*. He replied in writing as follows, "I considered the book unsuitable for circulation in the libraries".' Such banning is not confined to Dun Laoghaire. The County Dublin Librarian lists as unsuitable for general circulation all of Galsworthy's novels, Smollett's *Peregrine Pickle*, Sterne's *Tristram Shandy*, and Tolstoy's *Anna Karenina*. Kilkenny contributes Balzac's *Wild Asses' Skin*, Dumas' *Count of Monte Cristo*, Arnold Bennett's *The Card*, and Thomas Hardy's *Tess of the D'Urbervilles*. Cork has banned Croce's *History of Europe in the Nineteenth Century*. The list could be indefinitely expanded.[17]

If ignorance is equated with virtue the policy of the Irish censorship is defensible. It can only be understood when one appreciates the extreme puritanism of Irish Catholicism. As in Victorian England so in contemporary Ireland art is criticised from the standpoint of morality and a rigid system of sexual ethics.* In his *Apologia* Newman gave poetic expression to the attitude determining the Irish attitude to literature:

> The Catholic Church holds it better for the sun and moon to drop from heaven, for the earth to fail, and for all the many millions on it to die of starvation in extremest agony as far as temporal affliction goes, than that one soul, I will not say should be lost, but should commit one single venial sin, should tell one wilful untruth, or should steal one poor farthing without excuse.[18]

Literally applied such doctrines give rise to strange results.

[17] Taken from official lists in his possession kindly lent by Mr. Sean O'Faolain.

* Gaelic writers, whether ancient or modern, have never been inhibited. The Gaelic language is rich in sexual synonyms. See writings of Merriman, McNamara and O'Sullivan, criticised by Trinity's late Victorians as being 'indecent'.

[18] Newman, *Apologia pro vita sua*. Everyman Edition (1949), p. 222.

The Irish Censors hold that it is better to lose all the masterpieces of world literature, rather than risk the contamination of a single soul by admitting an impure book. This attitude is combined with a strong anti-intellectualism and a distrust of those who are contemptuously branded as 'literati'.* This view is well expressed in a letter from L. J. Walsh published in the *Irish Rosary*. Mr. Walsh describes those opposed to the censorship as 'dilettanti, mere poseurs and literary lapdogs . . . who claim for their writings and for the stage the abandonment of all those decencies and reticences which the divinely directed Church and the accumulated wisdom of ages have set up. . . . I would rather have the opinion of a shrewd old Irish mountainy mother as to what would be likely to be a source of moral danger to her boys and girls, than that of any person living in the unreal world of books, no matter what his status was.'[19] Another point made in defence of the censorship is that if the 'literati' made less fuss ninety per cent. of the people would be ignorant of its existence.

The principle of censorship as opposed to its practice is capable of a more rational defence. Publishing in Ireland is negligible, the overwhelming majority of books being imported from Britain or the United States. The common law offence of publishing an 'obscene libel' cannot, therefore, be invoked against publishers since they are outside the jurisdiction, and it would be inequitable to prosecute booksellers who cannot be expected to know the contents of every book they stock. Few in Ireland object to the principle of some censorship, but there is unanimous opposition amongst writers to the methods and policy of the present Board.

* Thus Mr. Kehoe in the Debate on the Censorship in the Senate, 18 November 1942: 'Having fathered George Moore and others of his ilk—I do not know if that added one jot to our national reputation'.

[19] *The Irish Rosary*, November 1941.

CHAPTER IX

OBSCENITY, LAW AND SOCIETY

OBSCENITY in literature and the arts * raises intricate legal problems, but these are only reflections of issues of a wider social nature. It is maintained by some that there should be no law for the suppression of obscenity, because far from being an evil, it is a necessity in modern conventional society. Havelock Ellis held this view, maintaining that the conditions of contemporary society require relief from oppressive conventions just as the conditions of childhood create the need for fairy stories. Obscene books, therefore, are not aphrodisiac, but act as safety valves protecting society from crime and outrage. The average reader of obscenity is not socially undesirable, but quite harmless, and deprived of this outlet would turn to others, directly harmful to society.

A more convincing argument is that obscenity forms a necessary and valuable part of human life. The sexual appetite must be satisfied and find expression both in art and life. When we look at a nude by Renoir, Mr. Noël Annan recently pointed out,[1] the minds of most of us are not possessed by questions of significant form.

> Half the great poems, pictures, music, stories of the whole world [wrote D. H. Lawrence] are great by virtue of the beauty of their sex appeal. Titian or Renoir, the 'Song of Solomon' or *Jane Eyre*, Mozart or 'Annie Laurie', the loveliness is all interwoven with sex appeal, sex stimulus, call it what you will. Even Michael Angelo, who rather hated sex, can't help filling the Cornucopia

* Obscenity is not confined to literature, sculpture or painting, but sometimes occurs in music. Thus when Shostakovitch's opera *Lady Macbeth of Mensk* was performed in Philadelphia in 1935 'some obscene trombone notes so shocked certain ladies at the opening night that a large number walked out. As the first trombone player refused to play the notes a substitute did so'. (*Philadelphia Daily News*, 6 April 1935.)

Gilbert and Sullivan wrote an obscene opera, *The Sod's Opera*. Characters included Count Tostoff, The Brothers Bollox, a pair of hangers on, and Scrotum, a wrinkled old retainer. For many years a copy of the opera was kept in the guard room at St. James's Palace.

[1] Third Programme Broadcast, 24 February 1955.

> with phallic acorns. Sex is a very powerful, beneficial and necessary stimulus in human life, and we are all grateful when we feel its warm, natural flow through us, like a form of sunshine.[2]

On this point Havelock Ellis wrote: 'Obscenity is a permanent element of human social life and corresponds to a deep need of the human mind, or, for all we know to the contrary of mind generally'.[3] Thus to outlaw obscenity is to falsify life, to separate the sexual appetite from everyday living and ultimately to degrade it. Lawrence spent the greater part of his life struggling against this attitude and its consequences, and was branded as an obscene writer and a peddler of dirty books, whereas his attitude to sex was essentially integrated and ultimately religious. In his last years he inclined ever closer towards Catholicism as the one religion which had raised the sexual life to the level of a sacrament. His views are of course expressed in his novels, but he crystallised them in his essay 'Pornography and Obscenity.'

> Without secrecy [he wrote] there would be no pornography. But if pornography is the result of sneaking secrecy, what is the result of pornography? What is the effect on the individual. The effect on the individual is manifold and always pernicious. But one effect is perhaps inevitable. The pornography of today whether it be the pornography of the rubber goods shop or the pornography of the popular novel, film, and play, is an invariable stimulant to the vice of self-abuse, onanism, masturbation, call it what you will. In young or old, man or woman, boy or girl, modern pornography is a direct provocative of masturbation. It cannot be otherwise; when the grey ones wail that the young man and the young woman went and had sexual intercourse, they were bewailing the fact that the young man and the young woman didn't go separately and masturbate. Sex must go somewhere, especially in young people. So in our glorious civilisation it goes in masturbation. And the mass of our popular literature, the bulk of our popular amusements just exist to provide masturbation.

Lawrence was using the word 'pornography' in a wider sense than that of ordinary usage, but he and Ellis were in agreement in distinguishing obscenity from pornography, and in maintaining that it was only by artificially excluding the discussion of sex from literature that a market for pornography was created. Thus Ellis wrote: 'Obscenity there will be under all systems for it has a legitimate and natural foundation; but the vulgar, disgusting and stupid form of

[2] 'Pornography and Obscenity.'

[3] Revaluation of Obscenity', *More Essays of Love and Virtue* (1931).

obscenity called pornography—the literature and art that are a substitution for the brothel and of the same coarse texture, has its foundations not on Nature but on artificial secrecy'.[4] In effect Lawrence and Ellis were attacking the whole industrial and urban society of modern England which alone makes possible the separation of life and sex. Neither Lawrence nor Ellis attempted to justify pornography, they both attacked it, but they went further to condemn the conditions of life which stimulated the demand.

FREEDOM OF DISCUSSION

Obscenity raises the whole problem of censorship and the freedom of discussion in contemporary society. The one point on which all involved in the obscenity debate are agreed is that a censorship of books before publication is undesirable. 'The liberty of the press', wrote Blackstone, 'is indeed essential to the nature of a free state: but this consists in laying no previous restraints upon publications and not in freedom from censure for criminal matter when published.' [5] General agreement exists in Britain that whatever the theoretical arguments in favour of a censorship—and Plato has shown that they can be weighty, in practice the advantages that follow from a wide freedom of publication are far greater than those benefits which might be gained by a system of censorship.*

Freedom of discussion is perhaps the basic doctrine of the liberal society, and springs not from a cynical contempt for truth, but from the conviction that no one man or body possesses truth in its entirety. To attain the truth the human mind must be free: free to speculate, to express, to make mistakes and to try again. Further the liberal ethic presupposes an adult society with a certain minimum of education and the ability if left to itself to choose the right thing freely.

[4] From 'Revaluation of Obscenity'.

[5] 4 Comm. 151, 152.

* Thus Plato in *The Republic*:

SOCRATES: 'Then shall we carelessly and without more ado allow our children to hear any casual stories told by any casual persons, and so receive into their souls views of life for the most part at variance with those which we think they ought to hold when they come to man's estate?'

ADEIMANTUS: 'No we shall certainly not allow that.'

SOCRATES: 'Our first duty, then, it seems, is to set a watch over the makers of stories to select every beautiful story they make, and reject any that are not beautiful. Then we shall persuade nurses and mothers to tell those selected stories to the children. Thus will they shape their souls with stories far more than they can shape their bodies with their hands. But we shall have to throw away most of the stories they tell now.' (Everyman Edition (1935), p. 58.)

Such freedom has, however, always been limited, although the limits have varied from decade to decade. Orators speak of the difference between 'liberty' and 'licence', but how does one distinguish? No logical point exists at which liberty can be distinguished from licence, just as there is no numerical point at which the number of constraints imposed by the state changes a free into a slave society. The liberal doctrine is one of the 'minimum' state in which constraints are kept to the minimum necessary for good government, and not imposed for their own sake. Thus a man may publish what he wishes subject to the constraints of the law of civil and criminal libel. He must not defame, he must not blaspheme, he must not be seditious and he must not be obscene, but within these limits he is free to publish what he pleases. Dicey did not think the freedom extensive. 'Freedom of discussion', he wrote, 'is then in England little else than the right to write or say anything which a jury consisting of twelve shopkeepers think it expedient should be said or written.'[6] Dicey was, of course, a Whig and was exaggerating; blasphemous and seditious libel are now dead letters and the worst features of the libel law have been modified by the Defamation Act of 1952. Today obscene libel is the only effective legal limitation on freedom of discussion.*

AUTHORS' RIGHTS

Underlying the dispute about obscenity is a real clash of social interests. Authors have a right to communicate their thought and work freely. They must, as E. M. Forster has pointed out, feel free if they are to give of their best, and they cannot feel this if they are in continual fear of prosecution.

> The police magistrate's opinion is so incalculable, [wrote Virginia Woolf]—he lets pass so much that seems noxious and pounces upon so much that seems innocent—that even the writer whose record is hitherto unblemished is uncertain what may or may not be judged obscene and hesitates in fear and suspicion. What he is about to write may seem to him perfectly innocent—it may be essential to his book; yet he has to ask himself what will the police magistrate say: and not only what will the police magistrate say, but what will the printer say and what will the publisher say? For both printer and publisher will be trying uneasily and anxiously

[6] *The Law of the Constitution*, 9th edition, p. 246.

* There are obviously many non-legal limitations, direct and indirect, from prevailing standards of taste to the existence of monopoly institutions like the B.B.C.

> to anticipate the verdict of the police magistrate and will naturally bring pressure to bear upon the writer to put them beyond reach of the law. He will be asked to weaken, to soften, to omit. Such hesitation and suspense are fatal to freedom of mind and freedom of mind is essential to good literature.[7]

Such freedom must extend to every sphere of human conduct including that of sexual morality and behaviour. This is more than ever true today, when literature and especially the novel is so closely concerned with psychological problems and the realistic portrayal of sex. It can hardly be suggested that the Victorian solution of omitting sex from literature or confining the representation of sexual relations to those of an impeccably regular kind, which a reverend mother could contemplate with equanimity, should be readopted today. Such an attitude would maim contemporary literature by artificially restricting its range and shutting out from its vision what François Mauriac has called 'that place of desolation, the human heart'. Not all authors, of course, find conventions cramping. Dickens was happy to accept those of his own time, and a skilful writer like Thackeray was able to exploit them. It is true also, as C. S. Lewis has written, that to banish prudery from literature is to 'remove one area of vivid sensibility' and 'to expunge a human feeling'. But the obscenity problem is acute for writers such as Lawrence who are not following but leading their readers in directions to which they have not grown accustomed. For such writers literary reticence and obscenity laws can be destructive.

But if authors have a special position in society they also have duties since they are not writing in a vacuum but writing to be read. 'Literature is a social institution using as its medium language, a social creation. Such traditional literary devices as symbolism and metre are social in their very nature. They are conventions and norms which could have arisen only in society.' [8] Literature may or may not have a social purpose, but it certainly has social implications and writers cannot be totally emancipated from the customs of the community in which they live. If a great literature cannot be created without freedom, neither can it be sustained without a sense of responsibility on the authors' part. The greater the power and the less the external restraint, the more urgent the need of interior sanctions voluntarily imposed. Ultimately, the working of a free society is dependent on this intangible, a sense of self-discipline, the only alternative to which is regimentation. A free and, therefore, a great literature has grown up in England because of the high sense

[7] *The Nineteenth Century and After*, Vol. DCXXVI, April 1929.
[8] *Theory of Literature*, Austin Warren and René Welleck (London 1949), p. 89.

of responsibility felt by authors for their work. Freedom and responsibility go together one extending the other, so that freedom is possible only in a confident and mature society. It is no accident that the three great English contributions to civilisation have been law, literature, and parliamentary government, all dependent upon self-restraint and an unwritten law of liberty.

Those authors who pretend that there is no problem, and that the whole question of 'obscenity' has been created by a group of unenlightened Grundys and Comstocks only bring discredit on their own cause. Nor is the inevitable quotation from Milton—out of its historical and literary context—of any practical utility in the social conditions of the present time.*

> The whole problem of propaganda [said Mr. Ifor Evans, at the P.E.N. Congress of 1944], the dissemination of opinion, the distribution of printed matter, has changed entirely since Milton's day. Milton's conception of the circulation of ideas was that which might have prevailed in Greece—a small audience all of whom are capable of forming their own judgements, with discussion to correct false emphasis. He has in mind the formulation of an adequate judgement by the Socratic method. Even the England of his own day did not fit into that picture altogether, and the world of our day does not fit into it at all. One man or group of men can by subtle psychological methods and by use of the newspaper and radio effect a secret tyranny over the minds of millions.

To use the language of Milton to defend the immunity of commercial interests whose only object is to make money by the sale of degrading pornography is only to mislead.

On the other hand, those who pose the question as a clash between a group of irresponsible intellectuals, leaders of a minority literary coterie, striving to impose their extravagances on the virtuous and sober-living majority are equally wide of the mark. Authors certainly have an interest in a free literature, but it is one shared by the rest of society. Consciously or unconsciously a nation's literature mirrors

* The following passage from the *Areopagitica* is not so often quoted: 'I mean not tolerated popery, and open superstition, which as it extirpates all religious and civil supremacies, so itself should be extirpate, provided first that all charitable and compassionate means be used to win and regain the weak and the misled; that also which is impious or evil absolutely either against faith or manners no law can possibly permit, that intends not to unlaw itself: but those neighbouring differences, or rather indifferences, are what I speak of, whether in some point of doctrine or discipline, which though they may be many, yet need not interrupt the unity of spirit, if we could but find among us the bond of peace'.

its life and values, being at once the repository of its culture and the guarantee of its continuance. If authors have an interest in writing freely the public in general has an equal interest in being able to choose what to read. Society, however, also has an interest in preventing the exploitation of literature by those who wish to make money through the stimulation of the baser appetites and passions. Racketeers are especially tempted today by the emergence in every modern state of a new public who can read, but who are only semi-literate. On the whole, perverts excepted, educated people do not read pornography, since their taste for reading is fully formed, and they find it dull and uninteresting, but the barely literate masses have had no such opportunity and here the purveyors of filthy sub-literature find a profitable market.

Presumably it is this consideration which determines the policy of prosecuting only those books which are sold at popular prices. Publishers certainly act on the presumption that a high-priced book will not be prosecuted, and sometimes produce editions of the same book, one bowdlerised at a low price, and the other unexpurgated at a high one. Thus *The Mint*, by T. E. Lawrence, recently published, came out in two editions: the 'popular' edition at seventeen shillings and sixpence, 'from which certain Anglo-Saxon words have been omitted', and a full edition at three pounds thirteen shillings and sixpence, which included the offending words.* Some see in this practice a certain class discrimination, distinguishing an élite who can be trusted from the majority who cannot. It would be absurd, however, to suggest that the rich are either incorruptible or even beyond further corruption, and the Director of Public Prosecutions is probably actuated by the belief that the social gain in suppressing a high-priced book with a limited circulation is not worth the trouble of launching a prosecution. When this practice is extended to deprive the general public of literary works it is indefensible, but the protection of the mass of the people from the corrupting effects of pornography is not so much class prejudice as a realistic recognition that the present educational level leaves them open to victimisation.

DOES PORNOGRAPHY CORRUPT?

It has been assumed so far that pornography does have a corrupting effect on its readers, but this assumption must be further examined. Such an assertion rests not on scientific evidence but on what is called 'common sense'. A further assumption is made that even if there are legitimate doubts about the effect of reading upon adults

* The full edition was heavily oversubscribed.

there can be no doubt that reading does have a positive effect on youth and especially children.

Undoubtedly, the general moral standards and social customs prevailing in a community are frequently formed or changed by the influence of books. 'I am convinced', wrote Bernard Shaw in his preface to *Mrs. Warren's Profession*, 'that fine art is the subtlest, the most seductive, the most effective instrument of moral propaganda in the world, excepting only the example of personal conduct'. In our own time we have the example of André Gide, whose books changed the outlook of a generation. The law, however, cannot be invoked to protect prevailing moral standards, first because this assumes a finality which such standards do not possess, since much of what passes for morality is merely convention, and secondly, because in a country such as England there is no common agreement on ultimate moral attitudes. A book advocating divorce will appear 'obscene' or 'corrupting' to one group, while another will regard it as an argument for a necessary freedom. Similar considerations apply to books about such subjects as birth control or homosexuality, on which there is no agreed opinion. Unless there is universal agreement on any subject, such as, for example, compulsory education, the liberal state cannot impose coercive sanctions. The situation is different in a state such as Southern Ireland, where there is an almost universal agreement on certain moral principles, and which enables a censorship to be imposed which would be intolerable in England.

The justification for the laws against pornographic books is that such books have a directly undesirable effect on sexual behaviour. Unhappily, there is little scientific evidence to support this view since hardly any research has been carried out on the causal relation between reading and behaviour. Social sciences can never hope to be as exact as the natural sciences since their study is man not matter, and with regard to sexual behaviour man is subject to so many differing stimuli that it is difficult to isolate one and to gauge its effect. Furthermore, it is at least as probable that it is sexual desire, especially if frustrated, that creates the taste for pornography and not pornography which stimulates sexual desire.

THE KINSEY REPORT

One of the very few investigations into this field was carried out by Kinsey and he gives the result of his researches in the second of his two reports.[9] He concludes that for the pre-adolescent and the late

[9] *Sexual Behaviour in the Human Female*, Saunders (London 1953). An attempt to suppress this work as 'obscene' failed at Doncaster in 1954. See *The Times*, 20 March 1954.

teen-ager erotic literature is not an important factor in arousing sexual desire. The age group most likely to be aroused by vicarious experience is that of the adult male, especially in the upper social groups. Women are less likely to be aroused by erotic literature than men.

> A great deal of pornographic literature [wrote Kinsey] turns around detailed descriptions of genital activity, and descriptions of male genital performance. These are elements in which females according to our data are not ordinarily interested. The females in such literature extol the male's genital and copulatory capacity and there is considerable emphasis on the intensity of the female's response and the insatiability of her sexual desires. All of these represent the kind of female which most males wish all females to be. They represent typically masculine interpretations of the average female's capacity to respond to psychologic stimuli. Such elements are introduced because they are of erotic significance to the male writers, and because they are of erotic significance to the consuming public, which is almost exclusively male.

Kinsey compiled the following tables, the first showing the response to erotic reading materials, and the second the response to hearing erotic stories:

TABLE I. READING LITERARY MATERIALS

Erotic Response	*Females* per cent.	*Males* per cent.
Definite and/or frequent .	16	21
Some response . .	44	38
Never	40	41
No. of cases . . .	5,699	3,952

TABLE II. STIMULATION BY EROTIC STORIES

Erotic Response	*Females* per cent.	*Males* per cent.
Definite and/or frequent .	2	16
Some response . .	12	31
Never	86	53
No. of cases . . .	5,523	4,202

He further stressed that sex information comes as much from experience and word of mouth as from reading matter. Unfortunately he grouped together information from the verbal and printed word, and it is not possible to establish from his tables the proportion between these two sources of information. However, in 1938 the New York City Bureau of Social Hygiene carried out some researches and showed that books play a very small part in the dissemination of sex information among women. One thousand two hundred women out of 10,000 college and school graduates were questioned about the sources of their sex knowledge. Of the 1,200 only 72 mentioned books and none of these were of the pornographic type. Asked what they found most sexually stimulating 95 of the 409 who replied answered, 'Books'; 208 said, 'Men'! [10]

Behaviour is a function of both personality and environment, the dominant influence being personality. However, as the Jesuits have long known and modern psychologists stress, the personality is formed at a very early age, normally before the reading habit is formed. Environment, of course, influences behaviour, but direct experiences have a much greater influence on human behaviour than vicarious experiences through books. Once again there is no direct evidence in point, but the research into drug addiction and voting which has been carried out in the United States shows that reading matter and even mass mediums of communication have much less influence on attitudes than is generally supposed.[11] Mass communications confirm and reinforce existing attitudes, but they rarely cause a fundamental change of outlook.

YOUTH AND COMICS

Youth and children are probably more open to influence, because their attitudes have not yet been fully formed, and they have little residue of past experience on which to draw. There is no evidence that the reading of horror comics for instance leads directly to the committal of delinquent acts, but they may well have the more general effect of deadening a child's sensitivity and accustoming him to accept brutality and violence as a normal part of human conduct. In 1946 George Orwell noted the change which had come about in boys' papers after the war, and pointed out that bully worship and the cult of violence entered into the comics in a way they

[10] Alpert, 42 Harvard Law Review 40, at pp. 73, 74 (1938). One of the books from which sexual information was derived was Motley's *Rise of the Dutch Republic*!

[11] See *Studies in the Epidemiology of Drug Use*, I. Chein, E. Rosenfeld, D. Wilner. Research Centre of Human Relations, N.Y. University (1954). Also *The People's Choice*, P. F. Lazarsfeld, etc. Duell, Sloan and Pearce (New York, 1944).

never did in the old *Gem* and *Magnet* and even the *Hotspur* and the *Wizard*.

> There is a great difference in tone [he wrote] between even the most bloodthirsty English paper and the threepenny Yank magazines *Fight Stories*: *Action Stories*: etc. (not strictly boys' papers but largely read by boys). In the Yank magazines you get real blood-lust, really gory descriptions of the all-in, jump-on-his-testicles style of fighting written in a jargon that has been perfected by people who brood on violence.[12]

Dr. Wertham in his book *Seduction of the Innocent* stressed this brutalising effect that horror comics have on children and supported this view by experiments carried out by himself and other psychologists. In the 'Thematic Aperception' test children were shown pictures and asked to tell stories about them. Many children showed themselves obsessed with stories of murder and violence and this reaction was stronger in the case of children who read horror comics than in those who did not.

> The most subtle and pervading effect of crime comics on children [wrote Dr. Wertham] can be summarised in a single phrase: moral disarmament. To put it more concretely it consists chiefly in a blunting of the finer feelings of conscience, of mercy and sympathy for other people's sufferings and of respect for women as women, and not merely as sex objects to be bandied around, or as luxury prizes to be fought over. Crime comics are such highly flavoured fare that they affect children's taste for the finer influences of education, for art, for literature, and for the decent and constructive relationships between human beings and especially between the sexes.

He refuted the argument that such reading provides a necessary 'catharsis' for children's emotions because emotion is stimulated without being given any adequate outlet. The child identifies itself with the characters in the comic and is left with only a limited scope for release in action. These actions, he wrote, can only be 'masturbatory or delinquent'.

His argument that the reading of horror comics leads to juvenile delinquency is less convincing. He gives numerous examples of juvenile delinquents who had many comic books in their possession, but so have many children who never commit a delinquent act. He quotes the case of Howard Lange, a thirteen-year-old boy who killed his seven-year-old companion. He stabbed him with his

[12] 'Boys' Weeklies', *Critical Essays* (1946).

pocket knife, choked him, stamped on him and dropped four blocks of concrete on his face. He then hid his victim under a pile of leaves. In court the judge took judicial notice of Lange's possession of twenty-six comics 'of homicidal and near-homicidal and brutal attacks upon the persons of the character depicted by means of knives, guns, poison arrows and darts, rocks of cliffs, etc.' The argument is the old one of *post hoc propter hoc* and is open to the same objections. Sheldon and Eleanor Gluck in their study 'Unravelling Juvenile Delinquency' [13] gave little prominence to reading among the ninety factors they listed as causes of juvenile delinquency. They showed in fact that delinquent children read much less than the law-abiding.*

Horror comics have now been banned in England and in many Commonwealth and European countries. Such a step can be justified as a precautionary measure, if only to protect abnormal children, since there is no literary or social interest in the horror comic to be weighed against its possible harmful effect. Further, children are clearly in need of protection, whereas adults can be expected to choose for themselves. The irony of the horror-comic situation is that they are read—at any rate in the United States—as much by adults as by children.† Forty-one per cent. of male adults and 28 per cent. of females in the United States read horror comics regularly.

Pornography and obscene books on the other hand do not appear to be widely read by children, nor do children glean their sexual information principally from books‡ as Table III (opposite) setting out the results of some American research shows.

[13] New York, *The Commonwealth Fund* (1950).

* Of 500 delinquent children 2·7 per cent. were found to read either books or comics while for the 500 non-delinquents the percentage was 7·8 per cent.

† Norbert Muhlen, 'Comic Books and Other Horrors'. *Commentary*, Vol. VII, No. 1, January 1949. Of children between 6 and 11 in the United States, 95 per cent. of the boys and 91 per cent. of the girls read fifteen per month. Between the ages of 12 and 18, eight out of every ten children read at least twelve per month. There are no detailed figures for the United Kingdom, but J. E. V. Birch (Taunton Borough Librarian) estimates that 30 million comics of the American type are sold annually in Britain, mainly to children between the ages of 7 and 13.

‡ Adults according to Kinsey are not, however, generally aroused by sado-masochistic stories, as is shown here:

AROUSAL FROM SADO-MASOCHISTIC STORIES

Erotic Response	*By Females* per cent.	*By Males* per cent.
Definite or frequent . .	3	10
Some response . . .	9	12
Never	88	78
No. of cases . . .	1,016	2,880

TABLE III. FIRST SOURCES OF SEX INFORMATION FOR BOYS*

	Origin of Babies (%)	*Ejaculation* (%)	*Nocturnal Emission* (%)	*Contraception* (%)	*Menstruation* (%)	*Intercourse* (%)	*Prostitution* (%)	*Venereal Disease* (%)
Conversation: Male Companions	52·5	67·4	68·0	92·1	57·6	90·8	93·0	65·5
Conversation: Female Companions	0·7	—	—	0·5	4·3	1·7	—	—
Mother	27·5	1·3	2·8	2·7	20·2	0·5	1·5	4·8
Father	3·5	2·6	2·8	1·6	4·3	1·0	1·9	4·8
Printed Matter	4·4	2·2	1·6	1·0	5·1	2·1	1·3	14·3
Adults	3·0	1·3	2·4	0·5	4·3	0·5	1·3	6·8
Observation	4·1	11·3	—	—	2·1	0·7	—	—
Experience	—	10·9	22·4	—	—	—	—	—
Others (School, Radio, etc.)	2·2	—	—	—	—	—	—	3·8
Unknown	2·1	3·0	—	1·6	2·1	2·6	1·0	—

The causal relation between reading and behaviour is so uncertain, the number of sexual stimuli so diverse, and the subjective factors are so numerous, that the law in the sphere of obscenity should proceed with caution. One point seems evident, that literary standards should not be regulated by law. Literature is creative, imaginative, and æsthetic, with no extrinsic purpose, its one criterion being fidelity to its own nature. It is the study of the universal, but in the light of the individual and the particular, an expression of man's creative faculty, intent on beauty not on utility. Law is not creative but regulative, seeking not a special ideal harmony, but a generalised justice and the application of universally valid principles. Thus it is impossible to attempt to confine literature within the Procrustean bed of the law.

On the other hand the law is rightly used to suppress the social evil of pornography and to punish those who seek to benefit by its distribution. The point has been clearly put by Virginia Woolf.

> There can be no doubt [she wrote] that books fall in respect of indecency into two classes. There are books written, published and sold with the object of causing pleasure or corruption by means of their indecency. There is no difficulty in finding where they are to be bought nor in buying them when found. There are others whose indecency is not the object of the book but incidental to some other purpose—scientific, social, æsthetic, on the writer's part. The police magistrate's power should be definitely limited to the suppression of books which are sold as pornography

* Taken from Glen V. Ramsey, 'The Sex Information of Younger Boys,' *Journal of Orthopsychiatry* (1943), Vol. XIII, pp. 347–352. The boys were selected from the middle and upper middle classes of a Mid-Western city with a population of 100,000.

> to people who seek out and enjoy pornography. The others should be left alone. Any man or woman of average intelligence and culture knows the difference between the two kinds of book and has no difficulty in distinguishing one from the other.[14]

George Moore made the same distinction in *Avowals*. He denied that pornography and literature overlap.

> On the contrary the frontiers are extremely well defined so much so that even if all literature was searched through and through it would be difficult to find a book that a man of letters could not instantly place in one category or the other. The reason is that real literature is concerned with description of life and thoughts about life rather than with acts. The very opposite is true in the case of pornographic books.

THE RÔLE OF THE LAW

The law then should provide a formula enabling a jury or magistrate to distinguish between the two. The value that society derives from freedom of discussion in the sexual sphere together with the value to society of the particular book in question must be weighed against the benefit of protection from a harmful effect on sex conduct which may reasonably be expected to result from reading a book. Even if a book presents unpopular or unconventional views about sexual morality it should be tolerated, provided its manner of presentation is not pornographic. The simplest way to achieve this result is to frame a law which takes into consideration the purpose with which a book has been written or published. When judging the effects of a book the standard to be taken should be that of a reasonable man unless it is a publication expressly intended for children, when the possible effects on children should be considered. There are many works that despite their merit are not suitable for children, but the law cannot reduce the standard of literature to that of a child's library. The law must protect children, but the primary responsibility is that of the educator, parent or schoolmaster. Ultimately, the solution to the child's reading problem is the provision of well-written wholesome books and comics.

It has been suggested that the courts are not the proper place for decisions of this kind and that either an independent board of review should be set up, or that publishers should impose their own censorship, as is done in the film industry. These suggestions must be rejected since they would be open to abuse. There is no parallel between books and films sufficient to justify the conferring of wide

[14] *Nineteenth Century and After*, Vol. DCXXVI, April 1929.

powers on publishers, and the English tradition has always been that issues of liberty or freedom of expression must be decided in the ordinary courts of the land. A special jury for such cases might be empanelled, but the difficulty of an ordinary jury's making up their mind about a literary or scientific work would be adequately solved by the admission of expert evidence.

In this sphere administration of the law is as important as the substantive law itself. By making all prosecutions subject to the consent of the Director of Public Prosecutions or the Attorney-General vexatious prosecutions would be avoided. Ill-advised prosecutions which fail, serve only to advertise a book, and do more harm than good to public morals. There is something to be said for an independent board to advise whether a prosecution should be brought, but such a board would be an additional safeguard and is not a necessary condition for a reasonable and intelligent administration of the law.

As can be seen from the historical chapters of this book standards of literary taste fluctuate from decade to decade, and the law makes itself ridiculous by endorsing with legal sanctions opinions which are essentially contemporary and ephemeral. The obscenity problem involves a conflict of rights, and thus no perfect solution is possible, the best one can hope for being a compromise. Some compromises are, however, better than others, and there is general agreement that the compromise embodied in the present law is unsatisfactory and out of date. Shaw described law as 'the intolerance of the community', but commended it as a 'defined and limited' intolerance.[15] It is precisely because the present law of obscene libel is neither defined nor limited, and confers a wide measure of discretion on the individual judge or magistrate that its reform is urgent, for it is only limitation that makes the restraints of the common law preferable to an administrative censorship. For this reason the proposals contained in the draft Bill, Appendix II of the book, are desirable and necessary reforms of the law. Their implementation would not only restore the traditional common law doctrine of criminal responsibility, but would bring the law governing obscene publications into accord with the changed conditions and needs of modern times.

[15] Preface to *The Showing-Up of Blanco Posnet.*

APPENDICES

APPENDIX I

ANOMALIES OF ENGLISH LAW

1. The intention or purpose of the author, artist, publisher, etc., is ignored.

2. No certainty in theory or practice exists as to the meaning of the words 'deprave or corrupt' nor to which class of persons these words apply.

3. It is doubtful whether there is any defence that a work is of literary, artistic or scientific merit, or whether these are relevant considerations to be taken into account by a judge or jury in declaring a book 'obscene' according to law.

4. Expert evidence on literary or artistic merit is not admissible in court, and it is doubtful whether evidence of scientific value is admissible.

5. The punishment for committing the offence of 'publishing an obscene libel' is nowhere defined or limited.

6. Any private person may bring a prosecution for obscene libel, and the police although under an obligation to consult the Director of Public Prosecutions need not listen to his advice. Thus there is no standard of uniformity in the administration of the law. A book condemned in one place may be acquitted in another.

7. Under the Obscene Publications Act, 1857:

(*a*) The author, publisher, printer, etc., have no *locus standi* in the court and may not give nor call evidence.

(*b*) Although the police are bound to consult the Director of Public Prosecutions before bringing a prosecution for obscene libel there is no obligation to consult him before invoking the Act. Private persons may set the Act in motion.

(*c*) The magistrate is not bound to make any finding of obscenity based on evidence given in court, nor need the prosecution make out a *primâ facie* case of obscenity nor indicate in what respects a book is considered obscene.

(*d*) No time limit exists within which proceedings under the Act must be brought. Thus after books have been seized the police can hold them indefinitely without bringing them before a court.

The Summary Jurisdiction Act, 1848, requiring a complaint to be made within six months of the time when the offence arose does not apply to proceedings under the Act.

8. No certainty exists as to whether the test of a book's obscenity is an 'isolated' passage or a book's 'dominant effect'.

9. It is no offence to have obscene articles, prints, etc., in one's possession with intent to publish them.

10. The Customs authorities may destroy books, etc., as obscene without any application to a court. The burden of invoking a court's jurisdiction rests on the aggrieved party.

11. No provision is made for a uniform policy to be pursued by the Department of the Director of Public Prosecutions, the Post Office and the Customs authorities.

12. The law relating to obscene offences is a mixture of common and statute law. Apart from the common law offence there are eleven statutes dealing with 'obscenity' and numerous local acts and ordinances The law is in need of consolidation.

APPENDIX II

THE OBSCENE PUBLICATIONS BILL, 1955

Obscene Publications

A

BILL

To amend and consolidate the law relating
to obscene publications.

Ordered to be brought in by
Mr. Roy Jenkins, Mr. John Foster, Mr. Foot,
Mr. Angus Maude, Mrs. Eirene White,
Mr. Nigel Nicolson, Mr. Kenneth Robinson,
and Mr. Simon

EXPLANATORY MEMORANDUM

1. The Bill makes changes in both the substance and the language of the law. The common law misdemeanour of obscene libel disappears and is replaced by a new statutory offence.

2. The question of intention is declared to be relevant, and the court is required to consider among other factors:—

(*a*) the dominant effect of the publication;

(*b*) evidence of its corrupting influence if any;

(*c*) the literary or other merit of the publication; and

(*d*) the class of persons among whom it is likely to circulate.

3. The word 'obscene' is extended to cover publications that unduly exploit horror, cruelty, and violence.

4. Whereas the common law sets no limit to the punishment for obscene publication, the Bill defines maximum penalties.

5. It also amends and consolidates the provisions in numerous existing acts which deal with obscene matter, and provides penalties for a number of summary offences.

6. Further, the Bill amends the law relating to 'destruction orders' by magistrates in the following ways:—

(*a*) by introducing the same test of obscenity as that prescribed for criminal offences;

(*b*) by giving the author, publisher, printer and distributor the right to give and call evidence.

7. The destruction of obscene publications by the customs authorities is made dependent on the issue of a destruction order by a magistrate.

8. Provision is made for uniformity in the operation of the law by making all proceedings in England or Wales subject to the consent of the Attorney General.

ARRANGEMENT OF CLAUSES

Clause

A

BILL

TO

Amend and consolidate the law relating to obscene publications.

BE it enacted by the Queen's most Excellent Majesty, by and with the advice and consent of the Lords Spiritual and Temporal, and Commons, in this present Parliament assembled, and by the authority of the same, as follows:—

1. Offences under this Act. Any person who shall distribute, circulate, sell, or offer for sale, or write, draw, print or manufacture for any of the aforesaid purposes, any obscene matter shall be guilty of an offence:

Provided that no person shall be convicted of an offence under this section unless it is established by the prosecution either—

(*a*) that the accused intended to corrupt the persons to or among whom the said matter was intended or was likely to be so distributed, circulated, sold, or offered for sale; or

(*b*) that in so distributing, circulating, selling or offering for sale, or writing, drawing, printing or manufacturing for any of the aforesaid purposes, he was reckless as to whether the said matter would or would not have a corrupting effect upon such persons.

In this Act 'reckless' shall connote advertence in the mind of the accused person as to the corrupting consequences of his action, although there is no desire that such consequences shall take place:

Provided also that in any proceedings under this Act a person who wrote, drew or composed, or printed or published the work in respect of which the proceedings are brought shall be entitled, if he desires, to appear and to be represented in the proceedings and to be heard by the court upon the question whether the work is obscene.

2. Evidence as to obscenity. In deciding, for the purposes of any of the provisions of this Act, whether any matter is or is not obscene, the court shall have regard to the following considerations:—

(*a*) whether the general character and dominant effect of the matter alleged to be obscene is corrupting;

(*b*) evidence, if any, as to the literary or artistic merit, or the medical, legal, political, religious, or scientific character or importance of the said matter; and for this purpose expert opinion shall be admissible as evidence;

(*c*) evidence, if any, as to the persons to or among whom the said matter was, or was intended, or was likely to be distributed, circulated, sold or offered for sale;

(*d*) evidence, if any, that the said matter has had a corrupting effect.

3. Evidence as to sale, &c. In deciding whether, for the purposes of any of the provisions of this act, any matter alleged to be obscene was distributed, circulated, sold, or offered for sale, or written, drawn, printed or manufactured for any of the aforesaid purposes with the said intent or recklessness, the court shall have regard, *inter alia*, to the following considerations:—

(*a*) the general character of the person charged, and where relevant, the nature of his business;

(*b*) the general character and dominant effect of the matter alleged to be obscene;

(*c*) any evidence offered or called by or on behalf of the accused person as to his intention in distributing, circulating, selling or offering for sale the said matter.

4. Interpretation. For the purposes of this Act the word 'obscene' shall be deemed to include any matter which, whether or not related to any sexual context, unduly exploits horror, cruelty, or violence, whether pictorially or otherwise.

5. Penalties. Except where otherwise provided, any person who commits any offence against this Act shall be liable on summary conviction to a fine not exceeding one hundred pounds or to imprisonment for a term not exceeding four months, or to both.

6. Penalties for printing, &c., obscene matter.—(1) Any person who prints or causes to be printed in any newspaper, periodical, or circular, or exhibits or causes to be exhibited to public view or distributed in any street or public place, whether a building or not, any picture or any printed or written matter which is obscene, shall be liable on summary conviction to a fine not exceeding fifty pounds or to imprisonment for a term not exceeding one month.

(2) Any person who affixes, distributes, delivers, inscribes, or throws down in any street, public place, or area any such matter as is described

in subsection (1) of this section shall be liable on summary conviction to a fine not exceeding five pounds or to imprisonment for a term not exceeding fourteen days; and any constable may arrest without warrant any person whom he shall find committing any offence against this subsection.

7. Postal packets containing obscene matter. Any person who sends or attempts to send or procures to be sent a postal packet which—

(*a*) encloses any obscene print, painting, photograph, lithograph, engraving, cinematograph film, book, card, or written communication, or any obscene article whether similar to the above or not, or

(*b*) has on such packet or on the cover thereof any words, marks, or designs which are grossly offensive or of an indecent or obscene character,

shall be guilty of an offence against this Act.

8. Power to search for, and dispose of, obscene matter.—(1) It shall be lawful for any magistrate, upon information on oath that—

(*a*) any obscene matter is kept in any premises within his jurisdiction for the purposes of sale or distribution, exhibition for gain, letting upon hire, or being otherwise circulated for gain, and

(*b*) one or more articles of the said character have been sold, distributed, exhibited, lent, or otherwise circulated as aforesaid, at or in connection with such premises,

and if it shall appear to him that the said sale, distribution, exhibition, lending on hire or otherwise circulating would have a corrupting effect on persons into whose hands the said matter was likely or was intended to fall, to issue his warrant authorising any constable to search for and seize all such matter within seven days from the issue of the said warrant, and forthwith to bring the matter so seized before him.

(2) The said magistrate shall forthwith report the facts to the Attorney General and to the persons, if any, whose names appear on the matter alleged to be obscene as those of the author, publisher, printer or manufacturer thereof.

(3) If the Attorney General then gives his consent to further proceedings, but not otherwise, the said magistrate shall within seven days issue a summons requiring the occupier of the said premises to appear before the appropriate court of summary jurisdiction and show cause why the matter seized should not be destroyed.

(4) The said author, publisher, printer, distributor or manufacturer of the matter alleged to be obscene shall have the right to give and call evidence in order to oppose the making of an order for the destruction of the said matter; and it shall be the duty of the prosecutor to indicate to

the court wherein lies the alleged obscenity of the matter under consideration.

(5) The court, if satisfied after considering the evidence that the matter seized is obscene and has been kept for any of the purposes aforesaid, shall order that such matter be destroyed:

Provided that such order shall not be carried into effect until the expiration of the fourteen days allowed by section eighty-four of the Magistrates' Courts Act, 1952, for the giving of notice of intention to appeal to quarter sessions against the said order.

(6) If the magistrate before whom the matter alleged to be obscene was originally brought, or the court which proceeds to hear the aforesaid evidence, decides that the said matter is not obscene, or if proceedings have not been instituted within a reasonable time, the matter shall be returned forthwith to the person from whom it was seized.

9. Prohibition of importation of obscene matter.—(1) The Commissioners of Customs and Excise are hereby empowered to seize and detain any obscene matter which is in course of being imported into or exported from the United Kingdom.

(2) When any such matter is so seized, the Commissioners of Customs and Excise shall forthwith take proceedings under the last preceding section for the order of a court of summary jurisdiction that the matter seized be either destroyed, delivered to the consignee or returned to the person from whom it was seized.

10. Enactments nullified. The provisions of any act, whether public, general, local or private, which are in identical or similar terms to any provisions of this Act, are hereby declared to be of no effect.

11. Saving. Nothing in this Act shall affect the operation of the Judicial Proceedings (Regulation of Reports) Act, 1926, or the Law of Libel Amendment Act, 1888.

12. Obscene libels. It is hereby declared that obscene libel shall not be punishable at common law.

13. Repeals. The enactments specified in the Schedule to this Act are hereby repealed to the extent specified in the third column of that Schedule.

14. Initiation of proceedings. No proceedings in England and Wales under this Act shall be initiated unless by or with the consent of the Attorney General.

15. Short title. This Act may be cited as the Obscene Publications Act, 1955.

SCHEDULE

Enactments Repealed

Session and Chapter	Short Title	Extent of Repeal
5 Geo. 4. c. 83	Vagrancy Act, 1824 ..	In section four, the words 'every person wilfully exposing to view in any street, road or highway, or public place, or in the window or other part of any shop or other building situate in any street, road, highway, or public place, any obscene print, picture or other indecent exhibition'.
10 & 11 Vict. c. 89.	Town Police Clauses Act, 1847.	In section twenty-eight, the words 'or publicly offers for sale or distribution or exhibits to public view any profane, indecent, or obscene book, paper, print, drawing, painting or representation'.
20 & 21 Vict. c. 83.	Obscene Publications Act, 1857	The whole Act.
39 & 40 Vict. c. 36.	Customs Consolidation Act, 1876.	In section forty-two, the words 'Indecent or obscene prints, paintings, photographs, books, cards, lithographic or other engravings, or any other indecent or obscene articles'.
52 & 53 Vict. c. 18.	Indecent Advertisements Act, 1889.	The whole Act.
15 & 16 Geo. 6. and 1 Eliz. 2. c. 55.	Magistrates' Courts Act, 1952.	Paragraph 16 of the first Schedule.
2 Eliz. 2. c. 36.	Post Office Act, 1953 ..	Paragraphs (*b*) and (*c*) of subsection (1) of section eleven.

APPENDIX III

COMPARATIVE LAW

The law of Scotland and the British Commonwealth countries have been set out in full as these will be of interest to English-speaking readers. Recent developments in Australia and New Zealand are of particular interest. A selection has also been made of the law in foreign countries. France and Germany have been chosen because of their importance in European life and culture. The smaller countries are represented by Belgium, Greece and Switzerland, countries of widely differing culture. The law of Denmark and Sweden has been included because of the more liberal attitude to sexual morality in Scandinavian countries. Asiatic countries are represented by the law of the Soviet Union and of Japan. Finally the Roman Index has been included as the only censorship system of international importance.

COMMONWEALTH LAW

1. Scotland

Scots law is very similar to English law but there are certain points of difference.

1. To publish, circulate, or expose for sale any obscene work devised and intended to corrupt the morals of the community and to create inordinate and lustful desires is an indictable offence. (*Henry Robinson* (1843), 1 Broun 590 and 643.)

No corrupt intention need be proved. (Anderson, *Criminal Law of Scotland* (1904).)

2. Whether the offence has been committed will depend on extrinsic circumstances, e.g. manner of offering for sale, etc. (*McGowan* v. *Langmuir*, [1931] S. C. (J) 10.

3. The Post Office Act, the Customs Acts, the Indecent Advertisements Act, 1889, apply to Scotland.

4. The Obscene Publications Act, 1857, does not apply to Scotland.

5. The Burgh Police (Scotland) Act, 1892 (55 & 56 Vict., c. 55, s. 380) provides:

> Every person who publishes, prints or offers for sale or distribution or sells, distributes, exhibits to view or causes to be published, printed, exhibited to view or distributed any indecent or obscene book, paper, print, photograph, drawing, painting, representation, model or

figure, or publicly exhibits any disgusting or indecent object, or writes or draws any indecent or obscene word, figure, or representation in or on any place where it can be seen by the public, or sings or recites in public any obscene song or ballad is liable to a penalty of ten pounds or alternatively without penalty to imprisonment for sixty days.

2. AUSTRALIA

'Obscene Offences' in Australia fall under the jurisdiction of the six state legislatures and provisions for punishing them vary from state to state. Customs and Postal regulations are, however, laid down by the federal parliament and apply in all the states. Despite legislative differences between the states, the common law in each is based on the English common law and the offence of 'obscene libel' remains, although in practice prosecutions are few. The English interpretations of the common law are accepted in all the states. The Hicklin judgement is thus part of Australian law.

I. FEDERAL LAW

A. Customs

(*a*) Under the Customs Act (1901–1950, No. 80 of 1950) indecent or obscene works or articles may not be imported into the Commonwealth under penalty of a hundred-pound fine. A similar penalty applies to the export of such articles. (S. 50, s. 52 (c), s. 111.)
The articles are also liable to forfeiture.

(*b*) The Minister for Trade and Customs may make regulations under the Customs Act to prohibit the importation of literature which whether in words or pictures in his opinion:

(i) unduly emphasises matters of sex or crime;

(ii) is calculated to encourage depravity.

He may also prohibit the exportation of any goods 'the exportation of which would in his opinion be harmful to the Commonwealth'. (S. 112.)

(*c*) Notice must be given of seizure to the person from whom the goods were seized or the owner of the goods. (S. 205.)

(*d*) 'Whenever any goods have been seized by any officer and claim to such goods had been served on the Collector by the owner of such goods, the Collector may retain possession of the goods without taking any proceedings for their condemnation and may by notice under his hand require the claimant to enter an action against him for the recovery of the goods and if such claimant shall not within four months after the date of such notice enter such action the goods shall be deemed to be condemned without any further proceedings.' (S. 207.)

(*e*) A five-year limit for prosecution applies. (S. 249.)

B. Post Office. (Post and Telegraph Act, 1901–1950. Statutory Law Revision Act No. 80 of 1950.)

(*a*) 'Every postal article received in a post office which contains an enclosure contrary to the provisions of this Act or the regulations or of any other Act or on the outside of which any profane, blasphemous, indecent, obscene, offensive or libellous matter is written or drawn: shall be deemed to be posted in contravention of this Act.' (S. 40.)

(*b*) 'The Postmaster General or any other director may at any time cause any postal article having anything profane, blasphemous, indecent, obscene, offensive or libellous written or drawn on the outside thereof or any obscene enclosure in any postal article to be destroyed. No action shall be brought against the Postmaster General or any officer of the Department for anything done under the provisions of this section, but any person aggrieved by anything done by the Postmaster General or a Director under this section may appeal to a justice of the High Court or to a judge of a Supreme Court of a state by summons or petition in summary manner.' (S. 43.)

(*c*) The Postmaster General may refuse to deliver such articles and order them to be destroyed. (S. 44.)

(*d*) 'If the Postmaster General has reasonable ground to suppose any person to be engaged either in the Commonwealth or elsewhere in receiving money or any valuable thing in connexion with a fraudulent obscene, indecent or immoral business or undertaking: he may by order under his hand published in the *Gazette* direct that any postal article, received at a post office addressed to such person either by his own or fictitious or assumed name or to any agent or representative of his or to an address without a name, shall not be registered or transmitted or delivered to such person.' (S. 57.)

(*e*) It is an offence punishable by a fine of one hundred pounds or not more than two years' imprisonment with or without hard labour to 'knowingly' enclose in a packet any indecent or obscene article, etc., or to write on the outside of such packet any obscene, indecent, grossly offensive remarks, etc. (S. 107.)

II. STATE LAW

A. New South Wales

1. Obscene and Indecent Publications Act, 1901–1955. (Act No. 12, 1901, as amended by Act No. 12, 1908; Act No. 36, 1946, and Act No. 10, 1955.)

(*a*) A police magistrate or any two justices may issue a warrant authorising police officers 'to enter in the daytime into any house shop room or other place and to search for and seize all obscene publications found therein together with all printing presses engines types plates stones working plant and material used for the purposes of or in any way in connection therewith and to carry all the articles so seized which are capable of removal before a police magistrate or any two justices'. (S. 5.) The conditions under which the warrant may be issued are identical with those prescribed by the Obscene Publications Act, 1857, e.g. as to information on oath, sale from the premises, and the satisfaction of the magistrates that publication would amount to a 'misdemeanour proper to be prosecuted as such'. Powers of destruction are identical with and subject to the same restrictions as those conferred by the Obscene Publications Act, 1857.

(*b*) 'Any police officer above the rank of an ordinary constable may forthwith seize and carry to the nearest police office any obscene publication found hawked about or carried in any street or public place for sale or for exhibition distribution or publication for gain and shall report the fact of such seizure in writing to the magistrate there presiding.'

Such magistrate may—

(a) if within seven days after such seizure the person who hawked about or carried the publications seized or some person claiming to be their owner does not appear and demand possession or

(b) if such person appears and demands possession and it is found that the publications are obscene and were hawked about or carried for any of the purposes aforesaid order such books to be destroyed as provided in section 9. The magistrate shall if not satisfied that the publications are obscene or were hawked about or carried for any of the aforesaid purposes order them to be forthwith restored to the claimant. (S. 14.)

(*c*) Offences.

1. Every occupier of the house etc. where articles such as those described in s. 5 have been seized or anyone who appears to be the owner of such articles shall for a first offence be liable to a penalty not exceeding fifty pounds or to imprisonment for not more than three months, and for subsequent offences to a fine of not more than a hundred pounds or to imprisonment for not more than six months. (S. 15.)

2. Everyone who prints, photographs, lithographs, draws, makes, sells or has in his possession apparently for the purpose of sale, publishes, distributes or exhibits any obscene publication or assists in doing so, etc., etc., shall be liable to a penalty not exceeding fifty pounds or to imprisonment for any term not exceeding six months. (S. 16.)

3. Every person printing or publishing in relation to any judicial proceedings 'any indecent matter or indecent medical surgical or physiological details, being matter or details the publication of which . . . would tend to encourage depravity, or would tend to injure the morals of the public or of any class or section thereof',

is liable to a fine of not more than five hundred pounds or to four months' imprisonment or both. (S. 19.) The only persons liable under this section are proprietors, editors, master printers, and publishers. *Bonâ fide* law reports, etc., are exempted.

(*d*) Registration.

The 1955 amending Act requires all distributors of printed matter to be registered. If such distributors are guilty of any offence under the Act or are found guilty of publishing an obscene libel the court may order their registration to be cancelled and they are thus prohibited from any further publishing or distributing. Full details of the exceptions and operation of these provisions are given in the Act. (Ss. 20–29.) They are identical with those provided by the Police Offences Act of Victoria 1954. (See p. 231 where the Victorian legislation is described.)

(*e*) Works of Literary Merit, etc.

'The provisions of this Act, other than sections twenty to twenty-nine, both inclusive (the provisions requiring registration, etc.) do not apply to the printing, publishing, making, possessing, selling, delivery or distribution or the exhibiting in the window of any shop or the posting or causing to be posted of—

(a) any work of literary or artistic merit; or

(b) any *bonâ fide* medical or scientific book, pamphlet, magazine or periodical,

unless the court is satisfied that notwithstanding its literary or artistic merit or its character as a medical or scientific book, pamphlet, magazine or periodical, the printing, publishing etc. was not justified in the circumstances of the particular case having regard, in particular, to the persons, class of persons or age groups into whose hands it was intended or likely to come.' (S. 4.)

(*f*) Meaning of Obscene and Indecent.

1. 'Without prejudice to the generality of the meaning of the word "obscene" any publication or advertisement shall be deemed to be obscene if it unduly emphasises matters of sex, crimes of violence, gross cruelty or horror.' (S. 3 (2).)

2. 'Any advertisement in relation to contraception or contraceptives shall be deemed to be an indecent advertisement.' (S. 3 (1).)

3. 'In determining for the purposes of this Act whether any publication or advertisement is obscene the court shall have regard to—

(a) the nature of the publication or advertisement; and

(b) the persons, class of persons and age groups to or amongst whom the publication or advertisement was or was intended or likely to be published, distributed, sold, exhibited, given or delivered; and

(c) the tendency of the publication or advertisement to deprave, corrupt, or injure the morals of any such persons, class of persons or age group.

to the intent that a publication or advertisement shall be held to be obscene when it tends or is likely in any manner to deprave, corrupt or injure the morals of any such persons or the persons in any such class or age groups, notwithstanding that persons in other classes or age groups may not be similarly affected.' (S. 3 (3).)

(*g*) Selected Cases.

1. *Bremner* v. *Walker* (1885), 6 L. R. (N.S.W.) 276; 2 W. N. 44.

The Defendant gave a lecture in support of the views of Mr. Bradlaugh and Mrs. Besant as expressed in *The Fruits of Philosophy*. Diagrams were exhibited consisting mainly of male and female human organs of generation.

Held. That the drawings were obscene, but that they would not be so if exhibited to those for whom they might be necessary instruction such as medical students.

2. *Ex parte Collins* (1888), 9 L. R. (N.S.W.) 497; 5 W. N. 85.

A conviction for publishing *The Laws of Population*, by Mrs. Besant, was set aside.

Wundeyer, J.: 'A court of law has now to decide for the first time whether it is lawful to argue in a decent way with earnestness of thought and sobriety of language the right of married men and women to limit the number of children to be begotten by them . . . the test in this case is not whether the tendency of the book is to promote immorality but whether the language of the book itself is obscene.' (At pp. 506 and 510.)

3. *Thompson* v. *Storer* (1933), 50 W. N. (N.S.W.) 199.

In this case expert medical evidence was admitted given by a professor of medicine at Sydney University and two ministers of religion who testified that the work in question was 'a medical treatise' and, therefore, exempted from the operation of the Obscene Publications Acts.

4. *Boyd* v. *Angus & Robertson Ltd.* (1946), 63 W. N. (N.S.W.) 189.

We Were the Rats, a novel by Lawson Glassop, was held to be obscene.

Studdert, D.C.J.: 'A first-rate war book and a first-rate novel . . . the author who had no need to rely upon pornography or blasphemy to hold the attention of the readers has thought it necessary or desirable to descend to both. . . . I have borne in mind the life of the soldier in Tobruk for which I imagine no one could get a better picture than from the book itself . . . but it seems to me that not everything a man says or does can be the subject of publication to the general public. . . . Finally, I should like to refer to what I consider one of the most objectionable features of the book. The dialogue from beginning to end teems with the irreverent use of the name of the founder of Christianity.'

B. Queensland

1. Criminal Code. (4 Geo. 5, No. 28 of 1913.)

'Any person who knowingly and without lawful justification or excuse:

(1) Publicly sells or exposes for sale any obscene book or other obscene printed or written matter, or any obscene picture, photograph, drawing or model or any other object tending to corrupt morals; or

(2) Exposes to view in any place to which the public are permitted to have access, whether on payment of a charge for admission or not, any obscene picture, photo, drawing, model, or any other object tending to corrupt public morals; or

(3) Publicly exhibits any indecent show or performance whether on payment of a charge for admission to see the show or performance or not; is guilty of a misdemeanour and is liable to imprisonment with hard labour for two years.

It is a defence to a charge of any of the offences defined in this section to prove that it was for the public good that the act complained of should be done. Whether or not the doing of any such act is or is not for the public good is a question of fact. (S. 228.)

2. The Vagrants Act. (22 Geo. 5, No. 27 of 1931.)

(*a*) It is an offence under this Act to publish, print, etc., any indecent or obscene matter. A first offence is punishable with a twenty-pound fine or three months' imprisonment. A second offence is penalised with a fifty-pound fine or six months' imprisonment. A third offence is punished with a one-hundred-pound fine or one year's imprisonment. If the offending publication is a newspaper its registration may be cancelled by the court. (S. 12.)

(*b*) Prosecutions under this Act may only be brought by a police officer and he must have the consent of an inspector or sub-inspector of police. A prosecution for exposing indecent cards may only be brought after a warning has been given. (S. 14.)

(*c*) The Act contains provision for search and seizure similar to the 1857 Obscene Publications Act. (S. 15.)

3. The Objectionable Literature Act, 1954. (3 Eliz. 2, No. 2 of 1954.)

(1) The Act sets up a Board to be called 'The Literature Board of Review', consisting of a Chairman and four members. Members hold office during the pleasure of the 'Governor in Council' for a period not longer than three years. (S. 6.)

(2) Three members must be present to form a quorum. (S. 7.)

(3) 'The Board shall—

(i) Examine and review literature with the object of preventing the distribution in Queensland of literature which or any part of which is objectionable: Provided that the Board shall not at any time examine or review any part of any literature consisting solely of public news, intelligence, or occurrences, or political or religious matter, or any remarks or observations therein.

(ii) Furnish to the Minister, when and as often as may be required, a report generally upon, or, as may be requested, any information in relation to, all or any matters affecting or having relation to the object for which the Board is constituted or to the Board's carrying out, and giving effect to, the provisions of this Act.' (S. 8.)

4. 'Objectionable' is defined in the Act. 'In relation to literature or any part of any literature, regard being had to the nature thereof, the persons, classes of persons, and age groups to or amongst whom that literature is or is intended to be or is likely to be distributed and the tendency of that literature or part to deprave or corrupt any such persons (notwithstanding that persons in other classes or age groups may not be similarly affected thereby), objectionable for that it—

(i) Unduly emphasises matters of sex, horror, crime, cruelty, or violence; or

(ii) Is blasphemous, indecent, obscene or likely to be injurious to morality; or

(iii) Is otherwise calculated to injure the citizens of this State.' (S. 5.)

5. 'Nothing in this Act shall apply with respect to any newspaper containing only public news, intelligence, or occurrences, or political matter, or any remarks or observations therein, or advertisements which are not objectionable under and within the meaning of this Act, or only a combination of any of these, or with respect to any publication of a medical, pharmaceutical, legal or other professional character *bonâ fide* intended only for circulation among members of the profession concerned, or any publication intended only for *bonâ fide* political purposes, or which represents in good faith and with artistic merit any work of recognised literary merit, or any scriptural, historical, traditional, mythical, or legendary story only.

Moreover the Governor in Council may from time to time by order in Council exempt any literature from the operation of this Act and while that order in Council remains in force such literature shall be exempted accordingly:

Provided that in any proceedings whatsoever it shall lie on the person alleging the fact to prove that any literature the subject of the proceedings falls within the provisions of this subsection or, as alleged is exempted hereunder from the operation of this Act.' (S. 4.)

6. Powers of the Board.

(*a*) 'The Board may by its order prohibit the distribution in Queensland of any literature if that literature or some part thereof is in the opinion of the Board, objectionable.' (S. 10.)

(*b*) A person shall not in Queensland—

(i) Distribute; or

(ii) Either in writing or otherwise howsoever promise, offer, represent, or advertise that he will distribute (whether the actual distribution is to be in Queensland or elsewhere) any literature at any time when the distribution in Queensland of that literature is prohibited by an order of the Board. (S. 10.)

(*c*) Orders may be revoked by the Board when the book, etc., has been 're-constructed so as to be no longer objectionable'. (S. 10.)

(*d*) Any person aggrieved by the Board's decision may appeal to a court which will decide whether the publication is 'objectionable'. (S. 11.)

7. Powers of Seizure.

Any member of the police force may enter and search premises of distributors of literature and seize and remove any literature under the ban of the Board. The owner may appeal to a court for a restitution order. (S. 14.)

8. Punishment.

(*a*) 'Any person guilty of an offence against any provision of this Act shall be liable, if no specific penalty is provided for that offence to a penalty not exceeding one hundred pounds or in the case of a second or any subsequent offence to a penalty not exceeding five hundred pounds.'

(*b*) All trial is summary.

(*c*) 'A prosecution for an offence against this Act may be instituted at any time within twelve months after the commission of the offence or within six months after the commission of the offence comes to the knowledge of the complainant, whichever is the later period.' (S. 17.)

9. Contracts.

'Every contract with respect to the distributing of any literature, whether made before, on, or after the coming into operation of this Act, shall be deemed to contain a provision that if, by reason of any order of prohibition with respect to that literature made under this Act by the Board, any of the parties to that contract would in carrying out that contract or any part thereof commit an offence against this Act, then he shall be excused from carrying out the contract or part as aforesaid; and every other term, provision, or condition of that contract or of any other agreement between the parties shall be read subject to such provision.' (S. 21.)

C. South Australia

1. Criminal Law Consolidation Act, 1935. (No. 2252 of 1935.)

S. 270. 'Any person convicted of any of the following common law misdemeanours that is to say:

(*a*) Any public selling or exposing for public sale or to public view of any obscene book, print, picture, or other indecent exhibition: shall be liable to be imprisoned for any term not exceeding two years.'

2. South Australia Police Act, 1936. (No. 2280 of 1936.)

(*a*) It is an offence to sell, exhibit or distribute indecent advertisements. For a first offence the punishment is a fine of not more than ten pounds and for a subsequent offence not less than fifty pounds. (S. 108.)

(*b*) Indecent details of judicial proceedings may not be reported save in law reports, etc. (S. 109.)

(*c*) News accounts relating to sexual morality in newspapers are restricted. No one report may occupy 'more than 50 lines of 13 ems wide or the equivalent thereof in any kind of type or carry a heading composed of type larger than ten-point capitals'. For breach of this provision or (*b*) above the penalty on first conviction is a fine of not more than two hundred pounds and on a second conviction a fine of not more than five hundred pounds or six months' imprisonment or both (S. 110).

(*d*) No proceedings under ss. 109 or 110 may be taken without the consent of the Commissioner of Police. (S. 115.)

D. Tasmania

1. The Criminal Code, 1924. (14 Geo. 5, No. 69 of 1924.)

(*a*) Any person who knowing or having a reasonable opportunity of knowing the nature thereof publicly sells or exposes for public sale or to public view or distributes to the public any obscene book or other printed or written matter, or any picture, photograph, model or other object tending to corrupt morals or publicly exhibits any disgusting object or indecent show is guilty of a crime.

(*b*) In any prosecution for a crime under this section it shall be a defence to prove that the act alleged was done for the public good. The question whether any such act as aforesaid was capable of being for the public good, and whether there is any evidence in the circumstances of excess beyond the requirements of the public good are questions of law. The questions whether such act as aforesaid was for the public good and whether there was any such excess as aforesaid are questions of fact. (S. 138.)

2. Police Offences Act, 1935. (26 Geo. 5, No. 44 of 1935.)

(*a*) It is an offence to sell, print, deliver, etc., any indecent matter. Punishment is a fine of fifty pounds or if the offence was committed 'wilfully' a fine of one hundred pounds or three months' imprisonment. (S. 26.)

(*b*) 'In determining whether any document, representation or other matter is of an indecent nature or suggests indecency within the meaning of this division, the magistrate shall take into consideration not merely the nature of that document, representation or matter itself, but also the nature and circumstances of the act done by the defendant with respect thereto and the purpose with which the act was done, and the literary, scientific, or artistic merit or importance of the document or matter: and no document, representation or matter shall be held to be indecent unless having regard to these and all other relevant considerations the magistrate is of the opinion that the act of the defendant was of an immoral or mischievous tendency.' (S. 27.)

(*c*) Publications advocating the prevention of conception are deemed 'indecent'. (S. 28.)

(*d*) A master is vicariously liable for the act of a servant if the act is done in the course of his employment. (S. 28.)

(*e*) Absence of guilty knowledge is not a defence. (S. 28.)

(*f*) Powers of seizure and destruction are given by S. 29.

(*g*) No prosecution may be brought without the consent of the Attorney-General. (S. 30.)

3. Objectionable Publications Act, 1954. (No. 80 of 1954.)

(*a*) The Act sets up a 'Board of Review' of not more than five persons appointed by the Governor. (S. 4.)

(*b*) Powers of the Board.

(1) 'The Board shall

(i) examine and review publications with the object of preventing the distribution in this State of objectionable publications, or any part thereof, and in particular and without prejudice to the generality of this sub paragraph, examine and review any particular publication that is referred to it by the Minister for examination and review.

(ii) furnish to the Minister as and when required by him, such reports and information as he may require (either generally or in a particular case or in respect of a particular matter) in relation to the administration of this Act or the exercise or performance of the Board's functions or duties under this Act.' (S. 7.)

(2) 'Where in the opinion of the Board any publication consists in substantial part of pictures (whether with or without the addition of words) and—

(*a*) is of an indecent nature or suggests indecency; or

(*b*) portrays, describes, or suggests acts or situations of a violent, horrifying, or criminal, or of an immoral nature,

the Board may, having regard to the matters, referred to in section ten, determine that the publication is an objectionable publication.' The Board may by order prohibit the distribution of that publication in this State. (S. 8.)

(3) Objections may within fourteen days of the publication of a decision of the Board be lodged with its secretary. The Board must then fix a time and place for the hearing of the objection. An objector is given the right to appear before the Board and may call witnesses. (S. 9.)

(4) 'For the purposes of this Act in determining whether a publication is objectionable the Board shall have regard to—

(*a*) the nature of the publication;

(*b*) the persons, class of persons, and age groups to or amongst whom or which the publication is intended, or is likely, to be distributed;

(*c*) the tendency of the publication to corrupt those persons, class of persons, or age groups, or any of them, notwithstanding that other persons or classes of persons, or persons in other age groups, may not be similarly affected thereby;

(*d*) the nature and circumstances in which the publication is distributed in this State; and

(*e*) the literary, scientific or artistic merit or importance of the publication;

to the intent that a publication shall not be deemed to be objectionable unless, having regard to the foregoing matters and all other relevant considerations, the Board is of the opinion that the distribution of the publication in this State would have an immoral or a mischievous tendency or effect.' (S. 10.)

(5) 'Publication' means 'any book, pamphlet, magazine, or printed paper, and (without prejudice to the generality of this definition) includes a publication of the type that is commonly or popularly known as a comic, comic paper, comic strip, comic book, or crime comic, but does not include:

(*a*) a newspaper; or

(*b*) a publication that is of a purely official, religious, or professional or scholastic character.' (S. 2.)

(*c*) Offences.

'No person shall:

(a) distribute in this State any publication to which a subsisting order under s. 8 applies;

(b) fail upon payment or tender by an authorised officer or by a police officer of the current market price therefor or at the prescribed rate of payment, to sell to that officer any publication that is demanded by him; or

(c) contravene or fail to comply with any other provision of this act that is applicable to him.

Penalties: For a first offence fifty pounds; for a subsequent offence, not less than five pounds or more than one hundred pounds, or imprisonment for three months or both.' (S. 15.)
In addition the publication may be confiscated. (S. 12.) Trial is summary. (S. 18.)

(*d*) Contracts.

'Notwithstanding any contract or any term or condition of any contract (whether entered into before or after the commencement of this Act and whether the contract is oral or in writing or is express or implied) a person is not liable for breach of contract by reason only of his rejecting any publication that is delivered to him, or of his refusing to accept delivery of, or to deal in any manner in, any publication if he is in good faith and reasonably believes that his acceptance of delivery of, or his possession of, or his dealing in, that publication may render him liable to be prosecuted under this Act or under section one hundred and thirty-eight of the Criminal Code or under Division IV or Part II of the Police Offences Act 1935.' (S. 16.)

(*e*) Powers of Search and Seizure.

These are conferred on authorised officers and police officers by s. 11.

E. Victoria

1. Police Offences Act, 1928. (No. 3749 of 1928.) As amended by Police Offences (Obscene Publications) Act of 1938. (No. 4573 of 1938.)

(*a*) 'Every person who

(a) knowingly keeps or knowingly suffers or permits to be kept any obscene articles for the purpose of gain in any house or place of which he is the occupier; or

(b) being the owner of any obscene articles knowingly keeps or knowingly suffers or permits to be kept such obscene articles in any house or place for the purpose of gain; or

(c) prints photographs, lithographs, draws, makes, sells, publishes, distributes or exhibits any obscene articles or assists therein,

shall for a first offence be liable to a penalty of not more than fifty pounds or to imprisonment for a term of not more than twelve months and for a second or any subsequent offence be liable to a penalty of not more than one hundred pounds or to imprisonment for a term of not more than two years.' (S. 171 as amended.)

(*b*) 'Every person who exhibits in any picture theatre or place of public resort any film or cinematograph display which is of an indecent or obscene nature or is of a disgusting nature etc. . . . shall be liable to a penalty of not more than five pounds or to imprisonment for a term of not more than three months.' (S. 173.)

(*c*) It is also an offence for any newspaper to include any pictures or advertisements of an indecent, obscene or disgusting nature. (S. 177.) No prosecution for this or a number of allied offences (Ss. 178, 179, and 180) may be undertaken except by a 'member of the police force under the authority of the Chief Secretary or of the Minister of Public Health or of the Chief Commissioner of Police given either generally or in a particular case'. (S. 181.)

(*d*) 'No action suit or information or any other proceedings of what nature soever shall be brought against any person for anything done or omitted to be done or purporting to be done in pursuance of this part or in the execution of the authorities under this part unless notice in writing is given by the party intending to prosecute such action, suit or information or other proceeding to the intended defendant one month at least before prosecuting the same, nor unless such action etc. is brought or commenced within three months next after the act or omission complained of, or in case there is a continuation of damage then within three months next after the doing such damage has ceased.' (S. 183.)

(*e*) 'Obscene (without limiting the generality of the meaning thereof) includes:

(a) tending to deprave and corrupt persons whose minds are open to immoral influences; and

(b) unduly emphasising matters of sex, crimes of violence, gross cruelty or horror'. (S. 2 of 1938 Act, amended by s. 2 of 1954 Act.)

(*f*) S. 170 of the Act as amended by the 1938 Act confers similar powers of search, seizure and destruction as under the 1857 Obscene Publications Act. Instead of the words 'publication of them would be a misdemeanour and proper to be prosecuted as such' the words 'satisfied that any of the articles . . . are obscene' have been substituted. (S. 2 of 1938 Act.)

2. Police Offences (Obscene Publications) Act, 1954. (No. 5779 of 1954.)

(*a*) The Act gives the court new instructions as to the judging of a work 'obscene'. 'In determining for the purposes of this Part whether any article is obscene the court shall have regard to:

(a) the nature of the article; and

(b) the persons classes of persons and age groups to or amongst whom it was or was intended or was likely to be published, distributed, sold, exhibited, given or delivered; and

(c) the tendency of the article to deprave or corrupt any such persons class of persons or age group—

to the intent that an article shall be held to be obscene when it tends or is likely in any manner to deprave or corrupt any such persons or the persons in any such class or age groups, notwithstanding that persons in other classes or age groups may not be similarly affected.' (S. 2.)

(*b*) A new section is substituted for s. 184 of the 1928 Act.

'The provisions of this Part shall not apply to the printing, publishing, delivery, distribution, posting, keeping or possession of any work of recognised literary or artistic merit or of any *bonâ fide* medical political or scientific book pamphlet magazine or periodical unless the court is satisfied that notwithstanding its literary or artistic merit or its character as a medical political or scientific book pamphlet magazine or periodical, the printing, publishing etc. was not justified in the circumstances of the particular case having regard, in particular, to the persons, class of persons or age groups into whose hands it was intended or was likely to fall.' (S. 3.)

(*c*) Registration.

(1) The Act requires all distributors of printed matter to be registered. This does not apply to newspapers or to printed matter 'of a purely official, religious, social, professional, scholastic, commercial, business, advertising or trading character'. The Chief Secretary may create further exceptions from time to time. Every distributor is entitled to be placed on the register. 'After the first publication of the register any distributor of printed matter shall not sell; or distribute for sale any printed matter unless he is registered under this Act.' Every publication must also be marked with his name and address.

(2) 'Where any distributor of printed matter is convicted:

(a) of the indictable offence of publishing an obscene libel; or

(b) on summary conviction before a court of petty sessions consisting of a stipendiary magistrate sitting with or without other justices:

(i) of an offence against part V of the Principal Act (1928) or of aiding abetting counselling or procuring the commission of any such offence;

(ii) of an offence against this Act:

the court before which he is so convicted, in addition to and without prejudice to the imposition of any other penalty to which he may be liable, may in its discretion by order direct that his registration as a distributor of printed matter be cancelled or that the said registration be suspended for such period as the court directs.' On this point an appeal must always be allowed. 'After cancellation or during the period of suspension of any registration the distributor in question shall be deemed and taken for all purposes to be unregistered and shall be ineligible to be re-registered unless, upon application made in the prescribed manner to a court of petty sessions constituted as aforesaid after the prescribed notice in writing of intention so to apply has been served upon the Chief Secretary, the court directs that the said distributor be so re-registered.' (S. 8.)

(3) Penalties for breaches of the provisions of the Act are for a first offence a fine of not more than fifty pounds or imprisonment of not more than twelve months and for a second or any subsequent offence a fine of not more than one hundred pounds or to imprisonment for a term of not more than two years. (S. 12.)

(*d*) Contracts.

Exemption is provided for breach of any contract by rejection of printed matter by a bookseller etc. if he *bonâ fide* believes its acceptance would make him guilty of some obscene offence and he gives notice to the other party in writing of his reasons for rejection of a consignment etc. (S. 10.)

Note: 'Distributor' is defined as

'(a) in respect of any printed matter published in Victoria the publisher thereof; and

(b) in respect of any printed matter published outside Victoria, the person primarily responsible for its distribution or sale in Victoria.'

3. *R.* v. *Close*, [1948] V. L. R., 445.

This case is of interest since the law on obscene libel was fully reviewed by the judge. The author and publisher of *Sailor Beware* was prosecuted. They were found guilty.

Herring, C.J., applied the Hicklin test and declared it to be the law. On 'intention' he said: 'That there are cases where it may be rebuttable (i.e. the presumption of criminal intention) may be conceded. Thus, for example, it may be proper to ascertain the actual intent where a book is published for a limited class of people, for example the medical profession. But where publication is indiscriminate I think the decision in Hicklin's case must be taken as laying down the law.'

Gavan Duffy, J.: 'Put into plain terms the applicant's contention is that if a book is skilfully written and its obscenities faithfully mirror the scene and characters the author has chosen he has not infringed the law. This is not the rule here whatever it may be in some states of America. Literature is not yet a sanctuary or an Alsatia.'

Fullagar, J., held that literary merit was a relevant factor even at common law. 'It would not be true to say that any publication dealing with sexual relations is obscene. The relations of the sexes are of course legitimate matters for discussion everywhere. They *must* be dealt with in scientific works and they *may* be legitimately dealt with —even very frankly and directly—in literary works. But they can be dealt with cleanly and they can be dealt with dirtily. There are certain standards of decency which prevail in the community and you are really called upon to try this case because you are regarded as representing and capable of justly applying those standards. Do you think that the publication now before you is one in which these matters are dealt with artistically and with whatever frankness clearly? Or do you think that there are passages in it which are just plain dirt and nothing else, introduced for the sake of dirtiness and from the sure knowledge that notoriety earned by dirtiness will command for the book a ready sale.'

The judges doubted whether the exemption given by Stephen, J., in his digest about works published 'for the public good' was as wide as he stated.

F. Western Australia

1. Act to Suppress Indecent and Obscene Publications, 1902. (No. 14 of 1902.)

(*a*) The sale, publication, distribution, etc., of indecent or obscene works and articles is punished by a fine of not more than twenty pounds or not more than six months' imprisonment. (S. 2.) Trial is summary. (S. 3.)

(*b*) No newspaper may be prosecuted without the authority of the Attorney-General. (S. 6.)

(*c*) 'Nothing in this act relates to any work of recognised literary merit or to the delivery or exhibiting in the window of any shop, or the posting or causing to be posted for transmission by post for any lawful purpose of any *bonâ fide* medical work or treatise, but in any prosecution for an offence against this Act the burden of proof that a publication is a *bonâ fide* medical work or treatise, or a work of recognised literary merit shall lie on the defendant.' (S. 5.)

2. Criminal Code. (4 Geo. 5, No. 28 of 1913.)

'Any person who knowingly and without lawful justification or excuse:

(1) publicly sells or exposes for sale any obscene book or other obscene printed or written matter, or any obscene picture etc. or any other object tending to corrupt public morals; or

(2) exposes to view in any place to which the public are permitted to have access, whether on payment of a charge for admission or not, any obscene picture etc. or any other object tending to corrupt public morals; or

(3) publicly exhibits any indecent show or performance whether on payment of a charge for admission to see the show or performance or not; is guilty of a misdemeanour and is liable to imprisonment with hard labour for two years.'

It is a defence to a charge of any of the offences defined in this section to prove that it was for the public good that the act complained of should be done. Whether the doing of any such act is or is not for the public good is a question of fact. (S. 204.)

3. Canada

I. PUBLICATION OF OBSCENE MATTER (Criminal Code, 2 Eliz. 2, 1953, s. 150)

1. Everyone commits an offence who:

(*a*) makes, prints, publishes, distributes, circulates or has in his possession for the purpose of publication, distribution, or circulation any obscene written matter, picture, model, phonograph record, or other thing whatsoever; or

(*b*) makes, prints, publishes, distributes, sells or has in his possession for the purpose of publication, distribution or circulation, a crime comic.

2. Everyone commits an offence who knowingly without lawful justification or excuse:

(*a*) sells, exposes to public view or has in his possession for such a purpose any obscene written matter, etc.;

(*b*) publicly exhibits a disgusting object or an indecent show;

(*c*) offers to sell, advertises, publishes an advertisement of, or has for sale or disposal any means, instructions, medicine, drug, or article intended or represented as a method of preventing conception or causing abortion or miscarriage; or

(*d*) advertises or publishes an advertisement of any means, instructions, medicine, drug, or articles intended or represented as a method for restoring sexual virility or curing venereal disease or disease of the generative organs.

3. No person shall be convicted of an offence under this section if he established that the public good was served by the acts that are alleged to constitute the offence and that the acts alleged did not extend beyond what served the public good.

4. For the purposes of this section it is a question of law whether an act served the public good and whether there is evidence that the act alleged went beyond what served the public good, but it is a question of fact whether the acts did or did not extend beyond what served the public good.

5. For the purposes of this section the motives of the accused are irrelevant.

6. Ignorance of the nature or the presence of articles mentioned in sub-s. 1 is no defence.

7. In this section 'crime comic' means a magazine, periodical or book that exclusively or substantially comprises matter depicting pictorially:

(*a*) The commission of crimes real or fictitious or

(*b*) Events connected with the commission of crimes, real or fictitious, whether occurring before or after the commission of the crime.

Note: S. 151 restricts the reporting of 'indecent matter' in relation to judicial proceedings, unless the Attorney-General gives his consent. The restriction does not apply to law reports intended for the use of the legal or medical profession or to matter published by order of the court. S. 494 (1) provides 'No count for publishing a blasphemous libel, etc., or for selling or exhibiting an obscene book, pamphlet, newspaper, or other written matter, is insufficient by reason only that it does not set out the writing that is alleged to be obscene'. Under s. 497 the court may order that such writing be set out.

II. THEATRICAL PERFORMANCES (Criminal Code, s. 152)

1. Everyone commits an offence who being the lessee, manager, agent or person in charge of a theatre presents or gives or allows to be presented or given therein an immoral, indecent or obscene performance, entertainment or representation.

2. Everyone commits an offence who takes part or appears as an actor, performer or assists in any capacity in an immoral, indecent, or obscene performance, entertainment or representation in a theatre.

III. POST (Criminal Code, s. 153)

Everyone commits an offence who makes use of the mails for the purpose of transmitting or delivering anything that is obscene, indecent, immoral or scurrilous. (Law reports, etc., excepted.)

IV. PUNISHMENT (Criminal Code, s. 154)

Offences under the preceding heads are punishable by: on indictment, imprisonment for two years; on summary conviction, a fine of five hundred dollars or six months' imprisonment or both.

V. CUSTOMS

Item 1201 of the Canadian Customs Tariff prohibits 'the importation of books, printed papers, drawings, paintings, prints, photographs, or representations of any kind of a treasonable, seditious, immoral or indecent character'.

VI. SELECTED CASES

1. *R.* v. *Britnell*, [1912] 4 D. L. R. 56 (C.A.).

'Knowingly' must be proved affirmatively by the prosecution. A bookseller with a large business was held not responsible for the sale by a clerk of an obscene book. No evidence was offered that the accused knew of the presence or the character of the book.

2. *R.* v. *St. Clair*, [1913] 12 D. L. R. 710 (C.A.).

A bulletin circulating amongst clergymen and containing descriptions of obscene theatrical performances was itself held to be obscene.

Per Hodgins, J.A.: 'The public good must be actually served, and an intention to serve it will not be sufficient.'

3. *R.* v. *Ballentine*, [1914] 22 C. C. C. 385 (N.B.).

Per Carleton, C.C.J.: 'A publication may be technically obscene, yet it is only when it tends to corrupt the morals by inflaming the passions and inciting to immoral conduct that it is punishable.'

4. *Conway* v. *R.*, [1944] 2 D. L. R. 530.

A tableau of actresses nude above the waist and standing motionless to represent 'living statuary' was not an obscene theatrical performance within the meaning of s. 208.

Per Lajure, J.: 'At the basis of every criminal offence there must be a criminal intent or *mens rea.* According to the evidence the show given by the appellant and for which the charge is laid was a tableau in which three girls stand perfectly motionless for the purpose of forming a background for a scene: they did not move, did not talk, and evidently tried to effect living statues. It is clear that the manager of the theatre wished to show a beautiful scene, some kind of artistic background. I do not say that he succeeded: he perhaps completely missed the effect he was after, but, nevertheless, the object sought by the appellant was to create a beautiful background and not an immoral scene. . . . I have come to the conclusion that in presenting the tableau the appellant had no intention of presenting an immoral or obscene show, but rather a background more or less artistic let us say, but not in itself indecent.' The judge then laid down the Hicklin test. 'So according to the defendant it would be necessary for a show to have a tendency to depravity. In the present case that was certainly not the appellant's intention.'

Theatrical critics, etc., were admitted to give evidence of the show's artistic and decorative purpose.

4. New Zealand

I. THE PENAL CODE (Crimes Act, 1908, s. 157)

1. An offence punishable with two years' imprisonment with hard labour is committed by anyone 'who knowingly without lawful justification or excuse publicly sells or exposes for public sale or to public view any

obscene book or other printed or written matter . . . or other object tending to corrupt public morals'.

2. No one is liable under this section if he proves that the public good was served by the acts alleged to have been done.

3. It is a question of law whether the occasion of the sale, publishing or exhibition was such as might be for the public good, and whether there is evidence of excess beyond what the public good requires in the manner, extent or circumstances in, to, or under which the sale, publishing, or exhibition was made, so as to afford a justification or excuse therefore: but it is a question for the jury whether or not there was such excess.

4. The motives of the seller, publisher or exhibitor shall in all cases be irrelevant, and it shall not be a defence that he did not know the matter or object or show, as the case may be, forming the subject of the charge was obscene or tended to corrupt public morals, or was disgusting or indecent, unless he satisfies the court not only that he did not in fact know it, but also that he had no reasonable opportunity of knowing it, and further that in the circumstances of the case his ignorance was excusable.

This is an indictable offence.

II. THE INDECENT PUBLICATIONS ACT, 1910 (as amended by the Act of 1954 (3 Eliz. 2, No. 78)

1. It is a summary offence punishable with a fine of fifty pounds, or a fine of one hundred pounds or three months' imprisonment if the offence is wilful, to publish an indecent document. (S. 3.) Trial is always before a magistrate sitting alone.

2. In determining whether a document, etc., is indecent a magistrate shall take into account:

(*a*) The nature of the document or matter.

(*b*) The nature and the circumstances of the act done by the defendant with respect thereto and the purpose for which the act was done.

(*c*) The literary or artistic merit or medical, legal, political or scientific character or importance of the document or matter.

(*d*) The persons, classes of person or age groups to or amongst whom the document or matter was or was intended or was likely to be published, distributed, sold, exhibited, given, sent or delivered: and the tendency of the matter or thing to deprave or corrupt any such persons, class of persons, or age group (notwithstanding that persons in other classes or age groups may not be similarly affected thereby). (S. 5 (1).)

3. No document or matter shall be held to be indecent unless having regard to the aforesaid and all other relevant considerations the magistrate is of opinion that the act of the defendant was of an immoral or mischievous tendency. (S. 5 (2).)

4. Subject to the provisions of s. 5 any document or matter which relates or refers or may be reasonably supposed to relate or refer to any disease

affecting the generative organs of either sex, or to any complaint or infirmity arising from or relating to sexual intercourse, or to the prevention or removal of irregularities in menstruation, or to drugs, medicines, appliances, treatment or methods for procuring abortion or miscarriage, to preventing conception, or which unduly emphasises matters of sex, horror, crime, cruelty or violence, shall be deemed to be indecent within the meaning of this Act.

5. If any act relating to publication of an indecent document is done by a servant in the course of his employment then the master is liable whether he authorised the act or not.

6. The 1954 Act requires all printed matter to have the name and address of the distributor printed upon it. Further all distributors, etc., must enter their names on a government register. After the date of publication of the register no distributor, etc., may sell or distribute for sale any printed matter unless his name is entered on the register. For any offence against s. 157 of the Crimes Act, 1908, or against the 1910 or 1954 Acts, the court may order the registration to be cancelled or suspended for a period. A registration can only be made by order of the court. Penalty for a first breach of this provision is a fine of fifty pounds or not more than one year's imprisonment, and for subsequent breaches a fine of one hundred pounds or not more than two years' imprisonment.

Newspapers, official publications, religious magazines, etc. are exempted from the necessity of registration.

7. Newsagents and booksellers are not liable for any breach of contract by refusing to accept printed matter if they believe its sale may involve them in an offence.

8. *Destruction Orders.* Under s. 10 of the Act a constable after laying a complaint on oath may obtain a search warrant and search premises for indecent documents. These may be seized and brought before the magistrate who may order their destruction after the expiration of fourteen days.

9. No person may be prosecuted under the Crimes Act, 1908, AND the Indecent Publication Acts.

10. The consent of the Attorney-General must be obtained before any proceedings are taken.

III. POST, CUSTOMS, RAILWAYS, ETC.

1. The importing of all indecent documents or articles within the meaning of the Indecent Publications Act is forbidden. (Customs Act, 1913, s. 46.)

2. Anyone who posts a postal packet containing any indecent or obscene print, etc., or having thereon (i.e. on the cover) any indecent words, etc., commits an offence and may be fined not more than twenty pounds. (Post and Telegraph Act, 1928, s. 106 (*e*) (*f*).)

3. It is an offence punishable by imprisonment of two months or fine of ten pounds to sell obscene books on railway property. (Government Railways Act, 1926, s. 31.)

IV. EVIDENCE

All courts and persons acting judicially may in matters of public history, literature, science or art refer for the purposes of evidence to such published books, maps or charts as such courts or persons consider to be of authority on the subject to which they respectively relate. (New Zealand Evidence Act, 1908, No. 56, s. 42.) In *Sumpter* v. *Stevenson*, [1939] N. Z. L. R. 446, Professor Savill was allowed to give evidence on literary value.

V. SELECTED CASES

1. *Clarkson* v. *McArthy*, [1917] N. Z. L. R. 624; G. L. R. 401.

Held: that to exhibit a photographic reproduction of Giorgione's 'The Sleeping Beauty' in a shop window was an act of an immoral or mischievous tendency.

Per Cooper, J.: 'It is a reasonable inference from the manner in which it was exhibited that it was placed by the appellant in the shop window for the purpose of attracting the attention by its nudity of passers-by.'

2. *Walsh* v. *Strathmore* (1932), 27 M. C. R. 97.

Salmon, S.M.: 'The word "bloody" however coarse it may appear in print cannot by any standard be described as indecent, but the word "bugger" is frankly obscene.'

3. *Sumpter* v. *Stevenson*, [1939] N. Z. L. R. 446.

Held: that no offence was committed by the London Book Club by selling *The Decameron* at sixpence to their subscribers.

A material factor was that the Club had not advertised the book in such a way as to indicate that it was indecent.

Blair, J., laid down certain principles:

(1) Proof that certain portions of a classical work offend against modern ideas of decency is not enough to support a conviction, and the nature and circumstances of selling or hiring of such a work, and its literary value and purpose must be considered.

(2) Not only must the matter be indecent but the circumstances of publication must be such as to bring the indecent element somewhat into the forefront, or to put it in another way, no offence is committed unless the purpose behind the publication is shown to be such as to give prominence to indecent portions of the work.

5. SOUTH AFRICA

I. OBSCENE OFFENCES

1. Any person who sells, distributes, offers for sale or distributes or wilfully exposes or causes to be exposed to public view any indecent or obscene publication commits an offence. (Act 31, 1892, (C), para. 2.)

(*R.* v. *Narroway*, C. P. D. 23 September 1927: Held that exhibition to two persons in a private room was not a 'public view'.)

2. An offence is committed by 'writing or transmitting or knowingly being a party to the writing or transmission of any communication containing threats of bodily injury or indecent or obscene matter: manufacturing, selling, exposing for sale, or exhibiting any obscene or indecent figure, cast, statue or model; selling, making, printing, circulating, exhibiting, or publishing any indecent book, paper, pamphlet, photograph, card, picture or other representation, advertising, etc., any means for the prevention of conception or procuring of abortion; and selling, buying or using anything intended to excite carnal desire'. (Act 38, 1909, (T) para. 2.)

3. In Natal it is an offence 'lewdly to give or send any indecent letter, etc., to any woman and anyone who does so exhibit any letter, etc., so as to be likely to give offence to women is declared guilty of indecency'. (Act 22, 1898.)

This does not apply to newspapers.

Note: (1) The Hicklin test of obscenity is part of South African Law. (2) It is a defence that publication was for the public good.

II. POST OFFICE (Union Statute)

Anyone who puts into the post office any article 'in or with or upon which there is any indecent or obscene matter or anything of a profane, libellous or grossly offensive character' commits an offence. (Act 10, 1911, para. 96 (1) (c).)

III. CUSTOMS (Union Statute)

(*a*) The importation of goods which are indecent or obscene or on any other ground whatsoever are objectionable may be prohibited. (Para. 21 (1) (*f*) of Customs Act, 1944.)

(*b*) The Minister may declare certain literature to be indecent. 'In the event of any question arising as to whether any goods are indecent or obscene or objectionable the decision of the Minister of the Interior shall be final: provided that in respect of engraved, printed, lithographic and photographic matter the decision shall be given after consultation with the Board of Censors appointed in the terms of sub-s. (1) of s. 2 of the Entertainments (Censorship) Act (No. 28 of 1931). Provided further that if any printed, engraved, lithographic, or photographic matter is according to the decision of the said minister indecent, obscene or objectionable, and is contained in any publication which in the opinion of the said minister is one of a series he may by notice in two consecutive issues of the *Gazette* publish the name of such publication and every issue of that publication shall thereupon and until such notice is withdrawn by him for the purposes of this section be deemed to be indecent, obscene, or objectionable as the case may be.

(*c*) Any goods imported contrary to the provisions of the Act are liable to forfeiture. (S. 122.) Anyone importing such goods is liable to a fine of not more than one thousand pounds or treble the value of the goods whichever is the greater, or imprisonment for not more than five years or both. (S. 124.)

(*d*) Where a notice has been issued under sub-s. 2 of s. 21 anyone 'who sells, offers or keeps for sale or distributes or exhibits' the named publications is guilty of an offence punishable with a fine of two hundred pounds or to imprisonment without the option of a fine of not more than twelve months or both. (S. 133.)

(*e*) Any prohibited goods intended for export may be confiscated. (S. 137.)

Note: *Commissioner of Customs* v. *Watchtower Bible and Tract Society*, [1941] C. P. D. 438. In arriving at a decision the Minister is obliged to afford the importer of the articles in question an opportunity to submit contentions upon the question as to whether the articles are indecent, obscene, or objectionable.

IV. ENTERTAINMENTS (Censorship Act, No. 28 of 1931, amended by Act 6, 1934)

Applies to any public entertainment, cinematograph films, etc.

(1) No person may exhibit any film or advertisement for a film without the approval of the Board of Censors (p. 1).

(2) The Board may not approve any film which in its opinion is calculated to be offensive to decency. A special prohibition applies to films which in the Board's opinion depict in an offensive manner nude human figures, passionate love scenes, vice or loose morals.

(3) Additional powers exist in Cape Province. (Ordinance 9, 1926, s. 2.)
The administration may prohibit the exhibition of a picture other than a film, play, or entertainment:

(*a*) Calculated to give offence to religious convictions or feelings of any section of the public.

(*b*) Calculated to bring any section of the public into ridicule or contempt.

(*c*) Contrary to morals or public policy.

(4) Additional powers of an administrative nature exist in Natal, Transvaal, and the Orange Free State.

6. INDIA AND PAKISTAN

1. The Indian Penal Code, 292. Whoever:

(*a*) sells, lets to hire, distributes, publicly exhibits or in any manner puts into circulation, or for purposes of sale, hire, distribution, public exhibition or circulation, makes, produces or has in his possession any obscene book, pamphlet, paper, drawing, painting, representation or figure or any other obscene object whatsoever, or

(*b*) imports, exports, or conveys an obscene object for any of the purposes aforesaid, or knowing or having reason to believe that such object will be sold, let to hire, distributed or publicly exhibited or in any manner put into circulation, or

(*c*) takes part in or receives profits from any business in the course of which he knows or has reason to believe that any such obscene objects are for any of the purposes aforesaid made, produced, purchased, kept, imported, exported, conveyed, publicly exhibited or in any manner put into circulation, or

(*d*) advertises or makes known by any means whatsoever that any person is engaged or is ready to engage in any act which is an offence under this section, or that any such obscene object can be procured from or through any person, or

(*e*) offers or attempts to do any act which is an offence under this section,

shall be punished with imprisonment of either description for a term which may extend to three months, or with fine, or with both.

Exception. This section does not extend to any book, pamphlet, writing, drawing, or painting, kept or used *bonâ fide* for religious purposes or any representation sculptured, engraved, painted or otherwise represented on or in any temple, or on any car used for the conveyance of idols, or kept or used for any religious purpose.

2. The Hicklin test of obscenity has been adopted by the courts. (Thakur Dutt (1917), P. R. No. 25 of 1917; Ghulam Hussein (1916), P. R. No. 5 of 1916.)

3. Works of art are never considered obscene. (Ranchhoddas, *The Indian Penal Code* (Bombay 1936).)

4. Indian Penal Code, s. 293 (*b*). Whoever sells, lets to hire, distributes, exhibits or circulates to any person under the age of twenty years any such obscene object as is referred to in the last preceding section, or offers or attempts so to do, shall be punished with imprisonment of either description for a term which may extend to six months, or with fine, or with both.

5. S. 294. Whoever, to the annoyance of others,

(*a*) does any obscene act in any public place, or

(*b*) sings, recites, or utters any obscene songs, ballad or words, in or near any public place,

shall be punished with imprisonment of either description for a term which may extend to three months, or with fine, or with both.

7. Ceylon

PENAL CODE

1. S. 285. Whoever sells or distributes, imports or prints for sale or hire or wilfully exhibits to public view any obscene book, pamphlet, paper, drawing, painting, photograph, representation or figure or attempts or offers so to do shall be punished with imprisonment of either description for a term which may extend to three months or with fine or with both.

2. S. 286. Whoever has in his possession any such obscene book or other thing as is mentioned in the last preceding section for the purpose of sale, distribution or public exhibition shall be punished with imprisonment of either description for a term which may extend to three months or with fine or with both.

3. S. 287. Whoever sings, recites or utters in or near any public place any obscene song, ballad or words to the annoyance of others shall be punished with imprisonment of either description for a term which may extend to three months or with fine or with both.

FOREIGN LAW

1. Belgium

A. OBSCENE OFFENCES

1. It is an offence to distribute, sell, or exhibit any books, prints, articles, etc., 'contraires aux bonnes mœurs', punishable with imprisonment from eight days to six months, and a fine from twenty-six to five hundred francs. It is also an offence punishable with the same penalties to distribute, import, or transport such articles for the purpose of commerce. (Article 383, Penal Code, Loi du 14 juin 1926.)

2. In such cases the author also commits an offence, punishable with imprisonment from one month to a year, and fine of from fifty to one thousand francs. (Art. 384, Loi du 14 juin 1926.)

3. Youth.

(*a*) Whenever a minor is involved in the above offences, the penalties are doubled. (Art. 386.)

(*b*) It is an offence punishable by a fine from twenty-six to five hundred francs to distribute to those under sixteen or to expose to public view any articles, etc., 'de nature à troubler leur imagination'. (Art. 386 (*b*), Loi du 31 mars 1936.)

4. Meaning of Obscene.

There is no statutory definition although the preamble to the 1936 statute refers to 'ce qui blesse ouvertement la pudeur'. (Pasinomie (1936), p. 353.)

A jurist's definition is: 'de nature à éveiller ou à surexciter des passions sensuelles'. (Nypels, *Code pénal belge interprété* (1897), T, II, p. 519.) There have been various attempts by judges to define the meaning of the word.

(*a*) 'Pour constituer le délit d'outrage aux bonnes mœurs, il ne suffit pas que des dessins, figures ou images aient, abstraction faite du texte imprimé, un caractère érotique, provoquant ou même légèrement licencieux; ils doivent avoir un caractère obscène, de manière à produire, à la simple vue un sentiment de réprobation. (Liège, 29 octobre 1901. Pas. (1902), II, p. 65; J. T. 1908, 1353; Jur. Liège, 1901, 291; P. P. 1902, 306.)

(*b*) 'Le nu n'a point, par lui-même, un caractère licencieux.' (Liège, 21 novembre 1950. Pas. (1951), II, p. 79.)

B. ADMINISTRATIVE POWERS

1. The king may by decree forbid the importing into Belgium of obscene foreign publications. Breaches of these decrees are punishable by fine and imprisonment. (Loi du 11 avril 1936.)

2. The judicial police—with the warrant of a magistrate—may seize and destroy obscene articles that are being exhibited, sold or distributed. (Art. 386 bis.)

3. Courts may destroy obscene articles which have been the object of a criminal charge; and obscene publications imported contrary to royal decree may be destroyed by the police.

4. The Minister of Communications may forbid by decree the transportation of any obscene articles within Belgium. This applies to the Post Office and all means of transport. (Art. 22 de la loi du 25 août 1891 sur le contrat de transport. Art. 78 de l'arrêté royal du 10 septembre 1936.)

5. Customs: officers may seize those publications which have been forbidden entry by royal decree. In the case of other publications they may seize them provisionally but must submit them to a magistrate for a decision. (See circulaire du Ministre des Finances du 31 mai 1948.)

6. No offence may be prosecuted more than three years after it has been committed.

C. ARTISTIC, LITERARY OR SCIENTIFIC MERIT

There is no legal obligation to take these matters into consideration, but this is done in practice, as the following extracts from judgements show.

(*a*) 'La représentation des formes humaines, même dans leur nudité integrale peut être offerte avec une harmonie de lignes, de contours, ou de couleurs qui satisfait et charme l'œil en provoquant une simple et pure émotion esthétique, sans éveiller dans le cœur du spectateur bien intentionné aucun sentiment mauvais, aucune excitation que 'auteur n'a, du reste, pas cherchée. Mais il en est tout autrement quand, sous prétexte d'art, l'auteur des dessins, images ou figurines n'a pas cherché à produire ou à reproduire une forme esthétique ou à provoquer une saine admiration de son œuvre, mais a, au contraire, créé un tableau auquel on ne peut trouver d'autre fin que de remuer les plus mauvais instincts de ceux quie le verront.' (Verviers, 3 juillet 1908, J. T. 1908, 1345; P. P. 1908, 1160; Rev. dr. pén. 1908, 764.)

(*b*) 'Le nu n'ayant pas nécessairement par lui-même un caractère licencieux et les attitudes figurées n'apparaissant pas comme le résultat d'une recherche voulue d'immoralité, le commerce de pareilles images s'adressant a une clientèle d'artistes et s'entourant de précautions speciales pourrait être toléré. Exposées aux yeux des passants ou mises dans un but de lucre à la portée du premier venu, semblables images sont incontestablement de nature à impressioner de façon malsaine l'imagination de la jeunesse et peuvent, à ce titre, donner prise à l'action de la justice. (Trib. Bruxelles, 29 décembre 1909. P. P. 1910, 132; Rev. dr. pén. 1910, 170.)

(*c*) 'Si le talent du dessinateur est, à l'exclusion des sujets traités, à même d'accaparer l'attention de quelque autre spécialiste du dessin, le caractère obscène de ces sujets n'en subsiste pas moins. Si les images obscènes ont, en vue de la vente, été réunies en catalogue avec d'autres qui sont irréprochables, les tribunaux doivent prêter attention à l'avis d'artistes avertis pour connaître l'utilité plus au moins grande de cet ouvrage pour l'étude et le perfectionnement de la technique de leur art. Il peut résulter de l'intérêt documentaire et de l'utilité technique même de l'ouvrage qu'il constitue un véritable instrument de travail et ne peut, en conséquence, aux yeux de législateur, être rangé dans la catégorie infamante des ouvres contraires aux bonnes mœurs.' (Corr. Liège, 26 février 1930. J. T. 1930, 221; P. P. 1930, 400; Rev. dr. pén. 1930, 402.)

(*d*) 'Les travaux de la science, utilisés dans le but en vue duquel ils sont faits, sont, par l'intention qui les inspire et par leur nature, étrangers à toute notion d'outrage aux mœurs, fussent-ils insérés dans un catalogue, et il est licitie d'y insérer des éléments graphiques quels qu'ils soient. Il en serait autrement si, sous prétexte d'œuvre scientifique, il avait été tenté de couvrir des faits punis par la loi.' (Cass. 7 décembre 1931; Pasic. (1932), I, p. 2.)

N.B. Whenever an offence involving a book is tried the case goes before la Cour d'Assises and not before the ordinary tribunals. Trial is by jury. (Art. 48 de la Constitution.)

2. Denmark

A. OBSCENE OFFENCES

1. The Danish Press Law prohibits the circulation of printed matter, the obscenity of which is obvious on a cursory reading. (S. 15 (2).)

2. The Danish Penal Code also punishes the distribution of obscene publications.

(*a*) Any person is liable to fine or, under aggravating circumstances, imprisonment for not more than six months who:

(a) offers or delivers obscene publications, pictures or articles to a person under eighteen years of age,

(b) publishes or distributes or for this purpose manufactures or imports obscene prints, pictures or articles,

(c) arranges any public shows or exhibitions of an obscene nature. (S. 234 (1), No. 1.)

(*b*) If the publication or importation is part of a general business in obscene articles affecting the whole public the penalty is increased to twelve months' imprisonment. (S. 234 (1), Nos. 2 and 3.)

(Taken from Act of 15 April 1930 as amended by Act of 15 March 1939.)

3. Post: Obscene or indecent articles are forbidden to be sent through the post. (Danish Post Law, 1919.)

4. Limitation of Proceedings.

(1) No prosecution may be brought more than two years after the offence has been committed.

(2) No prosecution may be commenced without the consent of the Attorney-General.

B. ADMINISTRATIVE POWERS

1. The Penal Code provides that where a conviction has been recorded all the obscene articles concerned can be confiscated. Such articles may also be confiscated if they are kept for the purpose of committing an offence. A court decision is necessary. (S. 77 (1), No. 1.)

2. The police in an emergency may impound obscene articles but must report the impounding to a court within twenty-four hours, which decides whether their action be upheld. (Code of Criminal Procedure, s. 746.)

C. ARTISTIC, LITERARY OR SCIENTIFIC MERIT

Works which seriously discuss sexual questions on a scientific basis or are a genuine attempt at literary or artistic creation are not considered obscene. It does not matter that the creation in itself has little artistic or æsthetic value. Works are normally judged as a whole but there have been instances of books being condemned on the basis of obscene passages.

3. FRANCE

A. GENERAL

The French law governing obscene offences or 'outrages aux bonnes mœurs' was originally contained in the Penal Code and in the law of 29 July 1881, but is now governed in essentials by the 'Decret-Loi' of 29 July 1939. Offences against youth were specially dealt with in a new law of 16 July 1949 (Loi No. 49—956) passed as a result of widespread concern about the literature and 'comics' being distributed to French youth. The question was first raised in 1947 and a Commission appointed to draft a new law. Under the 1949 Law a special Commission was appointed to supervise literature intended for children. Its functions were to propose positive measures for the improvement of children's literature; to bring any infractions of the law to the notice of the authorities; and to give advice to the Minister as to the foreign periodicals intended for youth which should be admitted into France. Their first report for the year 1950 laid down a code for comics and other forms of literature intended for children or young persons. (*Compte rendu des travaux de la commission de surveillance et de controle des publications destinées a l'enfance et l'adolescence*, Paris, 1952.)

B. OBSCENE OFFENCES

1. It is an offence punishable with imprisonment for a period from one month to one year and a fine of from 24,000 to 1,200,000 francs to make, possess, transport, distribute, sell, import, or export, for commercial purposes, or even for distribution or exhibition, any writings or designs, etc., 'contraires aux bonnes mœurs'. The meaning of this phrase is nowhere defined. (Art. 119, 'Decret-Loi' of 29 July 1939, D.P. 1939, 4, 369.)

2. It is an offence similarly punishable to advertise any such articles. (Art. 120.)

3. When a publication involving the Press is concerned the editor is held primarily responsible; then the author; then the printer, distributor, etc. The author, however, may always be joined as an accomplice.

4. If one of the above offences is committed and within the five years immediately following a further offence is committed the maximum penalties are increased to two years' imprisonment or a fine of up to 12,000,000 francs. (Art. 123.)

5. Accounts of criminal trials, etc., may not be published to be read by the general public nor may photographs or other representations of crimes or their surrounding circumstances be published. Penalties for the infractions of these provisions are fines from 12,000 to 240,000 francs. (Art. 38 de la loi du 29 juillet 1881 et Art. 128, 'Decret-Loi', 29 juillet 1939.) The judge may, however, authorise such publication.

6. Youth.

(*a*) When any of the above offences involves publication to a minor the penalties are doubled. (Art. 122, 1939 loi.)

(*b*) Publications intended principally for youth are subject to severe restrictions. Such publications 'ne doivent comporter aucune illustration, aucun récit, aucune chronique, aucune rubrique, insertion présentant sous un jour favorable le banditisme, le mensonge, le vol, la paresse, la lâcheté, la haine, la débauche, ou tous actes qualifiés crimes ou délits ou de nature a démoraliser l'enfance ou la jeunesse. Elles ne doivent comporter aucune publicité ou annonce pour des publications de nature à démoraliser l'enfance ou la jeunesse.' In 1954 the following words were added to this clause: 'ou de nature à inspirer ou entretinir des préjugés ethniques'. (Loi 29, II, 1954.)

Penalties for publishing the above are imprisonment from one month to a year and a fine of 50,000 to 500,000 francs. Penalties are increased for subsequent offences. (Art. 2 et Art. 7, Loi No. 49—956 du 16 juillet 1949.)

(*c*) It is also an offence to give or sell to any minor any publication which has been designated by the Minister of the Interior as being dangerous to youth. (Art. 14.)

(*d*) Publishers of periodicals, etc., intended for youth must be registered in a special manner, and if they are found guilty of one of the above offences may be suspended from publishing either temporarily or permanently. (Art. 7.)

7. No prosecution may be brought more than three years after the offence has been committed.

C. ADMINISTRATIVE POWERS

1. The judicial police may seize and destroy any obscene prints, books, articles, etc., provided that they are publicly exhibited. (Art. 126, 1939 loi.)

2. The court may order the destruction of any obscene articles involved in a trial, but if they have artistic or literary value may donate them to one of the state museums. (Art. 126, 1939 loi.)

3. The judicial police may seize obscene articles at the frontiers. (Art. 126, 1939 loi.)

4. The Post Office may refuse to accept obscene articles, etc., such as obscene postcards.

D. INTENTION

Under French law no crime is committed unless the accused realises the criminal nature of his act. In the case of offences 'contraire bonnes mœurs' such knowledge is presumed from the act itself, but it is open to the accused to rebut this presumption. If he realises the criminal nature of his act, his motives are irrelevant.

(Arrêt de la Chambre Criminelle de la Cour de Cassation du 23 juin 1928. Recueil, Dalloz, 1928, I, 161.)

E. ARTISTIC, LITERARY OR SCIENTIFIC MERIT

1. When a book is the object of the charge no prosecution can be brought without the consent of a special Commission set up to give advice in such matters. The Commission advises the Minister of Justice. (D. L., juillet 1939, art. 125; Décret 5 septembre 1945 (J. O. II. septembre); Décret 15 janvier 1948. (D. 1948, 62 B. L. D. 1948—117).)

2. Literary or other merit is no defence to the charge, but such merit may be taken into consideration when imposing the penalty.

Expert evidence on such matters is not admitted.

Note: In all judgements reasons must be given for the court's finding of any work obscene. If no indication is given the conviction is quashed. (Chambre Criminelle, 7 janvier 1937. Dalloz, 1937, I. 53.)

F. A NEW LAW

Under a law of 25 September 1946 a court decision holding a book obscene may be reviewed after twenty years. The right to commence the process rests either with the condemned author or publisher, any surviving relative, or 'la Société des Gens de Lettres de France'. Under this law the judgement against Charles Baudelaire, Poulet-Malassis and de Broise for publishing *Les fleurs du mal* was annulled by the Court of Cassation on 31 May 1949.

The following are extracts from the judgement.

> Le fait d'outrage aux bonnes mœurs se compose de trois éléments nécessaires: le fait de la publication, l'obscénité du livre et l'intention qui a dirigé son auteur.
>
> Les poèmes contenus dans les Fleurs du Mal et faisant l'object de la prévention ne renferment aucun terme obscène ou même grossier et ne dépassent pas en leur forme expressive les libertés permises a l'artiste.
>
> Si certaines peintures ont pu, par leur originalité alarmer quelques esprits à l'époque de la première publication, et apparaître aux premiers juges comme offensant les bonnes mœurs, une telle appréciation, ne s'attachant qu'à l'interprétation réaliste de ces poèmes et négligeant leur sens symbolique, s'est révélée de caractère arbitraire et n'a été ratifiée ni par l'opinion publique, ni par le jugement des lettrés.
>
> Par suite, le délit d'outrage aux bonnes mœurs relevé à la charge de l'auteur et des éditeurs n'etant pas caractérisé, le jugement intervenu doit être cassé et leur mémoire dechargée de la condamnation prononcée.
>
> (Du 31 mai 1949. Ch. Crim. MM. Battestini, pr.; Falco, rap.; Dupuich, Av.-Gén.) (See Dalloz (1949) *Jurisprudence*, p. 348.)

4. GERMANY

A. OBSCENE OFFENCES

1. By the Penal Code it is an offence punishable with a term of imprisonment up to one year and a fine:

(*a*) To offer for sale, sell, or distribute indecent (pornographic) publications, illustrations or pictures in places accessible to the public. Displaying, manufacturing, advertising, or keeping such objects for sale is also an offence.

(*b*) To sell or offer indecent (pornographic) publications, illustrations or pictures to a person under sixteen years of age.

(Par. 184, Penal Code, 1871, in published version of 25 August 1953. *Federal Law Papers*, Vol. I, p. 1083.)

2. It is also an offence to sell or distribute publications, etc., which without being pornographic offend grossly against the concept of decency. (Para. 184 (*a*).)

3. Under the Press Law an additional liability is imposed on editors, publishers, printers and distributors of periodicals. Their liability is first tested under the ordinary criminal law, but even if they have not been participants, they may still be held responsible for the publication of indecent matter, unless they can prove that they exercised due care and have not been negligent. (Paras. 20 and 21 of the Press Law, 7 May 1874. *Reichs-Law Gazette*, p. 65.) (Similar provisions are contained in the special Press Laws of Bavaria and Hesse. See Bavarian Press Act, 3 October 1949. B.L.A.R.G., p. 243, and Hessian Act for Freedom of Press, 23 June 1949. H.L.A.R.G., p. 75.)

4. *Youth.* In 1953 a special Act was passed by the Bonn parliament designed to protect the youth of the country from corrupting publications. The Act set up a special Federal Office to compile a list of publications 'liable to corrupt minors morally' including 'indecent publications and also publications extolling crimes, wars and racial hatred'.

A two-thirds majority of those in the 'office' is required to include a publication in the list.

(S. 1.) No publication may be inserted in the list:

(1) If it serves the purpose of art, or science, research or education.

(2) Its publication is in the public interest, unless the presentation gives offence.

(3) Merely on the strength of its political, social or ideological contents.

As soon as a publication is placed on the list, and this has been made public, it may not be offered for sale to a minor under eighteen years of age or made available to him. Nor may such publications be sold, distributed or lent by vendors outside business premises, nor sold from house to house by hawkers. Once a publication has been placed on the list it may not be commercially advertised, except in trade papers. A periodical publication may be placed on the list for a period from three to twelve months if more than two issues have previously been placed on the list. Newspapers, and magazines of a political nature, are exempted from this provision. Publications which obviously would be corrupting to minors to a serious degree are subject to the above restrictions without being placed on the list.

Penalties:

(*a*) Contravention of the above provisions with intent to do so, is punishable with imprisonment for up to one year, or a fine, or both.

(*b*) If the publication is merely negligent, then only a fine may be imposed.

(*c*) Confiscation of the publication may be ordered if it is not possible to prosecute or the publication has been with intent.

(*d*) If the publication has been made available to the minor by 'the person responsible for his upbringing' or another minor, there is no punishable offence.

Federal Office. This Office is made up of assessors presided over by a chairman appointed by the Minister of the Interior. The assessors are to be selected by the Minister from those connected with

(1) Art.
(2) Literature.
(3) The Book Trade.
(4) The Publishing Trade.
(5) Youth Organisations.
(6) Youth Welfare.
(7) Teaching Bodies.
(8) The Churches, the Jewish Religious Bodies, and other religious communities which are legal bodies.

Evidence. The Publisher and the Author are entitled 'as far as possible' to give evidence before the Office.

Appeal. The normal appeal procedure under administrative law is applicable. The time limit for an appeal is one month from the publication of the decision.
(Act of 9 June 1953. Published at Bonn, 16 June 1953. *Federal Law Gazette*, No. 27, p. 377.)

5. The concept of 'indecency' is not defined by statute, but has been defined by the judges as that which is 'offensive to the sense of shame and decency with regard to matters of sex'. (Supreme Criminal Court, Vol. IV, p. 87; Vol. XXI, p. 306; Vol. LVI, p. 175.) The determining factor is the reaction of the ordinary unbiased member of the public. (Supreme Criminal Court, Vol. XXXII, p. 418; Vol. XLVIII, p. 230.)

6. (*a*) Offences under the Penal Code and the Juveniles Publications Act, 1953, must be prosecuted within five years. (Penal Code, para. 67, sub-para. 2.)

(*b*) Offences under the Press Acts must be prosecuted within one year. Shorter periods apply under the Bavarian and Hessian laws.

B. ADMINISTRATIVE POWERS

1. Where a prosecution is not possible a destruction order may be applied for. (*Penal Code*, para. 42.)

2. Where there has been a conviction an order should be made ordering the destruction of all copies of the relevant works in the possession of the author, printer, publisher or bookseller, and which are publicly displayed or offered for sale. (*Penal Code*, para. 41.)

3. See under *Youth* above for powers under the 1953 Act.

4. Seizure of publications can ordinarily only take place under a court order, but in urgent cases the police may take action. For destruction of the articles seized, a court order is always necessary. (Para. 94 & 98, Criminal Proceedings Act.)

5. (*a*) Customs authorities are to search for pornographic prints, books, etc., and on discovery to inform the local police so that they may take action. (*Guiding Principles*, No. 232, sub-para. 4.)

(*b*) The Post Office have power to seize goods of an indecent nature sent through the post. Under para. 48 of the Postal Regulations the authorities are required to return such goods to the senders. (Postal Regulations, 30 January 1929, N.L.G., I, p. 33.)

C. INTENTION

1. An express criminal intention is not necessary to constitute an offence under the Penal Code, but to be convicted the accused must know that the contents of the publication are liable to offend against the general sense of shame and decency. (Supreme Criminal Court, Vol. XXXVII, p. 315.)

2. In the cases of offences involving youth the accused must be aware that the person he dealt with was under sixteen or eighteen years of age, before he can be convicted of any offence.

3. Special provisions with regard to 'intent' and 'negligence' apply under the 1953 Act. See under *Youth* above.

D. ARTISTIC, LITERARY OR SCIENTIFIC MERIT

1. If a publication treating of sexual matters is of a scientific or artistic nature, then it is not considered obscene. The artistic purpose is taken to 'ennoble' the subject-matter and there is no offence against shame or decency. (Supreme Criminal Court, Vol. LVI, p. 176.)

2. Publications must be judged as a whole and in relation to the whole work indecent passages may become insignificant. (Supreme Criminal Court, Vol. XXIII, p. 390.) The publication of the indecent passages by themselves would, however, be an offence. (Supreme Criminal Court, Vol. XXIII, p. 388; *New Legal Weekly*, 1953, p. 1317.)

E. UNIFORMITY IN ADMINISTRATION

Principles for administering the law on obscenity have been laid down by the Länder and are binding throughout the federal republic. (*Guiding Principles*, 1 August 1953, Nos. 224, 225, 229, 231.) Information on prosecutions, etc., is collated by the Federal C.I.D. office which makes this available to the local police, etc.

5. GREECE

A. OBSCENE OFFENCES

1. The printing, acquisition, possession, transportation, importing or exporting of obscene publications of any sort for the purpose of trade,

distribution or public exhibition is an offence punishable by fine and imprisonment. (Law 5060 of 30 June 1931 and Law of Necessity 1092 of 21–22 February 1938, modified by the Law of Necessity 1683 of 27 March/1 April 1939.)

Obscenity is defined as 'a direct or indirect prejudice to the moral conceptions of the public' and as 'an offence to decency in accordance with public feeling'. The test of obscenity may be an isolated passage or the whole book.

2. *Customs and Post.* Neither of these bodies has any special powers.

3. *Limitation of Proceedings.* No prosecution may be instituted more than eighteen months after the date of publication.

B. ADMINISTRATIVE POWERS

The police may obtain destruction orders from the courts.

C. INTENTION

An intention to sell, exhibit, or circulate is necessary to establish the offence. The author and the publisher are primarily liable, but if they are not known the printer is held responsible.

D. ARTISTIC, LITERARY OR SCIENTIFIC MERIT

1. The regulations do not apply to such works of established value.

2. No work of art or science can be considered obscene unless it is sold or given to a person under eighteen for a non-educational purpose.

6. JAPAN

A. OBSCENE OFFENCES

1. 'A person who distributes, sells or exhibits publicly obscene literature, drawings, etc., shall be subject to imprisonment for a term not exceeding two years or to a fine not exceeding five thousand yen.' (Article 175 of the Criminal Code.) Authors are indicted as accomplices.

2. *Definition of Obscenity.* There is no statutory definition, but the concept has been defined in the courts.

'Obscene objects are those objects which stir up and excite sexual desire, spoil the normal sexual modesty of the ordinary human being and are contrary to good sexual morals.' (Supreme Court, 10 May 1951.)

'Obscene literature is, generally speaking, literature which includes the expression stimulating sexual desire by which one shall become sexually excited to the extent that even restraint by reason would be impossible or extremely difficult and which makes one feel immodest or repulsive.' (Tokyo Regional Court, 18 January 1952.)

'Obscene literature is literature which excites or stirs up sexual desire by the undisguised and minute description of sexual organs or sexual behaviour, spoils normal sexual modesty and is contrary to good sexual morals. The scope of obscene literature tends to become gradually narrower with the progress of time, and judgement of it should be made in the light of the good sense of the people in the generation in question.' (Tokyo High Court, 10 December 1952.)

3. The test of obscenity is normally the whole book and not isolated passages, but in the *Lady Chatterley's Lover* case the court said: 'Even when isolated passages are considered to come under the definition of obscenity, the whole book will be treated as obscene literature, unless some measures are taken to eliminate those isolated passages. (Tokyo High Court, 10 December 1952.)

4. *Post and Customs*

(*a*) Obscene articles, etc., may not be sent through the post. (S. 4, Art. 14 of Postal Law, read with Art. 175 of Criminal Code.)

(*b*) 'Books, drawings, etc., which are injurious to good morals' may not be imported. (S. 3, para. 1, Art. 21 of Customs Tariff Law.) The Customs authorities may confiscate and destroy such articles or order the person importing them to return them to the country of origin. (*Ibid.*, para. 2.)

B. ADMINISTRATIVE POWERS

1. The prosecutor, procuratorial official, and judicial police are authorised to seize obscene matter. (Law of Criminal Procedure, para. 1, Art. 222.)

2. The Court may also order the seizure and destruction of obscene matter. (*Ibid.*, Art. 99. See also: S.I., Para. I, Art. 19 Criminal Code.)

N.B. The Film Industry has established an organisation, 'The Japan League of Film Production', which endeavours to eliminate anything of an obscene nature from films by providing 'ethical regulations for film production'.

C. INTENTION

'The criminal intention of selling obscene literature is sufficiently established when the accused is aware of the fact that obscene descriptions are contained in the book, and that he is selling such a book. It is not necessary that the accused should be able to judge the measure of obscenity of descriptions contained in the book.' (Tokyo High Court, 10 December 1952.)

'In order to establish the crime of distributing obscene literature, it is not necessary that the accused should be aware of the obscenity of its contents.' (Nagoya High Court, 26 April 1950.)

D. ARTISTIC, LITERARY OR SCIENTIFIC MERIT

Scientific books dealing with sexual subjects are not generally regarded as obscene, but literary or artistic merit does not constitute a defence. 'Obscene literature and drawings are those which tend to mislead the general public in their just understanding of sexual life and to corrupt good morals, and their artistic merits shall not be taken into consideration when judging their obscenity.' (Nagoya High Court, 26 April 1951.)

In 1952 *Lady Chatterley's Lover* was condemned as obscene. An appeal to the Supreme Court is now pending but the judgement of the High Court is of interest. 'In general the aim of literature lies in enquiring into every problem of human life, and it is undeniable that love and sex, which play an important part in human life, have been favourite subjects of writers. Literature lives in and depends on human society; it deals with the problems of men in their social lives. It must abide by the conditions which form and maintain social order. It is, therefore, impossible to give literature such absolute liberty as to enable it to neglect these conditions. Such conditions bring about a certain limit to the manner in which literature can express itself. Literature becomes liable to the measures of punishment which are enacted to maintain social order, when its manner of expression goes beyond that limit and renders the contents of literature subject to the definition of the above-mentioned 'obscene literature'. . . . However, there can be a case in which the artistic character of literature attenuates and sublimates sexual impulse created by the sexual description in certain passages, or in which the persuasive of the philosophy or the idea of literature, does away with the character of obscenity.' (Tokyo High Court, 10 December 1952.)

7. SWEDEN

A. GENERAL

The provisions controlling the sale and distribution of obscene literature are contained in the Press Law of 1949. This is one of the four fundamental laws in which the Swedish constitution is contained, and which can only be repealed by special procedure. The Act provides that: 'Every Swedish citizen shall have the right to express his thoughts and opinions in print, to publish official documents and to make statements and communicate information on any subject whatever, subject to the regulations set forth in this Act for the protection of individual rights and public security'. (Chap. 1, Art. 1.) The Act further provides that: 'No publication shall be subject to censorship before being printed nor shall the printing thereof be prohibited'. (Chap. 1, Art. 2.) Finally, it is provided that: 'A person whose duty it is to pass judgement on abuses of the freedom of the Press or otherwise to ensure compliance with this Act shall constantly bear in mind that freedom of the Press is the foundation of a free society and should always pay more attention to illegality in the subject-matter and thought than in the form of expression, in the aim rather than in the manner of presentation, and in doubtful cases, should acquit rather than convict'. (Chap. 1, Art. 4.)

Under Swedish law all authors whether of articles or books have the right to remain anonymous and if they exercise this right may not be subjected to any criminal proceedings. (Chap. 3.)

B. OBSCENE OFFENCES

1. *General*

(*a*) 'Statements in printed matter shall be considered unlawful when they include representations generally punishable according to law as amounting to actions offensive to decency.' (Chap. 7, Art. 4, s. 12.) The penalty for making such statements is a fine or imprisonment for not more than two years. (Chap. 18, para. 13, of Penal Code.)

(*b*) Under the Press Law responsibility for publication of obscene matter is always limited to a single person. If responsibility cannot be placed on this person (because of the anonymity rule, etc.) it passes to another specified in the law.

2. For periodicals the editor, who must be appointed by the owner, is primarily responsible; secondly, it rests on the editor's representative; thirdly, on the owner; fourthly, on the printer. For non-periodical publications the author is primarily responsible, provided his name is given; secondly, the publisher; thirdly, the printer. (Chap. 8.)

3. *Youth.* 'The circulation among children and young persons of printed matter, the contents of which may have a brutalising effect, or may otherwise involve serious danger to the moral upbringing of young persons', is governed by special provisions and is forbidden. (Chap. 6, Art. 2.) The penalty provided for this in a draft Bill, not yet approved in the Riksdag, is imprisonment for not more than six months or a fine.

In Spring 1954 'horror comics' were the subject of a debate in the Riksdag.

4. *Customs and Post.* No special restrictions can be imposed on the sending of printed matter through the post or other public transport organisation on the grounds of its contents. The Customs authorities have no rights to impose restrictions. They are expressly forbidden. (Chap. 6, Art. 4.)

5. *Limitation of Proceedings*

(*a*) Proceedings must be taken within six months of publication. (Chap. 9, Art. 3).

(*b*) No prosecution can be undertaken without the advice of the Minister of Justice and the consent of the Attorney-General. (Chap. 9.)

6. *Trial is by Jury*

C. ADMINISTRATIVE POWERS

1. When any person has been convicted of an obscene offence all copies of the publication intended for circulation may be confiscated.

2. Instead of a prosecution a petition for confiscation may be brought.

3. The Minister of Justice may order the seizure of alleged obscene matter, but legal proceedings must be commenced within a fortnight or the seized matter returned to its owner. Furthermore, pending a decision of the court a ban on further publication may be issued. After proceedings have been

commenced the court itself may issue a seizure order or a publishing ban, pending its own decision.

4. If matter 'manifestly constitutes an offence against decency' the police may temporarily impound matter, but they must then apply for a seizure order. (Chap. 10, 'On Special Co-ercive Measures'; Chap. 7, Art. 7.)

5. All administrative decisions must be confirmed by a court.

D. INTENTION

This is not relevant to the offence except so far as the provisions of Art. 4 of Chapter 1 apply. (See A. General)

E. ARTISTIC, LITERARY OR SCIENTIFIC MERIT

The Law contains no specific provision about these matters. In practice such works are never prosecuted, only flagrant cases of pornography reaching the courts. (The average number of cases is five per annum.) The matter is judged by its general character and a defendant may cite in his defence statements by witnesses or experts regarding the literary or other qualities of the work.

8. SWITZERLAND

A. OBSCENE OFFENCES

Swiss federal law draws a fundamental distinction between publications which are 'obscene' and those which are 'immoral'.

1. It is an offence to distribute, exhibit, import or export any obscene articles, 'en vue d'en faire le commerce ou la distribution ou de les exposer en public'. Punishment is a fine of up to 20,000 francs or up to three years' imprisonment. Unless the general public is involved, there is no offence. Private transactions are thus outside the scope of the law. (Art. 204, Code penale suisse.)

2. Meaning of 'Obscene'. No statutory definition is given to the word, but it has been left to judges and legal writers to define its meaning. Two definitions may be cited:

(*a*) 'tout ce que blesse la pudeur, tout ce qui s'adresse a l'esprit de license et de débauche. D'où un povoir d'appréciation abandonné à la sagesse du juge. Ce qui, en revanche, est obscène, c'est le licencieux qui s'étale brutalement, par la recherche voulue de sujets, de dessins, de situations visant directement a éveiller dans l'imagination des idées malsaines, et dénotant chez l'auteur l'intention perverse de s'adresser principalement a l'esprit de luxure et de débauche . . . un image peut-être contraire aux bonnes mœurs (immorale) sans aller jusqu'à l'obscenité.' (*Revue suisse de jurisprudence*, Vol. XXII, cahier 19, 1 avril 1926, p. 294, renvoi 2.)

(*b*) In a 1927 case the Tribunal Federal gave the following definition which has been generally accepted: 'La notion de l'obscenité est relative et complexe. Il faut que la publication soit objectivement, par son sujet et la façon dont il est traité, de nature à blesser la pudeur sexuelle; que son but soit essentialement d'exciter les passions sexuelles et qu'elle ne se propose pas des fins scientifiques ou artistiques; que par le mode de diffusion est des personnes atteintes, elle risque d'exercer une action corruptrice sur les mœurs et en outre que le délinquant se rende compte de l'effet qui sera ou qui pourra être produit'. (*Recueil Officiel* 53, Vol. I, p. 234, 7 juillet 1925.)

3. It is an offence to display in any public place, e.g. in a shop window anything 'de nature à compromettre le développement moral ou physique des enfants et des adolescents, en surexcitant ou en égarant leur instinct sexuel'. It is also an offence to give such objects to anyone under the age of eighteen. These publications are described as immoral, but no definition is given of the word, except that it is confined to sexual matters. In the case of 'immoral' publications, sale to an adult is no offence. (Art. 212, Code penale suisse.)

4. After a conviction the court may order the destruction of the articles.

B. ADMINISTRATIVE POWERS

1. *Post*. . . . any immoral articles may be seized and destroyed by the postal authorities. (Art. 25, Loi fédérale sur les services des postes.)

2. *Customs*. . . . any immoral articles may be seized by the Customs authorities and subject to the approval of the Minister may be destroyed. There is no appeal to the courts. (Art. 36, al. 4, and Art. 55, Loi fédérale sur les douanes.) Under the constitution, however, there is an appeal to the Minister of Justice. (Art. 23, 2, 1914 Federal Administration Act.)

C. ARTISTIC, LITERARY OR SCIENTIFIC MERIT

1. Such works are not subject to the law since their purpose is artistic or scientific. (Trib. Fed., 7 juillet 1927, *Recueil Officiel* 53, Vol. I, p. 234.) In 1949 the Cantons were consulted on this point and replied unanimously in favour of their exclusion. 'L'État n'est pas le dépositaire des règles de la morale traditionelle, et il ne doit pas se mêler d'un domaine que reste celui des associations ou des personnes privées . . . Légiférer, c'est aussi standardiser la pensée, la réduire à un commun diviseur . . . indésirable, qu'il soit cantonal ou fédéral. C'est aussi supprimer la vérité en même temps que l'erreur, l'œuvre d'art en même temps que celle qui ne merite pas de survivre.'

2. Should the question arise concerning any seized work the Minister consults experts, e.g. Professors of Literature, etc.

9. U.S.S.R.

A. GENERAL

Since all publishing and printing is in the hands of public bodies such as the State, local authorities, trade unions, etc., very little pornography circulates in the Soviet Union. There are no reported cases on the subject.

B. OBSCENE OFFENCES

The Soviet Criminal Code makes it an offence punishable by five years' imprisonment to 'prepare, distribute, or advertise pornographic collections, printed matter, pictures and other objects, and also trading in the same or possession of the same with intent to sell them'. (S. 182 (a).) This section was inserted in the 1926 Code by a law of 25 November 1935. (Collected Statutes No. 22, Art. 214.) Before 1935 no law on the subject existed.) This is the only provision punishing the sale of pornography.

C. ADMINISTRATIVE POWERS

All pornography is liable to confiscation. (S. 182 (a), Criminal Code.)

D. ARTISTIC, LITERARY OR SCIENTIFIC MERIT

Such merit is considered inconsistent with the term 'pornography', and such works are not liable to forfeiture, etc.

APPENDIX IV

THE ROMAN INDEX

The Christian Church has banned books from the earliest times, but it was not until the Council of Trent (1564) that a full-scale censorship was introduced. One reads in the Acts of the Apostles that the Ephesians burnt their bad books at the instigation of St. Paul and this tradition was maintained by the early Christian fathers.

St. Isidore: 'To read books subversive of religion is to offer incense to the devil.'

St. Augustine: 'By means of immoral matter nice language is not acquired but by means of nice language immorality is learned. I do not accuse the language but the intoxicating wine of error that we drink in from it.' (On Terence.)

In 325 the Council of Nicea condemned the errors of Arius and proscribed his writings. The works of Nestorius were condemned at the Council of Ephesus (431). In 496 Pope Gelasius issued a list of sixty books which were not to be read. In 1121 the works of Abelard were condemned, and in 1418 at the Council of Constance those of Wyclif and Huss. In 1520 Leo X in a bull 'Exsurge Domine' condemned not only the existing works of Luther but also any that he might write in the future! Paul IV issued a list of banned books and brought the matter before the Council of Trent.

The first comprehensive list of banned books, afterwards to be known as the Index, was issued by the Council of Trent in 1564, which also published ten rules to govern publishing and reading of books in the future. Apart from banning heretical works and allowing no book to be published without the permission of the bishop, the rules provided that all books treating *ex professo* of obscene subjects should be banned. (*Decreta Con. Trid.*, p. 298.) These rules lasted two hundred years until the pontificate of Benedict XIV. The Congregation of the Index, a group of cardinals and priests who were to supervise the application of the rules and to revise the list of banned books was set up by Pius V, and put on a permanent basis by the bull 'Sollicita ac Provida' (1753). Pius IX mitigated the rules in 1848 and a general reform was agreed upon. This resulted in the promulgation of new rules in 1897 and in 1900 a new Index was issued. The rules were further altered in the new code of canon law prepared by Pius X and issued by his successor Benedict XV in 1917.

Today the Index system is divided into three parts: the Congregation of the Index; the rules or legislation contained in the code of canon law; and the list of prohibited books, last issued in 1948. The following rules are selected from the canon law and must not be considered exhaustive:

1. No Roman Catholic priest or layman may publish book without prior ecclesiastical approval if it deals with scripture, theology, canon law, etc. (Canon 1385.)

2. The right to prohibit books is reserved to the Holy See and to the bishops. A papal prohibition applies to the whole church, an episcopal prohibition to the bishop's diocese only. (Canons 1395 and 1396.)

3. Certain books and classes of books are automatically prohibited by canon law. These include heretical and schismatic books, books supporting divorce, duelling, and suicide, or which evoke spirits, advocate magic, etc. In particular books which 'professedly treat of impure and obscene subjects, narrate or teach them' are forbidden. (Canon 1399.)

4. When a book has been prohibited it may not without due permission be published, read, retained, sold, or translated, or communicated in any way to others. Catholic booksellers may not keep forbidden books in their shops without permission from the Holy See if the ban is papal, or the bishop if it is episcopal. Even with such permission they must only sell the books to those they reasonably think have permission to read them. (Canons 1398 and 1404.)

5. Cardinals and bishops are not bound by the prohibitions. (Canon 1401.)

6. Permission to read individual banned books may be given by local bishops if there is an urgent need to read the book. If bishops have a general faculty from the Holy See to allow their subjects to read forbidden books they may grant this permission, but only for good and reasonable cause. (Canon 1402.)

7. Penalties:

(*a*) An excommunication specially reserved to the Holy See is automatically incurred by those who publish books written by apostates, heretics and schismatics in defence of apostasy, heresy or schism; and by those who defend, or read, or keep such books in their possession, without permission. This also applies to books forbidden by apostolic letters. To incur the excommunication there must be knowledge of the ban. (Canon 2318.)

(*b*) Authors and publishers who publish texts or commentaries on the scriptures without permission incur a simple excommunication. (Canon 2318.)

(*c*) Apart from these penalties—referring to the classes of books mentioned above—no specific penalties are laid down. There is thus no excommunication for reading an obscene book.

N.B. Leo XIII in the constitution 'Officorum ac Munerum' forbade obscene ancient and modern classics to all except those whose office or position as teacher made their reading necessary. The new code contains no such ruling. In 1927 Cardinal Merry del Val issued instructions to archbishops and bishops urging them to take action against obscene books. ('De Sensuali et de sensuali-mystico litterarum genere.')

Select List of Books from 'Index Librorum Prohibitorum', 1948. (*Typis Polyglottis Vaticanis.*)

BALZAC. All novels.
CASANOVA. *Mémoires.*
D'ANNUNZIO. All novels and plays.
DÉSCARTES. Seven philosophical works.
DUMAS. All novels.
FRANCE, ANATOLE. All works.
GIBBON. *The Decline and Fall of the Roman Empire.*
GOLDSMITH, OLIVER. *An abridged history of England from the invasion of Julius Cæsar to the death of George II.*
HUGO, VICTOR. *Notre-Dame de Paris; Les Miserables.*
HUME, DAVID. All works.
LA FONTAINE. *Contes et nouvelles en vers.*
MAETERLINCK. All works.
MILL, J. S. *Principles of Political Economy with some of their applications to social philosophy.*
MIVART, ST. GEORGE. 'Happiness in Hell' (*Nineteenth Century*, December 1892, February and April 1893).
MORGAN, LADY SYDNEY. *Italy, a journal of a residence in that country exhibiting a view of the state of society and manners, art, literature* (1822).
PASCAL. *Pensées.*
RENAN. *Life of Jesus* and seventeen other works.
RICHARDSON. *Pamela.*
ROSMINI. *Five wounds of the Church; Constitution on Social Justice.*
ROUSSEAU. *Social Contract; Julie.*
STENDHAL. All novels.
VOLTAIRE. *Œuvres* (1748).
WILKINS, JOHN. *Discovery of a new world or a discourse tending to prove that 'tis probable there may be another habitable world in the moon, with a discourse concerning the possibility of a passage thither* (1701).
ZOLA. All works.

APPENDIX V

SELECTED LIST OF BANNED BOOKS

ABÉLARD, *Lettres d'Hélöise et Abélard*, Rome 1140.
ANON., *The Confessional Unmasked*, England 1868.
ANON., *Venus in the Cloister*, England 1727.
BAUDELAIRE, C., *Les Fleurs du Mal*, France 1857.
BLAND, M., *Julia*, England 1954.
BOCCACCIO, G., *The Decameron*, England 1954.
CALDWELL, E., *God's Little Acre*, U.S.A. 1950.
CASANOVA, *Mémoires*, Roman Index 1834.
CHARLES, E., *The Sexual Impulse*, England 1935.
CONNELL, V., *September in Quinze*, England 1954.
DE MONTALK, P., *Poems*, England 1932.
DREISER, T., *An American Tragedy*, U.S.A. 1930.
ELLIS, H., *Sexual Inversion*, England 1898.
GREENIDGE, T., *The Magnificent*, England 1934.
HALL, RADCLYFFE, *The Well of Loneliness*, England 1928.
HANLEY, J., *Boy*, England 1935.
HUXLEY, A., *Antic Hay*, U.S.A. 1930.
HUYSMANS, *La Bas*, England 1934.
JAMES, NORAH, *The Sleeveless Errand*, England 1929.
JOYCE, JAMES, *Ulysses*, England 1923.
KINSEY, A., *Sexual Behaviour in the Human Female*, South Africa 1953.
KNOWLTON, C., *The Fruits of Philosophy*, England 1877.
LAWRENCE, D. H., *The Rainbow*, England 1915; *Lady Chatterley's Lover*, Japan 1952 (never published unexpurgated in England).
LOUŸS, P., *Aphrodite*, England 1934; *The Songs of Bilitis*, England 1934.
MILLER, H., *Tropic of Cancer*, U.S.A. 1953; *Tropic of Capricorn*, U.S.A. 1953. (Neither has ever been published in England.)
MOORE, G., *A Story Teller's Holiday*, U.S.A. 1929.
OVID, *Elegies*, England 1599.
PETRONIUS, *Satyricon*, England 1934.
RABELAIS, F., *Pantagruel*, France 1533; All works, South Africa 1938.
REMARQUE, *All Quiet on the Western Front*, U.S.A. 1929.
RUMBOLD, R., *Little Victims*, England 1934.
SADE, D. A. F., *Justine*, France 1791; *Juliette*, France 1798.
SANGER, M., *Family Limitation*, U.S.A. 1915.
SMITH, L., *Strange Fruit*, U.S.A. 1944.
SMITH, W., *Bessie Cotter*, England 1935.
STERNE, *A Sentimental Journey*, Roman Index 1819.
WILSON, E., *Memoirs of Hecate County*, U.S.A. 1946.
ZOLA, E., *La Terre*, England 1888.

APPENDIX VI

BIBLIOGRAPHY

1. LEGAL

ARCHBOLD, J. F., *Criminal Pleading and Practice* (33rd edition), London 1954. Sweet and Maxwell.

BENTHAM J., (Ed. Harrison, W.) *Introduction to the Principles of Morals and Legislation*. Oxford. 1948. Blackwell.

CAMPBELL, J., *Lives of the Lord Chancellors* (Vol. VIII: *Lord Lyndhurst*), London 1869. John Murray.

CHESTER, S. B., *Anomalies of the English Law*, London 1911. Stanley Paul.

COPINGER, W. A., *Law of Copyright* (8th edition), London 1948. Sweet and Maxwell.

D'AUTREC, L., *L'Ouvrage aux Mœurs*, Paris 1929.

DICEY, A. V., *Lectures on the relation between Law and Public Opinion in England during the Nineteenth Century*, London 1914. Macmillan.

GARDINER, F. J. and LANSDOWN, C. W., *South African Criminal Law and Procedure* (Vol. II), Cape Town 1936. Jura and Co.

GARDINER, S. R., *Reports of Cases in Courts of Star Chamber and High Commission*, London 1886. Camden Society.

HALE, W. H., *A Series of Precedents and Proceedings in criminal causes from 1475–1640: extracted from Act Books of Ecclesiastical Courts in the Diocese of London, illustrative of the discipline of the Church of England*, London 1847.

—— *Precedents in Causes of Office against Churchwardens and others, etc.*, London 1841.

HALLIS, F., *The Law and Obscenity*, London 1932. Harmsworth.

HALSBURY (Ed. Viscount Hailsham), *Laws of England* (2nd edition): Vol. IX, Part XI, paras. 667–671; Vol. XXXII, Part III, paras. 87–89 (*Plays*); Vol. XXXII, Part IV, paras. 90–108 (*Films*), London 1933. Butterworth: (3rd edition) Vol. X, paras. 1274–1279, London 1955. Butterworth.

HOLDSWORTH, W., *History of English Law*, Vol. IV, Vol. VIII, London 1937. Methuen.

KENNY, C. S., (Ed. Turner, J. W. C.), *Outlines of Criminal Law* (16th edition), Cambridge 1952. Cambridge University Press.

LEADHAM, I. S., *Select Cases before the King's Council in the Star Chamber A.D. 1477–1509* (Vol. XVI), *1509–1544* (Vol. XXV), 1903 and 1911. Selden Society.

LUXFORD, J. H., *Police Law in New Zealand*, Wellington 1950. Butterworth.

McDONALD, J. H. A., *On the Criminal Law of Scotland* (5th edition), Edinburgh 1948.

NOKES, G. D., *History of the Crime of Blasphemy*, London 1928. Sweet and Maxwell.

PHIPSON (Ed. Burrows, R.), *The Law of Evidence* (9th edition), London 1952. Sweet and Maxwell.

RANCHHODAS, R. and THAKORE, O. K., *The Indian Penal Code*, Bombay 1936. The Bombay Law Reporter Office.

ROSCOE, H., *Criminal Evidence* (16th edition), London 1952. Stevens.

RUSSELL, W. (Ed. Turner, J. W. C.), *On Crime*, Vol. II (10th edition), London 1950.

SALMOND, J. W. (Ed. Heuston, R. V.), *On the Law of Torts* (11th edition), London 1953. Sweet and Maxwell.

SCHROEDER, THEODORE, *'Obscene' Literature and Constitutional Law*, New York 1911. Privately Printed.

SIMPSON, S. P. and STONE, J., *Law and Society*, Book II, St. Paul, Minn., 1949. West Publishing Co.

STEPHEN, J. (Ed. Sturge, L. F.), *Digest of the Criminal Law* (9th edition), London 1950. Sweet and Maxwell.

STEPHEN, J., *History of the Criminal Law of England*, London 1883. Macmillan.

Stone's Justices' Manual, London 1955. Butterworth.

TREMEEAR, W. J. (Ed. Harvey, A. B.), *Annotated Criminal Code, Canada and Supplement* (1953), Toronto 1944. The Carswell Company.

WILLIAMS, GLANVILLE, *Criminal Law*, London 1953. Stevens.

—— *The Reform of the Law*, London 1951. Gollancz.

Report of Criminal Code Commissioners, London 1879. Stationery Office (Cmd. 2345).

Report of Joint Select Committee on Lotteries and Indecent Advertisements, London 1908. Stationery Office (Cmd. 275).

The Modern Approach to Criminal Law, London 1948. Macmillan.

Codex Iuris Canonici, Pius X, Rome 1931. Typis Polyglottis Vaticanis.

SELECTED ARTICLES (References to newspaper articles, etc., are given in the text)

ALPERT, L. M., 'Judicial censorship of obscene literature', *Harvard Law Review*, November 1938 (**52**: 40–76).

ANONYMOUS, 'Obscene Publications' (articles and notes). *Justice of the Peace*, October, November, December 1954 (**118**: 664–6, 680–2, 694–7, 709–11, 725–6, 812–18).

B. L., 'Criminal Law—Artistic purpose', *Canadian Bar Review*, June–July 1944 (**22**: 553–5).

CAMPBELL, I. D., 'Indecent Publications Amendment Act 1954: a commentary', *New Zealand Law Journal*, September 1954 (**30**: 293–4).

EDDY, J. P., 'Society of Authors' Draft Bill'. *Criminal Law Review*, April 1955 (218–26).

EHASBURG, W. G., 'Art: immoral or immortal', *Journal of Criminal Law*, September 1954 (**45**: 274–8)

FORBES, M. Z., 'Obscene Publications', *Australian Law Journal*, July 1946 (**20**: 92–4).

LOCKHART, W. B. and MCCLURE, R. C., 'Literature, the law of Obscenity and the Constitution', *Minnesota Law Review*, March 1954 (**38**: 295–395).

MACKAY, R. S., 'Recent Developments in the law on obscenity', *Canadian Bar Review*, November 1954 (**32**: 1010–18).

MARKS, S., 'What is obscene literature today', *United States Law Review*, April 1939 (**73**: 217–23).

MOSKIN, M., 'Inadequacy of present tests as to what constitutes Obscene Literature', *Cornell Law Quarterly*, Spring 1949 (**34**: 442–7).

NIGHTINGALE, G. M., 'Vulgar Postcards', *Justice of the Peace*, January 1954 (**118**: 5–6).

NUTTING, C. B., 'Definitive standards in federal obscenity legislation', *Indiana Law Review*, November 1937 (**23**: 24–40).

ST. JOHN-STEVAS, N. A. F., 'Obscenity and the Law', *Criminal Law Review*, November 1954 (817–33).

WHITWORTH, F., 'Law as to Obscenity', *Law Journal*, December 1935 (**80**: 397–8).

2. GENERAL

ALDINGTON, RICHARD, *D. H. Lawrence*, London 1950. Heinemann.

ALLEN, WALTER, *The English Novel*, London 1954. Phœnix House.

ANDERSON, M., *My Thirty Years' War*, London 1930. Knopf.

Annual Register, 1798.

ANON. (An Old Bibliophile), *Forbidden Books*, Paris 1902. Privately Printed.

ANON., *Letters from a friend in Paris*, London 1874. Privately Printed.

ANON., *Life of M. G. Lewis*, London 1839.

ANON., *The Romance of Lust*, 1873. Privately Printed.

APOLLINAIRE, G., FLEUVET, F. and PERCEAU, L., *L'Enfer de la Bibliothèque Nationale*, Paris 1913. *Icono-bio-bibliographie descriptive, critique et raisonnée . . . et tous les ouvrages composant cette célèbre collection.* (See Mus. Brit. P.C. 28 June 1928 for subsequent additions. Supplement edited by Alfred Rose.)

ARBER, E., *A Transcript of the Registers of the Company of Stationers of London, 1554–1640* (5 Volumes), London 1875–1876; Vol. IV, London 1877; Vol. V, Birmingham 1894. Privately Printed.

ARMITAGE, GILBERT, *Banned in England*, London 1932. Wishart.

Articles in *The Bell* on Irish Censorship, September 1941 *et subsq.*

ATKINSON, E. TINDAL, *Obscene Literature in Law and Practice*, London 1937. Christophers.

BAGEHOT, WALTER, *Literary Studies*, London 1879. Longmans.

BAKER, E. A., *The History of the English Novel* (10 Vols.), London 1924–39. H. F. and G. Witherby.

BELL, CLIVE, *On British Freedom*, London 1923. Chatto and Windus.

BESANT, A., *Autobiography*, London 1893. Fisher Unwin.

BEVINGTON, M. M., *The Saturday Review, 1855–68*, New York 1941. Columbia University Press.

BIRREL, A., *Essays About Men, Women and Books*, London 1894. Elliot Stock.

BLAKEY, D., *The Minerva Press, 1790–1820*, London 1939. The Bibliographical Society.

BLANSHARD, PAUL, *The Irish and Catholic Power*, London 1955. Verschoyle.

BLUNDEN, E., *Leigh Hunt's 'Examiner' Examined*, London 1928. Cobden-Sanderson.

BONNER, H. and FORDER, *The Queen* v. *Charles Bradlaugh and Annie Besant*, London 1877. Free Thought Publishing Co.

BONNER, H. B., *Charles Bradlaugh*, London 1894. Fisher Unwin.

BONNER, H. P., *Penalties Upon Opinion*, London 1934. Watts (Thinkers' Library).

BOSWELL, J., *Life of Johnson*, London 1872. Bell and Daldy.

BRENTFORD, LORD, *Do we need a Censor?*, London 1936. Faber.

BRIGHTFIELD, M. F., *John Wilson Croker*, London 1940. Allen and Unwin.

British Museum Papers:

11851. i. 21. Brief for the Defence, *People of State of New York* v. *Donald Friede and Covici Friede.* (*Well of Loneliness.*)

11851. i. 19. Brief for the Defence and Judgement in *U.S.* v. *Married Love* (1931).

11851. i. 20. Report of Police Proceedings re *Boy.*

11853. v. 57. Report of the *Sexual Impulse* case.

BROME, V., *H. G. Wells. A Biography*, London 1951. Longmans, Green and Co.

BROWN, H. and LEECH, M., *Anthony Comstock, Roundsman of the Lord*, London 1928. Wishart.

BUCHANAN, ROBERT, *On Descending into Hell*, London 1889. George Redway.

BUCKLEY, J. H., *The Victorian Temper*, London 1952. Allen and Unwin.

BENNETT, E. A., *Books and Persons, 1908–11*, London 1917. Chatto and Windus.

CARPENTER, E., *My Days and Dreams*, London 1916. Allen and Unwin.

Catalogue of Thomason Tracts, London 1908. British Museum.

CAUSTON, B. and YOUNG, G. G., *Keeping it Dark or the Censor's Handbook*, London 1930. Mandrake Press.

CHAPMAN, R. W., 'Authors and Booksellers', article in *Johnson's England*, Oxford 1933. Clarendon Press.

CLOWES, SIR W. C. (Speculator Morum), *Bibliotheca arcana seu catalogus librorum penetralium, being brief notices of books that have been secretly printed, prohibited by law, seized, anathematised, burnt or bowdlerised*, London 1884–5. Privately Printed.

COCKBURN, H., *Life of Francis Jeffrey*, Edinburgh 1872. A. and C. Black.

GOLDBERG, I., *Havelock Ellis*, London 1926. Constable.

COLLIER, JEREMY, *A Short View of the Immorality and Profaneness of the English Stage: Together with the Sense of Antiquity upon this Argument.* London 1699.

CORMAN, HERBERT, *James Joyce*, London 1941. John Lane.

CRAIG, ALEC, *Above All Liberties*, London 1942. Allen and Unwin.
—— *The Banned Books of England*, London 1937. Allen and Unwin.
CRAIG, ALEC, *Sex and Revolution*, London 1934. Allen and Unwin.
CRUSE, A., *After the Victorians* (On the books that were most widely read between 1887 and 1914), London 1938. Allen and Unwin.
—— *The Englishman and his Books in the early Nineteenth Century*, London 1930. G. G. Harrap.
—— *The Victorians and their Books*, London 1935. Allen and Unwin.
DANCE, E. H., *The Victorian Illusion*, London 1928. Heinemann.
DECKER, C. R., *The Victorian Conscience*, New York 1952. Twayne.
DE MONTALK, P., 'Whited Sepulchres' (*Right Review*), London 1936.
DENNETT, MARY WARE, *Who's Obscene?*, New York 1930.
DE SELINCOURT, O., *Art and Morality*, London 1935. Methuen.
DICKENS, CHARLES, *Letters to Wilkie Collins, 1851–70* (selected by G. Hogarth), London 1892. Osgood and McIlvaine.
DINGWALL, E. J., 'Erotic Literature' (*Cassell's Encyclopædia of Literature*, Vol. I, London 1953. Cassell.
D'ISRAELI, I., *Curiosities of Literature* ('Destruction of Books'), London 1807. John Murray.
DITCHFIELD, P. H., *Books Fatal to Their Owners*, London 1895. Elliot Stock.
DOBSON, H. A., *Samuel Richardson*, London 1902. English Men of Letters Series.
DOUGHTY, O., *A Victorian Romantic: Dante Gabriel Rossetti*, London 1949. Frederick Müller.
Drive for Decency in Print (Report of Bishops' Committee), New York 1939.
DUDDEN, F. H., *Henry Fielding: His Life, Works and Times*, Oxford 1952. Clarendon Press.
DUFF, E. G. *et al.*, *Hand-Lists of Books printed by London Printers, 1501–1556*, London 1913. The Bibliographical Society.
—— *A Century of the English Book Trade*, London 1905. The Bibliographical Society.
EGAN, BERESFORD, *The Sink of Solitude*, London 1928. Hermes Press.
EGAN, BERESFORD and STEPHENSEN, P. R., *Policeman of the Lord*, London 1929. Sophistocles Press.
ELLIS, HENRY HAVELOCK, *More Essays of Love and Virtue*, London 1931. Constable.
—— *My Life*, London 1940. Heinemann.
—— *A Note on the Bedborough Trial*, London 1898. Privately Printed.
—— *Studies in the Psychology of Sex*, New York 1936. Random House.
ELWIN, M., *Charles Reade*, London 1931. Jonathan Cape.
ENGLISCH, P., *L'histoire de l'érotisme en Europe*, Paris 1933.
ERNST, M. and SEAGLE, W., *To the Pure*, London 1929. Cape.
ERNST, M. L. and LINDEY, A., *The Censor Marches On*, New York 1940. Doubleday, Doran and Co.
EVERETT, E. M., 'The Party of Humanity', *Fortnightly Review and Contributors, 1865–74*, Chapel Hill 1939. University of North Carolina Press.

FARRER, J. A., *Books Condemned to be Burnt*, London 1892. Elliot Stock.

FAY, W. G. and CARSWELL, C., *The Fays of the Abbey Theatre*, London 1935. Rich and Cowan.

FORMAN, H. B., *The Vicissitudes of Shelley's 'Queen Mab'*, London 1887. Privately Printed.

FORSTER, E. M., *Abinger Harvest*, London 1946. Arnold.

FOWELL, F. and PALMER, F., *Censorship in England*, London 1913. Palmer.

FRAXI, P. (H. S. ASHBEE), *Index Librorum Prohibitorum*, 1877. Privately Printed.

—— *Centuria Librorum Absconditorum*, 1879. Privately Printed.

—— *Catena Librorum Tacendorum*, 1885. Privately Printed.

GALLICHAN, W. M., *The Poison of Prudery*, London 1929. Werner Laurie.

GALSWORTHY, J., *A Justification of the Censorship of Plays*, (Satirical pamphlet), London 1909. Heinemann.

GASKELL, E. C., *The Life of Charlotte Brontë*, London 1947. John Lehmann.

GAY, JULES, *Bibliographie des principaux ouvrages rélatifs à l'Amour, etc.*, Paris 1861–1900.

GILDERSLEEVE, V. C., *Government Regulation of the Elizabethan Drama*, New York 1908. Columbia University Press.

GRAHAM, W., *English Literary Periodicals*, New York 1930. T. Nelson.

—— *The Beginnings of English Literary Periodicals, 1665–1715*, New York 1926. Oxford University Press.

GREG, W. W., *The Library*, London, Vol. IX, No. 4, p. 242. Oxford University Press.

GREG, W. W. and BOSWELL, E., *Records of Court of Stationers' Company*, London, 1930. The Bibliographical Society.

GREGORY, LADY, *Our Irish Theatre*, London 1907. Putnam.

HAIGHT, A. L., *Banned Books*, London 1955. Allen & Unwin.

HAIGHT, G. S., *George Eliot and John Chapman*, New Haven 1940. Yale University Press.

HAIRE, NORMAN, *Sexual Reform Congress London 1929*, London 1930. Kegan Paul.

HALDANE, E. S., *Mrs. Gaskell and her Friends*, London 1930. Hodder and Stoughton.

HANSON, L. and E. M., *The Four Brontës*, London 1949. Oxford University Press.

HARDY, EVELYN, *Thomas Hardy*, London 1954. The Hogarth Press.

HARE, HUMPHREY, *Swinburne: a biographical approach*, London 1949. Witherby.

HARRIS, FRANK, *Bernard Shaw*, London 1931. Gollancz.

HEWLETT, D., *A Life of John Keats*, London 1949. Hurst and Blackett.

HONE, J., *The Life of George Moore*, London 1936. Gollancz.

HOPKINS, A. B., *Elizabeth Gaskell: Her life and work*, London 1952. John Lehmann.

House, H., *The Dickens World*, London 1942. Oxford University Press.

Hurley, T., *Commentary on the Present Index Legislation*, Dublin 1907. Browne and Nolan.

Index Librorum Prohibitorum, Rome 1948. Typis Polyglottis Vaticanis.

Jackson, Holbrook, *The Fear of Books*, New York 1932. C. Scribner's Sons.

Joyce, James, *Ulysses*, London 1936. John Lane.

Kinsey, A., *Sexual Behaviour in the Human Female*, London 1953. Saunders.

Knowles, D., *The Censor, the Drama and the Film, 1900–1934*, 1934. Allen and Unwin.

Knowlton, C., *Fruits of Philosophy*, London 1877. C. Bradlaugh.

Ladd, H. A., *The Victorian Morality of Art*, New York 1932. R. Long and R. R. Smith.

Lafourcade, G., *La Jeunesse de Swinburne, 1837–1867*, Paris 1928. University of Strasbourg.

—— *Swinburne: A literary biography*, London 1932. G. Bell.

Laporte, A., *Bibliographie clérico-galante*, Paris 1879. Privately Printed.

Lawrence, D. H., *Pornography and So On*, London 1936. Faber and Faber.

—— *Sex, Literature and Censorship*, (essays edited by H. T. Moore), London 1955. Heinemann.

Lockhart, *Life of Walter Scott*, London 1893. A. and C. Black.

Macaulay, T. B., *Critical and Historical Essays*, Vol. III, p. 256. 1843. Longman and Co.

Marchand, L. A., *The Athenæum: A mirror of Victorian culture*. Chapel Hill 1941. University of North Carolina Press.

Martin, T., *A Life of Lord Lyndhurst*, London 1883. John Murray.

Maurois, A. M., *Byron*, London 1930. Jonathan Cape.

Mayne, E. C., *Byron*, London 1924. Methuen.

McKerrow, R. B., Article on Booksellers in *Shakespeare's England*, Vol. II, London 1916. Oxford University Press.

—— *A Dictionary of English Printers, 1557–1640*, London 1910. The Bibliographical Society.

Melville, L., *The Life and Letters of Laurence Sterne*, London 1911. Stanley Paul.

Meredith, G., *Modern Love* (with an Introduction by C. Day Lewis), London 1948. Hart-Davis.

Meredith, Wm., *Letters of George Meredith*, London 1912. Constable.

Milton (Ed. Arber), 'Areopagitica', London 1868. Alex Murray.

Montagu, I., *The Political Censorship of Films*, London 1929. Gollancz.

Moore, George, *Avowals*, London 1919. Privately Printed.

—— *Literature at Nurse or Circulatory Morals*, London 1885. Vizetelly.

Neill, S. D., *History of the English Novel*, London 1951. Jarrolds.

Nesbitt, G. L., *Benthamite Reviewing* (*Westminster Review, 1824–1836*), New York 1934. Columbia University Press.

Orioli, G., *Adventures of a Bookseller*, Florence 1937. Privately Printed.

Orwell, George, *Critical Essays* (Boys' Weeklies), London 1946. Secker and Warburg.

PALMER, J., *The Censor and the Theatres*, London 1912. Fisher Unwin.

PETERSON, H., *Havelock Ellis*, London 1928. Allen and Unwin.

PINTO, V. DE SOLA, *Rochester*, London 1935. John Lane.

—— *Sir Charles Sedley*, London 1927. Constable.

PLACE, FRANCIS, Collection British Museum (180 Volumes), 1792–1852.

PLATO (trans. F. M. Cornford), *The Republic*, Oxford 1941. Clarendon Press.

PLOMER, H. R., *A Dictionary of the Booksellers and Printers who were at work in England, Scotland and Ireland from 1641 to 1667*, London 1907. The Bibliographical Society.

—— *A Dictionary of the Booksellers and Printers who were at work in England, Scotland and Ireland from 1668 to 1725*, Oxford 1922. The Bibliographical Society.

PLOMER, H. R., BUSHNELL, G. H. and DIX, E. R. McC., *A Dictionary of the Printers and Booksellers who were at work in England, Scotland and Ireland from 1726 to 1775*, 1932. The Bibliographical Society.

POLLARD, A. W. and REDGRAVE, G. R., *A Short-Title Catalogue of Books Printed in England, Scotland, and Ireland and of English Books Printed Abroad, 1475–1640*, London 1926. The Bibliographical Society.

PRAZ, MANIO, *The Romantic Agony*, London 1951. Oxford University Press.

QUINLAN, M. J., *Victorian Prelude*, New York 1941. Columbia University.

READE, CHARLES, 'The Prurient Prude' (*Readiana*), London 1883. Chatto and Windus.

READE, R. S. (A. ROSE), *Registrum Librorum Eroticorum*, 1936. Privately Printed.

REED, A. W., *Early Tudor Drama*, London 1926. Methuen.

Report of Police Committee of House of Commons, 1817.

Reports of Public Morality Council, London 1900–1955.

Reports of Society for Suppression of Vice, London 1800–1825.

Reports of the British Board of Film Censors, Wardour Street, London.

Report of the Committee on Evil Literature, Dublin 1926. Stationery Office.

Report on Pornographic Materials (Gathings Committee), Washington. Union Calendar 797, 82nd Congress, 2nd Session, House Report No. 2510.

Report of Senate Committee on Comic Books and Juvenile Delinquency, Washington. 84th Congress, 1st Session, No. 62, 1955.

ROCHESTER, *Collected Works* (Ed. J. Hayward), London 1926.

ROSSETTI, D. G., *Letters from D. G. Rossetti to Algernon Charles Swinburne, regarding the attacks made upon the latter by Mortimer Collins and upon both by Robert Buchanan*, London 1921. Privately Printed for T. J. Wise.

RUTLAND, W. R., *Thomas Hardy*, Oxford 1938. Basil Blackwell.

SADLEIR, MICHAEL, *Nineteenth-Century Fiction*, London 1951. Constable.

—— *Things Past*, London 1944. Constable.

SAMPSON, GEORGE, *The Concise Cambridge History of English Literature*, Cambridge 1949. Cambridge University Press.

SANGER, M., *My Fight for Birth Control*, London 1932. Faber.
SCOTT, G. R., *Into Whose Hands*, London 1945. Gerald G. Swan.
SEAGLE, W., *Cato or the Future of Censorship*, London 1930. Kegan Paul.
SENCOURT, R. E., *The Life of George Meredith*, London 1929. Chapman and Hall.
SHAW, G. B. *et al.*, *Censorship of Plays in the Office of the Lord Chamberlain. The Case for Abolition*, London 1908. Arden Press.
SHAW, G. B., *Prefaces by Bernard Shaw*, London 1934. Constable.
—— *Statement of the Evidence in Chief of George Bernard Shaw before the Joint-Committee on Stage Plays* (*Censorship and Theatre Licensing*), London 1909. Privately Printed.
STEPHENSEN, P. R., *The Well of Sleevelessness*, London 1929. Scholartis Press.
STOPES, M. C., *A Banned Play* (*Vectia*) *and a preface on the Censorship*, London 1926. J. Bale.
—— *Contraception: Its Theory, History and Practice*, London 1923.
STRAUS, R., *The Unspeakable Carll*, London 1927. Chapman and Hall.
SWEENEY, JOHN, *At Scotland Yard*, London 1904. Grant Richards.
SWINBURNE, A. C., *Contributions to the Whippingham Papers*, London 1888. Privately Printed.
—— *Notes on Poems and Reviews*, London 1866. J. C. Hotten.
—— *Under the Microscope*, London 1872. D. White.
TENNYSON, CHARLES, *Alfred Tennyson*, London 1950. Macmillan.
THOMAS, W. B., *The Story of the Spectator, 1828–1928*, London 1928. Methuen.
THRALL, M. H. T., *Rebellious Frasers*, New York 1934. Columbia University Press.
TILLOTSON, G., *Thackeray the Novelist*, Cambridge 1954. Cambridge University Press.
TILLOTSON, K., *Novels of the 1840's*, Oxford 1954. Clarendon Press.
UNWIN, STANLEY, *The Truth about Publishing*, London 1950. Allen and Unwin.
VIZETELLY, E. A., *Émile Zola, Novelist and Reformer*, London 1904. John Lane.
—— *Extracts from English Classics*, London 1888. Privately Printed.
WAGNER, G., *Parade of Pleasure*, London 1954. Verschoyle.
WARD, A. W. and WHALLER, A. R., *Cambridge History of English Literature*, Vol. XI, Chap. XIV, 'Book Production and Distribution, 1625–1800. Cambridge 1953. Cambridge University Press.
WARREN, A. H., *English Poetic Theory, 1825–1865*. Princeton 1950. Princeton University Press.
WEBB, R. K., *The British Working Class Reader*, London 1955. Allen and Unwin.
WEBER, C. J., *Hardy of Wessex*, New York 1940. Columbia University Press.
WELLEK, R. and WARREN, A., *Theory of Literature*, London 1949. Jonathan Cape.
WERTHAM, F., *Seduction of the Innocent*, London 1955. Museum Press.

WHITE, N. I., *Shelley* (2 vols.), London 1947. Secker and Warburg.
WING, D. G., *Short-Title Catalogue of Books printed in England, Scotland, Ireland, Wales and British America and of English books printed in other countries, 1641–1700* (supplemented 1953 by Fry, M. I. and Davies, G.), U.S.A. 1945–51. Index Society.
WOOD, ANTHONY À, *Athenæ Oxonienses*, Vol. IV, 1813–20. F. C. and J. Rivington.
WOOLF, V. *et al.*, Articles on the Nineteenth Century, April 1929.
YOUNG, G. M., *Early Victorian England, 1830–1865* (2 vols.), London 1934. Oxford University Press.
—— 'Today and Yesterday' (*The Age of Tennyson*), London 1948. Hart-Davis.

JOINT SELECT COMMITTEE OF THE HOUSE OF LORDS AND THE HOUSE OF COMMONS ON STAGE PLAYS (CENSORSHIP), *Verbatim Report of The Proceedings and full text of The Recommendations*. The Stage. London. 1910.

APPENDIX VII

OBSCENE PUBLICATIONS: PROCEEDINGS IN ENGLAND AND WALES

		1935	1936	1937	1938	1939	1950	1951	1952	1953	1954
OBSCENE PUBLICATIONS ACT, 1857: Number of destruction orders		39	33	44	66	11	76	271	115	154	132
Number of articles ordered to be destroyed	Books and magazines	900	1,506	5,314	24,727	3,006	40,404	65,277	31,842	44,130	167,293
	Photographs	8,347	11,492	8,737	2,064	344	7,182	28,956	8,329	20,141	10,803
	Postcards	78	7,784	Nil	17	Nil	297	11,662	16,029	32,603	16,646
	Miscellaneous	176	705	622	5,006	7	160	2,150	2,546	1,950	18,609
Common law misdemeanour: publishing an obscene libel											
Number of persons found guilty		39	18	31	39	7	19	51	34	49	111
Total amount of fines		£1,048.15	£244	£675	£370.15	£69	£451	£5,938	£906	£2,786	£12,677
Range of sentences		6 weeks–12 months	6 months–2 years	1–6 months	1 month–2 years	12 months	3–12 months	6 weeks–2 years	6–18 months	3–12 months	3–18 months

(Written answers Nos. 5 and 6, 3 May 1955, given by the Home Secretary in the House of Commons in reply to questions put by Roy Jenkins, M.P., on 29 April 1955.)

APPENDIX VIII

LIST OF ENGLISH STATUTES*

(N.B.—Numbers in bold type are index references).

1 Ric. 3, c. 9 (Aliens, 1483–4), **6.**
25 Hen. 8, c. 15 (Printers and Binders, 1533–4), **6.**
3 Jac. 1, c. 21 (Plays, 1605–6), **14*n*.**
13 & 14 Car. 2, c. 33 (Licensing of the Press, 1662), **22.**
16 Car. 2, c. 8 (Licensing of the Press, 1664), **22.**
16 & 17 Car. 2, c. 7 (Licensing of the Press, 1664–5), **22.**
10 Geo. 2, c. 19 (Plays and Wine Licences, 1736–7), **21.**
21 Geo. 3, c. 49 (Sunday Observance, 1780–1), **30.**
32 Geo. 3, c. 60 (Libel, 1792), **145–7.**
5 Geo. 4, c. 83 (Vagrancy, 1824), **38, 131.**
1 & 2 Vict., c. 38 (Vagrancy, 1837–8), **131.**
2 & 3 Vict., c. 47 (Metropolitan Police, 1839), **132.**
6 & 7 Vict., c. 68 (Theatres, 1843), **53, 157–8.**
6 & 7 Vict., c. 96 (Libel, 1843).
10 & 11 Vict., c. 89 (Town Police Clauses, 1847), **132.**
11 & 12 Vict., c. 43 (Summary Jurisdiction, 1847–8), **131*n*.**
14 & 15 Vict., c. 100 (Criminal Procedure, 1851), **129*n*.**
16 & 17 Vict., c. 107 (Customs Consolidation, 1852–3), **66.**
20 & 21 Vict., c. 83 (Obscene Publications, 1857), **54, 66–9, 129–31, 136, 152.**
24 & 25 Vict., c. 94 (Accessories and Abettors, 1861).
24 & 25 Vict., c. 100 (Offences against the Person, 1861).
33 & 34 Vict., c. 75 (Elementary Education, 1870).
33 & 34 Vict., c. 79 (Post Office, 1870), **70.**
39 & 40 Vict., c. 36 (Customs Consolidation, 1876), **132–3.**
51 & 52 Vict., c. 64 (Law of Libel Amendment, 1888).
52 & 53 Vict., c. 18 (Indecent Advertisements, 1889), **131–2.**
55 & 56 Vict., c. 55 (Burgh Police (Scotland), 1892), **217–18.**
8 Edw. 7, c. 48 (Post Office, 1908), **133.**
9 Edw. 7, c. 30 (Cinematograph, 1909), **93.**
5 & 6 Geo. 5, c. 90 (Indictments, 1914–6), **144.**
7 & 8 Geo. 5, c. 21 (Venereal Disease, 1917–18), **132.**
15 & 16 Geo. 5, c. 86 (Criminal Justice, 1924–5), **134*n*.**
16 & 17 Geo. 5, c. 61 (Judicial Proceedings (Regulation of Reports), 1926), **132.**
15 & 16 Geo. 6 & 1 Eliz. 2, c. 44 (Customs and Excise, 1951–2), **132–3.**
15 & 16 Geo. 6 & 1 Eliz. 2, c. 55 (Magistrates Courts, 1951–2), **133–4.**
15 & 16 Geo. 6 & 1 Eliz. 2, c. 66 (Defamation, 1951–2).
1 & 2 Eliz. 2, c. 36. (Post Office, 1953), **133.**
3 & 4 Eliz. 2, c. 28 (Children and Young Persons (Harmful Publications) Act, 1955).

* References to Commonwealth Statutes will be found in Appendix III.

APPENDIX IX

LIST OF REPORTED CASES

(N.B.—Numbers in bold type are index references).

ENGLISH AND COMMONWEALTH*

Abingdon (1794), 1 Esp. 226, **148.**
Ackroyd v. *Barret* (1895), 11 T. L. R. 115, **148*n*.**
Ballentine (1914), 22 C. C. C. 385 (N.B.) (Canadian case), **236.**
Barnadiston (1684), 9 St. Tr. 1334, **146*n*.**
Barraclough, [1906] 1 K. B. 201, C.C.R., **144.**
Betterton (1702), Coram Rege Roll, Mich. 13 Wm. 3 (P.R.O. 2147) Rex Roll, r. 9, **21*n*.**
Bottomley v. *Woolworth's* (1932), 48 T. L. R. 521, **157.**
Boyd v. *Angus and Robertson Ltd.* (1946), 63 W. N. (N.S.W.) 189 (Australian case), **222.**
Bradlaugh (1878), 3 Q. B. D. 509, 607, **70–4, 134, 135, 145, 154, 155.**
Bremner v. *Walker* (1885), 6 L. R. (N.S.W.) 276; 2 W. N. 44 (Australian case), **222.**
Britnell (1912), 4 D. L. R. 56 (C.A.) (Canadian case), **236.**
Bryan (1951), 35 Cr. App. Rep. 121, **121*n*.**
Burdett (1820), 4 B. & A. 95, **149.**
Burns (1886), 16 Cox C. C. 355, **142*n*.**
Capital and Counties Bank v. *Henty* (1882), 7 A. C. 741, **148*n*.**
Carlile (1819), 3 B. & A. 161: 4 St. Tr. (N.S.) 1423; 1 St. Tr. (N.S.) 1389, **35, 48*n*, 132*n*, 150*n*.**
Carlile (1845), 1 Cox C. C. 229, **125.**
Carr (1680), 7 St. Tr. 1114, **145.**
Cassidy v. *Daily Mirror*, [1929] 2 K. B. 331, **148*n*.**
Clarkson v. *McArthy* (1917), N. Z. L. R. 624; G. L. R. 401 (New Zealand case), **239.**
Close (1948), V. L. R., p. 445 (Australian case), **232.**
Collins, Ex parte (1888), 9 L. R. (N.S.W.) 497; 5 W. N. 85 (Australian case), **222.**
Comm. of Customs v. *Watchtower Society* (1941), C. P. D. 438 (S. African case), **241.**
Conway (1944), 2 D. L. R. 530 (Canadian case), **150*n*, 236.**
Cox v. *Stinton*, [1951] 2 K. B. 1021; [1951] 2 All E. R. 637, **130, 131.**
Creevey (1813), M. & S. 273, **132*n*.**
Curl (1727), 2 Stra. 788, **23, 24.**
De Libellis Famosis (1606), 5 Co. Rep. 125a; 77 E. R. 250, **12*n*.**
De Marny, [1907] 1 K. B. 388, C. C. R., **125*n*.**
De Montalk (1932), 23 Cr. App. R. 182, **106–7, 125, 145*n*, 151.**
Dixon (1814), 3 M. & S. 11, **141.**
Dugdale (1853), 1 E. & B. 435, **125*n*.**

* References to unreported cases will be found in the text.

UNITED STATES

INDEX